'It is a modern *Pilgrim's Progress*...
technique, which powerfully anal
is that it shows the range of spirit
which have given rise to the Cath
celibacy.'

Fergus Pyle, *The Irish Times*

'Sensitive, carefully researched, concentrated on the human agonies.'

Belfast Telegraph

'In these pages there is a strong sense of the urgent need for rationality, openness and compassion in responding to what is a truly vast crisis.'

Professor Adrian Hastings, *The Tablet*

'An unforgettable and affecting love story – better than *Thorn Birds*, as memorable as *The Nun's Story*.'

The Australian, Australia

'A compelling, unique work that allows the reader to hear the heartbeat of troubled people. Thomas is a world-class writer who has an evocative, almost magical ability of story telling. He combines the language of the heart and soul.'

Professor Glen van Warreby, *Philadephia Enquirer*

'An amazingly intimate insight into struggles of the celibate life... the psychological insights are invaluable. This is a mirror in which, whether or not we have been called to a celibate life, we see ourselves.'

The Rev Dr John Gosling, *Church Times*

'Fascinating reading... it is the first example of an attempt to bring together all aspects – biblical, historical, doctrinal, legal, psychological – which go to make the issue of celibacy such an intractable one. I was particularly impressed that every viewpoint is represented from the most trivial and self-deluding to the most sophisticated and profound.'

Professor Hubert J. Richards

'A real life *Thorn Birds* which grabs you from the first page to the last. Five lives in torment trapped in a world few of us suspected even existed today... It is also a worthy successor of that classic, *The Nun's Story.*'

BBC Radio Ulster, Northern Ireland

'The book reads like a novel, rushing from one drama to the next, and has a fly on the wall compulsion... It is sensational in the best sense of the word – not least because the Vatican want to hound out of office those who shared their intimate lives.'

Edinburgh Evening News, Scotland

'Absorbing, sensitively written... the effect is to bring home to the reader just how hard it must be to reconcile one's faith with a strong physical and emotional need to love someone else completely.'

Ottawa Times

'Epic account of the clergy's struggle with their sexuality. The wrenching conflict between spirit and flesh that Gordon Thomas defines leaps over the wall of the cloister and becomes surprisingly relevant to the secular world beyond.

Anne Harris, Sunday Independent

'Arouses powerful emotions... it reveals how individuals attempt to reconcile their quest for spiritual growth with the demands for celibacy.'

Michael Delmonte, RTE Radio

'Powerful and compassionate... challenges our attitude to a way of life we have accepted for hundreds of years.'

Irish Independent

'A time bomb of a book, tackling in unflinching detail the ultra-sensitive subject of chastity/celibacy in the Roman Catholic Church.'

Today

TRESPASS INTO TEMPTATION

TRESPASS INTO TEMPTATION

GORDON THOMAS

THE REALITY OF CELIBACY IN THE CHURCH

A LION BOOK

Published by
Lion Publishing plc
Sandy Lane West, Oxford, England
ISBN 0 7459 3802 7
Albatross Books Pty Ltd
PO Box 320, Sutherland, NSW 2232, Australia
ISBN 0 7324 1655 8

Originally published as *Desire and Denial*, 1986
This edition first published 1997
10 9 8 7 6 5 4 3 2 1 0

A catalogue record for this book is available
from the British Library

Printed and bound in Great Britain
by Caledonian International Book Manufacturing, Glasgow

For EDITH
*and her determination that no one
would take unfair advantage or
distort reality for any reason.*

NOTE TO THE READER

All the people in this book are real. A few asked for, and were given, guarantees their identities would be suitably protected because their experiences still traumatize them.

Behind their motives for breaking silence is a plea that religion must not continue to exact its penalty and claim more victims.

The principal participants were interviewed from a questionnaire prepared with the help of Professor Noel Walsh, Professor of Psychiatry at University College Dublin, and head of the Department of Psychiatry at St Vincent's Hospital, Dublin. Each participant was given a list of 550 questions about their lives and personal experiences. Interviews were conducted over an eighteen-month period.

As well as their personal recollections, all the principal interviewees made available their diaries, private papers and other personal documentation. In all places where dialogue is used, this was produced from the written records.

Transcriptions of all the interviews were made for all interviewees; some ran to almost 1000 pages of typescript. All interviewees were given the right to change or amend what they had said. After reading back their interviews, often over several readings, not one interviewee made a single change in what he or she had originally said. It is a tribute to their courage and honesty.

Gordon Thomas
Delgany, Ireland
November 1996

CHAPTER ONE

Exodus

Day and night they continue to depart, leaving their church in deepening crisis and their own futures uncertain. They are Roman Catholic priests who find they cannot cope with their vow of celibacy.

Compulsory celibacy distinguishes Catholicism from all other Christian denominations, despite Christ not making it mandatory and choosing married men to be among his disciples. Saint Paul, while regarding celibacy as superior, left it a free choice: 'Concerning celibacy, I have no commandment of the Lord' (1 Cor 7:25).

It was not until the Second Lateran Council of 1139 that the church barred priests from taking wives and remodelled the priesthood to what we know today: a body of men too often struggling to live a lifestyle which increasingly makes no sense to them. As this century draws to a close, one which has seen a sexual revolution in so many areas, many priests find it increasingly hard to accept a vow that asks of them: 'Are you resolved, as a sign of your interior dedication to Christ, to remain celibate for the sake of the kingdom and in lifelong service to God and mankind?'

Those who cannot, leave. Many attract headlines and further the debate on compulsory celibacy.

In September 1996, it was the turn of the Catholic Church in Scotland to be gripped by the revelation that one of its princes, Monsignor Roderick Wright, the Bishop of Argyll and the Isles, could no longer live a celibate life. His love for a woman, a parishioner he had counselled through her own broken marriage, was greater than the promise he had made at his ordination twenty-two years previously. The news reverberated far beyond the parishes of his Highlands fiefdom.

Cardinal Basil Hume, Primate of All-England and Wales cautiously suggested the possibility of looking again at compulsory celibacy because it was a 'church law, not a divine one'. For a moment it looked as if his Eminence had broken ranks after a lifetime of promoting the virtues of a celibate priesthood. Next day, he was back on the spiritual ramparts insisting he was not suggesting compulsory celibacy was about to be abolished; far from it. Outwardly the church's style of crisis-management – the least said, the sooner forgotten – seemed to have once more triumphed. The traditional attitude towards any priest who fell in love would remain: abandon the woman and repent the sin.

Only the Pope and a handful of his advisers knew the full truth behind Bishop Wright's sudden departure. As well as the woman he had driven off with into the Scottish night, he had fathered a love-child by another woman. The boy was now sixteen and living with his mother on the south coast of England in reduced circumstances. For all those years Bishop Wright had managed to keep his secret from surfacing, though only recently had he begun to provide support for his son. Those in the Scottish Hierarchy who had suspected were reassured by the bishop that the whispers were baseless rumours.

On the night he decided to resign, Bishop Wright confessed to church officials the truth. When the Vatican was told, the first reaction was: could the matter still be kept quiet? The decision was taken to wait and see.

On the fifth day after Bishop Wright's resignation, Joanne Whibley, the mother of his son, Kevin, approached the BBC saying she could no longer live 'the life of the lie'. The story she told on national television was wretchedly familiar, of a woman who had tasted forbidden love with a priest and carried his child, only to have their son rejected at birth by his father. From Bishop Wright there had only been a repeated promise that 'one day' they would all be together 'as a real family'. Instead, like the rest of Britain, Ms Whibley had learned her lover had gone off with another woman who had abandoned her own children to follow him.

Like a bush fire the uproar once more spread across the front pages, into every news bulletin and onto radio talk shows. Cardinal Hume and every other Catholic bishop in good standing with media training, were trundled out to try and calm the renewed anger and upset in the Catholic world. The Pope, on a pastoral visit to France, announced compulsory celibacy would stay. His spokesman urged perspective – 'after all there have only been six bishops these past ten years who have behaved like this'. It seemed an unusual attempt at justification, perhaps an indication of how badly rattled the Vatican was.

In Ireland there was a sense of *déjà vu*. The revelations from Scotland were a mirror image of the now notorious case of Eamonn Casey, the former Bishop of Galway – an old friend of Bishop Wright.

They had met at church conferences, sat on work parties. Both were regarded as modern-day thinkers on church affairs and tipped as potential Cardinals – perhaps even possible candidates for the highest office of all, the throne of St Peter. Outside their clerical duties they shared a common interest in good food and wine and walking. The intriguing question was whether they shared with one another their common secret of fatherhood.

It cannot be discounted. Both men possess the kind of personality that would require them to seek a safety-valve. The strain of having to keep a common secret would have been great. This may well account for Bishop Wright, at the time of Casey's outing, urging there should be compassion and understanding for his fellow bishop and that the law of celibacy needed rethinking. Shortly after expressing such thoughts he was warned by the Vatican to stay silent on the subject. He also became a subject of scrutiny into his own private life. That such scrutiny did not go far enough became self-evident by the story the mother of his son told.

But in 1992 it was Casey who, under intense pressure from the mother of the child he had fathered, admitted the affair, including that he had 'borrowed' £70,000 from Diocesan funds to give to her. The money had subsequently been returned to church coffers from an anonymous source. While a stunned nation digested this information, Casey – again very much in the style of Bishop Wright – confessed these truths to church officials at the last possible moment before fleeing Ireland, esconced in a first-class airline seat. Wright chose to go by car.

Both men left behind them a scandalized and deeply offended and hurt Catholic faithful. In Scotland the same questions were asked as had been asked in Ireland four years previously. How could a Catholic bishop use his high office to continue a sexual liaison, while at the same time casting out any priest who strayed? How many fellow bishops suspected what was going on? If they had chosen to look the other way, that was indeed Christ-like, but did it not make a mockery of the rules of celibacy they were all expected to live by? How had they rationalized the dichotomy between sexuality and spirituality? A clue can be found in the words of Annie Murphy, the mother of Eamonn Casey's son, Peter. In her subsequent account of the affair she wrote:

> one snicker from me would have torn apart Eamonn's closely-woven web of self-deceit. He and I had been brought up with the same moral code. We both knew there was no justification for what he was doing. I had one advantage over him: guilt was not my enemy but my friend and accomplice. Being a bad Catholic is the best religion there is.

Both Eamonn Casey and Roderick Wright fled their responsibilities. But, while giving up their comfortable lifestyle, they have remained bishops with all the respect that goes with the office. Casey, now a parish priest in Ecuador, is treated with veneration when he returns to Ireland. Wright, when the dust settles, has no reason not to expect a similar welcome should he choose to return to Scotland. Both retain the title of bishop.

Such treatment, in the case of Casey, has caused understandable resentment among other, less-exalted priests who have resigned for similar reasons to follow their heart's desire into an uncertain world. They have all too often found themselves in the dole queue because they have no special skills except an ability to preach and pray.

But for Eamonn Casey the church provided security from the moment he left Ireland. In May 1992 he was taken to a convent in San Antonio, Texas. He received personal counselling from a distinguished American psychiatrist. At some point it is reasonable to assume he would have been asked to give a full explanation to the Vatican of his relationship with Annie Murphy – and try to explain how he came to 'borrow' a huge sum of money to – she has claimed – buy her silence.

In March 1993, Casey was moved to a convent in Mexico. It was there I spoke to him. Close to sixty-seven years of age, he appeared a tragic figure, filled with bitterness against Annie Murphy for revealing their relationship.

I had met Casey some nine years earlier during the preparation of the first draft of this book. It seemed a good idea for me to obtain the views of Catholic opinion-makers.

Bishop Casey was an obvious choice, given his high profile. He had accompanied Pope John Paul II during the pontiff's tour of Ireland; Casey was frequently on Irish radio and television. He seemed to have a view on everything clerical. I assumed Casey would surely join in the debate on celibacy I hoped to launch.

He greeted me with words which have remained in my mind. 'Well now,' he said. 'This is an interesting theme, right enough. But not one I can readily identify with. Celibacy has never been a problem for me.'

At the time the bishop's own son, Peter, was nearly ten years old. I reminded Eamonn Casey of this during our interview in Mexico. His response was to abruptly break off all further discussion and disappear into the somewhat bemused Mexicans on the street. I did not pursue him.

In the past quarter of a century over 100,000 Roman Catholic priests have given up their vocations. It has left the Vatican with the greatest crisis it has faced since the Reformation, leaving the largest church in Christendom without priests, and its congregations starved for the Eucharist. It is a virus poisoning the body of Christ. Yet the Vatican remains intransigent under the iron rule of the present supreme pontiff, Pope John Paul II.

It is certain that the church will react similarly to the next headline-making desertion. Each desertion is recorded on computer in the Vatican Statistics Office, along with details of how long the priest had served and what efforts were made to stop him leaving. There is no space to detail the trauma, the deep spiritual pain and emotional hurt each priest undoubtedly felt at renouncing his calling because he could not cope with the conflicts in his body and mind.

Ironically, in the eyes of the Vatican they remain priests, on the basis that 'once a priest, always a priest'. In the United States of America those who leave to wed are known as 'married priests'. Others who simply prefer to live with the woman of their choice are called 'resigned priests'. In Austria they are termed 'priests without a role'. In France they are called 'veteran priests'.

The analogy with survivors of combat comes closest to describing what they have all experienced – a shattering conflict of the soul. Many leave their ministry in the dead of night, making the sign of the cross and walking into the darkness which momentarily hides their agony. Others march boldly away after a final confrontation with their superior over the shadow life they have had to live.

The Vatican keeps no formal record of the number of resigned priests who do marry – because the church does not recognize such unions. Those marriages sometimes work, but they are often turbulent. A love affair which brought a man out of the active priesthood can turn out to be a symptom of deeper maladjustment and the relationship founders. A common reason was articulated by a former priest in the wake of the Bishop Wright resignation – 'Being married is harder than being celibate. I did not realize how selfish celibacy had made me.'

The reason for leaving is overwhelmingly a need to maintain, or consummate, a physical love for a woman they have each secretly cherished in their priestly life. Only a few priests leave over a physical relationship with a man; perhaps it is easier to maintain such an alliance within the church.

Nuns mostly resign having fallen in love with a man. Sometimes it is a priest, more often someone they have met through their work, usually teaching or social and community duties. Few nuns renounce their vows because of a physical attraction for another woman. They, too, claim it is easier to maintain such a relationship within the sisterhood. Outwardly, at least, the church seems largely indifferent to the thinning of the ranks of its women. But the emotional pain nuns suffer before leaving is assuredly as great as that of the priests.

Present trends indicate that the number of priests in ministry within the United States will have halved by the year 2000. That will leave less than 15,000 to deal with the spiritual needs of 70 million Catholics.

Currently one in five US priests resign from active ministry within ten years of their ordination. In 1996 over 2000 US parishes had no full-time priest. By the start of the new millennium – upon which Pope John Paul II pins so many hopes – the average age of US priests who can transform those aspirations into reality will be sixty-five years – retirement age. How many will opt to do so? How many will actually live to reach that milestone? The trend continues to rise in the number who die before retirement. Stress, from a lifetime of trying to cope with celibacy, is given as a major reason in a study commissioned by the US Catholic hierarchy.

Vocations continue to decline. In 1965 there were 48,000 students enrolled in US seminaries. Today the figure is under 10,000.

A study of the Catholic Directory showed that the number of vocations in the United Kingdom between 1968 and 1987 had fallen by 1526. During the same period the Catholic population rose by 20,000 to 4,164,000. The number of priests continues to decline in Britain though the exact figures are still carefully kept from public scrutiny.

One English support group set up to help women involved with priests, Seven-Eleven, reported in 1995 that there were currently over eighty such ongoing liaisons in England and Wales, and added that the global figure could run to many thousands.

In Ireland, David Rice, a former priest, had details of over ninety clandestine relationships in the Republic, 'some involving well-known clerics'. He claimed that in 1996 there were ten such relationships in one single diocese, affairs which had produced eight children by priests. Four other parish priests had asked their lovers to have abortions. Rice said these were only some of the 'sinister fruits' of compulsory celibacy.

Elsewhere there is little to comfort Rome. In Spain one in four priests have left in the past twenty years. The average age of those who remain was, in 1996, fifty-seven years. The numbers to replace them have grown steadily less.

At the start of the new millennium France is likely to have only 25,000 diocesan priests; in 1980 there were 40,000. In Italy almost 10,000 priests have resigned in the past twenty years. In Holland in the same period the figure currently exceeds 3000. Ireland, long a bastion for vocations, has seen almost 500 priests leave, the majority to get married. Throughout the Catholic world in 1986, 160,000 of 375,000 parishes did not have a full-time priest.

But this is not another book about the abundant statistical evidence of a powerful church in crisis. It documents instead an anguish, even terror, that those who have not experienced cannot begin to comprehend. Those who have experienced it, have found that the very authority and doctrine of their church, which had once comforted, protected and supported them, faced instead an unyielding position repeatedly and defiantly expressed by his Holiness, Pope John Paul II – 'Celibacy is a sign of the undivided love of the priest for God's people.'

Written in what amounts to papal stone, that declaration ensures that, for his priests, earthly passion is laced with guilt, women are branded as temptresses and physical frustration co-mingles with spiritual hunger.

In 1940, when Father Breslin entered an Irish seminary there were no detectable signs that the church's autocratic attitude towards celibacy would ever be challenged. It was compulsory. There was no more to be said.

Sister Victoria entered her convent in the United States in 1958. By then the first murmurs were surfacing within the US church for a change in compulsory celibacy. The discussion would affect her attitudes and behaviour and eventually make her part of the pressure for reform. Her behaviour would mark a turning point in the attitudes of many priests and nuns.

By 1966, when Father Philippe became a seminarian in the United States, the protest movement within the church had become part of the anti-authority movement worldwide. Father Philippe became convinced that the US church could no longer remain rigid about the right of its priests to fully express their sexuality. He knew he certainly could not function fully as a priest without taking that into account.

Sister Clare embarked upon her commitment in Ireland in 1973, when the sheer speed of change had begun to create a deepening and demoralizing crisis in the church, though she herself was still too young to understand the reasons until the Second Vatican Council gave full vent to the sexual revolution.

Father Breslin, by then middle-aged and with an accumulation of experience and pain in coping with his own sexuality, found the freedoms that had followed the Council's edicts, had left him disappointed, surprised and often angry. Like many other priests of his generation he wondered if his years of constant struggle to remain celibate had been worthwhile. Father Philippe and Sister Victoria felt the church had not gone far enough. Committed young nuns like Sister Clare often alternated between excitement and confusion.

When Andrew entered a seminary in Rome in 1982, almost forty - two years to the day that Father Breslin became a seminarian, the need for change within the church was not a matter for debate. It was there. The only question was how far it could go.

While their accounts are of intense personal experiences, they are also about growth and the profound spiritual change needed to live the quasi-mystical state called religious celibacy. It is also a story of coming alive again.

CHAPTER TWO

A Way of Life

Father Seamus Breslin had lost count of the number of persons he had helped to die in peace by this, the forty-first year of his ministry. But he wondered how much longer any priest would retain final custody over the dying. The campaign to admit women into the ranks of the Catholic clergy was mounting. For Father Breslin a nun nowadays often denoted a revolutionary in a modified habit – hoping among other things to administer the last rites he was about to give.

Father Breslin was sixty-three years old and had no living relatives to share his sorrow over that and other predicted changes: church-recognized divorce, contraception, ordained women priests and optional celibacy.

The call from the hospital that Eileen's time had finally come reminded him of his promise to her. 'You will die in peace because I will be there to see you do.'

It had taken him years to recognize that the customs and rituals surrounding dying served two purposes: to try and reduce its frightening aspects by placing it in a recognizable system of values and to support those who are about to be bereaved. One of his many skills is that he always managed to make the words associated with dying sound as if he had never used them before.

Standing in the hospital room doorway he was a short slight figure, his face dominated by sharply intelligent eyes. Eileen's heartbeats continued moving across the monitor screen, blips reducing her grasp on life to an endless trace. It had been a long and painful illness but now it was ending. Eileen was forty-six years old, a wife for twenty-five of them, the mother of four grown children. Her husband and three sons were grouped around the bed. Her daughter, working abroad, had been summoned. Father Breslin was certain she would arrive too late.

The emotions aroused by approaching death were already emerging. He could detect the fear, sorrow, despair and helplessness of the family and the resignation of the doctor and nurse. While he well understood their responses, it was Eileen who mattered.

Father Breslin had visited her regularly during her months in hospital, reminding her that when the time came, God would receive her. He had told Eileen in a dozen ways that her own strong religious conviction was the best preparation for the life hereafter and it would actually protect her from any fear of death. Nevertheless, it had taken him several talks to foster the idea that she must accept the possibility of a growing and inevitable sense of separation from her family, doctors and nurses. It might be the only way they could tolerate what was happening to her.

Eileen had once said she was glad to be a Catholic because it gave her a priest with no ties other than to his ministry. Until then he never thought of Eileen as having even a rudimentary interest in his vocation. But she had spoken knowledgeably about the holiest and greatest of celibates, that their deeds and writings were influenced by their complete consecration to God. And he had thought, 'How could I have even had the notion of telling her otherwise? Of explaining that celibacy is a continuing education in human frailty.' That would have been too revealing a glimpse into his mind.

Now he watched her eyes, dilated with pain-killing drugs, drift towards where he stood in his surplice and stole. The family gathered around the bed were caught in some deep, primitive and instinctive ritual. Her husband held Eileen's hands, his fingers barely brushing her skin as if afraid even such small contact might cause her pain. The eldest son was at the foot of the bed, head bowed, a hand resting close to his mother's feet. This contact, too, was light yet deeply poignant. The other sons stared silently at their mother as if no words could communicate their true feelings.

Father Breslin bent over Eileen and in a soft and clear voice said he would give her Holy Communion for those close to death. He took a wafer from its case and made the sign of the cross before Eileen's face. After murmuring a prayer he bent closer to listen. From Eileen's lips came a weak 'Amen'. He placed the wafer upon her waiting tongue and gently closed her mouth. She stared at him, too weak to swallow. He gently lifted her chin, allowing the wafer to slide down her throat. From a pocket he produced a tiny silver vial containing holy oil, unscrewed the top and used his thumb to moisten the skin, anointing her eyes, mouth and ears, murmuring further prayers. After the rites were over, he placed Eileen's rosary in her hand. He glanced at the monitor.

The family, followed by the doctor and nurse, returned to the bedside. Eileen's husband resumed holding her hand, fingering the rosary beads and praying softly. His sons stood at his shoulder, Father Breslin between them. Suddenly, irregular beats appeared on the screen. A red light flashed on the monitor. The doctor checked Eileen's pulse. A straight, unbroken line had replaced the blips. The light no longer flashed. The nurse glanced at Eileen's husband.

'She's gone.'

The family turned and stared at Father Breslin.

'She has found God's peace,' were his first words of reassurance.

He nodded to the doctor and nurse to leave.

The silence in the room was broken when Eileen's husband said, without bitterness or self-pity, that Father Breslin should be glad he would never feel the pain of losing a loved wife.

Father Breslin remained silent. How could he explain at this moment that his past was a potent aphrodisiac, that somewhere in his subconscious those halcyon summers of long ago still lived on, that while outwardly he appeared to barely tip the scales at his emotional weight, inwardly he still carried secret memories.

He began to comfort Eileen's family. He had prepared them these past months to face the painful and difficult adjustment her death would bring. He had urged them to recognize and resist an impulse to isolate themselves. In their close-knit community it would be especially sad if they turned away the helpful intentions of their relatives and friends. And, if some did not rally round, it would be because they would not know what to do or say.

His voice was calm and certain, devoid of any pity, but filled with a deep sense of sympathy. He urged them to regard Eileen's death not solely as a terrible blow. Nor must they blame themselves or those who cared for her, the doctors and nurses. No one could have done more. There must be no misplaced anger. Above all they must resist temptation to turn away from God.

Then quietly, without fuss, he detached himself from the bedside tableau. For the moment there was no more he could do. The family would draw sympathy and strength from each other. This was no place for outsiders to be part of their shedding of tears.

Driving back to the parochial house he pondered that unequivocal statement of Eileen's husband about loving and losing a woman. Father Breslin had never told anybody that he once squandered that chance, that he had carried forward this memory year after year. For so long he had dangled on the rope of conscience. He had often wondered where Mary was and who she was with; whether if he had behaved differently, he would not now be returning to a loneliness which, in spite of all his efforts, he could not totally pray away. Whenever he thought about her, he always came back to Kierkegaard's dictum: 'To cheat oneself out of love is the most terrible deception: it is an eternal loss for which there is no reparation, either in time or in eternity.'

Victoria was late: not that she minded. She had been making well-managed entrances all her life – from that morning when, barely four years old, she had paraded into her parents' bedroom draped in a black cloth with a handkerchief on her head announcing she was a nun. Her mother had called her cute. Her lateness today would give Paul time to explain to his other guests about her.

During the cab ride across the city she mused again how prurient people were when they learned her profession, asking her to differentiate between sexual love and genital sex, or to discuss mortification of the flesh and the Pope's latest reminder that masturbation was still a mortal sin. And of course, because of what she was, they asked her about chastity.

Such questions used to make her feel uncomfortable. But nowadays she answered them fully. Being able to do so was one of her talents.

Another was her clothes sense. She wore a Dior scarf at the neck, a Thai silk blouse and a fashionable skirt with matching blue shoes but no make-up or jewellery; nothing to detract from her natural good looks. She looked younger than her forty-four years.

Paul was waiting for her at the door to the apartment he had gutted and remodelled from a slum attic. Being introduced to his guests she was impressed with how well he now handled his homosexuality. An understanding of her own sexual needs had enabled her to help him overcome a broken marriage and a number of gay encounters before Paul had settled into a steady relationship with his live-in lover, Mario.

After introducing her to a dress designer who made a modest living copying Paris originals, Paul ushered her to a group listening to an actor describing why he had refused yet another offer from Hollywood. Victoria knew the man's only source of income was dubbing English language films into Italian.

Finally they reached Jim, standing by a window, holding a glass of white wine for her. He was strongly built with an honestly happy smile. He wore loafers, a sports shirt and linen pants. He too did not look his age – close to fifty. Accepting her wine, she kissed Jim on the mouth.

After a few pleasantries, the conversation turned to an article just published in one of the specialist journals they both read. It confirmed their own observations: a high percentage of those in religious life had no clear idea of how to handle their emotional and physical demands.

Jim was enraged by Pope John Paul II who, by a stroke of his pen soon after being elected in October 1978, had ended official dispensation from the priesthood. For months Jim had been trying unsuccessfully to obtain figures from the Vatican on the numbers who have abandoned their vocation. He told her he was still trying.

Victoria murmured: '*Tu es sacerdos in aeternum.*' The words were from the ceremony of ordination used when a bishop placed his hands on a man's head symbolizing he would be a priest forever.

Victoria squeezed Jim's arm. She understood his deep frustration over the situation. They were still discussing the matter when Paul called them to dinner. He was a fine cook, the meal an epicurean delight. Jim and Victoria were seated at opposite ends of the table. The conversation, as she had expected, had a distinctive undertone. The actor related that when he was with a touring company he regularly visited gay public baths because they were always the cleanest.

'Nice soft lighting and music. If somebody gave you the fish-eye you just said "I'm resting". It was an accepted code. Nobody bothered you. Now I guess it's different.'

Another guest boasted of his latest acquisition. He had persuaded a sculptor friend to create a representation of two young men making love.

'I tell my straight friends it's a surrealist impression of the Alaska pipeline.'

Paul interrupted to say gay hedonism bored him. Mario looked hurt. Another guest enquired of Jim if he had read *The Church and the Homosexual*? Jim had. Its author was a respected Jesuit. The essence of his argument was that a man knew he was a true homosexual only when he fell in love with another man; even if he was a priest the experience should not affect his calling.

Victoria sensed the focus of interest switching and narrowing. She quoted from Willa Cather's novel, *Death Comes for the Archbishop*, the words of the character, Father Martinez, who had an illegitimate son – '"Celibate priests lose their perceptions. No priest can experience repentance and forgiveness of sin unless he falls into sin."' Pausing she looked at Jim.

He completed Martinez's speech. '"Since concupiscence is the most common form of temptation, it is better to know something about it."'

The questions came. Paul kept a watchful eye, ready to intercede and deflect any inquiries he judged to be too pointedly personal. However they were searching enough.

Afterwards, on the way back to her apartment, Jim and Victoria agreed that it had not been hard to convince the other guests that, while they frequently shared the same bed, and kissed and caressed, they did not actually make love because she was a professed nun and he a priest in good standing. That was why he would not sleep with Victoria on this night, because in the morning he must celebrate early Mass.

Some things, he reminded himself, never changed. They still called him Father Philippe.

He concentrated on the activities around the altar, conscious of Cap beside him. His son was five years old, tall for his age, with his mother's fair hair and still too young to understand the whispers directed at them.

Father Philippe had hardened himself against the tongue-waggers who said his clothes were no longer custom-made, his after-shave not the expensive cologne he once imported from Paris. Yet he knew there was still a sense of style about him. What really offended his detractors was his refusal to move out of the parish to escape their hostility.

Supported by Margot and her family he had stood his ground. Part of this resolve was to appear at Mass.

The scandalized stares had followed him all the way from the vestibule and past the confession boxes as he had led Cap, arm protectively around the boy's shoulder, to their seats. Father Philippe knew what they were saying – he was putting on weight, and his face, which had always been soft and boyish, had suddenly caught up with his forty-two years. That's what happened, he imagined them murmuring to each other, when a priest did what he had done.

He took care they could not see his right thumbnail scraping the skin of his left hand; it was a nervous habit going back to his days as an altar boy. Being a priest had then been his only ambition.

The sanctuary windows sparkled in the diffused morning sun, giving Christ on the stained glass the appearance of being crucified against a purple sky tinged with red, darker than blood. In one of his last conversations with the diocesan chancellor, Father Philippe had rejected the authenticity of the depiction. The chancellor, of Irish descent, had listened with a splintering stare as Father Philippe explained he believed Jesus was pinioned through the wrists, feet nailed so they sloped downwards, forcing him to stretch upwards, racking the limbs. This was the unique torture of the cross. The torment of having to constantly rise and fall would only have ended with asphyxiation and death. The chancellor had coldly replied that he should have taken up medicine instead of the priesthood.

Watching him now concelebrating Mass with the bishop, Father Philippe wondered whether the chancellor had any idea of what it was like to realistically follow Christ? Did he not see that celibacy was a lost dream? Would the chancellor ever begin to understand that if a priest had never had a relationship with a woman, then he could not know what he was giving up?

The preparations at the altar were complete. The sacred host had been removed from the tabernacle and the sanctuary lamp burned steadily. In orderly file, pew by pew, people approached the altar rail which separated the sanctuary from the rest of the church.

Father Philippe scooped Cap in his arms and, eyes fixed on the bishop and chancellor who were moving back and forth behind the rail dispensing Holy Communion, he joined the lengthening procession.

He knew people were genuinely shocked to see him in line. He ignored them, determined to partake in the extraordinary miracle by which Jesus gave his body and blood for spiritual nourishment.

Close to the rail, Father Philippe lowered Cap to the floor and grasped his hand, smiling reassurance. For the moment every space at the rail was occupied with kneeling supplicants, waiting for either the bishop or chancellor to pause before them. As each received a wafer, rose and left, their places were taken by others.

A space had become vacant at the chancellor's side of the rail. Father Philippe motioned for a woman behind him to take it. She stepped forward, ignoring him and the child. A communicant rose from before the bishop. Father Philippe moved swiftly, tugging Cap with him and knelt in the vacant place.

Shafts of sunlight flooded the sanctuary. High above him Father Philippe could see the crucified Christ. He quickly lowered his eyes.

There was a burning look in the chancellor's eyes and a faint and familiar odour from his cassock: the unmistakable mixture of incense, sweat, hospital antiseptic and the aroma of funeral parlours – an odour that eventually permeated every cassock.

Voices softly intoned the hallowed, *the body of Christ*, as each wafer was taken from the chalice. Father Philippe continued to stare ahead, willing himself that, having come this far, he must remain kneeling. He could sense the chancellor's puffy, red-rimmed and angry eyes on him. Then the bishop impassively placed a wafer on Father Philippe's tongue, murmured the incantation and moved on.

Father Philippe closed his eyes to squeeze back the tears. God loved him. For a moment longer he knelt in prayer, then holding Cap's hand, he walked back to their pew.

Father Philippe knew he would never again say Mass, sit in the priest's box of the confessional, or receive new holy oils or bury the dead. Yet in the eyes of the church he would remain a priest until he died or his Holiness the Pope changed his mind about granting him dispensation.

He suspected not even Margot understood his feelings over being denied a vocation because he had chosen to love her. Father Philippe had been married twice. With the covert help of the church, his first union had been dissolved so that he could return to his ministry. While still a priest in the eyes of the church he had wed Margot and fathered two children, Cap, and at home, baby Daniel.

Clare prepared the table without a fuss. She would again eat by herself, for this was Friday evening, the start of the weekend, when she would not be answerable to school bells and the repetitive questions of children. She made the preparation as part of an automatic gathering-up of the past into the present.

The Mistress of Postulants and Novices had instilled the principle that no matter what the task, it must be carried out with no commotion. Those were the days when Clare had devoutly accepted that the Mistress had total control over her life, deciding among other things when she should receive a new pair of shoes, take a bath or obtain a new toothbrush.

Sometimes Clare was ashamed of the anger that surfaced when she recalled those times. God only knew how hard she had tried to live with her body and not feel alienated from it.

Clare finished setting the table, cup, saucer and place in symmetrical order with the cutlery. This meticulous alignment had formed part of what the Order's Rule called Preparation. The Mistress had expanded its meaning – 'You must symbolically put your flesh to death so that your love becomes absolutely focused on God's will.'

Yet love was the word Clare least associated with her cloistered life. From the outset it was drummed into her, the Mistress emphasizing her points with sharp taps of a ruler on her desk, that all Clare's ideas on love must change. 'What matters is being able to love selflessly; being loved in return by any other person is beside the point, indeed is actively discouraged. You must accept the constant presence of only three persons in your life, God, Christ and the Blessed Virgin Mary. If ever you feel the onset of loneliness or despair it can only be because you are no longer expressing love the way you must. You are never alone. God is there. Look at him and his love as if it were a mirror. When you love God you become his mirror and he becomes yours. To live in God's love is your greatest challenge.'

To signify her commitment, Clare had accepted her hair must be covered with tight bands of linen and her body enveloped in shapeless cloth. The garments were intended to eliminate sensual feelings. She wore a veil to proclaim she was consecrated to Christ. She was given a new name, biblical and familiar, together with a number and listed in the Order's name book as Sister Mark Luke – 136. She was told she must not see this as depersonalizing, but to accept it as part of relinquishing the past.

Clare had voluntarily agreed to forgo other rights: the freedom to travel at will, to visit or entertain friends as she wished, to go home when she felt like it, to have her family visit her without seeking special permission. She could not wear beneath her heavy serge robe one single item which was feminine or frivolous. She was told those restrictions were all necessary to help her become spiritually formed.

She had been a virgin when she joined the Order at eighteen years of age. Now it was different; girls frequently had full sexual experience before entering religious life. Yet, at the age of thirty-four, she accepted she might live the remainder of her life without physically knowing a man. Still strong within her was another idea the Mistress had also instilled. 'Sexuality is the enemy of chastity. The demands of the body can be overcome. Chastity becomes easier through prayer. Bodily urges die by reciting the rosary.'

Because of Tom she now knew differently. She kept his photograph thumb-tacked to the inside of her wardrobe door: a tall, smiling man, not unhandsome and in his early forties. She had taken the snapshot on a Saturday morning, outside the city's main art museum. Later she had raised the subject of their relationship, and then only to say she would never ask him to go beyond what he wanted, that she realized it had to be a relationship without promises. She had known she was deceiving herself.

So it began. They would speak on the phone each Friday evening when she was back from school, planning where they would go during the weekend. Usually it would include a pub for a drink, and sometimes a restaurant for dinner. She would insist on paying her way and, after some protest, he accepted.

Gradually she came to realize she wanted more. She wanted to take his arm as they stood waiting to cross a street; to surprise him with a kiss as they sat watching a movie. But Clare did none of these things because of who Tom was.

She began to notice little traits in him. He was at pains never to commit himself fully; always holding back something of himself and yet at the same time showing he could be vulnerable and needed reassurance. This had increased her desire for him. At times she felt the tension both exquisite and unbearable and that he, too, must have realized the space between them was charged with sensuality.

After about a month Tom began to suffer crippling backache and headaches, so severe he had had to cancel their weekend plans. She would be consoling and understanding, all the while suffering the special disappointment of unfulfilled love.

After the third Friday in a row when he had offered a particularly bad headache as a reason for not meeting her, the blow fell. Next day she had impulsively telephoned Tom to learn he had gone away for the weekend. The woman at the other end had sounded cold and suspicious. Clare had risked one more question, asking if Tom had recovered from his sickness. The woman had said there was no one sick at this house and hung up without saying another word.

Two weeks passed before Tom rang. He said he would pick her up next day and they would drive into the hills. When he collected her he wore jeans and a sweat-shirt. She had never seen him look more casual or relaxed. She knew something was seriously wrong when they drove out into the country in silence. Usually he would have found a dozen things to talk about. He parked on the edge of the road and she thought he had stopped to admire the view. Instead, he told her he could no longer meet her. In a small voice she asked why. Tom restarted the car and drove a full mile before answering. He merely said she should not make it harder than it was for him.

She had wanted to question him, as though by pushing the knife ever deeper into herself she could perform an operation which would cure her forever of love. She wanted to ask him about the weekend when he had lied to her, to confront him with evidence, convicting him in her eyes forever – anything which forced her to recognize the extent of her illusions. Clare had said nothing as he drove her home.

When Tom dropped her off he said she must always have known there was a part of his life he could never share. Then as he drove away, she knew she would never see him again. Yet, in the months which had followed, she had never stopped loving him. She had tried to delude herself she only wished he would accept her love as a gift; that he, of all men, could do that. Tom was a priest.

Past midnight, Andrew continued to write at the desk. From somewhere beyond the massive walls of the seminary bedroom, voices on a radio argued. Suddenly they were gone, as an unseen hand switched to a music station. Formulating his thoughts about love into words, Andrew had decided, was even more of a commitment than the sexual act itself. Words forced him to give substance to moments plucked from the recesses of his mind. There were times when he felt he was writing about somebody else instead of trying to recall his own relationship with Jane.

He had kept the diary since his first day in the seminary. It was his way of reminding himself that, in the rigidly structured routine of the seminary, he still managed to keep a little piece of himself which only the Almighty knew about.

A polaroid of Jane was scotch-taped to a board festooned with notes from his tutors and his spiritual director. In the photograph she had a halo of blonde hair and a generous mouth, slightly crooked because she was smiling. The photograph was over three years old, taken just before he became a seminarian.

He had sometimes wondered what God might think of some of the diary entries. About his admission to a powerful ambition to rise high in the church, 'perhaps even become Pope'. That he found some of the other seminarians social bores, and a few of the tutors spouted pointless dogma. He had also confided his own shortcomings: his impatience, his lack of humility: 'I must learn to give, give, give and keep on giving because that is what the Lord wants of me.'

But what would God say about his feelings now for Jane? Her presence was there on page after page: words and descriptions reflecting the kind of emotional pain he had never thought possible. That was why he hesitated over how much he could commit onto paper. It still hurt too much. And his deeply-felt emotions for Jane constantly threatened his progress towards priesthood.

Once more the physical memory of Jane – her musky scent, the sheen of her hair, the smooth hardness of her nipples under his touch – permeated the monastic room. The familiar excitement coursed through him.

Andrew went to the books on the shelves along one wall. They were old friends, the pages well thumbed, some passages underscored. He began to read a comforting interpretation of Genesis, the very first account of the creation, the one which said God was clearly concerned about man and aware of his struggles with loneliness. He turned to the New Testament. On a slip of paper inserted between the pages of the Gospel of Matthew he had written his own interpretation of the apostle's views on marriage. 'It is not possible for everyone because of its special demands. But nor is celibacy. And Matthew seems to be saying that either are acceptable as long as a person chooses to follow Jesus. But there seems to be a choice. Marriage or celibacy.'

He skimmed one book after another, seeking the confirmation and reassurance they contained. Andrew returned to his desk pondering, mentally framing a thought, conscious again of Jane. Once more he began to write, quickly, the way he did when taking notes during lessons on moral theology.

No one can say that sexual abstinence is better than sexual intercourse. Nor is it less perfect. Both intercourse and abstinence are New Testament values. They cannot be presented as the supreme Christian value. That value is giving one's life to Christ. Doing that means the highest form of lasting love is possible. One nothing can shake.

Andrew stopped writing. Tears began to blot the page. He pushed the diary aside.

A scene from a novel came to mind – Huxley's *Point Counter Point*. Andrew had read it at university. A couple had shared a bath and one said 'of such is the kingdom of heaven'. He knew why that image remained vivid. He had regularly shared a tub with Jane.

Andrew began to scribble on a piece of paper, two words. Celibacy. Jane. Each time he completed either, he added a question mark. Then he drew a line through the word and wrote the next one. In this way he quickly filled another page of his diary. He closed his eyes. In his mind's eye the images had once more become stronger, detail after detail retained in all their crystal and destroying clarity. He could recall the bedroom they had shared, the way she had positioned each item of furniture. Some of it had been there when they rented the apartment: the double bed with a missing leg, propped up with a stack of old text-books; the faded yellow cotton curtains; the Victorian painting of the

Forth Bridge in the dark wooden frame he thought ghastly but she loved. They had bought a number of items at car boot sales, afterwards carrying home their purchases in triumph. There was a mahogany cabinet with an inlaid black marble top which she had placed on her side of the bed. In it she stored her curlers, setting lotion, diaphragm and gel. He had squatted naked on the bed and watched her, totally nude, cream and insert the cap. Then he had reached for her.

There was the hardback Edwardian dining-table chair they had argued over; he thought the price inflated, she not. She had placed the chair beneath the bedroom window. They used it as a clothes-horse, dumping their Levis, T-shirts and underwear on it when the urge to make love became overpowering.

Their love-making was always a secret triumph between them, a communion of bodies and minds, producing a shared sense of wonder and jubilation. In the long deep bath that was big enough for them both, they had soaked, bodies pressed together, and made love, joined like sea urchins, her eyes closed as though she were alone at the end of some journey. The last time they had bathed together she had begged him not to rush, to see how long he could remain inside her. To encourage him she had whispered those three words which still held him captive. 'I love you.'

Andrew opened his eyes, brushing away tears with the back of his hand and rose to his feet. From a jacket he fished out a handful of coins. He looked at his watch. Almost one o'clock in the morning, close to midnight where Jane was.

He began to pace the room, twelve paces by eight. His belongings were scattered everywhere: shoes, shirts, shorts, exercise books, old newspapers, letters. Jane had often complained about his untidiness and he had tried to make light of it by saying being in love made everyone careless of everything. She had looked at him carefully before turning away.

He came to a decision. Bare-footed, he padded from his cell-like room, hurried down the corridor, past all the other identical rooms. Dark though it was, he knew his way: he had made this journey many times at this hour. He was excited now as he reached the top of the staircase. At the bottom he turned into the Corridor of the Cardinals: the portraits of their Eminences peering down from the walls.

The seminary's payphone was beside the massive sixteenth-century front door. Nothing disturbed the silence. He paused, breathing slowly, getting his emotions under control. He began to insert the coins into the telephone box. Careful though he was, the noise of each one dropping through the slot was loud.

He began to dial, slowly, careful not to make a mistake and have to repeat the long sequence of numbers. He knew he should feel guilt, but love, as he once told Jane, could turn him into a monster. He pressed the receiver to his ear. A series of clicks, then silence. He groaned aloud; he must have misdialled. He was about to start again when the ringing tone began. A sleepy woman's voice answered. With infinite gentleness Andrew kissed the receiver and replaced it, breaking the connection with Jane.

Slowly he retraced his steps, head bowed, dejected, once more shocked and disgusted at his adolescent longing and lust, more so because Jane was now another man's wife. But he was convinced that a nocturnal telephone call to hear for a few brief seconds the voice of the girl he rejected to become a priest was one way for him to cope with a life of celibacy.

Safely back in his room, Andrew sat at his desk and recorded what he had done and how he felt afterwards. He believed God would understand his weakness. That was why Christ died on the cross, to help sinners like him.

In the end is it like this for every priest? Are the demands on their sexuality not only sacred but cruel? Is it possible to live in the midst of the world without enjoying its pleasures?

CHAPTER THREE

Once a Priest

Seamus Breslin found pleasure in the most ordinary of things. One was awakening promptly and, in the few moments there was time, lying quietly under the bedding, trying as the Dean of Studies repeatedly urged, to see himself as a sentient cog in the vast, intricate machine of life. Rhetoric was one of the Dean's indulgences. The other was drinking hot, scalding tea, punctuated with loud sighs. The sounds of a solitary mind, Seamus had decided, pleased at his growing faculty to judge a personality.

Observation, he was certain, would help to make him a good priest. While mastering Latin, Gregorian chant and the mystery of prayer were important – especially Latin, the language of the church – they were still only a part, along with lilies on the altar at Easter, burnt incense, the taste of wine from the chalice, the sorrow of so much organ music, the daub of grit on the forehead for Ash Wednesday, a reminder of human mortality. All this had combined to create what mattered to Seamus: the immensely comforting faith of Catholicism.

For as long as he could remember, he had always been stirred by the language and rituals which distinguished it from all other religions. There was fish on Friday and the sign of the cross to be made when passing a funeral or graveyard; confession and penance; plenary indulgences and papal encyclicals; and overseeing it all, the Holy Father in Rome, a figure almost as mystical as God. It all fused to make Catholicism different. That was why he wanted to be a priest. It was no ordinary job.

On his first day in the seminary of Clonliffe in Dublin, the Dean had said he assumed Seamus understood that sexual abstinence was absolutely necessary. The spiritual director had added that celibacy was ultimately a personal mystery, not to be explained away by argument.

Seamus was twenty-one years old on this summer morning in 1945 and a virgin; he had never taken out a girl or kissed any woman except his mother and sisters on their cheeks. Almost all of his heroes and heroines had 'Saint' before their names.

Having meditated as the Dean had suggested, Seamus dressed and then began to pack the clothes he would need for the summer break. On top of the clothes he placed his Bible.

In spite of the long hours he devoted to various sports, he was puny: short and wiry; slope-shouldered and bespectacled. But there was about him an alertness beyond his years and in his two years at Clonliffe he had shown he was nobody's fool – and that he suffered fools badly. It still worried him; humility was among the essentials of being a good priest. Yet, try as he might, Seamus could not tolerate stupidity. In this respect he was very much like his father. The thought did not please him.

On his last visit home his father had wanted to know if Seamus didn't at least feel a twinge of longing at the news that one old classmate was getting married, and another had fathered a child. Didn't that stir something in him? His father had hooked thumbs into his braces and said there was nothing in the Gospels to show that Christ recommended celibacy. In vain Seamus tried to argue but his father had cut him off, growling about fancy words never winning the day and had gone off to the pub. His mother had sat in her chair, silent, too proud to show her hurt.

As an afterthought, Seamus tucked a pair of shoes into the suitcase; they needed mending. But it would be a while longer before he would take them to the cobbler. The family budget was already fully stretched to keep him in Clonliffe. Battered though it was, the suitcase was unusual in that it had sturdy, tin locks. This was the fifth year of World War II and metal of any sort from neutral Ireland was being sent to England to help build planes and make bomb casings.

Seamus had been ambivalent about the outcome of the struggle between Germany and Britain until the day bombs fell on Dublin not far from the seminary. The dust from the debris barely settled before the gossip swirled through the cold and forbidding corridors of Clonliffe that Winston Churchill had personally authorized the air raid as a warning of what would follow unless Ireland openly committed itself to the Allies, or that Hitler was behind the attack, launching it as a brutal reminder that nowhere in Europe was beyond his reach. There were almost as many rumours as seminarians.

Born and raised in a staunchly Republican family, Seamus had surprised himself by having no doubts who dropped the bombs: the same sort of Nazi pilots he had seen on the newsreels attacking Warsaw and Rotterdam. The strength of his hatred for them continued to astonish him. He wondered if it was appropriate for priestly life.

There were other, very different emotions which had also troubled him. One disturbed him so much that, at the time, he felt unable to go to his regular confessor at Clonliffe. Instead, in the semi-darkness and total privacy of a confession box in a church he had never entered before or since, he accused himself, as rite demanded, of mortal sin. After reciting the opening prayer of the Confiteor, part of the sacrament of Penance, Seamus confessed how Brigid was the first woman to bring him face to face with sexual temptation.

The Mass of Deposition, one of the great celebrations in the Catholic calendar, was reaching its climax in the parish church in Carlow. Faith was visible on the faces of those packed tightly in their pews: men in blue serge suits, women in print dresses, boys and girls in the garments they had worn for First Communion.

To be among them was to remind Seamus of his roots. Though his parents had moved to Dublin when he was a baby, the tug of the land was still in him; he liked nothing better than to feel bog moss under his feet or smell pungent burning peat. Since entering Clonliffe he had come here every summer, staying on an uncle's farm, training the parish choir for this Mass, initiating them in the intricacies of Gregorian chanting. He worked them hard, and always thrilled at how well they responded. Broad country accents, often rough in spoken speech had, under his tutelage, become unified and mellifluous in the responses, introits and antiphons; their psalmody and hymnody had soared to the rafters of the church.

As the choir led the congregation in a final hymn, Seamus watchful as always, ears attuned for a false note, felt intensely proud of what he had achieved.

He only wished he could say the same about Brigid. In the front row of the choir, singing in perfect harmony, her eyes were fixed intently on him. She was petite, the way girls from Carlow often were: jet-black hair, bobbed in the front and falling to her shoulders, velvet-black eyes set in an oval face, her skin free of make-up and tanned – for this was August, and it had been an exceptionally hot summer for Ireland.

They had known each other for less than a month; twenty-three days to be exact. But he could remember every hour he had spent with this nineteen year old who worked in the village store. Brigid's father was dead, and her mother in domestic service with one of the area's landed gentry families.

After the first nightly choir practice, he had escorted Brigid home, sweltering in his black clerical suit, cycling beside her through the country lanes which led to her mother's cottage. Brigid had told Seamus of her dream of moving to Dublin. To her it was as remote and exciting as the New York, Paris or London she saw on the weekly film screenings in the church hall. Perhaps, she had added, if she came to Dublin, there might be an opportunity for them to meet. He had remained staring blankly ahead, knowing Brigid could become an occasion of sin. He knew he should have told her plainly why, even as a seminarian, they could not meet again.

The next night he escorted her home once more, pedalling slowly and saying little. Approaching the cottage she dismounted and he followed, being careful to keep their bicycles between them. She looked at him quizzically and had quietly asked what the problem was. He said there was none, and had laughed, trying to hide his embarrassment. Brigid had looked at him steadily. He had waited for her to say something but instead she turned and went inside.

During the next few days he had felt increasingly unsettled. His lectures had not prepared him for this. There had been oblique, guarded cautions about 'temptresses' and 'wanton women sent by the Devil' to seduce priests from their celibate calling. He knew she was none of these. Brigid's commitment to her faith was as deep as his own.

Yet he also knew he wanted to hold her in his arms and kiss her with a passion he had never realized he possessed. His desire had left him in a state of increasing anxiety and guilt, feeling a sense of failure, shame and unworthiness. In a desperate effort to find an answer, he had tried to intellectualize his emotions, applying the same techniques he used successfully in Clonliffe to analyze a scriptural passage. But academic rationalization and being in love, he had discovered, have nothing in common.

As the hymn ended, Seamus realized that throughout the entire service his own eyes had never left Brigid's except when closed in prayer.

Later, outside her cottage, he put down his bicycle. Then, without a smile, with no word, but with great seriousness, he took her hands and gently tried to remove them from her bicycle handlebars. She resisted, gripping the bars tightly.

'Why?' she had asked.

He could not understand the question.

'Do you really want to?' she asked.

'Of course.' He had paused, frightened by his own boldness. 'Do you?'

She had not answered, but stood there, stiffly silent, his hands gripping hers. Finally, when she spoke, it was softly, like the trembling in her fingers. 'Do you want to kiss me?'

From inside the cottage came a voice. 'You'll not be doing that! Get to bed, girl! At once. And you, young man, remember who you are!'

Seamus had jumped on his bicycle and pedalled away furiously. Long after he was out of earshot, he could still remember the angry words of Brigid's mother. Next day he returned to Dublin.

The confessor in that unfamiliar church had reassured Seamus he had not put his vocation in jeopardy – but that he should look upon the incident as a warning. He determined that when he returned to his uncle's farm to once more train the choir, he would avoid Brigid.

Before taking the train to Carlow he must go home. His mother would be eagerly waiting to hear how the semester had gone. He was less certain about his father's mood. He had lost count of the times he had sat in his seminary room and prayed for God to give his father the strength to stop drinking. But he knew that, apart from the progress of the war, there was no subject he could discuss with his father without the risk of provoking one of those sudden, volcanic outbursts. As long as he could remember the explosions were the dominant feature of their relationship, reaching back into his childhood.

Barely eight years old, Seamus had dismantled his father's long defunct pocket watch and, having replaced the useless workings, was unable to close the case. In his anxiety to do so, he clenched it between his jaws, leaving his teeth marks on the casing. That night his father found the watch. He held it up demanding to know who had dared touch it. Seamus, close to terror, blamed one of his sisters. His father ordered the girl to place the watch in her mouth. Her teeth did not fit the grooves. He told Seamus to try. His teeth matched the indentations. His father beat him mercilessly.

Seamus' dominant characteristics came from his mother. They shared the same determination to see something through, the same thirst for knowledge. There were other strong ties: God, and a rooted belief that the family was a storehouse of secrets, and it was a vital function of each of its members to keep them intact. There could be no greater crime in Gertrude Breslin's eyes than to display in public so much as a bone of any family skeleton. Her son had the same passionate conviction. In a way it had helped him to be a model student from the outset.

Geographically, his journey to Clonliffe had been insignificant, a few short miles from the family home in the suburbs of Dublin. Spiritually, his experiences in the seminary had placed an unbridgeable distance between himself and his past. The signposts were many – discovering that Lent meant giving up something precious, in his case sport, learning from an older boy it was a mortal sin to enter a Protestant church, perfecting the distribution of his weight between elbows and knees when he knelt on bare boards during devotions, being instructed by a priest on how to become a dependable altar server. One day he was told by a nun who was a relative that it would be a fine thing to one day get married, but even finer if he became a priest. That was the first time he had heard religious vocation being placed above wedlock and it was an energizing thought. He began to think seriously about the priesthood, and wonder if God was indeed calling him. It seemed the most natural of things.

When Seamus first seriously thought of the priesthood, money, never easy to come by in the Breslin family, was at a premium. Pennies were literally counted and recounted. Every Friday night his mother sat at the kitchen table and counted out what she already owed local tradesmen. To ensure the family had three nourishing meals a day, Gertrude Breslin virtually stopped spending anything on herself. Yet she hid their poverty well. At Mass no one could tell how many hours she had spent mending clothes; and, no matter how worn, the family's shoes were always polished. She set great store by such matters, just as she did about her religion and telling the truth.

The night he had sat across from her at the table and, as calmly as he could, said he had prayed for weeks, and was finally convinced he had really been called – her eyes had fixed intently on him. Then she had quietly asked, 'And where would we get the money?'

He was shattered, his dreams and hopes gone. In all those weeks of praying, he had never thought of asking God if he would provide. His mother had risen and stood over him, placing a hand on his shoulder, pressing firmly as if to physically reinforce her next words. The money, she said, would be found. He'd impulsively hugged her.

Events moved swiftly then. Seamus had obtained one of the handful of scholarships to Clonliffe. It was worth £80 a year for the first three years. By careful budgeting his mother calculated the bursary could be stretched to help cover his final years in the seminary. She would ensure, somehow, that the balance would come out of the family coffers. That settled, she took him to a clerical outfitters, a shop where his father knew a salesman who agreed to a discount. That night Seamus dressed for the family, first in his black serge suit and white shirt and black woollen tie. Then, as a climax, in his soutane and Roman collar.

'My God,' his father had said, 'he looks like a priest already.'

Next day Seamus arrived at the office of the seminary's doctor. The man was determined to explain his importance.

'God may have called you, young man, but the Almighty has left it up to me to pass you.'

He sat down behind his desk, adjusted his pince-nez and drew a form towards him.

'Do you know about the impediments?'

Seamus was baffled. In years of regular church attendance, conversations with his parish priest, reading of religious books, there had been no mention of impediments.

'The impediments,' the physician repeated. 'I've got to ask you about them. Illegitimacy. That apply? It's a bar. You can't be a priest if you're a bastard.'

Seamus felt his face redden. 'My parents have been married for...'

'Good. No illegitimacy impediment.'

The doctor scribbled on the form.

'Any convictions?'

'Convictions?'

'Come, boy. You know, convictions for crime, particularly sexual.'

Seamus shook his head rapidly.

The doctor made another notation. He suddenly looked up. 'You ever hit the bishop?'

'Sir?'

Seamus was astonished by the question.

'Relax, young fella. I have to ask these questions. If you hit a bishop or even a priest, that is a bar. Surely you can see that?'

Seamus nodded, too stunned to speak.

'Strip off. Everything. As naked as the day your ma saw you.'

Completely naked, the first time he had ever undressed before a stranger, Seamus felt mounting panic. Why was the doctor peering so intently at his sexual organs?

'You can't be ordained unless you're a whole man. You've got to have all your sexual faculties. Eunuchs can't become priests.'

The doctor walked to his desk and made a further notation. Then he returned to walk slowly around Seamus.

'Move your left leg.'

'Which way?'

'I don't care. Just move it.'

Seamus did so.

'Move the other one.'

Seamus repeated the action, moving his right leg back and forth.

'No wooden legs,' said the doctor. 'You can't be ordained if you've a wooden leg. It would mean you are not a complete person.'

The doctor pointed towards a curtained alcove.

'Go in there and give me a specimen. Just pee in the pot.'

Seamus could not pass a drop of urine. Beyond the curtain the doctor paced impatiently.

'Come on, come on boy, bring me the specimen.'

Seamus emerged with the empty jug.

The doctor sniffed. 'You're the first one I've ever had who can't pee, but not being able to pass water on command is no impediment.'

He made a final notation on the form, signed it and addressed the envelope to the Dean of Clonliffe.

'Okay, young fella, God called you and I passed you. Good luck.'

From the outset his tutors had constantly reminded him that the demands for a place in one of Ireland's main seminaries far exceeded availability, and that his call from God was no guarantee he had the staying power to survive both the spiritual and physical rigours of seminary life.

The threat of dismissal was invoked for a list of infractions: missing chapel; talking during periods of silence; not knowing the name and history of the saint of the day; failing to make full use of study time; being seen in the company of a woman except a nun or a student's own relatives; entering another seminarian's room. Staff paid particular attention to monitoring all friendships. But homosexuality belonged to a wider ban on all discussion on sex. Clonliffe was an authentic asexual haven where all energies were focused on creating worthy successors to the original fisher of men. Coping with sexual urges simply had no part to play. You just put it out of your mind, his spiritual director had said very firmly.

Nevertheless, Seamus had managed to establish one friendship. Seamus realized he was dissimilar to Patrick Gallagher. There was a worldliness about Patrick; he knew as much about jazz as chant. He had travelled in Europe and spoke French and Spanish as fluently as Gaelic. He made everything seem easy, engagingly deprecating his efforts by saying he was making up for misspent years at school. Patrick's particular skill, Seamus thought, was that he could gut a book quicker than anyone for salient facts. Directed by Patrick's unfailing sense of where information was buried in leather-bound tomes which had often lain undisturbed for years, Seamus had read about the *bramacarya* of Hinduism, with its emphasis on total discipline and education, and how poverty and celibacy are at the centre of Buddhism. He had discovered that during the first three centuries of the Catholic Church there were no barriers placed upon any cleric wishing to marry.

He had traced back the earliest legislation to the fourth century when the Spanish council of Elvira ordered all clergy to 'abstain from their wives'. The decree did not actually forbid marriage but merely demanded abstinence. Total celibacy only came with the rise of monasticism, and the Madonna became the new martyr as Christianity spread through the Roman empire. Her virginity became universally accepted as a Catholic tenet, forming a cornerstone for celibacy.

In the Clonliffe library, Patrick had unearthed a dissertation by a former President of the Seminary arguing that, as well as any form of forbidden physical sex for a priest, there was an equal danger from sensuality engaging the mind.

Patrick asked about this in the Dean's next class. The Dean stared at him in stony disbelief, pinching his nose with his thumb and finger. Finally, he said celibacy was a gift and that no one refused a gift, especially when it came from God. They should pray every day to keep it intact. Seamus already knew prayer was a mysterious factor working in an unfathomable and unilateral manner, divorced from all other mortal thoughts.

In one of his first essays he had described prayer. 'Utter and self-giving, with nothing held back. It is the kind of love which always demands giving of our best, not only to those we love, like family and friends, not even to those we find it hard to like, but most important of all to those towards whom we are largely indifferent.'

Later he had been asked for an explanation of what he thought faith was exactly. In his neat hand he wrote an interpretation he hoped would stand the test of his time as a priest. 'Faith is the total acceptance of an unseen power superior to me; an invisible and different order of beauty to which I must adjust if I wish to attain to the supreme good. Linked to this belief is also a total desire to communicate with faith.'

His explanation had earned him a word of praise from the Dean, but more important, Seamus' progress was something to tell his mother, to reinforce her belief that all the sacrifices she continued to make to keep him in Clonliffe were worthwhile.

It had been exciting: learning to genuflect and venerate; accepting he could smoke only at certain times, in all an hour a day, and then only in one of two specially designated 'smoking sheds', their walls brownish-yellow from years of nicotine; that he must rise at six o'clock each morning and must be to bed sometimes a full hour before dark, for it was light until 11.30 at night in high summer; that he must learn how to meditate silently and to examine his conscience; that he must never walk with his hands in his pockets in case, as the Dean had put it on the first day, he might be tempted to let the Devil do his handiwork.

His life was governed by bells which punctuated a schedule that directed him from chapel to classroom, from early morning prayers to Latin translation, then back to chapel before returning once more to the classroom. Short breaks for meals and recreation were signalled by a clap of the bell. In all, the bell rang forty-three separate times through the day, each a sonorous tocsin. The noise emphasized that Clonliffe was a place of books and prayer.

He felt pleased with how much he had learned. He knew all the anniversaries of the deaths of saints. He had studied the *Deposition Fidei*, the sum of revealed truths given by Christ to the church. He knew the history of the Ember Days, days of fasting. He had analyzed the victims of the Euchites and Quietists, heretical sects. He had read the Euchology, the book which contains the rituals of the Greek Church, so similar in many ways to the Church of Rome. He had listened to lectures on heaven, accepting it was not only a state but a place of beatitude where God imparts his glory to the blessed and clearly shows himself to them. He had concluded that hell is a place of eternal torment. He had come to grips with pastoral theology, the science of the care of souls which is a mixture of dogmatic and ascetical theology and canon law. He understood the deeper meaning of the Pater Noster, the prayer Christ taught to his disciples; he had learned to use the liturgical name for the last three days of Holy Week, *Triduum sacrum*, and to examine the mystery of the holy Trinity. He knew the historical significance of the sacred vessels, among them the chalice, paten and pyx. He had learned about vestments and the meaning of their various colours: white to be worn on feasts of confessors and virgins; red to commemorate martyrs; black in the penitential seasons and Masses for the dead, and green for ordinary occasions. He had learned that when bishops celebrated pontifically they took their vestments directly from the altar, but ordinary priests robed in the sacristy.

Through all this – and much else – Seamus had come to realize the many roles a priest had to play – all important. He was there to provide a sense of spiritual comfort to his flock; to convince them to accept that there is a time to live and a time to die; to create a mutual trust between those who govern and those who are governed, to work, in every way, towards a purification of the religious sense of those he would be responsible for when he finally left Clonliffe.

But that was still a long way ahead. He would need three more hard years to absorb all else he had to learn. For the moment though, Seamus could take a pause on his road to ordination. His taxi had finally arrived.

The taxi was ancient but this was 1945 and any vehicle which qualified for a petrol allowance was pressed into service. The driver was torn, like many Irishmen, over his loyalties about the outcome of the war. In the past, when he had picked up Seamus, the man had sported a Nazi swastika in his lapel; the buttons were freely handed out by the German Embassy in Dublin. Now the cabby wore a Union Jack emblem, and for good measure a pair of RAF flying wings sewn on his jacket sleeves.

When the taxi dropped him off, Seamus felt familiar emotions. After the vastness of Clonliffe, the house seemed tiny. Yet so many lives had been lived behind its front door, the brass letter box shining from a daily polishing by his mother. In a window was a plant, his Christmas gift to her. He reached a hand inside the letter box and pulled out a key on its string, the way he used to do as a child. He opened the door quietly, intent on surprise.

His mother was waiting. He put down the suitcase and she hugged him, as she always did when he came home. Behind her, framed in the kitchen door, was his father. Even in the gloom, Seamus sensed the raw, whisky-inflamed eyes measuring him. He greeted him politely.

Abruptly his father turned away, returning to the kitchen to sit by the range. Warm though the day was, he felt the cold.

Seamus followed his mother into the kitchen. The table was set; for her, food and affection were synonymous. Over the years the stove had deposited a sheen of black on the ceiling and walls. The kitchen had always been the focal point of the house, where the family ate and received the occasional visitor, usually a relative or the parish priest. The front parlour was only used at Christmas and on feast days.

Beginning to eat, Seamus described how the term had gone, how he hoped he had done well in his examinations. His mother nodded from time to time. Her slate-coloured eyes were as alert as ever, but they were rimmed with more lines than he remembered, and he noticed she had an even smaller appetite. Once more an old fear nagged him.

His father pushed away his plate, noisily cleared his throat and lit a cigarette, using a jam-jar lid in which to flick his ashes, and began to talk about the war, attacking Churchill and British policies. Seamus began to relax: this was safe ground.

Suddenly, his father was off on a new tack. The government had just promised to supply electricity to every home in Ireland by the 1950s. It would mean a bathroom and hot water in every home. He sat back, staring at the hairs on the back of his hand, the way he always did when about to attack. Seamus waited, knowing there was nothing he could do.

His father asked if he would disagree that clean bodies make for clean minds. 'Clean bodies *do* make clean minds.' Liam Breslin let the repeated words hang for a moment. 'Fact is, makes it easier for a priest to tell a man to swear off beer and cigarettes. That's so, isn't it, boy?'

Seamus nodded, trying to relax by breathing slowly. He knew the tactic. His father would try and extract one admission after another. Priests used the same technique in the Inquisition. His father moved quickly, pushing the argument forward.

'No need to be sensitive, boy! There's no room in the priesthood for delicate stomachs. You've got to be tough to do God's work. Hardened to the core to tell a man to give up the bottle and his fags. You going to be able to tell me that one day? When you've got your collar on and you're apart from the rest of us? Being a bishop's lap dog! Yes, your Grace. No, your Grace. But never screw your Grace. Though they know about that, don't they?'

Seamus prayed silently for God to save this frail and ruined old man he still could stop himself from loving.

But in no time his father had raised from the graveyard in his mind the story of the Failed Priest.

'What happened to him, boy? Remind me again, for my memory's not what it was.'

Seamus refused to be baited.

They both knew the story of the Clonliffe graduate who had thrown away seven years of study to set up home with a widow. They had been forced to flee Dublin, going north to Protestant Ulster where their two children were born. But the priest was unhappy, wishing to legitimize his offspring, yet feeling unable to marry unless the church blessed the union. He had returned to Dublin and begged the archbishop to grant him this one wish.

'Remember, boy, what happened then?' Liam had worked himself up, his nostrils flaring, enormous disbelief expressed as a loud clearing of the throat.

'I'll tell *you*. Our good archbishop sent the papers to Rome. And the Pope fired them straight back. No dispensation! Remember what you said the Holy Father wrote. "A priest should either be chaste or he should go to hell." Wasn't that it, boy? But he'd said it in Latin, hadn't he? How does that go? *Aut castus aut perinte*. Is that it, boy? Is that good Latin? I've forgotten. My memory's not what it was. But remember it, boy!'

Liam Breslin sat back, his victory over his son complete.

The platform for the train to Carlow was filling and there was still no sign of Patrick.

From force of habit Seamus checked again a small card in his breastpocket. Its face was covered with a grid, each square containing a Latin word. There were several pencil ticks in the squares. Each one indicated he was following the daily routine for all seminarians away from Clonliffe. So far today he had awoken at the prescribed hour, said his prayers, meditated, attended Mass, received Holy Communion, read passages from the Bible, recited the rosary and examined his conscience. There were spaces for more prayers and meditation. In all he must spend a total of almost four hours every day in devotions. If he failed he must place a cross against the relevant item. Ten crosses on the card could lead to expulsion. Seamus knew he could never cheat; he was on trust. But he was determined there would only be ticks on his card.

He put away the card and looked towards the station entrance. He saw Patrick then, hefting his suitcase in one hand, wearing a navy blue suit and a new cap. Clinging to his arm was a girl.

Seamus saw Patrick put down his case and gently pull her to him. He saw them kiss. She pushed her face against his shoulder, a gesture somehow more intimate than even their kissing. Then she turned and walked quickly away, not once looking back, hurrying out of the station.

Patrick stared down the platform, his eyes searching once more.

Panic gripped Seamus. He must hide. He must hide and then emerge from some place and pretend he had seen nothing. But it was too late. Patrick stood before him smiling broadly, apologizing and saying he had overslept, but that it didn't matter because he had marked it down on his card. Patrick did not mention the girl. Nor did Seamus. He realized how badly he wanted to preserve illusions.

They squeezed into a carriage containing a woman with a couple of children and some farmers. There was only time to place his suitcase beside Patrick's on the overhead rack before the train jerked out of the station, gathered speed and left the city behind, heading out through the fields. Seamus felt trapped in this box-like compartment. He closed his eyes, pretending to sleep. Patrick talked to the farmers. At Carlow, before they separated, Patrick arranged for Seamus to come to supper in a few days, adding that with five sisters, it would be nice to have another man at the table. He reminded Seamus that one of them, Mary, was in the choir last year.

Seamus pretended, but he couldn't recall her. Then he had eyes only for Brigid.

On the appointed day Seamus bicycled one mile after another, eight in all, from his uncle's farm to the Gallagher house. There was a glow in his cheeks which had not been there in Dublin. What his uncle called seminary pallor had been wiped away by fresh air and sunny days. The old parish priest had welcomed him warmly but his words were more weary than Seamus remembered from last year.

When Brigid did not attend the choir rehearsal, the priest explained. A travelling salesman from Galway – the priest made it seem as remote as the Arctic – had swept Brigid off her feet, taking her back there to marry. He was a Protestant. In this closed country community where no one married outside the faith, it would be a heavy burden for her mother to bear, having a daughter in a mixed marriage.

Seamus was stunned. A marriage between a Catholic and a person of another religion, such as a Protestant, was legally binding. But unless permission had been obtained from Rome, the union was invalid under canon law. Brigid was now a heretic, to be denied the blessed sacrament. She was effectively a person who did not exist in the eyes of the church.

Seamus promised himself he would include her in his prayers. He wished he could do more.

Dusk approached as he peddled up the Gallagher's farm track. He wheeled his bicycle round to the back; only strangers knocked on a front door in these parts. Across the yard the cow parlours produced enough milk for a sizeable portion of the county. Seamus knocked on the open kitchen door.

'Come in.' The voice was liltingly beautiful. 'Seamus, if you're coming in, come in.'

CHAPTER FOUR

Always a Priest

The kitchen was twice the size of his mother's. In the middle of the room was a wooden table with chairs for a dozen people. Along one wall were porcelain sinks, gleaming white with long wooden draining boards: against the far wall a range bigger than he had ever seen, each burner occupied by a saucepan. From the ceiling hung haunches of bacon, curing. On side tables were bowls of eggs and fruit. All this he saw without taking his eyes off her.

'Well, you finally made it. You're welcome. I'm Mary.' Her laugh was soft and throaty.

She came forward, moving away from the range, wiping her fingers on her apron. When she smiled her teeth were even and white.

He extended his hand. Her grip was cool.

'You look like you've seen a ghost.' Mary smiled again. 'Don't you remember? I was in the choir last year.' There was the gentlest of teasing in her voice. 'Next to Brigid.'

'Oh yes. Patrick told me.' His face reddened. In the silence a light rhythm of clocks ticked against each other: a mantle clock, a cuckoo clock above the sinks and glimpsed through a door leading from the kitchen, a grandfather clock.

She looked at him steadily. 'I can't come this year, though. Mammy died in the winter and I've got to run the house.' She brushed a strand of hair from her forehead. 'You must know how it is. Younger sisters, all at school and a father who works all the hours God has given him.'

Cycling here, he noticed that the Gallagher pastures faced southwards and had already been cut for hay and winter silage.

'He misses Pat, you know. He'd never say so. But he misses him. It's difficult when you have a son who's been called.'

Mary reminded him of a girl his sisters had played with at school.

She, too, had always been self-assured and direct. Mary seemed the same kind of girl. She murmured something he could not understand. It must have been French. Patrick had told him she had spent a summer in Paris before the war. He suddenly wished he had not had such a conventional education – taking mathematics and Gaelic in preference to art and a European language.

'We all want him to be a priest. Mammy most of all. That was the last thing she said. "Let our Pat be a priest." She once gave him a holy card and he learned it overnight. It took me a month.' She laughed.

'What did the words say?' He wished he hadn't asked the question. It made him sound such a seminarian.

She quoted: 'To be in God's service is to live in the midst of every family, yet belong to none. To share all suffering. To hear all secrets. To heal all wounds. To teach and instruct. To pardon and console. To bless and be blessed forever. To be a priest.' She laughed again. 'I suppose that's why only a few get called. You have to be very exceptional. Pat is exceptional. Mammy understood that.'

Seamus nodded, struggling to bring order to his mind. How could he not have remembered that terrible day when the Dean had received a sudden telephone call and sent Patrick home? Patrick had returned from his mother's funeral wan-faced and withdrawn, but composed. His grief had remained hidden for a while, until Patrick was discovered weeping uncontrollably in his room. The Dean sat with him for an entire afternoon. Afterwards they emerged together and spent several more hours in the chapel, praying.

Mary was speaking about the eggs. He realized he had been staring at the bowls. She was saying he could take some home to his mother. Fresh eggs were a luxury in the war-rationed cities. He thanked her, still absorbed by her face. Her cheekbones were high, eyebrows strong and slightly darker than her hair, nose perfectly straight, forehead rounded, wide and deep. Her mouth was not only large, but had a clear and distinct shape with corners which sloped upward. He had read that lips like hers denoted a person who was sensual and emotional. He felt a hot-wash of excitement he had never before experienced.

'Is something the matter?' The concern in her voice was genuine.

'Patrick. Is Patrick here?'

'He's helping with the milking.'

Once more he felt a consuming need to impress her. He could not believe she did not sense how he felt; that she could not see his heart on his face.

'I'll go and give Patrick a hand. I do most of the milking at my uncle's. He says I'm faster than his cowman and cheaper too.' Seamus half-turned, embarrassed over his boasting.

'You don't want to be getting that nice suit dirty over there.'

Seamus turned back to face her, a great blush pulsing across his face.

'Sit yourself down. You've had a long bike. Would you like something to drink?'

'Please. Thank you.'

She smiled at him.

'Don't they teach you to say anything but "please" and "thank you" at Clonliffe? Patrick said you never stopped talking!'

'You know Patrick, always paying a person a compliment.'

He sat at the table watching her pour milk from a jug.

'Take your jacket off. You must be hot in all that black. I couldn't imagine spending all my life in black. It must be worse for a nun,' Mary said. She turned, smiling, bringing him the drink.

'I'm glad you are not a nun.' He felt he was about to surrender his reason.

She burst out laughing. 'You don't really think I'd do something like that, do you?'

Seamus draped his jacket over the back of the chair and sipped the milk. However hard he tried, his eyes could not leave her.

The rest of the evening passed in a blur for Seamus. He was only aware of her: watching her bring dishes to the table, serving her father, then him as a guest, leaving Patrick and her sisters to help themselves. She had asked him to say grace, a visitor's privilege, bowing her head with the others while he murmured a blessing. At the end of the meal, she made a fresh pot of tea for the men while she and her sisters cleared away.

When she broke a drinking glass, slippery with suds from the sink, he half-rose from his chair, eager to help. She looked at him and quickly shook her head, asking lightly if they now trained a priest for housework.

He was overcome with new emotions: guilt and a feeling that he was betraying his mother's scrimping and the quiet optimism of his spiritual director that he would be a good priest. Above all, betraying himself. The words of the director drifted mockingly through his mind. *Your vocation will be safe as long as you never abuse it.*

Later, the emotions were still there as he prayed at his bedside, kneeling until all feeling went from his knees. They remained until he fell asleep.

He awoke to the sounds of stirring in his uncle's bedroom, hearing only her last words to him, as soft and clear as if she were standing at the foot of his bed. *We'll see you again, soon.*

He tried to drown out the words with silent *Pater Nosters*, remembering his spiritual director had said prayer was the only defence.

The spiritual director was close to fifty. He sat in an armchair in his study, Seamus opposite him. Every student came here regularly to receive guidance. The director's breadth of knowledge and understanding for all things human was a model of what a priest should be. On this day he had chosen to discuss celibacy, a matter not raised before in their informal sessions. He reminded Seamus that at the Last Supper there were no women present. And when Christ said, 'Come, follow me,' it was scripturally clear he meant the apostles were expected to leave everything – and everyone – else behind. They were not going to go forth and missionize the world with wives in tow. Christ was saying that at the core of every vocation was an essential emotional personal detachment in body and spirit that was only possible when there are no other ties. The director then spoke of the celibate as a torch bearer for the eternal life. 'You will come to accept that it is the detached celibate priest who best understands the commitment of what marriage is, because he is married to the Lord. Your soul lives in your body, and as long as you live you will have sexual impulses. It is for you to decide to let God help you to banish them.'

Mary was once more back in his mind.

The next day passed in silent, anguished inner debate and mechanical actions. He ate but had no appetite; conducted the choir by instinct; answered questions he did not appear to hear. He wondered what she was doing at particular times of the day. Was she with somebody else, bestowing her favours on another boy? Once, to wash away the idea, he held his head under the cold tap and let cold water soak his head. Cycling to another choir practice, he invented a game to torture himself further. A downward thrust of his right leg meant he must save his vocation. Using his left leg, the heart side meant he should accept his feelings for Mary.

Right foot down. *A vocation is a gift, self-sacrifice a small return for being called by God.*

Left foot down. *Human love is not to be condemned but developed and treasured. This is why I feel new confidence, a heightened perception and an increased compassion.*

Right. *Not true. Where was compassion for Patrick at the railway station?*

Left. *That's different. Patrick isn't in love. Not like I am.*

Right. *The greatest love any man can have is the love Christ gave.*

Left. *But I love her.*

Right. *Still not too late. Those feelings can be cut off cleanly, clearly.*

Left. *I love her.*

Right. *I love Christ.*

Left. *We both love Jesus.*

Right. *But not in the same way.*

Left. *Yes.*

Right. *No.*

When he reached the church, several members of the choir asked if he was unwell. Impulsively he said he was developing a summer influenza and would have to go home to bed. The choir watched silently as he climbed back onto his bicycle. A mile down the road he realized he was not on the road back to his uncle's farm, but cycling towards the Gallaghers'.

Half-broiled in his black suit, he arrived in the yard. He carefully knotted his tie and mopped his forehead. He knocked on the closed kitchen door and hesitantly stepped inside. Only the ticking clocks broke the silence. The door leading to the front parlour was on its latch. He paused, not certain what to do. When he rapped, there was no response. His hand reached towards the latch and lifted it.

'Why, Seamus, where would you be going?'

He whirled, crimson in the face.

Mary was standing in the doorway, a basket of eggs on her arm. She walked to the table and put them down and burst out laughing.

55

'Glory be! You should see your face. You look like somebody who's been caught with their hands in the till! But it's good to see you. You'll stay for tea, of course?'

He nodded, smiling foolishly.

Pedalling home in the darkness he had a new game.

Left foot down. *She loves me.*

Right foot down. *I love her.*

Left. *She loves me.*

Right. *I love her.*

Seamus careened through the countryside.

That night he was not certain he had been fully asleep when the spiritual director surfaced in his mind reminding Seamus that a good priest never judged anybody. People fail because they are people. Seamus must not think he had failed by accepting Mary's invitation to tea, by sitting opposite her at the table, watching her every movement and words. That was not failure, but a test, part of the same test which allowed him to play games on his bicycle. The real test was to win the right game.

Five full days and nights had passed since he had seen Mary. He had prayed. At times he felt as if God had left him in limbo, other times he was almost euphoric, imbued with a new lease of life.

Falling in love, he reasoned, was immune to discipline. It was not something that had to be done like working the choir, walking the horse into the barn, hefting the hay into the loft. Falling in love he decided, was something which just happened.

On the sixth night he begged God to help him to marry Mary. That night he slept deeply.

The Mass was four days away. The choir, Seamus knew, was pitch perfect. Pedalling towards the Gallagher house for the first time in ten days, he was certain. He would leave Clonliffe, get a teaching post and then ask Mary to marry him.

When he cycled into the yard, Mary was waiting at the kitchen door. There was no smile, no welcome.

'Oh, Seamus, it's you.'

'Who else?' he grinned.

'I thought you were the doctor.'

He felt suddenly chilled.

'The doctor? Why, what's wrong?'

'It's Norma. She's ill. I think it's her appendix. Dad sent Patrick for the doctor hours ago.'

She tried to conceal her yawning, saying she had been up most of the night with her sister. There was no warmth in her voice.

'Can I help in any way?' He saw her look and wished he had not asked.

'She needs medicine, not prayers.' Her voice was sharp for the first time he could remember.

She walked quickly past him to the corner of the yard, looking down the lane. Seamus slowly wheeled his bicycle towards her. She leaned against the house gable and closed her eyes.

'I'm sorry, Mary. I really am.' He tried to keep his voice calm.

She nodded, not opening her eyes.

He counted the number of times the cuckoo chirped in the kitchen before he made one last try. Would she be coming to the Mass?

She opened her eyes and looked at him.

'God, don't ask me now. Anyway, I'm sure you don't need me there to appreciate what you've done. And you know what they say about a priest? About him going straight to heaven because he's so good on earth.' She smiled then, the way she had smiled on their very first meeting. 'You're going to be a fine priest one day. Pat says so and I know so.'

It was not indifference he saw in her face, only certainty.

In the end Mary came. He could see her standing beside her father and sisters from his position near the altar. She wore a new hat and looked more lovely than ever.

Patrick had sent word that Norma would be out of hospital in a week and after Mass Seamus could join them for a meal. He politely refused. He had seen the way forward. It would no doubt be lonely. It would be hard, certainly, but it was the only way.

The Dean surveyed the ordination class. Seamus thought: this is very much his style – lengthy pauses between the archdeacon's carefully enunciated phraseology. When he'd first heard the Dean speak seven years before, he'd been overawed by the man's certainty. A man not troubled by so much as a knot in his conscience, who in every verifiable way knew he was doing and saying the right thing. On this morning the archdeacon struck Seamus as theatrical, his cultivated speech and elaborate grammar hard to concentrate upon.

Seamus' mind once more turned to his mother. She had finally told him she had a steadily progressing cancer, one beyond surgery. Nothing could change the inevitable outcome. Her faith, she had said, would sustain her to the very end.

Her reaction helped him cope. She had urged him to accept that her fate was part of a constant rhythm of life, that death and rebirth was the keystone of faith. She had wondered if she had always behaved well enough to feel justified in hoping for eternal life. He reminded her of what St Thomas Aquinas expounded: 'God's will is paramount but he recognizes mortal weakness and gives grace to those who persevere… in wanting to be delivered from sin.'

Gradually they came to accept her death by refusing to ignore it or deny its finality. He realized if he were to be a good priest, he must have full understanding into all the ramifications of dying. While his mother displayed an exceptional lack of emotional distress, very likely others he would meet would be unable to show such courage and calm. He would have to prepare himself to assist them to die.

His mother's positive attitude had helped in other ways. It strengthened his vocation, maturing him in a way he never realized was possible. He became more compassionate towards his father. He accepted his drinking was now a way to blot out what was happening. Death terrified his father; he was a man who believed he was condemned to endure beyond the grave the pains and uncertainties of this life. Seamus decided the best way he could help was to pray for his father's salvation.

When he prayed for his mother, he could see her clearly: shrunken by her wasting illness, her hair greyer, the veins standing out more prominently on the backs of her hands. He asked God to comfort her. He did not beg for his mother's life to be prolonged, only that her pain might be as little as possible, her death agony when it came, short.

The doctors dated the onset of the malignancy from around the last time he returned from Carlow two years before, in 1947, the year he called 'after Mary'. He dated events: *before Mary, after Mary*. It was another way to remind himself of his deepening maturity. He had thought a great deal about his feelings for Mary and concluded that he had, after all, confused love with a feeling of love; that he had allowed himself a brief spell of self-serving self-deception. He had come to see that, for him, bound daily closer to the priesthood, true love must always be an act of will which transcended ephemeral feelings. Genuine love required commitment and the exercise of wisdom.

After he received his Bachelor of Arts degree, a year of intensive work followed as he prepared for the diaconate.

A deacon was second only to a priest. He could help celebrate Mass, preach and baptize. Seamus had successfully rejected, to the satisfaction of his examiners, the Protestant argument that the original seven deacons were merely chosen to administer the alms of the church. Displaying a command of the scriptures which made even his spiritual director nod approvingly, Seamus had argued, with the same deadly accuracy his father once possessed, that the Bible clearly shows they were chosen for higher work than merely handling charities.

At the end of the year, having been questioned at length by the Dean, Seamus was created a deacon, the final step towards ordination.

Twice this past year on trips into Dublin he had seen Patrick with the girl. He finally took Patrick aside in the smoking shed, approaching the matter obliquely, saying everybody thought being in love was unique and that was understandable, because it was a gift from God.

Patrick stared at him. Seamus continued, saying there were various kinds of love: loving somebody who was physically attractive; loving a person whose personality was complementary; loving someone not realizing it was infatuation.

Patrick continued blowing one smoke ring after another, watching each one spiral and dissipate. Seamus plunged on. They both knew that some of those called to religious celibacy fell in love with another person. What was important was to be on the alert to resist even the first stirrings of such love; once its presence was discerned it should be dealt with swiftly and the relationship cleanly ended.

'You mean Helen?'

Patrick's use of her name jolted him. It gave the girl a new dimension, making her that much more of a threat.

'I can't bear to see you destroy yourself.' Seamus wished he had not sounded so emotional.

Patrick pinched his cigarette between his fingers, slipped the butt into a pocket and left the shed.

They had not spoken again for weeks until the evening Patrick rapped on his door. He stood there in the familiar blue suit, raincoat over his arm.

'I'm leaving. I've told the Dean about Helen and I've been given marching orders. Out before supper. I want to say goodbye,' Patrick announced.

Walking with Patrick through the main hall, Seamus was conscious of a sense of irrevocable separation. Patrick said Mary was in Dublin training to be a teacher, adding she was dating a bank clerk.

'They're talking of getting married.' Patrick laughed loudly, the sound echoing in the hall. 'Maybe we'll make it a double wedding. You'll come, of course.'

'I'll see.'

Patrick had not pressed. There was a sudden awkwardness between them. Without another word Patrick went out to the taxi, already loaded with his trunk.

The Dean was saying that Christ taught that if there are excesses of the flesh, there must be those who will give up even the legitimate pleasures of the flesh. He looked piercingly into each face.

'If any one of you feels a moment's doubt, the smallest of hesitations, then express them now. Just rise and leave the room. You will not be judged.'

A further pause. Seamus sensed the sudden tension in the air. No one moved.

Without a word the Dean walked away from the lectern and left the room.

Seamus enjoyed the choreography of practising saying Mass and performing its rituals. Under the watchful eye of the Dean, the ordination class had assembled in the sacristy attached to the seminary chapel. Surrounded by Clonliffe's precious church-plate and some of its rarest of books, the robed deacons stood before benches, each one the precise height of a church altar. Before them were the chalices and pyxes they would need.

Beside Seamus was a tall deacon with flaming red hair and the longest nose of any seminarian in Clonliffe. In unison they both bowed to venerate and kiss the bench; until they became fully-fledged priests they would not be allowed to use a real altar.

The face of Seamus' companion hovered a good three inches above his section of the bench. Only his nose touched it.

The Dean was before them, glowering. He jabbed a finger. 'Mister, why is your head at that angle?'

'It's my nose. It stops me kissing face-on!'

'Well, you can't say Mass with your head askew! What do you propose?'

Seamus intervened. 'He could come forward so that he rests his nose on the altar and kisses its edge.' He demonstrated how it could be done.

The Dean stood back, watching carefully. He pointed to the redhead. 'Now, you do it.'

Using Seamus' technique the awkward deacon managed to kiss the altar full face.

The Dean pronounced. 'Not perfect, but nearly. I suppose God will accept it, having given you such a nose in the first place!'

Seamus noticed several things as he greeted his parents in the cavernous hall where seminarians received relatives on one set day a week. His mother was more wasted than ever. The hospital had finally discharged her. No limit had been put on the time she had left to live but she had calmly told him it could not be more than a year.

The doctors and nurses had surrounded his mother with words and actions designed to suggest she was not mortally ill. She had finally told her senior doctor she had known the truth for some time. Even then he was reluctant to confirm the prognosis. Seamus had raised the matter with him, turning up at the hospital in his priestly garb to give further authority to his questions. The doctor spoke about white lies being kindly and the special responsibility of the medical profession to practice deceit because truth often produces distress. Seamus came away with the feeling that many doctors hid behind deliberate evasion because they did not know how to be properly candid with patients who were fatally ill.

Now there was no way of disguising reality. The stricken pallor on her face spoke for itself. Cancer was destroying her before his very eyes. Seamus sensed his father was close to being drunk. His hair was unkempt. He was wearing non-matching socks and a shoelace was undone. His inflamed eyes almost glowed in his face.

'How are you, Mammy?' Seamus asked.

'No complaints. I'm just glad to be here.'

Seamus took them to a corner of the great hall, far away from the other family groups. He concentrated on his mother, seating her, placing himself beside her. His father was almost jovial.

'You made it. You made it,' he almost half-shouted. 'Seven years. And in another week we'll be calling you Father. God bless you boy. I'm real proud of you.'

There were tears in his eyes.

Seamus was embarrassed and surprised. Since that night when the story of the Failed Priest had been dredged up, he had been careful to avoid any real discussion with his father about the priesthood, confining himself to generalizations: the work was hard but absorbing; there was talk of renovating part of the seminary and adding a new wing to cope with the anticipated influx of students in the next decade; some schools had as many as a score of final year pupils eager to enter the priesthood.

His father had listened and grunted, smoking furiously and saying there was plenty of work for them. England, he had roared, was in a state of moral decline, France in the religious doldrums, and the other great ally of the war, the United States, was turning into a cess-pool. Once more the priests of Ireland would have to go forth and save the sinners. Just as he had been uncertain how to respond to those remarks, so Seamus had, until now, no clear idea where he stood in his father's estimation. He leaned forward, keeping his voice down, hoping his father would take the hint.

'Thanks, Dad.'

'Your Daddy means it. We're all proud of you,' his mother said.

Liam Breslin produced a packet of cigarettes from his pocket. 'For you, boy. For the shed.' His barking laugh turned heads.

Seamus felt a flush on his face.

When the visit ended he led his mother out of the hall, her arm on his. His father trailed behind, staring at the paintings on the walls, saying they looked valuable enough to pay the tuition fees for all the seminarians at Clonliffe.

At five minutes to six on a Sunday morning in May 1947, Seamus awoke. He was filled with an excitement he had never before felt in this room he had occupied for one thousand, nine hundred and fifty-five days. He had just completed his last retreat before ordination.

During the retreat he had pondered the truth of religion, examined his conscience more carefully than ever before. Under the supervision of his spiritual director he had meditated on the penalties of sin, contemplated the full meaning of Jesus' life and death, reminding himself always that the way of the cross was not of this world. He had spent almost a full day meditating upon the greatest of Christ's miracles, the strongest proof of his divinity, the resurrection, reminding himself that all Christian truth, the very foundation of the church itself, stemmed from total acceptance that Jesus arose from the dead. He had let his mind dwell on the happiness of heaven. Finally, before going to sleep every night he had, through lengthy prayer, further united himself with God.

Now he was ready.

Entering the sacristy Seamus donned an alb, a vestment of pure white linen covering him from head to foot. He recited the words, 'make me white, O Lord, and cleanse me'. He took an oblong piece of cloth, the amice, rested it for the prescribed moment on his head, and then spread it across his shoulders, murmuring the traditional prayer, 'place on my head, O Lord, the helmet of salvation'. Next he tied a white cincture around his waist. He placed the maniple, a narrow vestment, around his neck. It symbolized not only the yoke of Christ, but also penance and sorrow for any sins he might have committed.

As Seamus adjusted the garment so that it hung from the left arm below the elbow, he uttered a further prayer, 'be it mine, O Lord, to bear the maniple of weeping and sorrow that I may receive with joy the reward of toil'. Finally, he draped a chasuble over his right arm. Until actually ordained he could not don this garment which, more than any other, would symbolize his calling. It was the principal vestment for celebrating Mass, a large round mantle covering his body both back and front and descending nearly to the knees.

From their stalls the choir chanted, the strong young voices rising and falling in perfect unison.

Seamus' eyes were fixed on the great altar and the figure of Christ on the cross. He felt the blood pulsing through his head. He had fasted since the previous day.

The spiritual director stood on one side of the altar, the Dean on the other. These two men, so very different in character and approach, had brought him to this climactic moment. What did it mean for them, he briefly wondered, to launch a new batch of priests? Seamus knew what it was to be one of those priests. The apostle John had recounted what Christ said: 'I have chosen you.'

The chanting stopped at the exact moment Seamus and the other deacons reached the altar steps and took their seats. The archbishop's procession appeared. A silence fell over the chapel. One by one the deacons rose and prostrated themselves on the marble floor below the archbishop's throne. His Grace recited a litany.

The stone was cold against Seamus' face. He concentrated, remembering what the spiritual director had cautioned about this moment.

'You are meant to feel humiliated. You will only be raised from the ground to a high dignity by the mystery of prayer while the whole church prays for God's grace to raise you to the priesthood. You must symbolically grovel in the dust, recognizing that God alone, not your brilliance or anything else, can raise you. You will remember his words "I have chosen you. You have not chosen me." Then, and only then, with those words in your head will you be able to rise.'

Seamus rose to his feet. His turn had come. He felt suddenly acutely alert. He waited before the archbishop's throne, head bowed.

The archbishop murmured a prayer, the Latin barely audible. Slowly, with infinite tenderness, he placed his hands gently on the head of Seamus. He left them in place for a moment. Then they were withdrawn.

Seamus stepped back and donned his chasuble.

He was now Father Breslin.

Next day he turned from the altar to cast his eyes over his first congregation.

He had barely slept in the twenty-four hours since ordination, yet he showed no signs of fatigue. He had eaten sparingly and sipped only water. After being admitted to Holy Orders, he had spent his last full day at Clonliffe. At meal times he sat with the staff at the high table, a sign of his new status. In between he had cleared his bedroom, packed his suitcase for the last time, received his new chalice and vial of anointing oil, and had a brief discussion with the archbishop about the future; there was plenty of pastoral work to be done in the diocese. Afterwards he prepared for his first Mass, reminding himself that until he died he was, as a priest, at the core of the Christian mystery.

He invited his family, relatives and friends to share the celebration, close to five hundred persons. In the front pew were his mother and father and his sisters. Gertrude Breslin had saved for almost a full year for this occasion, putting aside a set sum each week so that the family would be fittingly dressed. Liam Breslin wore a three-piece suit, his tie neatly knotted, his collar stud in place, his hair combed and sleeked down with hair oil. The girls had new dresses and hats. His mother had bought herself a grey two-piece outfit and matching hat. Rouge had put colour into her cheeks. But no make-up could hide the deepening dark rings under her eyes or put blood back into her lips or hands, which trembled with the effort of holding the missal. She had moved a little closer to death in the past week.

Father Breslin knew that by not so much as a flicker must he show his mother his own pain. She would not wish it. Nor would he.

He had laid down a strict rule for the meal that followed the Mass. He would not pay for, or encourage, more than one round of drinks. Yet already his father and a group of cronies were in a corner of the room, tippling from a bottle of whisky. They were already in a mellow mood.

His mother touched his hand. 'He's so proud, son. He really is!' Her voice had a pleading whisper. 'He's waited years for this. And found the money too, to pay for it. Let him have a sip or two. He'll not be a problem. Not today.'

Father Breslin looked down at her. There was a liveliness in her eyes he had not seen for a long time. It was as if she was determined to prove the doctors wrong.

There were printed place cards and individual menus. She had ordered the flowers and advised on the seating arrangements and asked the hotel to provide its best tableware. He could not spoil it for her.

When guests sat down at the long centre table for the meal, Liam Breslin remained standing, glass in hand, rock-steady on his feet, looking down at his son, eyes brimming with tears.

'It sounds strange for your own Dad to be saying this, but I'm real proud, son, to say "Welcome, Father."'

Then Liam Breslin addressed the guests. 'You know what they say! Once a priest...!'

In unison came a thunderous response, '...always a priest!'

That was the moment she chose to come. She was suddenly in his thoughts, reminding only him that she would never leave him. He may indeed be a priest until his dying breath, but to survive he would need her. Father Breslin told himself that was what Mary was saying.

CHAPTER FIVE

Illusions

Victoria began to laugh. Art could never hope to be a priest the way he was exploring her with his tongue and hands. In the darkness of his father's car, she deliberately avoided his mouth. 'I could have your baby and you'll have to marry me.' She hoped the threat would work but Art was nineteen, physically strong and impulsive.

He smothered her mouth with his, whispering urgently in her ear, saying she still had a week of freedom left and she should relax and enjoy.

He had not stopped trying to undress her since they settled in the back seat. Usually he was gentle, knowing this was how to arouse her; now he had a roughness about him that she found off-putting. She wondered if this was in any way related to what she had told him; that in just seven days she would be gone from him forever.

She had first been brought to this park – a trysting place for young lovers in this small Illinois town – by another boy when she was fifteen years old. That was two years ago and it had been Labour Day. She and Danny had shared a bottle of wine and watched the sun go down over the lake. Afterwards he had undressed her and they made love. She did not allow herself to admit any doubts about what she had done, not then. The guilt only came when Danny never called. She had felt soiled. She now knew the feeling had played an important part in her decision.

'Listen to me, will you, Art. Will you please stop and listen? I don't want this.'

He continued to press himself on her. She freed a hand to try and push him away. 'Stop. Do you hear? Stop.'

She knew he was holding her tightly to reassure her, just as she knew her resolve was weakening. His hand left her breast to turn on the radio. The music of Eddie Duchin filled the car. Only Art knew how Duchin affected her; there was something about his fluid keyboard music. She could feel her moistness as his finger entered her.

A school of tiny fish seemed to be swimming up inside her, her arms came round his back and pulled him down on her.

She felt his weight bearing down as he laboured to a climax.

After a while she spoke. 'Can we go home, please?'

He nodded, at the same time doing something he had never done before. Art slid out of the car to dress himself in the darkness while she adjusted her clothes. She found his solicitude surprising and tender. Perhaps he had now accepted her life would never be the same again. In a week's time she would enter a convent to become a nun.

The first seeds may have been planted when she tottered into her parent's bedroom, insisting she was a nun. That was the morning her mother called her cute. Her father was alive then, a fine, strapping man, always in robust health and because of this, his death came as a greater shock. He left a widow and four girls – Victoria and three younger sisters.

Her mother continued leading the family in saying the daily rosary and encouraging them not to be ostentatious about their faith, as many families were in their Catholic community. Rather, they must regard faith as a gift from God and use it as an inner driving force.

When she was six years old Victoria acquired a piece of old blanket which she pinned to her hair forming the semblance of a veil and habit. Then she would join the neighbourhood boys who used strips of white paper pinned around their necks as Roman collars. They would play a game called Gas Company in which they collected fuel bills through the neighbourhood. There was keen competition for the roles to persuade the company not to turn off the supply if a family couldn't pay the bill.

Victoria's neighbours were a mixture of Irish, Polish and other mid-European races whose faith and values were simple: love of God, love of family, love of neighbour. Catholicism was embracing and bracing, comforting and forgiving, demanding unswerving obedience and no challenge.

When Sister Stephen counselled about the dangers of necking, every one in the senior grade class knew she was really warning that girls could get pregnant if they allowed boys to French kiss. This physiological miracle had stayed with Victoria well into her teens. When

Father Bruce said at Mass one Sunday that Padre Pio regularly bled from his hands because he had inherited Christ's suffering for the world, everyone accepted it. When Brother Arnold, one of the monk teachers at the high school pronounced *Catcher in the Rye* an obscene book, no one doubted they were doomed to hell for reading it. News from the Pope in Rome was sacrosanct; if the Holy Father was reported to have a cold, people lit candles for his recovery. It was a world ruled by the penance of Hail Marys and Glory be to the Fathers. Nothing was too great a sin to be absolved. Sister Beverly Rose who taught the graduation class religion had stated as a fact that even murder could be absolved in the sanctuary of the confessional.

Confession had a powerful appeal for Victoria. It meant dressing up, putting on a hat to stand in line, edging towards the box itself, remembering sins since the last time. The box itself was like a tomb. In its confines she sometimes imagined she was a pharaoh's daughter, buried alive for all time, or an assistant to Houdini, about to emerge in triumph on some celestial stage. Sometimes she did not have much to confess. But the routine was always the same: down on the cushioned kneeler, face against the fine mesh of the dividing screen. She knew her confessors on the other side of the screen by their odours. Father Bruce reeked of after-shave; there was a perpetual whiff of onions from Father Doyle; Father MacDonald gave off an aroma of sweat and the peppermints he sucked while delivering absolution.

Between them they supervised a world where many of the pre-war values had survived into the 1950s. The source of social stability remained the family. Young people were still expected to ask their elders for permission to do many things: borrow the family car, stay out extra-late, sleep over at a friend's house. A counter-culture, either as a word or a concept, did not exist: the thought of demonstrating against the government was too absurd to be considered. The work ethic was strong. People continued to believe in themselves and in their country.

In this close-knit community, priests and nuns were cast as people apart; figures to be turned to in times of trouble; the first to be invited to a wedding breakfast, a christening party or a funeral wake. Through them God spoke: he was incarnate in their flesh and blood. They seemed to be aware of everything that went on: they knew what to do about a Catholic drunk, a Catholic wife-beater, a Catholic adulterer or adulteress. They used their power of prayer to heal them. Victoria believed she had regularly seen this work in a neighbourhood where there were few Protestants and no blacks, where the houses were modest, each with its small back yard and basketball hoop. Out front were parked, for the most part, second-hand cars.

Victoria had walked along these streets to and from school for eleven years and still remembered the initial impact the Reverend Mother had made on her. She did not appear to have any feet; her robes rose in perpendicular folds to her neck where they were met by an equally imposing head covering, layers of white and black cloth. Victoria realized her strip of blanket was a poor substitute for the real thing.

It was the Reverend Mother who first raised the possibility of Victoria answering God's call. It happened after early morning Mass on Memorial Day when Victoria had been thirteen years old and the memory of her father's death was still painfully fresh in her mind.

Leaving the church the nun fell into step with her, relaxed and smiling, not at all the way she was at school. Victoria found it surprisingly easy to answer her questions. No: she did not have any definite idea about what she was going to do after graduation. Yes: she did like religious class. Yes: she read her Bible every day. No: she never thought marriage should be the only aspiration for a girl. Then casually, as they went their separate ways, the Reverend Mother posed the question: 'Victoria, have you ever thought of becoming a nun?'

For most of that Memorial Day she had sat in her room and imagined the sort of life the Reverend Mother led. Prayer, of course, must be at the centre of it. But how easy was it to go to the bathroom in all those yards of starched linen and stiff serge? And what was it like to pray for strangers, people in China, someone you never knew by name? Nuns had to pray for everybody. Brother Arnold said so. What was it like to work all day without wages, teaching an unruly class, running the altar boy practices, cleaning the church? Did nuns eat different food to make them more holy? They couldn't drink alcohol, but they always seemed to have a good time at weddings.

Victoria was certain of one thing. There was no secret underground passage linking the convent to the house where the priests lived. That was just one of those dirty Protestant stories. Anyway, she couldn't possibly, even in her wildest fantasies, connect sex with the Reverend Mother. She possessed the sort of fierce purity which made *The Nun's Story* required reading for all good Catholics.

Later there were other signposts to her decision to enter convent life. She began to read, discovering for a start, and to her utter astonishment, that between the death of Simon Peter the apostle in AD67, and the year 312, there were no fewer than thirty-one popes. Many of those had perished by garrotting, crucifixion, strangulation, poisoning, beheading or smothering. Some found no peace in the grave. Pope Formosus was dug up in 897, nine months after being put into the Roman soil, his rotting corpse robed in pontifical vestments and placed on a throne to stand trial before a religious court convened by his successor. The corpse of Pope John XIV was, in 984, while still warm enough to bleed, skinned and hauled through the streets of Rome.

Victoria avidly read about how the Emperor Constantine became a Christian and then, years later in 322, established Catholicism as the religion of the empire. The faith became the dominant political factor in Europe. The Pope, the most important ecclesiastical personage in the entire world, headed a hierarchic church with a centralized government and absolute authority. But behind the monolithic edifice was a world that no soap opera began to rival.

So shocked and excited was she by the story of Marozia that she read it by flashlight late into the night, under her bedcovers. Marozia: the mother of one pope, fathered by another pontiff, the aunt of a third pope, the grandmother of a fourth. Marozia: who arranged the election of no fewer than nine popes in eight years in the turbulent tenth century; standing by while two were choked to death, one suffocated with a pillow and four poisoned. Marozia: the greatest maker and unmaker of popes, whose own fate was hidden from Victoria when her torch batteries ran out. She had been forced to wait until dawn to read how two cowled monks had, on another dawn a thousand years earlier, arrived in Marozia's room with the tell-tale crimson-clothed cushion. They had locked the door and told Marozia there was no point in struggling. Then they placed the cushion over her face, steadily exerting pressure until all the life was smothered from the old woman. Another Pope John had ordered that this be done.

Victoria had sat in religious class and wondered why Sister Beverly

Rose did not discuss women like Marozia, explaining why, in spite of people like her, or perhaps because of them, the church has survived. Instead, Sister Beverly Rose dwelt on Our Lady, including that momentous day when the Mother of Jesus appeared to three children near the town of Fatima in Portugal in 1917. The event had been accompanied by a miraculous change of course of the sun, a feat witnessed by hundreds. The children had said Our Lady told them three secrets, to be confided only to each pope when he was elected. One morning Sister Beverly Rose had said the latest news from Rome was that Pius XII had reread the predictions and fainted. He had been revived by his faithful nun. The thought of a women actually being allowed that close to the Holy Father was a potent one for Victoria. Perhaps she, too, could reach such a dizzy height if she entered religious life.

The Reverend Mother had reduced the matter to an emotive question: 'Are you capable of stripping yourself, emptying yourself, so that Christ can enter you with his fullness of being?'

Victoria had said she was.

Father Bruce said that the formation of all those in religious life was built on the solid foundation of three vows: poverty, chastity and obedience. These were what made a vocation a state of perfection. Victoria had not thought the vows sounded very demanding. Poverty was probably another word for frugal. Obedience was nothing new to her. Her mother had instilled it. She guessed that chastity meant giving up boys forever. That too, need not be an insufferable problem.

Since Danny, Victoria had made love sixteen times with Art. Every occasion was code-marked in her diary. A pierced arrow symbolized the act; a tree or a tiny car indicated whether it occurred in the park or on the back seat of his father's Ford. Alongside the drawings were letters: T, G, N: terrific, good, and nothing. There were only two 'terrifics'. Ten of the entries were accompanied by an 'N'. There were gaps of weeks between them. Unlike some of her girl friends, she had never felt a need to make-out every week.

Even so, she wondered if she would miss sex. Some of her friends predicted she would. She'd told them that nuns had probably special instructions about how to cope. She had no idea if this were true, but she sought proof through reading. There was almost nothing written about how priests and nuns remained chaste. The prophets Jeremiah and Ezekiel barely touched upon it. Nor did the canticles of the Song of Songs. St Augustine merely offered chastity as a model for all women who wished to follow Jesus. But Victoria could find nothing to show her how to live as a celibate in a practical day-to-day way.

She began to watch the priests and nuns to see if, from their behaviour, she could get some clues. Sister Beverly Rose seemed to have an especially deep need to be loved, and expressed her own affection not only with words but with touch, putting her arm around a boy, hugging a girl or even kissing, quickly on the cheek, a nun she had not seen for days. Brother Arnold was incapable of uttering so much as a word of affection and shunned physical contact. Father Doyle seemed never happier than when on the sports field or at the pool, plunging into the activity with great energy. Father MacDonald prowled the school corridors after class, looking for boys and girls locked in some furtive embrace. Father Bruce seemed to have less a need to be loved than to nurture it in others.

Victoria began to see that each one seemed to have personal guidelines allowing them to live with, and within, their vows. She was confident she would be able to do the same. It was reassuring to know that – when the time came – her faith, as always, would provide the answer.

From the beginning the nuns had taught there were only two major religions in the Christian world: Catholic and 'Others'. Only Catholics went to her school, and in the long summer vacations played exclusively together. Unlike Catholics, who were encouraged to attend Mass every day, the 'Others' only went once a week, and then to a number of different churches.

No matter how the 'Others' mocked Catholicism, it contained for her a totally satisfying religious experience. Mass, when the strong resolute masculine voices were a reminder that faith was not for weaklings or doubters, religious classes at school, saying family prayers around the table in the kitchen: Catholicism contained all the world's truth she would ever need. Her religious world was a secure and all-embracing one. She could continue to confess her sins and be forgiven.

After her first sexual experience, she had whispered her guilt over what she had let Danny do. On the other side of the grille Father Doyle asked her if she was genuinely repentant. She said she was. He asked her if she would try not to do it again. She promised she would. He absolved her, murmuring the prescribed words of forgiveness.

She had returned several times to confess similar indiscretions with Art. Father Doyle was always sympathetic, never keeping her more than a few minutes, long enough to hear her invariable response: she was sorry and would try not to repeat her sin. Father MacDonald she disliked. She could always sense him sitting hunched on the other side of the grille, sucking one peppermint after another. It was not that he asked leading questions. It was his disconcerting habit of repeating everything she said, almost as if he wanted to savour and save the words for some future use. She had finally told Art who said that was probably how Father MacDonald got his kicks. The thought of her confession being a source of personal satisfaction to the priest had made her avoid going for weeks. Afterwards she had managed to ensure only Father Doyle heard her admissions. Each time he absolved her.

Victoria believed this was what made her church unique. It recognized and understood human failings. The 'Others' could never claim that. A church with such power and overwhelming authority was also irresistibly attractive. She wanted to be part of it, not on the outside, but as an insider. The only way was to become a nun.

The decision made, the arrangements were surprisingly easy and swift. There were several visits for Victoria to the Mother House where she met the Mother Superior and a person called the Mistress of Postulants, whom everybody called Mistress. After speaking to her about faith being rooted in undying hope, they promised they would say repeated prayers for Victoria to join them.

There was no pressure, there was no need to exert any. Vocations were booming: there was not an American convent with a vacant place. A Catholic, John F. Kennedy, was being groomed for the White House. Catholics held high office in Washington, and elsewhere Catholic-owned periodicals had boosted circulations to unprecedented levels. A Catholic veto could close a pop concert, empty a cinema, give the thumbs-down to a play.

During the pre-admission interviews neither the Mother Superior nor the Mistress raised the question of whether Victoria was a virgin, or if she clearly understood what the commitment to chastity meant. Instead the Mistress gave her a summary of the Rule of the Order. The guidelines would officially control her every movement and thought from the day she entered. There were twenty-five lines devoted to chastity. Victoria had yet to read them. But she spent long periods in her bedroom thinking about her future.

Her bedroom was a contemporary social history of a typical young American girl. Victoria's dark green chenille bed coverlet matched the curtains and carpet. The wallpaper design was of countless daffodils. The effect of perpetual spring was completed by the cream painted woodwork.

Tucked into her dressing-table mirror frame were snapshots: Victoria at a pyjama party; she and her sisters at a birthday celebration for their mother; Victoria with her father shortly before he died; Art in his football uniform; Art and Victoria sitting on the front porch drinking lemonade. That was the night they first made love.

A bulletin board above the mirror was festooned with pom-poms from a football game. Art had been on the winning team and presented them to her. That night, too, they made love. Below the paper tassels was a thumb-tacked invitation to a friend's bridal shower, Victoria's high school schedule, half-a-dozen birthday and Christmas cards including one from Art, and his Valentine from last February, red imitation silk and gold letters, saying 'I love you'. There was a withered corsage of flowers, a reminder of the day she had been a cousin's bridesmaid. Art had come with her, gotten drunk and nearly crashed the car on the way home. He was so shaken he did not even kiss her goodnight.

Neatly stacked in their stand were many of the pop hits of the day, albums featuring Frank Sinatra, Lester Lanin, Billy Vaughan, the Kingdom Trio, Nat King Cole and, of course, Elvis Presley and Bill Haley. Shelves contained a selection of current bestsellers: Herman Wouk's *Marjorie Morningstar*, Morton Thompson's *Not as a Stranger*, and Robert Ruark's *Something of Value*. Each had been evaluated and discussed at length with friends. Next to them were two books she constantly referred to, their pages well-thumbed, corners neatly turned down to help her locate passages. One was *The Scrolls from the Dead Sea*, by Edmund Wilson. The other was *Life is Worth Living*, written by Victoria's favourite Catholic author, Archbishop Fulton J. Sheen. They had helped her answer many questions about her faith.

Beside them was her copy of the Bible. Given by her mother on the day she was confirmed, it had in the past year become essential reading. Throughout the Old Testament Christ was expected. From Genesis onwards the messianic currents had flowed down the centuries leaving no room for doubt about that glorious moment when Mary received a sign she would conceive by the Holy Ghost and that when her time came she would deliver the Son of God in a stable.

For Victoria that image was powerful, as were all others which followed: of Christ strong and unshakeable, filled with compassion, self-discipline, restraint and self-mortification. She was eager to transfer to Christ all the love and devotion she would, in a marriage, give to an earthly husband. She had already envisaged her wedding in her diary. 'I am to wed the Risen Christ and like him walk humble and poor among his people. Among them, but not of them.'

Christ, she concluded, did not come to earth to live. He wanted to die, to sacrifice himself for the sins of all others. His commitment on that first Good Friday was to ensure there would always be an Easter Sunday. Such selflessness had enthralled her and fitted perfectly her own concept of why she wanted to be a nun.

In her diary for August 6, 1958, she wrote: 'I want to save souls. To continue Christ's work. To give myself to the Lord, fully and completely, in a way I have never given myself to anybody before. In two days time I will.'

Victoria sensed her sisters, like many of her friends, now looked upon her differently. This year there would be three other local girls embarking on vocations. She did not know how they felt, but Victoria enjoyed the respect she now received. Within her circle, the notion a girl should aspire to become something other than a housewife was unusual.

Victoria awoke early. She remained under the covers, enjoying the excitement. Her eyes roamed over a room she knew she would probably never occupy again. Last night the send-off party had flowed through the house and out into the yard. There were relatives, neighbours, classmates, even persons she hardly knew. Her mother said wistfully there were probably more people than even for Dad's funeral.

Beneath some of the banter there was a similar sadness. Why even begin to explain that, while she was leaving their world, she was not leaving the world; that all she was doing was entering into a deeper relationship with God. Why say anything except to thank them for their farewell gifts? There were dozens, mainly expensive and beautiful, but not hers to keep. The Mistress of Postulants had given her a list of what was 'acceptable' to receive: solid silver candlesticks, goblets, napkin holders, cutlery, hand-polished glassware, pure linen table-cloths and napkins. On arrival at the Mother House she must hand them all over. It was Victoria's first practical experience of how the vow of poverty was interpreted by the Order.

The gifts covered the carpet of the bedroom, over a hundred items. All she could personally keep were a statue of St Joseph and a simply-framed picture of Our Lady. And her Bible. Now, in her mind's eye, she recalled moments from the party.

Victoria was admiring a candelabra when Sister Beverly Rose appeared beside her. She squeezed Victoria's arm. Her voice was soft and reassuring. She took the candelabra and gently led the way to Victoria's room. Sister Beverly Rose closed the door behind them and placed the gift on the floor beside the other gifts. Possessiveness, she explained, was one of the sins of secular life, a destructive force. Victoria's new life would enrich her beyond all worldly goods.

Victoria reached for her Bible on her bedside table, and turned to the words of her favourite apostle, Luke, reading a sentence she knew by heart. 'Whoever puts his hand to the plough but keeps looking back is unfit for the reign of God.' To look back was to covet possessions and lose any hope of acquiring the far greater treasure of heaven. She was more anxious than ever to start her process of dispossession.

Father Bruce had been among the first to arrive at the party. He stood for a while beside her as she received the first of her gifts. More than ever he seemed to have descended from some perpetual height others could not climb. As they stood there, Father Bruce murmured in her ear: 'The affectation of an elaborate headdress, the wearing of golden jewellery, or the donning of rich robes is not for you. Your adornment is rather the hidden character of the heart expressed in the unfading beauty of a calm and gentle disposition.'

She smiled, thinking she was perfectly content to give up what St Peter demanded. She knew there would be no more sunbathing in a skimpy swimsuit, no more make-up or wearing a pretty dress and no more making love to Art, to anybody.

Climbing out of bed, staring at herself in the mirror, her nightgown was of cotton flannel, the only kind permitted by the Order. She had worn it these past few nights to get used to the cloth. Victoria continued to stare at the mirror. Slowly and deliberately she plucked the photographs of Art from the frame. She tore them into pieces and dropped them into the waste basket. Next she removed the pom-poms and the corsage of withered flowers. Then the Christmas cards, not bothering to tear them but letting them fall into the bin. Finally, she took down Art's Valentine which she shredded. It was her way of exorcizing what had also happened the previous night.

Victoria was losing count of how many gifts she had carried to her room. She returned from yet another trip when she stopped, suddenly tense. Art had arrived, his back was to her, head thrust forward, listening to a girl who lived a few doors away. She looked up at him adoringly.

Victoria wondered why she felt a sudden pang of jealousy. Then Art was cutting through the crowd to reach her, using his arms the way he swam to propel himself forward, a bantering look in his eyes. He asked if she was still mad at him. She pretended not to understand. He rested his hand lightly on her arm, bent down and whispered in her ear, reminding her. She saw Sister Beverly Rose watching them.

She removed Art's hand, determined to show the watching nun his attention was not welcome, that he had no right to make such a proprietary display. Art laughed, asking why she was blushing. For a moment she felt resentment. She had not seen him since that night in the park. Nor had she invited him here tonight. Yet he was behaving as if she were still his, as if this were just an ordinary party, not her farewell from his world.

Sister Beverly Rose edged towards them. Art smiled, a sudden stiff smile. Father Bruce was at her elbow. He looked at Art steadily, his face more granite-like than ever.

From his pocket Art produced a small package. He thrust it into her hand and Father Bruce told her to open it. It was an expensive wrist-watch. The priest said it was a fine gift. Ignoring him Art told her the watch was to remind her of their time together. He abruptly turned and left, pausing only to take the blonde girl with him. She looked over her shoulder and smiled at Victoria. Sister Beverly Rose examined the watch. 'A nice piece, child, but you have a watch. I think it would be best to hand this in when you get to the convent.'

Victoria nodded. The watch, like Art, was no longer part of her world.

Bathed and dressed in a simple black cotton dress and sandals, Victoria sat in her room, waiting. She wished the time would pass more quickly. She wondered whether she should write Art a letter explaining she still wanted him as a friend. The restless surgings continued to create tension in her, putting her on edge.

When the party was over Victoria, her mother and sisters returned the house to its neat-as-a-pin condition. On their way to bed her mother paused in the doorway, staring at the spread of presents. 'You got far more than I did when I married your Dad.'

'Mother, it's because they're for the Community. It's people's way of showing their appreciation for all the Order means.'

Her mother nodded, trying to understand. She pointed to the collection of silver and linen. 'But what will the Order do with all this? Keep it? Sell it? Or what?'

Victoria smiled. 'I don't know. But God will find a use for it.'

Her mother kissed her on the forehead and without another word went to her room.

Victoria's mother turned and checked her three younger daughters were settled in the back of the car. Victoria sat beside her, hands on her lap, hair neatly brushed, staring ahead.

The girl who had left with Art was playing records on her porch. Further down the road a gang of boys were loading six-packs into a convertible. They were off to the lake, Victoria guessed. Some of their parents were mowing the little squares of grass in front of their houses.

Her mother held her rosary beads, old and worn now, like her hands. The final ritual before they could depart was about to begin.

Victoria cleared her throat. In a strong voice she announced, 'Saint Christopher, patron saint of travellers'. From her mother and the back seat came a responsive chorus. 'Guard and protect us on our journey'. Her mother added 'Amen'.

She checked the mirror. The two cars parked immediately behind had started their engines. They contained twelve of Victoria's closest relatives, aunts and uncles who had insisted on escorting her. The gifts she was taking to the Community filled the trunks of all three cars, together with Victoria's holdall filled with the clothes on the list the Order had given her.

The three cars moved down the road. Victoria stared straight ahead ignoring the neighbours' waves, wondering why she felt she suddenly wanted to cry.

Silence, deeper than any Victoria had known, enveloped her. She began to undress, first positioning her shoes beside the bed. She unclasped her garters releasing new black stockings. She laid them carefully on the bed.

The nun who escorted her here had cautioned she must take good care of everything, that these were the only clothes she would have for the foreseeable future. She had been controlled and calm, her face serene. When she spoke her voice was remote, as if living in this consecrated place required her to maintain a distance from everybody and everything except God. Victoria silently promised herself she would strive to become as perfect.

Victoria unhooked her postulant's cape. It was clasped at its pristine white collar and dropped without flare to her waistline. It was so designed, the nun had explained, to ensure custody of the hands. She had shown Victoria how to bend her elbows and clasp her fingers together beneath it. Henceforth, in public, whenever she was beyond the confines of the convent, she must walk like this. When she had work to do, or prayers to say, she could pin back the cape. The nun demonstrated how it could be buttoned at the shoulder but otherwise the cape must completely cover Victoria's hands until it became natural for them to be still.

She placed the garment on the bed beside the stockings and unbuttoned her dress. It was medieval black, relieved only by cuffs as white as the cape's collar, with a featureless bodice cut to disguise any suggestion that she possessed breasts. She pulled it over her head revealing a round-necked T-shirt and white cotton underpants and a garter belt.

These had all been ordered and paid for by her mother from a mail-order house specializing in clothes for nuns. She removed the T-shirt. Under it she had a bra which complied with the Order's specifications: black, without lace or fancy stitching. She unclasped her garter belt placing it on top of her other clothes. The belt was also black, without frills.

Victoria pulled on a cotton-flannel nightdress covering herself to her ankles. She felt inside her nightie and unclasped her bra and wriggled out of her panties letting the garments fall inside her nightdress to her feet.

The nun had explained that was how she must always undress. The procedure was part of the Order's ritual. Victoria stooped and in one quick movement picked up the panties and bra and placed them in the top drawer of a wooden chest with her other underwear. She folded her dress and cape and stored them in the second drawer. The bottom one held her toilet articles. When she bent Victoria was careful not to turn her back on the bed. Jesus – in his passion on a carved crucifix – was lying on the pillow.

The nun had shown Victoria how to place the cross, its top resting against the very centre of the pillow, at an angle of forty-five degrees. The precise position was laid down in the Order's holy Rule. While the crucifix was there, she must not sit on the bed. The nun's explanation had riveted her. 'Our Lord is watching while you go about his work.'

Before going to bed Victoria removed the crucifix and reverently placed it on top of the chest. She was not ready for sleep yet. Her surroundings continued to fascinate her. Hemmed in by white cotton curtains on three sides, the cubicle was in the middle of a long barrack-like room. The drapes were suspended from hooks in the ceiling and reached to precisely a quarter of an inch above the spotless and shining linoleum floor. On her way down the room Victoria counted: there were fifty identical pens. She had shivered when the nun called them cells. She really was embarking upon a monastic life. All the saints, monks, friars and hermits had lived in cells. She had an image of tortured-faced men struggling to ward off evil before reaching peace with God. But until the nun led her into the postulant's dormitory, Victoria had no idea women also occupied cells.

The nun had explained everything in the cell had its proper place. The iron bedstead *must* always be exactly two inches from the wall. The straight-backed chair *must* stand at the foot of the bed, six inches clear of it. Her shoes, thick-heeled and laced, the sort her grandmother wore, *must* be lined up on the left-hand side of the bed. The dresser scarf, a white strip of cloth, *must* be placed horizontally. Only one statue was permitted on top of the chest, which *must* always be two clear feet from the bed.

A statue of Our Lady, pressed into Victoria's hand by her mother just before they said their final goodbye, *must* be kept in the bureau. She could take it out to look at it, or even change it for the statue of St Joseph. But only one item must be displayed. Even her Bible must be kept in a drawer. Victoria's bed must be made in a certain way. The nun had demonstrated: untucking and then remaking the sheets, folding the corners diagonally, the way a nurse made a bed. She took unusual care to place the pillow exactly flat with an equal amount of undersheet on either side. Once satisfied, she had positioned the crucifix.

Victoria had noticed her movements had been deft and economical. When the nun moved, she not so much walked as glided, only the swish of her habit indicating her passage. Standing at the foot of the bed, the nun had eyed Victoria steadily.

In the same gentle, distant voice, she delivered her final instructions. 'Remember you have been chosen for this life. But it is sometimes not easy, especially for parents to understand God has called a daughter. You can help them, and please him, by remembering that the best kind of advertising for what he wants of you is the "show me" kind. You remember the saying, "by their fruits you shall know them"? So let your family know you, in your new life, as someone who is glad to have been called. That you have been chosen to serve others. Remember what Jesus said, "the harvest is good but labourers are scarce. Beg the harvest master to send out labourers to gather the harvest." You are now one of his labourers. You will learn here how to reap a harvest which is far more worthwhile than any other. So say goodbye to your family with that certainty. Be happy. For them. For God.'

The nun had paused and indicated the crucifix. 'And for him.' Without another word she turned and glided away.

Despite the nun's words and Victoria's determined efforts to follow the homily, the parting had not been easy.

As she rejoined her family everybody said how nice she looked in her postulant outfit. She took her mother by the arm, conscious time was running out and that soon they must say goodbye. They walked along the convent's path, past the chapel, and the seemingly endless red brick of the convent itself; roof below roof, eaves and narrow windows, all combining to give a totally enclosed feeling.

Near the chapel Victoria held her mother's hands in hers. She chose her words carefully, insisting she was genuinely glad to be no longer her own person, free to do as she pleased, that when professed she could be sent by the church to do whatever work was needed; that all she would do from now on would be based on selfless love, given without fear and offered in joy. There were tears in her mother's eyes.

The final act of parting was swift. A bell rang. The relatives of the nineteen other postulants admitted with Victoria were shown out by nuns. There was no time for clinging or last minute appeals for daughters to change their minds.

The father of one girl tripped and lurched against a wall. His nun escorts stood scandalized. The man was close to being drunk. Then the massive convent door closed on the girl's father, Victoria's relatives, and the entire secular world.

The Mother Superior appeared. Small and rotund with piercing grey-green eyes, Victoria suddenly thought she was far more forbidding than when they had met at her final pre-admission interview. Though reserved then, the nun was friendly. Now she appeared separated from the postulants by some invisible barrier.

Victoria remembered the words of the Mistress of Postulants. 'When you come here, you must always remember that, in the spiritual sense, the Mother Superior is neither man nor woman. She is Christ among us and as such is loved, obeyed and looked up to by us all. You must always remember that.'

The Mother Superior spoke. 'You are welcome. We have all prayed for this day, that God, having called you, would give you the strength to answer that call. Your presence here shows he wishes you to be part of this congregation. To remain you will need continuing strength and understanding.'

She turned and looked across the entrance hall. As if by some invisible command a nun appeared from a room carrying a pile of loose-leaf books. The Mother Superior turned back to the postulants. 'Strength and understanding. Those are the most important qualities you will need. Strength to maintain your faith in God and do what he wishes of you. Understanding to show you why you must do certain things for him. Always for him.'

She smiled, giving her face a radiance that a moment before was not there.

'It is not easy to recognize that you have been called. That you must know. But, having answered, it is even harder to remain faithful to the call. To be a nun in this world is always difficult. The temptations to abandon your calling are many. And you should be warned, the life here is hard. It was never meant to be anything else. You will be tested to the limit, not in your faith, but in your ability to turn that faith into what God wishes from you. He, not you, will in the end decide if you have the capacity to perform his work. You are here because you heard the call. To live up to it you must listen every day.'

The Mother Superior waited, letting her words settle, her eyes scanning the group before continuing to outline the difficulties.

'In an age of increasing selfishness you have been chosen to lead lives of sacrifice. There are some people who say it is a life against nature. You already know something of what is expected of you. Poverty, chastity and obedience. You have been told, briefly, about these vows in our correspondence with you.' Victoria realized she had never read up the vows. Thankfully, it appeared not to matter.

The Mother Superior spoke of the challenge of their new life. They were here because they were neither half-hearted in their religious determination or unsure why they had been chosen. Equally, they must recognise they would live a life which most women would find impossible. But they should not feel a need to apologize to themselves or anybody for the role for which they had been selected.

They need not give, or seek, an explanation for their chastity. But, just as a good marriage required working at, so did living a full celibate life, perhaps even more so, for it required disciplining nature's instincts and personal inclinations. They should recognize that self-control was what distinguished a human from other species. In many ways the ability to live naturally in a state of chastity was the apex of discipline. Some would find it a greater struggle than others. A few would undoubtedly discover the commitment too hard. They would not be judged but simply returned to the secular world.

For those who remained, the celibate life would shape their views and values in a way they would find totally satisfying. Chastity demanded a renunciation of several things but not of one's self. Only God has the power to choose who will receive such a gift. They had been chosen. They must not disappoint him.

The Mother Superior turned to the nun standing beside her with the books. Each one contained a mimeographed copy of the full holy Rule of the Order. The pages listed every requirement for living in this cloistered world. Every day, she added, her voice pitched to reach no further than the caped postulants, they would read and memorize a portion of the Rule. It would take them weeks.

Once more she paused, surveying the group. The time, she continued, would be well spent, their discoveries standing them in good stead for the rest of their lives. The Rule would teach them how, as celibates, they could undertake tasks which even married clergy in other faiths might find difficult to perform, unable or unwilling to take their families to areas of danger. But because they would not have husbands or children to consider they could when the time came, work in such places; with almost no worldly possessions they could travel quickly to where they were needed without having to be concerned at uprooting loved ones. Being celibate and impoverished they could obey their call with an undivided heart.

The Mother Superior nodded to the nun who began to hand out the books. The task completed, she left, with the same glide-walk Victoria was determined to acquire.

The Mother Superior continued. 'Read and inwardly digest. Silence here is a virtue which is to be used to recharge our spiritual batteries. You must always remember that. You cannot do God's work if you are being constantly distracted by other voices.'

Her right hand, plump and white, appeared from beneath her scapular and she made the sign of the cross over the postulants. She made it quickly. Then she glided away.

As if she had been standing in the wings waiting to make her entrance, thought Victoria, came the Mistress of Postulants. More than any other she would be the one responsible for their religious formation. She welcomed them in a voice that was sharp and distinctive. 'Tomorrow we start. You have just been told it will be hard. It will be harder than you imagine.'

'The nature of a vocation,' she continued, 'is not a job like teaching or nursing. It is following Christ. That means saying "yes" to the way of the cross. You must be prepared to strip and empty all the self in you so that Christ can be in you.'

She reinforced what the Mother Superior had said. They should see their chastity as an adventure, just as others regarded marriage. But marriages all too often failed because of the weakness of a husband. They would not ever face such a problem. Christ would never let them down. Only they could fail him – and only then if they attempted to rationalize the very mystery of chastity. It must be accepted as not something to be explained: trying to rationalize a commitment to celibacy could only lead to failure, dissatisfaction and a lack of fulfilment. She outlined the programme for the rest of their day: evening Mass, supper and then bed. Finally she told them about the Grand Silence.

It had descended while Victoria undressed.

Victoria continued to stand at her bedside, staring at the crucifix on her pillow. She knew that beyond her curtained enclosure, in identical cells, were eighteen other girls who had undressed, put away their clothes, said their prayers, read their Bibles and taken care not to touch their beds, each with its positioned crucifix. Yet there was not a sound. It was as if the Grand Silence had somehow made the other postulants vanish. Victoria felt utterly alone. She gently lifted the crucifix from her pillow and placed it next to the statue of St Joseph. Then she turned back the covers and climbed into bed.

At that moment two distinct sounds broke the Grand Silence. From close-by came intermittent snoring. From further up the dormitory was the sound of crying. Then it stopped as suddenly as it had begun. Victoria closed her eyes and was asleep almost at once.

CHAPTER SIX

Realities

Victoria began to prepare the essay, the last written test before going on retreat at the end of her postulancy. The subject was a favourite, canon law. There was precision about its language which appealed to her orderly mind. Her only worry, never voiced but confided to the diary she continued to keep, was the regulations were formulated by a male hierarchy.

Her preparatory work for the essay completed, Victoria began to write. She started with a quotation from St Augustine. 'If you can say "Enough" you are lost. Always increase, always progress, always go forward, step not on the way, turn not back, turn not aside.' Her second observation penned in her neat hand was from St Thomas Aquinas. 'The religious pledge their entire life to the zealous pursuit of perfection.'

She continued to write steadily, assembling her arguments in a clear, concise manner. A vow was a deliberate promise made to God. She began to expound the theological argument which distinguished between a mere promise and the totally binding commitment of her vows.

A vow must be an act of reason, ordered by the will. A sister who takes it upon herself to make such a deliberate promise must have full knowledge of what she is doing, must give her full consent to it, and in no way must she be coerced. In short, there must be no element present of ignorance, fear, fraud or force. A vow cannot be made to another person. Not even the Mother Superior, though she is the Christ amongst us, can accept our vow. This deliberate promise to God must be something that is good in itself. But even this is not enough. A vow must involve a choice. The choice between two good things.

She read back the passage. While she knew it would satisfy the Mistress, Victoria felt it needed an example which would strikingly clarify her argument. She thumbed through her Bible to the words of St Paul, noted the reference and resumed writing.

> *Marriage is a holy state, instituted by God. But St Paul says that the virginal state is better. Therefore, to vow oneself to that state, being the choice between two good things, is meritorious and pleasing to God. This is a perfect example of the object of a vow.*
>
> *A vow must be possible to carry out. God does not expect you to promise the impossible. Nor can a vow be made for useless, petty, foolish or unimportant matters unless the circumstances give them some semblance of moral good. For instance, you may vow never to go to a movie house because it once showed bad films, even though now it shows only movies that would be approved by the church. The act of going to the movie house now is not sinful, but if you made a vow to stay away because it was once a place of temptation, that vow would still be valid and acceptable to God. Remember the end in view in making a vow must always be God's glory.*

Victoria continued to compile her arguments, linking one thought with another, no longer surprised at how well she could manage this. She came to the core of her essay, the history of virginity.

Originally a pagan cult flourishing centuries before Christ, virginity reached back into the darkness of prehistoric times when totem gods demanded that untouched girls danced through the fields at dead of night to guarantee a good harvest. In Rome, virgins guarded the sacred fire outside the Senate, and were regularly whipped to death if caught in the arms of a soldier. In Babylon and Athens, in Thebes and Damascus, priestesses had to be virgins to exercise their supernatural power. To be a virgin was to be raised above all women and exalted in the eyes of all men.

In the two hundred years following the death of Jesus, celibate Christian girls were still routinely put to death. Not until the fourth century did the concept of religious celibacy find new favour. In Asia Minor, virgins banded together in communities. They spent their consecrated lives in prayer and spiritual counselling. Over the next 800 years the cloistered life assumed a definite form: rigid laws, isolation and, along with chastity, the vows of total poverty and obedience came into vogue.

Then, under the full fury of the Reformation, holy virginity was again threatened. The Protestant reformers, Luther and Bullinger, denounced chastity as wicked, dangerous for the body, and damaging to the mind. They proclaimed a woman's role was to be that of wife and mother; to be a virgin was to deny the creator's intentions. 'Celibacy is dismissed as a mask for impotence and sterility. It is evil.' It had taken centuries for the church to re-establish the paramount claim of chastity.

Her final thought completed, Victoria sat back in her hardback desk chair. There were still a few minutes to go before the examination ended that would formally mark the end of her nine months as a postulant.

Looking back, it was still hard to believe all that had happened and how much she had changed.

Without cosmetics, Victoria knew she could pass for a woman in her mid-twenties rather than a girl still to celebrate her nineteenth birthday. Yet she felt calmer and more responsible than she had ever done at home. She thought this was because she was free of all trivial decision-making, allowing her to concentrate fully on important things such as learning to communicate properly with God, recognizing her imperfections and correcting them.

She knew many of the postulants found the discipline oppressive. But Victoria constantly reminded herself that unquestioning obedience was important. Mother Superior's word was law. Until recently the Superior had been entitled to a bow on being passed in a corridor and a full curtsy from everyone who entered her office. Finally the Superior had convened a special council of the Mother House to announce she was relaxing such formality. But she remained authoritarian in other ways. She had once asked two postulants to clear snow in the midst of a blizzard. When they hesitated she sharply told them it was Teresa of Avila who ordered a nun to plant a cucumber sideways in the ground.

The Mother Superior was constantly looking for any sign that a postulant had forgotten the need for continual self-effacement. One had been caught glancing at her reflection in a polished brass plate and was publicly reprimanded. Another, discovered titivating her veil, was told there was no room for such feminine vanities. A third postulant forgot herself so far that curves could be discerned beneath her dress.

The Mother Superior assembled the postulants, lectured them on the virtue of being unattractive on earth, not only because attractiveness was a sexual lure, but to be unattractive showed they were saving themselves for eternal life. In eternity there are no men or women said the Superior, only souls. She then reminded them how many rules had been relaxed. When she was a novice it was forbidden to smell fragrant herbs, fruit and flowers. Now she permitted flowers in the parlours. When she had trained, she always sprinkled her food with a bitter flavouring to mortify her taste buds. That was no longer in the Rule, though she still did it out of choice. Life for a postulant had become easier but they should not abuse God's benevolence. Therefore, they would all spend an extra hour on their knees in chapel, praying for help not to do so.

While Victoria was a postulant, a new pope, the twenty-third to take the name of John, had been elected to the throne of St Peter. There was talk that he was planning a second Vatican Council when all the bishops would meet in Rome to examine the state of the church. On the agenda, ran the whisper in the Mother House, would be the future role of the sisterhood. Already nuns outnumbered priests by almost three to one, but they remained the same silent, compliant majority they were when Pope Boniface VIII decreed in 1298 that all religious women must obey without question the commands of their clergy. Even the Mother Superior looked upon Father Lowell, the priest who lived in an apartment behind the convent chapel, as her superior because only he had the power to turn bread and wine into the body and blood of Jesus.

Before every Mass a postulant laid out a special set of hand-stitched towels in the sacristy where Father Lowell robed. In all ways he was an exalted figure; a tall sandy-haired man in his thirties for whom nuns held open doors, laughed at his jokes and bowed demurely when he entered a classroom or one of their parlours. If they were seated and talking during an official period of recreation, they would instantly rise and stop in mid-sentence. Before he left, one nun always asked for his blessing and they would all fall to their knees while Father Lowell raised a consecrated hand and asked the Spirit of God to descend.

It was like this, she was certain, in all the convents of the 174 Orders in the United States. She had learned only those in contemplative communities – in perpetual enclosure – were strictly speaking, nuns. All others were what canon law termed Sisters-in-Christ. The same law also defined her Order as an active one: it provided teachers, nurses, prison visitors and social workers from its 35,000 members. It ran houses for unmarried mothers, trained nuns to care for alcoholics, junkies and the flotsam of city slums. Some sisters had been sent to train as doctors, economists and scientists. The teaching nuns spent their summers away from the classrooms helping handicapped children, ministering to grapepickers and assisting with an endless caseload of battered wives, pregnant schoolgirls and elderly who had been cast aside.

The Order was old, making it one of the aristocrats of the religious world, and the way its congregation lived had hardly changed in 300 years. Victoria's life was an unceasing round of prayer, penance, work and new understanding.

In her first month Victoria discovered tampons were banned. The Mistress explained the Order's doctor felt tampons were 'physiologically unsuitable' for a virgin. Only old-fashioned sanitary towels could be used.

The Mistress further astonished Victoria by adding that, when she had entered the Order after World War I, each postulant was given a diaper which was washed for reuse and when worn out, replaced by a new one. Those were the days, the Mistress said nostalgically, when it was accepted that a girl entering holy life was without any sexual experience. For a moment Victoria had a nagging fear that the Mistress knew about Art.

Though herself physically not a virgin, Victoria felt in her new life a purity that allowed her to cope and make sense of hundreds of rules and regulations – a veritable Baedeker of convent life. Obedience must be prompt; that 'not a word or a single instant intervene between the order given and its accomplishment unless there is obvious sin in it'. There were admonitions on how to show charity, compassion, unity, and above all, how to accept every 'penance and correction as if it were coming from the very lips of your heavenly Spouse, the Lord Jesus Christ'.

Acceptance was part of the preparation that would take her ever deeper into the disciplined routine of the Order. She had been certain that another postulant, Martha, would be among those who would complete the journey. So, she found it hard to believe that Martha was not seated at her desk, back ramrod straight, her marble-white face concentrating on her work, not so much as a muscle disturbing the fall of her cape. Martha had been the first in the group to master the twin virtues of custody of the eyes and hands. Later she had acquired, shortly before Victoria managed to do so, the art of walking like a nun. It was Martha who had sat there so attentively when the Mistress lectured on the meaning of interior silence, a required mental state that further distinguished a nun from other women. At its core was a total capacity to banish the past, to excise memories, to remove any distracting echoes from the outside world.

Victoria remembered when Martha had asked how long it took to acquire such control. The Mistress had frowned and pondered before she finally answered. *It could be years: many, many years. But it is worth waiting for.* Martha had smiled and said she was convinced that, with God's help, she would find the patience to wait. Victoria had left the chapel with Martha after evening Mass and Martha had stopped in midstride. Her eyes shone with excitement. 'I'm leaving.'

Victoria had been too stunned to speak, every word of Martha's ingrained in her mind.

'I'm leaving. Tonight. I'm going out. To get married.' Martha had explained that for months, on Sunday visits, her sister had been smuggling in love letters from her boyfriend.

'To get married...', Victoria had repeated. 'But you have already promised to be married to Christ.'

'That's what Reverend Mother said, Vikki. She wanted me to go with her and pray. I told her I've done all the praying. I just want Johnny.'

Victoria had looked at her, still stunned. 'But, Sister.' She'd stopped, uncertain. Should she be calling Martha 'Sister' now that she was about to re-enter the outside world? She didn't know. Nor, she thought, pulling herself together, did it matter. 'What time are you going?'

'Just before the Grand Silence. They've asked my father to drive to the back door. It'll be dark then.'

'But that's terrible. I mean, it's like you're doing something wrong. Not having a vocation isn't a crime.'

'They think it's the best way. Mother Superior said this is the way they always do it.'

Victoria had said she would be there to say goodbye. Martha vehemently shook her head.

'You must not come. You could get into trouble. You know what the Rule says about those going out? There must be no fuss and no goodbyes. I guess it can be upsetting and unsettling.'

Victoria was adamant. She would be there.

Shortly before nine o'clock she hurried to the back door of the Mother House. She was too late; Martha's father was already driving away. She could not be certain but she thought that Martha was weeping.

Victoria's own day continued to be ruled by the Canonical Hours, measuring not the passage of time as did a clock, but the liturgical hours of the Divine Office: Lauds, the first paean of early morning praise, Prime and its prayers. At nine a.m. the antiphons of Terce, a reminder of that moment when the Holy Spirit descended on the apostles at Pentecost. Sext at midday, the sixth hour, a pause to ponder passages of scripture. None, at three o'clock, the ninth hour, marking the moment when Christ died, and a time for silent meditation. Vespers recalled that first gathering in the Temple of Jerusalem. Compline, at eight o'clock, was another period of intimate prayer. At nine o'clock the Grand Silence descended, never to be broken except in the gravest of emergencies.

Next morning Lauds resumed the timeless passage of a new day of being instructed, initiated, shaped and spiritually formed to resemble in thought and deed all the other nuns in the Mother House, and those scattered throughout the world.

Victoria had come to recognize when the Mistress of Postulants had sensed the slightest wavering in her charges. That was the moment she would stop whatever she was saying or doing and repeat the guiding principle of the holy Rule. *You are sweetly dead to the world and the world dead in you.*

The Mistress frequently offered a memory of her own days as a postulant: how she had washed her clothes in cold water with soda crystals that left her hands coarse and red and slept on a pallet of straw from which she rose at the dead of night to offer thanks to God for giving her the means to scourge herself for sins great and small. In Europe, she would add, there were many sisters who still followed such a regime, and were better for it. She had instilled in Victoria that everything she did was preparation for an irrevocable break with her past, that to make it total and lasting there had to be severity; it was no more than the price Victoria must be expected to pay.

No visits home were allowed and her immediate family could see her only once a month, on a Sunday afternoon. All letters to her mother and sisters must first be read by the Mistress, who also censored all incoming mail. Art had written once. The Mistress had flatly told her she had torn up the letter. Victoria briefly wondered what Art had written. Now she could hardly remember what he looked like.

Once a week without fail, Victoria read aloud the Mistress' favourite quotation. *You must strip your heart of self, cut back hard on all the little shortcomings prompted by nature and the world.* The prospect of her individuality being excised did not daunt Victoria, indeed it was essential if she was to achieve this style of conformity. To do so required a complete understanding of the vows of poverty, obedience and chastity. Poverty and obedience were clear-cut. She must relinquish all her worldly possessions in order to identify more closely with those who possess little. The Order provided all her needs: food and lodging, clothes and shoes. When she was old there would always be a bed in the Mother House infirmary. Obedience was giving up the right to determine her own path in life, so that she would be available for God to use, if he so wanted. These were simple unequivocal vows. Chastity appeared, on the surface, equally easy to grasp. The Mistress had made her copy out its essentials. 'To abstain from any action, either internal or external, which is opposed to chastity. To practise continuous mortification of the mind and feelings. To take care at all times to avoid exclusive or particular feelings for others and maintaining a sensible modesty in all things.'

That night, after writing the words, Victoria awoke to find herself touching herself. She was so scared she wondered if she was ill. The next day she spent extra hours kneeling in chapel before she was once again able to accept chastity as a way to consummate her love for God.

Shortly afterwards she experienced, while asleep, an orgasm. Once more she prayed the experience away. But later, in the solitude of her cell, she dared again to wonder how it was going to be possible to commit her body to forfeit sex for the rest of her life. She finally found the courage to discuss the matter with Carmelita, the postulant who sat in the adjoining desk in class.

Carmelita, a tall, rangy girl from California, had a deadly gift for mimicry especially when taking-off the Mistress' clipped Boston accent. 'The spirit abolished the flesh in us. Anything physical must be avoided. Cross your legs and you're on the road to hell.' Carmelita had stooped and pulled her cape about her, twisting her face into the taut look the Mistress adopted when dealing with a sensitive topic. 'Now, Sister, remember the words of St Chrysostom. "The pangs of celibacy are a little crucifixion." So hang in there, Sister.' Victoria had laughed then. But Carmelita was no longer here.

The dark, icy clamp of winter had come early, freezing the ground and frosting the convent windows. Victoria wore a sweater beneath her flannel nightdress. Even then she felt cold, but she knew that was not the reason she had awakened. She glanced at her watch. It was almost two a.m. Other than the sound of the wind, nothing broke the Grand Silence. She closed her eyes hoping sleep would swiftly reclaim her. But the moaning sound, low, insistent and suppressed, was not the wind.

Victoria eased herself up on her elbow, listening hard, trying to identify from which cell the sound was coming. There was another urgent moan. She snuggled back under the bedclothes. Perhaps one of the postulants was having a bad dream.

The moaning came again, longer now, more uncontrollable. Victoria, with a sudden feeling of shock, recognized the sound. She slid out of bed, wincing at the iciness of the linoleum against her bare feet. She tiptoed out of her cell trying to locate the source, hoping she could still be wrong. The noise was coming from Carmelita's cell.

In spite of the cold, Carmelita had kicked back the bedding. Her nightdress was hoisted up around her waist. Her long legs were spread, hand clamped across her mouth to cut off the sound. Victoria wanted to rush forward; no, Carmelita, no. This is a mortal sin. You are committing a mortal sin. Stop it. Stop.

95

Instead she turned and hurried back to her cell, her face burning. Victoria remembered the words of the Mother Superior on that first evening she had addressed the postulants. A life against nature.

Time and again the theme had been taken up these past months by the Mistress. In one form or another she would remind them that religious life was one of self-abnegation. Any weakness that became known would be proof, the Mistress had said, that God did not want that person. Victoria wondered, standing by her bed, staring towards Carmelita's cell, whether she should not go and warn her of the terrible danger she faced. Carmelita could not surely have forgotten the lecture the Mistress had delivered. It had an uncompromising title: 'Masturbatory Activity'. The Mistress had explained that masturbation came from two Latin words: *manus* and *turbitio*, hand and agitation, and was a mortal sin. Those who indulged endangered their spiritual growth.

It was generally accepted by the Order's medical advisers that masturbation could cause grave psychological problems by inducing guilt and fear. They must always have before them the thought that a healthy mind did not need unhealthy stimulation. The Mistress had only spoken for minutes on the subject. But the silence had lasted far longer. Afterwards Victoria had told Carmelita they could have been listening to a discourse on the lifestyle of the bats which fascinated Reverend Mother.

Carmelita's moans were sharper and louder. Suddenly there was the sound of footsteps, then the voice of the Mistress, low and fierce. By the time the Mistress scuttled out of the dormitory, Victoria had crept back under the blankets, her eyes fixed intently on the crucifix on the bureau. Within hours Carmelita had packed her trunk and been driven from the Mother House to the airport to collect a one-way ticket. Her family had arranged to fly her home to California.

No one mentioned Carmelita after that morning when the Mistress briefly announced Carmelita's departure, adding that she had lost her struggle against pride and self-will. Those cryptic words officially closed the matter.

From the very outset Victoria realized her postulancy was a journey of self-discovery, designed to both test her faith and give her superiors a chance to assess her suitability: the scrutiny which had started at five o'clock on her first full day in the convent when the alarm bell broke, but did not end, the Grand Silence.

Victoria sat bolt upright and saw, standing in the doorway of the dormitory, the black-robed figure of the Mistress, lips pursed, eyes sweeping the area. She leaped from the bed and, donning a bathrobe, Victoria went to the communal bathroom. Other postulants were joining her. In complete silence they brushed their teeth and washed, the Mistress moving ceaselessly amongst them, ready to cut off with a warning finger any temptation to speak.

Victoria was the first to return to her cell. She removed her bathrobe, folded it neatly and placed it on the bed. She opened the top drawer of the bureau and, careful to conceal the garments from the crucifix, placed on the bed her bra, girdle, stockings and underpants. Stooping and straightening, she wriggled into her panties, taking care her nightdress continued to cover her body. She put on the bra, slipping it through the neck of her nightgown and securing it. She placed her postulant's outfit on the bed. From the bottom drawer of the dresser she took a tin of baby talc. Quickly pulling her nightgown over her head, standing sideways to the bureau, as instructed, to reduce the risk of exposing herself to the crucifix on the dresser top, she shook the talc under her arms and into her underpants. She then put on her black garter belt and stockings. She put on the black postulant's dress and her short black cape. Finally, she tied the laces of her sturdy rubber-soled shoes and put away the tin of talc.

Making her bed exactly as she had been shown, she turned to the bureau and, with infinite gentleness, cradled the crucifix in her hands and placed it in position on the pillow. Only then did Victoria glance at her watch. She was within the time allotted: twenty minutes from awakening to the placement of the cross. She pulled back the curtains around her cell and stepped out into the dormitory. Other postulants were emerging uncertainly.

Using her hands to issue silent commands, the Mistress lined up the girls in pairs. From now on – at meal times, in chapel, and in many of their duties around the Mother House – this would be how they would pair off. No postulant would be allowed to change her companion except at recreation, when they could move freely around. From that moment, too, their chronological ages had ceased and the only one they would be known by was their age in religious life, based on when they had been registered to enter the Order. Preceded by the Mistress, the procession filed out of the dormitory and down the main corridor to chapel. Victoria was still trying to imitate the effortless glide of the Mistress as she entered the chapel and genuflected to the altar, her body bending at the waist, her arms crossed beneath her cape.

By the end of her first day, Victoria saw what her daily life as a postulant would be. She would polish floors, wipe dishes and lay tables between study and prayer. At the end of her class work, she would resume her chores: helping to serve supper, polish more floors or work in the laundry before settling down to a further period of intensive study.

Then would come a final visit to the chapel when she would sink to her knees, emulating the professed nuns: her head bowed, spine soldierly straight and feet turned back. Bedtime ended her seventeen-hour day.

A feeling of spiritual fulfilment enabled her to cope with a dawn to darkness routine that totally governed her mind and body. She developed a habit of writing down and committing to memory key passages from the lectures which flowed from the Mistress about a world ruled by a discipline the like of which Victoria had never suspected existed.

It was November – three months since Victoria had entered, and the realization that Christmas was little more than a month away had percolated when the Mistress delivered her lecture on temptation.

'None of you can receive him if you yield to any one temptation. Let me be clear. I do not mean a temptation to commit a big sin. I am talking of the temptation to commit something small. Like not enjoying all your food. Like not putting enough effort into your domestic duties. Like complaining you are tired when you know you can continue to work longer. Small things. Little failures of duty. Tiny moments of self-indulgence. Thinking about candy when you should be thinking of God. Letting your minds wander, if only for a moment, into the past. Doing anything which compromises your promise to carry his cross.'

During the week before Christmas, the Mistress interjected into the curriculum an unscheduled talk on sin.

'You know, dear sisters, in your hearts you know this, that the more you try to serve God, the more you become aware of the sinfulness of sin. The closer you are drawn to him, the more you realize that things which did not seem like sins before, are now serious ones. But remember too: the greater the sense of your awareness of your sins, the greater is his love to take them away.'

On an icy January morning, the Mistress had returned to the virtue of purification.

'It is the furnace, dear sisters, in which we all have to be cleansed.

No one knows, except him, how many times we must be cast into that furnace before we emerge clean and worthy to serve him. But however painful the process is, you must accept it gladly. You must see it as a sacrifice you thankfully offer to him as a way of recognizing his suffering for you.'

In February, with rain sheeting down the convent windows, the Mistress ended her discourse on willpower with these words:

'Whatever evil there is in your nature, it can be excised. It may be a long and bitter struggle, especially if that evil involves the flesh and blood. They are weak. But your will is stronger if you allow it to be. You cannot win the fight alone. You can only achieve victory by praying as Our Lord prayed, allowing nothing to come between you and God. You will find, dear sisters, that the evil will then leave your body. This is a proven fact.'

In March the Mistress spoke about the dangers of satisfaction.

'My own prayer, dear sisters, for you is this. You will never, ever, allow yourself to be satisfied. For my part, while I have the power to do so, I will never allow you to be satisfied with any effort short of what you are capable of producing. I will encourage you to bear any trouble or pain if it brings the smallest advance in your spiritual growth. Indeed, I will continue to tell you that such travails are of no consequence if they stand between you and God. Your one aim is to be always with him whom you love. Being with him can give you joy beyond joy. You already have tasted that joy these past months. You can continue to do so if you stay true to your love, to your vows.'

In April the Mistress said she would escort them to the Chapter of Faults. In orderly file, paired as always, the postulants entered the study hall, hands clasped beneath their capes. On the index finger of each girl was a thick metal ring. Attached to it were nine separate strands of twisted steel wire; each braided piece was precisely three inches long. The strands were coiled to fit snugly into the palm of a postulant's right hand.

The Mistress explained the ring and strands were known as the Discipline. It was the instrument each nun in the Order, from its inception in 1650, had used to punish herself for any breach of the Rule. The Discipline was fashioned by the same nuns who threaded rosary beads for their sisters in Christ.

Every two months, after supper, the study hall was turned into the Chapter of Faults. Before going there the postulants had knelt in the chapel, lit only by the vigil light at the altar, and silently examined their consciences. This was essential preparation for what was to follow. Victoria had heard from a nearby pew a voice, low and breathy, murmuring: 'Mea Culpa. Mea Culpa'. The timeless words of self-accusation, a powerful reminder that no one is perfect in this world.

Standing before them in the study hall, the Mistress warned they must never reveal the secrets of the Chapter of Faults. Of all the rituals in their lives, none was more likely to be misunderstood. Religious penance would always hold a vicarious interest to outsiders.

The Mistress told them all to think of their faults. Victoria sank to her knees in her appointed place, bowed her head and began to meditate on her errors. She tried to remember every time she had failed to show humility, charity, compassion, understanding, sympathy and tolerance towards other sisters, to recall those occasions when, however briefly, her mind had drifted during silent meditation; when in chapel she had not concentrated totally on what Father Lowell was saying; of those times she had caught herself thinking of trivial and unimportant matters such as which record was in the top ten or what films were showing at the local cinemas.

The Mistress had said there was only one way the Rule allowed such lapses to be handled – through pain.

Victoria continued to silently question herself. Had she always prayed properly? Had she spoken out of turn? Had she displayed unseemly haste? Had she been silently resentful towards a superior? Spoken evasively? Not always got out of bed promptly? Failed to dress in the allotted time? Dawdled over some domestic chore? She was still working through her list when the Mother Superior entered and addressed them.

'We are here to seek to mortify ourselves by the power of the Holy Spirit. Remember the words of St Paul. "If ye through the Spirit do mortify the deeds of the body, ye shall live." Otherwise there is no mortification. The Spirit will enlighten you to see what requires mortification. But remember, too, what you have been taught.' The Mother Superior paused. The silence in the room stretched. Then she delivered her caution about the proper use of mortification.

'Beware of excessive violence. That can defeat the very purpose of mortification. It can create the very passion mortification is designed to crush. There is no victory if mortification provides pleasure. Mortification is designed to destroy the inner will, to break it, to crush it, to bring about its death. When this is done, then those evil passions will no longer be able to survive. There will be no validity remaining in you, dear sisters, which can nourish them. But remember, in this matter of the Discipline, in the endurance of pain, you must be careful not to go beyond your own strength in the matter. You may think it is a question of pride to allow yourself excessive mortification. But what you are doing then is to nourish those very passions you wish to excise. Not only is it your flesh which requires to be mortified, it is also your minds. Your thoughts have to be put to death, to be ground out of existence, so that your mind can be brought into subjection to the service of Christ. Every act of mortification must be an occasion of joyous thanksgiving.'

The Reverend Mother knelt and began to pray. Her lips moved but no sound came forth. She raised her eyes. 'Let us begin.'

There was a moment's hesitation. A nun kneeling beside Victoria rose to her feet. She stood, head bowed in contrition. In a voice so faint the words were barely audible, she announced, 'I accuse myself to you, dear Mother and to you all, my dear sisters.'

In a rush of words the nun begged forgiveness over being late for chapel and failing to polish the dining-room glassware properly. She returned to her kneeling position. Once more silence descended while they prayed that she would be forgiven.

Victoria rose to her feet. She clasped her hands even tighter under her cape, feeling the branded wire thongs against her skin and she began to speak.

'I have committed the fault of displaying indifference towards a sister.' She sensed that her voice sounded strange and disembodied. 'I have been moody.' She pressed the ring even harder against her skin, feeling the metal against a knuckle. 'I have been oversensitive.' She fought down an urge to forge ahead, to bring to an end this catalogue of faults. But she knew she must not do so. That would be a further failure – the fault of impatience. 'I have been thoughtless by excluding a sister from conversation during recreation.' Victoria revealed other failings. The morning in the communal bathroom when she had broken the Grand Silence by asking if she could borrow toothpaste because her own had run out. The afternoon when, late for Vespers, she almost ran into chapel. The evening when she had suddenly closed a door too loudly.

Finally she was finished. She stood for a moment, then slowly sank to her knees, her place taken by another postulant. Head once more bowed, hands clasped, Victoria waited, listening as one by one the other postulants recited their failings. Then there was only silence.

The Mother Superior's voice was suddenly firm and resolute. 'You may now use the Discipline. Do so in the knowledge it will advance your spiritual growth. I remind you again of the words of St Paul. "If ye through the spirit do mortify the deeds of the body, ye shall live".'

Victoria unclasped her hands and gripped the cat-of-nine tails in her left hand, her eyes staring at the floor. She half-rose, kneeling on her left leg. With her right hand she carefully raised her dress, exposing the flesh above the right leg of her stocking top. She lifted her left hand almost to shoulder height, letting the braided wires hang free. In a swift downward motion, she lashed her thigh with the metal thongs. She repeated the action.

Soon the sound of regular swishing of metal passing through the air and the distinctive sound of its impact against skin filled the room. There was not a whimper, nor a grimace of pain – only total concentration on the task in hand.

On Easter Sunday Victoria completed her seventh, and last, full day of the retreat. She had spent the last week in complete silence, neither exchanging a word with the other postulants, nor with anyone else in the Mother House. The Mistress' last instruction had been to pray and meditate from the moment she awoke until she returned to her bed. During meals she had continued the silent routine. She had found the experience exhilarating. The silence cleansed her mind, brought her closer to God. On this Sunday evening she had begun her final preparations to further deepen that relationship.

She stood in her cell behind the drawn curtains, staring at a pile of hairpins and rollers. During her absence at supper, the Mistress had placed them on the hard-back chair. Nearly nine months had passed since Victoria paid any attention to her hair, apart from clipping it once a week to keep it to the regulation length the Rule demanded. In preparation for her marriage feast, for the climactic moment she would become a bride of Christ, she must style it, trying to get her hair to resemble the fashionable way she once wore it.

She undressed, but did not fold away her postulant's dress and cape. She would never wear them again. After putting on her nightdress and bathrobe, she gathered up the curlers and went to the bathroom. Other postulants were already there, silently pinning up their hair. Victoria washed her hair and then wound it around the rollers, pinning them in place, frequently jabbing her skull in the process.

From time to time she paused to look in the mirror above the sink. As hard as she tried, her hair simply would not fall as it once had. Suddenly the Mistress stood behind her, shaking her head. Moments later she returned with a bottle of setting lotion. She handed it to Victoria and broke the silence of the retreat. 'Use it, sister. For God's sake, use it! Otherwise you will look a real mess!' She smiled and was gone.

Returning to her cell Victoria found her dress and cape had been removed. In their place was a white blouse with a ruffled bodice and flounced skirt hanging on a plastic hanger. Over the back of the chair were draped a white silk slip, cotton panties and seamed white stockings. On the floor where her granny shoes normally stood were a pair of white satin pumps.

Beyond her curtained enclosure Victoria heard a sudden burst of giggling. She peeped out and laughed: some of the postulants were staging an impromptu fashion show. Their clothes were from a special wardrobe next to the Mistress' office, a collection accumulated over the years. One postulant wore a full-length ballgown which was vintage 1940s, and she teetered along on a pair of incredibly spindly stiletto heels similar to some Victoria recalled her own mother wearing. Another was draped in a lace dress several sizes too big and wore a pair of pointy-shoes. A third girl was crowned by a white pill-box hat and veil. Each was about to become a bride of Christ.

Through reading, Victoria had learned the historical concept was over a thousand years old. As Christianity began to spread through the Roman empire, the birth of Jesus was presented as a divine incarnation

103

and Mary as the Virgin Mother. The early church decided a fitting reward for those who wished to emulate Mary was to symbolically take the Son of God as a husband.

Victoria had decided no other wedding could possible match her marriage to Christ.

Next day in her bridal dress, Victoria looked at her mother and sisters anxiously. In all there were twenty of her relatives coming to the clothing ceremony Mass on Easter Monday.

'Mother, how do I look?' she asked.

Her mother nodded. 'You look just fine.'

Victoria's youngest sister chimed in. 'You wearing the garter I sent you?'

Victoria blushed.

'Let me have it back. I want it for my own wedding day,' said her sister.

Her second sister asked, 'Where did you get the make-up? I thought nuns didn't wear the stuff!'

Her third sister interrupted. 'It's a wedding remember. Just like any other wedding.' She hesitated. 'That's right, isn't it, Vikki? That's why you're wearing Art's earrings.'

She felt her face burning. His name evoked a past she thought was dead.

Her mother intervened. 'She needed some jewellery to set off the dress.' She kissed Victoria quickly on the cheek. 'You look really beautiful. A beautiful bride.'

An uncle stepped forward, camera poised. Victoria shook her head explaining that no photographs could be taken. It's the Rule she added, knowing they would not understand. Her uncle looked puzzled. 'No pictures? And this is your wedding day?'

'I think we had better go in.' Her mother came to the rescue. 'We don't want to lose our places.'

Victoria watched her relatives walk towards the chapel. Then she went to the sacristy.

The sound of Bach's organ fugue, soft and restful, seemed to draw the procession into the chapel.

For the first time since entering, the postulants were not paired. They walked in single file, each carrying a spring posy and a Bible. Victoria was seventh in line. At the exact moment the first postulant crossed the threshold of the chapel, the organ music stopped. For a brief moment there was silence. Heads in the packed congregation turned and looked towards the door.

Suddenly the organ burst forth into *The Magnificat*, the hymn which praised Our Lady. The voices of the choir soared in support of the music. The sound reached its crescendo as the last bride took her place in the pews immediately in front of the sanctuary steps.

Seated on a massive carved chair before the altar was the bishop of the diocese. One by one the postulants rose and went forward to kneel before him. Victoria told herself how eagerly she had waited for this moment, how this was the final proof that she wished to totally commit her life to God.

It was her turn. She put aside her bouquet and Bible and went to the bishop. He looked down, peering intently into her face, as if seeking a final reassurance. She stared steadily back at him.

'My daughter, what do you wish?'

She repeated the words the Mistress had drilled into them. 'The grace of God and the habit of this holy Order.'

The bishop made the sign of the cross on her forehead, his spatulate thumb cool on the skin. He bent forward, whispering. 'The way of the cross, my child, is not of this world. But your reward will be that much greater in his world.'

Victoria rose and walked out of the sanctuary. Waiting for her was a professed nun. She silently led Victoria to the sacristy where the Mistress and several other professed nuns had gathered. There was an atmosphere of no-nonsense bustle.

The Mistress told Victoria to undress as quickly as possible. For a moment she hesitated. It had taken her almost two hours to dress, arrange her hair and put on her make-up, the cosmetics applied under the watchful eye of the Mistress. Afterwards the Mistress had gathered up the jars of creams, powders and brushes and returned them to a storage cupboard in her office.

'Sister, hurry! There's no time to daydream!'

Victoria kicked off her satin shoes, pulled her dress over her head and let it drop to the floor. A nun scooped it up and tossed it into a corner with other discarded dresses. Victoria peeled off her silk slip and rolled down her stockings. They joined the heap. In her bra and panties she was led to an adjoining room. It had a long table on which were stacked neat piles of black garments. Beyond the table the postulants who had preceded her were dressing. She thought how different they looked. But it was not just because they were wearing their new habits. With a sudden shock she realized their hair had been hacked off.

Victoria's eyes fixed on a wooden chair in a corner of the room. A nun dressed in unrelieved black stood behind it. In her hand she held a pair of tailor's scissors. Around the legs of the chair was a mounting heap of curls, tresses and locks.

The nun beckoned her to sit. She placed a cloth around Victoria's shoulders. Next she grabbed a handful of hair at the nape of the neck and cut it off. The nun gathered another large tuft and sheared it away. In moments only jagged pieces of hair sprouted from Victoria's scalp. The nun removed the cloth. During the entire procedure she had not said a word. As Victoria rose from the chair, stunned by the sheer speed with which she had been shorn, the nun was already motioning forward the next postulant.

The cutting of hair symbolized a readiness to die to the world, the last stage of eradicating sensuality.

The Mistress escorted Victoria to the table. She pointed to a pile of clothes and hurried back to watch the nun shear another bride. Victoria took the new black girdle belt from the top of the pile and slipped it around her waist. Next she put on the black stockings, then a black slip which reached down to the ankles. She picked up the habit – for which she had been measured weeks ago and which had been made by the Order's seamstresses – and shook out the folds. She held the heavy black serge-cloth garment before her. The habit had a lace bodice overlaid with a series of pleats at the front. The back was gathered so that the cloth fell gracefully from her shoulders to the ground. The Mistress had explained the habit was modelled from the mourning dress of high-born French widows in the Middle Ages.

Victoria donned the garment, her strong girlish limbs disappearing under the folds of black cloth. She moved a few steps, testing how she could walk in this outfit, far heavier than any of her old winter top-coats. Victoria put on the headpiece of stiffened cloth with two veils which distinguished the Order from all others. She fastened the chin strap. The shorter white veil hid her forehead. She pulled down the longer black veil made of fine-mesh nylon so that it completely covered her face. Her shoes were invisible beneath the folds of her new habit.

Once more the postulants formed into procession and re-entered the chapel to be greeted by a peal of triumph from the organ. The music stopped as they resumed their places. A tomb-like silence filled the chapel. The first postulant rose and, skirt swishing, walked up into the sanctuary. This time she stood, not knelt, before the bishop.

The choir softly chanted the *Gloria Patri* whose words for centuries had accompanied this moment of consecration for all the sisters of the Community when they become brides of Christ.

> Save Thy handmaiden, O Lord,
> For in thee is her hope.
> Let her be good and humble.
> Let her be exalted by obedience.
> Let her be content in prayer.
> Lastly, O Lord, we beg thee to
> receive gracefully her offering.

Victoria prayed.

Another postulant rose, stood before the bishop, and then returned. Each had been given an option of choosing one of three new names by which she would in future be known. The Rule specified there must be a suitable male name to accompany the choice. The Reverend Mother had approved Victoria's wish to use her dead father's Christian name as a prefix. She had chosen for her other name, Sarah, the wife of Abraham.

It was her turn to stand before the bishop, to hear him intone: 'Receive Sister Sarah John into the veil of holy religion.'

Victoria turned and walked from the sanctuary back to her pew, head erect and eyes shining. She joined in singing the evocative *Regnum Mundi*.

I have despised the kingdom of the
world and all worldly happiness,
For the sake of my Lord Jesus Christ,
Whom I have seen, whom I have loved,
In whom I have believed, and in whom
I am delighted.

At last, she told herself, she was really a nun, committed to a life of
obedience, poverty and chastity; that he, having chosen her for a life of
eternal celibacy, had freed her from all earthly cares and obstacles which
might impede her search for perfection in religion.

Then, in sudden panic she touched her earlobe. She had forgotten to
remove Art's earrings.

CHAPTER SEVEN

Encounters

Before walking to the lectern, Father Philippe ran over in his mind the key points of his lecture. How did the Virgin Mary become blessed among women? How had she avoided the ancient Hebrew ritual of the bitter water? What were the historical facts which led to hyperdulia, the ecclesiastical designation for the unique veneration of the Madonna? He mentally underscored the words which would allow him to evoke life 2000 years ago in *El Nasira*, the tiny village in a narrow Galilean gorge some 1200 feet above sea level and accepted by all Christians as the birthplace of Jesus. And again – strictly a reminder for himself – what about the pendant for Blanche Watts?

There were several weeks to go before his planned pilgrimage to Galilee yet he felt he knew, through reading, its people and their culture as well as he did those of his parishioners. Their warm encouragement for him to make this trip, and their obvious delight at having him as a priest, had deeply moved him. He would do nothing to embarrass them. That was why he continued to wonder about the pendant.

Parishioners remarked how well he chose and also wrapped a gift, expertly forming bows and twirls from ribbon, picking the right words to suit the occasion. They said he seemed to know all the quotations. They accepted this as much a part of his style as his formidable knowledge of the scriptures, his elegant off-duty clothes and his gourmet cooking. In this area of vast mysterious swamps, woodlands, swirling rivers and sluggish bayous, food was usually cooked simply. But he could skilfully create European cuisine and always served a good wine. They had told each other these attributes were to be expected in a priest with such a fine education, impeccable manners and polished accent.

No one asked about his past. Expansive though he was, Father

Philippe discouraged such questions. Nobody pushed. It was that sort of community.

Physically he was attractive. His dark hair shone, his hands were soft, with carefully manicured nails. He had a winsome little-boy quality which often aroused the mothering instinct in women – something it had never done in his own mother.

She formed part of the dossier kept in the diocesan chancellery. There, what he called 'the collection of papers', judged a priest's worth by the thickness of his file. His was already fat. From their urban citadel the chancellery staff still made discreet telephone calls to fill in the gaps, seeing if the damning words on record could be further added to. What hurt was that he had always tried to show them he had risen above his past.

He knew his superiors thought he was too aggressive in his preaching; that he failed to maintain a proper distance between a priest and his parishioners, especially women. The chancellery staff disapproved of the way he joked and joshed with the youngest and prettiest; gripped a woman's elbow when he ushered her out of the rectory, reluctant to end the intimacy and resume his business. They didn't like the way he sometimes gave a woman a little gift to mark her birthday or an anniversary. Priests did not behave like that.

He rejected such criticism and continued to enjoy the company of women. It made up for all those years when his mother had rationed affection.

From the beginning women in the parish came to him. They discussed their infidelities, the drug scene their children were involved with, the sheer boredom of their lives. He had nodded sympathetically as they apportioned blame. It was always somebody else's fault, usually a husband who drank too much, whose sex drive had gone, who was mean with money, who sometimes even was violent. He had tried to help, giving advice which did not always follow canon law, even recommending divorce, knowing how that would scandalize the chancellery staff.

What would they say about the pendant in his soutane pocket? It had caught his eye amid the jeweller's trays of paste necklaces, cheap bracelets and the rings boys gave their girls before being drafted for Vietnam. He wondered how this audience would react if he prefaced his lecture by asking them to vote: *Do I or do I not give Blanche Watts the pendant?*

For the chancellor's watchdog seated at the back of the hall, it would be enough and his mother had warned him this would be his fate; ruined by a woman. She had been going through one of her bouts of manic depression at the time. It was not her prediction that had frightened him but the idea that he could inherit her illness.

If he had not become a priest he would have studied medicine, believing he could have found a niche in psychoanalysis. Duty in the confessional was very similar, requiring the same observation of human functioning and behaviour. A confessor, like a psychiatrist, was skilled in understanding; both were products of intensive study and training which made them unusually sensitive to others.

In his final year at seminary he had evaluated the psychological make-up of Old Testament prophets and the people of the Gospels. He had decided Jesus could be labelled clinically obsessive in some of his behaviour. But, even more important, in presenting Christ as compassionate, gentle and loving – someone who touched people physically, psychologically and spiritually – the apostles had accepted as a fact his sexuality; not genitally, but in an affective way. Affectiveness – gentleness and tenderness – were an integral part of sexuality; it was those very qualities which elevated sexuality to a level where it was not a sin but an integrated part of human life. He had presented his conclusions to his spiritual director. He had been warned that, even at this late stage, months from ordination, he could be dismissed for daring to think such heresy. Crestfallen he worked on another project that concluded that Herod had all the traits of a severely disturbed personality.

Approaching the lectern, Father Philippe saw Simone wedged in the front pew. Even if she had not been unusually pretty, her clothes singled her out in the conservatively dressed audience.

Simone wore a floral skirt and plain white blouse which showed off her deep tan. Her chestnut hair fell naturally around her face. Even in repose, hands clasped in her lap, he thought there was something about her; more than mere beauty it was a quality which could best be described as presence. She accepted her looks as she accepted everything else: a secure home, a good job, an engagement ring on her finger. She was twenty-two years old with a love for the church and a fascination for scripture. For the past year she had taught Sunday school at Sacred Heart. A week ago he had met her in the street and enquired about Brad. She had hesitated, then explained that, though she still wore Brad's ring, she was no longer certain she wanted to marry him when he returned from Vietnam.

Next day Father Philippe had sent her a note inviting her to the lecture, signing it: 'Very affectionately, Philippe'.

Leaning on the lectern he thought how well the pendant would look around Simone's neck.

In pulpit class at his last seminary, standing at the podium, he had developed the trick of fantasizing that one of the seminarians was a girl. He would concentrate hard and imagine what it must be like to go with a woman. At the seminary they had a code for it: G.L. – getting laid.

Jay, another student, had gone G.L. one weekend, driving to a motel on an interstate highway to bury himself in the plump arms of a hooker. He had saved almost six month's allowance from his parents to pay her. When he returned to the seminary, the spiritual director had confronted Jay, then driven him to the railway station. The last Father Philippe had heard, Jay was a lingerie salesman in Memphis.

Six months later, the director – who always began Pulpit Class with the entreaty, 'O most precious blood of Jesus, oozing from every pore, grant us the grace to love thee more and more' – had one day driven out of the seminary dressed in a black mohair suit, white shirt and black tie. At Houston Airport he had purchased a one-way ticket to San Francisco where he had moved in with a stage director named Mark. When the shock subsided, everyone remembered the director had never done things by halves.

Father Philippe began his lecture by saying only two of the apostles actually mentioned Mary as the Mother of Jesus, and then only to reveal she had tried to dissuade him from his mission because she was certain he was mad. *Shock them, the spiritual director had said. Biff them in the gut. Take their breath away. John Kennedy had gone to Berlin and said he was a Berliner. A perfect example of audience identification. The director had been fond of using the language of the advertising world. Don't be wishy-washy, just hit them like the Marines did at Guadalcanal. He also liked war movies.*

He began to explore the very different genealogies of Mary and

Joseph in the Gospels of Matthew and Luke. Father Philippe reminded his listeners that the couple were part of a clearly defined society at a definite point in history and the source for what their life was like was the Gospels.

But the church did not say they must be taken as literal truth. They were written at least fifty years after the death of Jesus and united the hazy personal recollections of the disciples with the earliest christological speculations of the primitive Judeo-Christian community. Yet the Gospels remained documents that people used to interpret the reality of New Testament philosophy.

'Formgeschichte!'

He hurled the word into the hall, pronouncing it impeccably, pleased at the startle it created. He repeated the word, explaining it meant *form history*, a name coined by German Catholic scholars from their view that the Gospels, which contain myths and doctrines expressed as being true, were untrue. He saw that Simone was smiling.

'Mary and Joseph.' Father Philippe spread his hands as though balancing the biblical couple in his palms. He clasped his hands. 'Matthew and Luke.' Between them they offer perfect examples of historical fact and apocryphal truth.

Matthew had traced the ancestry of Jesus back to Abraham. Father Philippe's voice began to rise and fall like an auctioneer. 'Abraham begat Isaac and Isaac begat Joseph. Jacob begat Judas who begat Phares and Zara of Thamar.'

When he had finished reciting the first sixteen verses of Matthew's Gospel, a burst of applause greeted his performance. He cut it off with a swift wave.

'Luke takes the family tree of Jesus all the way back to Adam. They didn't have the advantage of an IBM computer to check all that begetting.' Now was the moment to lighten the mood. 'But they sure begot it wrong.' The sudden twang in his voice was a perfect imitation of Elvis Presley. It drew a burst of laughter.

He silenced the audience with a wave. He was serious as he went for his first point.

'But look what we have. Different names. Luke lists forty-one, many not on Matthew's list. He can only give us twenty-seven. That's a difference of fourteen generations.'

He allowed the silence to stretch knowing he had their attention – knowing he would. 'A generation in those days averaged twenty-five to thirty years. That leaves a gap of four centuries between the ages of Mary and Joseph. Four hundred years! Either Joseph was 400 years older than she was, or Mary was!'

The problem, he explained, had been neatly solved and historical truth rearranged. In the Gospels Joseph was the eldest brother of Mary's mother. Born and raised in Bethlehem, he had gone to Nazareth and married his young niece.

'If age did not weary them, neither did it matter when the facts were re-arranged!' He let the laughter subside before confiding he had always found a problem accepting the claims of hagiographers. He did not tell them that first and foremost had been the inventions of his mother.

'Holy Mary, Mother of Jesus!' His mother delivered the words at furious speed if a plate was not cleared, a pair of shoes needed mending, or a new dress was needed for one of the other girls.

In his early years, Philippe mostly wore hand-me-downs from his brother Donnie, who was tall and already muscular by the age of twelve. Philippe, five years younger, looked like a clown in Donnie's baggy trousers and floppy shirts. He had been almost eleven before his mother bought him a suit for the inaugural Mass of the new parish priest. For years she had refused to attend church because she thought his predecessors were too soft on sins of the flesh. He had died in his sleep on holiday in Las Vegas. Proof his replacement would be harder on the vices of the world was that at his first Mass he took as his text, 1 Corinthians 6:18 – Flee Fornication.

From then on, every Saturday, his mother marched the family off to confession, afterwards demanding to know how many Our Fathers and Hail Marys were doled out. At the end of the count she would invariably say, 'Holy Mary, Mother of Jesus'. By such repetition, Our Lady became fixed in Philippe's mind, a central part of his mother's world, in which heaven and hell were places just over the horizon and purgatory and plenary indulgence were staging posts along the road to a better life.

Philippe was twelve when he heard two more words. Premature Ejaculation. His mother shouted them at his father. Philippe should have been asleep, but even at night the heat and humidity of high summer permeated the house. Bathed in sweat, he had heard the anger in her voice which for years she had used on his father. She had stormed from their bedroom to the kitchen and begun to wash dishes, making a racket as if it were the middle of the day. Later, when he asked Irene, his eldest sister, what the words meant, she was shocked and made him promise he would never mention the incident again. She was fifteen at the time. Two years later she had married. By then her future husband had explained their meaning to Philippe.

At a cook-out held by Irene and her new husband, Donnie had slipped away with a girl, sneaking into the back seat of the family Chevvy. Philippe had crouched by the back of the car listening to the threshing and moaning from inside. Then the girl's sudden mocking voice had said his brother couldn't satisfy a corpse. Donnie had emerged from the car with the same hang-dog look their father perpetually wore. Philippe had walked the five blocks to the church and prayed for his father and brother, asking God to help them as he was helping him to become a priest.

Sometimes he thought he was doing so because he would be the first one in the family. Other times he wondered if it was to please his mother whose faith had been rekindled by their new priest. The only certainty was that his decision was welcomed by the nuns of the Holy Cross School.

When Sister Helen had set an essay for the scripture class – 'Why do you believe Jesus Christ is God?' – his answer was read out at morning assembly. 'I believe Jesus Christ is God because I speak to him every morning and evening in my prayers and I know he is God ever since I could read the Bible. I don't ever remember not believing Jesus is God, and not accepting he is my best buddy, even though I am not always his. But I want to try and be his best pal always.'

That evening Sister Helen had called for a long talk with his parents. He had stood outside the door listening. His father had said little, but his mother had finally asked how much it would cost. The nun insisted God would provide, adding a seminary was the right place for Philippe and reminding them their faith was rooted in hope and there could be no doubt God hoped their son would be allowed to answer his call. His mother had said, 'Holy Mary, Mother of Jesus'. For once there was no anger in her words.

After several meetings with the parish priest and Sister Helen, a seminary was chosen for Philippe to enter when he would be exactly seventeen and a half. He had yet to kiss or even date a girl.

There were other expressions at the seminary. 'Holy shit!' 'Holy damn!' 'Holy hell!' Philippe learned to use them as adjectives, nouns and imperatives, aware he was being profane, but then, so were all the seminarians. Besides, weekly confession wiped the slate clean.

A year after entering, he had learned that, to control her mood swings, his mother was on lithium and valium. On visits home she could plunge from elation to a profound depression so severe she often refused to attend Mass. One New Year's Day his mother had raced from one thought to another incoherently as she crossed over some frontier in her mind. Throughout the following summer she moved in and out of despair. She would refuse to speak, except to insist she was being punished for something she could not discuss. Philippe's father finally told him the doctor diagnosed her condition as manic-depressive psychosis. Philippe had hugged his father, the way he did as a child. Together they knelt on the kitchen floor and prayed for her to get well. Their entreaties were interrupted when she stood in the doorway shouting, 'Holy Mary, Mother of Jesus!' and screaming that premature ejaculation was the problem, all the time pointing at Philippe's father.

He was increasingly aware the seminary was pervaded with its own kind of sexuality. In the chicken fights when horse and rider charged each other around the gymnasium, he once felt a hand stroking his crotch. It was there in the way a seminarian suddenly put a hand around his shoulders, when he swam and someone dived underneath and grabbed at his trunks, when in the shower room several boys, soaped all over, wrestled with each other, ending in a heap on the floor. It was there at night in the movements under the bedclothes.

He finally began to think he should accept it, and there was also something exciting about it. He began to wonder if it was possible to make a theological case that Christian love and sexuality were compatible; that, far from being sinful, sexual feelings were an important part of being a total person and therefore made for a better priest. In Paul's letter to the Ephesians, the apostle took a positive position. 'A man never hates his own body but he feeds it; and that is the way Christ treats the church because it is his body, and we are its living parts. For this reason a man must leave his father and mother and be joined to his wife, and the two will become one body.'

Clearly Paul was also saying that making love was analogous to the relationship between Jesus and the church. The disciple would not have used a sexual analogy if he had thought it wrong. Paul was only explaining his loving understanding of Christ. In choosing to use sexual union as an example, he was

116

taking a positive attitude towards sexuality. Sex was sacramental, a sign of Christ's lasting love. Paul's only wish was for sexual fulfilment to be balanced against a life full of prayer. Verse 7:25 of Paul's first letter to the Corinthians says 'About remaining celibate; I have no instructions from the Lord.'

Paul was saying celibacy was a condition Jesus did not teach. Philippe began to ponder how the blessed Virgin could be fitted into this exciting, and for him, totally new and revealing interpretation.

Father Philippe was at the mid-point of his lecture. He had explained the role of angels as divine messengers from the time of the star worshippers of Assyria, guiding souls into bodies and, after death, escorting them to paradise or hell. He had led them, captivated, to that moment when Mary had come face to face with the Archangel Gabriel who announced she had been chosen to bear God's child. He explained that Mary, understandably perturbed for several days after Gabriel's visit, confided the extraordinary event to her elderly cousin, Elizabeth, who was also with child – later to be known as John the Baptist. He paused, eyes searching the hall, settling briefly on one rapt face after another. *Build them up. Just keep them waiting. Never fails.*

He related that, among the Jews at that time, marriage was a firm contract, so binding that, if a woman's intended husband died before they wed, she was entitled to the full legal protection of widowhood. Rabbinical teaching was equally strict on other matters. Preparations for a wedding could take up to a year while the rabbi satisfied himself the couple were aware of all their obligations and duties to their faith. During that time sexual relations were strictly forbidden. He described how adultery was punished by an ordeal known as the curse of the bitter water.

'A woman suspected of being unfaithful was led before her rabbi who poured consecrated water into a bowl to which was added powder. If she sipped and died, she was guilty. If she drank and survived, she was innocent. Since Mary was formally promised to Joseph, she should have been subjected to the test.'

Father Philippe quoted the nineteenth verse of Matthew's Gospel. 'Being a just man, and not willing to make her a public example, he was mindful to put her away privily.' Joseph didn't renege on his promise to marry Mary because an angel appeared to him and explained she was still pure. She was, said that angel, expecting God's child. Therefore there was no question of putting her through the test of the bitter water.

Walter, he remembered, had raised the question of what would have happened if the test had been applied to Mary. Walter had asked the question soon after Philippe had entered his second seminary.

His mother had started to telephone his first seminary, speaking voluntarily to anybody who answered. He tried to take as many of the calls as possible, listening while his mother rambled on about secrets in the Bible only she knew. Finally the administrator told Philippe he must stop her.

That was the day Philippe made a call of his own. The first was to Sister Helen to explain the situation and what he wished to do. She called back to say she had arranged for him to enter another seminary. He did so in the spring of 1967.

The new seminary was identical to the old. There was the same rote, the same sexual horseplay, the same petty cruelties, the same periods of stifling boredom. He continued to read everything on the subject of celibacy and sexuality.

Bookshops became a stalking ground. In one he found Schopenhauer and Comfort wedged between an early street guide to Baton Rouge and an account of De Soto's expedition down the Mississippi. Schopenhauer's *The World as Will and Idea,* was in mint condition. Comfort's *Sex in Society* was dog-eared. Philippe bought them both for a dollar and was coming out of the shop when a fellow seminarian strolled by. It was Walter.

'You read Schopenhauer?' Philippe asked.

'Yeah.'

'Good?'

'Depends what you want.'

'How about Comfort?'

'Depends if you want comforting.' Walter had a soft voice for so big a man.

They laughed together and walked back to the seminary discussing the two authors. Walter asked why Philippe was reading about sex.

'To see if I'm normal.'

'What's normal?'

They laughed again. As simply as that it had begun.

Walter became Philippe's catalyst for his need for a deep and lasting friendship, his desire to share permanent emotions, to have someone fill the void his mother could not. On that November afternoon Philippe was as hungry for love as Walter was to provide it.

Walking back to the seminary, Walter said that Schopenhauer was right about sexual impulse being the strongest and most powerful of motives. He took the book from Philippe and immediately found what he wanted.

> The sexual impulse is the ultimate goal of all human effort, interrupts the most serious occupations every hour, sometimes embarrasses for a while even the greatest mind, does not hesitate to intrude with its rash interfering with the negotiations of statesmen and the understanding of men of learning, knows how to slip its love letters and locks of hair even into ministerial portfolios and philosophical manuscripts. It breaks the firmest bonds, demands the sacrifice sometimes of life and health, sometimes of wealth, rank and happiness, nay, robs those who are otherwise honest of all conscience, makes those who have hitherto been faithful, traitors.

Walter snapped shut the book and thrust it at Philippe. 'What Schopenhauer is really saying is that love is more important than anything and is therefore quite worthy of the profound seriousness with which everyone pursues it. Always bear that in mind when you read Comfort. He tends to over-rationalize. But he's right about one thing. There's been a failure of social education as far as sex goes. Especially in the church. Too much emphasis on moral prohibition.'

It took Philippe a couple of days to read both books. Comfort had written there was no evidence to support the church's claim that celibacy could be directly linked to increased creativity; while it may be true that the tension of abstinence or of ungratified desire could be productively channelled into work, there was no acceptable evidence to relate continence with a capacity to work harder.

The following Saturday he and Walter spent two hours in the bookshop. Philippe had waited inside the door until Walter arrived and led the way to the back of the shop where a side room was filled with religious books.

'My private library,' Walter said. 'I found it a year ago. I crib all my answers for term papers here. You're welcome to use it.'

'Thanks.'

'Don't mention it. I like you.'

They sat on the floor, facing each other, knees bent and touching. From time to time Walter scrambled to his feet to locate a book and confirm some particular. As he rose, he rested a hand on Philippe's shoulder. It seemed the most natural thing to do. He said Comfort was right that all human relationships are sexual in the widest sense of the word, but wrong to say homosexuality was automatically unhealthy. There could be healthy and unhealthy homosexual relationships. The problem was that most people, including the church, didn't understand homosexuality.

'Why don't they use a different word?' Philippe asked.

'That would be dodging the question that healthy relationships can be homosexual.'

Walter had not pressed his point, but before they left separately, he had reached across and gently run his hand over Philippe's face.

Next Saturday Walter reminded Philippe of a line Scott Fitzgerald had written. 'A person's temperament is constantly making him do things he can never repair.'

'Fitzgerald was talking about a writer, not a budding priest, Walter.'

'*Touché*. But do you regret anything between us?'

Philippe shook his head. In truth he had never been happier.

It had become a routine to come to their hideaway and sit close together on a Saturday.

Philippe found his impatience mounting towards the end of his visits home, not only to escape his mother's delusions, but from a desire to return to the confined space where Walter and he continued to explore so many ideas.

He was now also comfortable with having Walter hold his hand and stroke his face. One Saturday, in November 1967, they sat in silence remembering the fourth anniversary of the news from Dallas that President Kennedy had been shot. Walter reached over and gently kissed Philippe on the mouth. Philippe returned the kiss. But when Walter placed a hand on his thigh, Philippe quickly removed it.

In the seminary they kept a distance, instinctively knowing this was the way to survive. Their relationship only flourished in the womb-like cavern of books. Philippe attacked his studies with a new zest. His marks in moral theology were second only to Walter, his altar practices were graded as exemplary; several of his sermons were preached by tutors in the seminary chapel.

One Saturday in the cubbyhole, Walter said, 'The Snot is getting curious. He gave me a funny look today.' The Snot was the prefect of discipline.

Philippe had reached over and squeezed Walter's hand. 'He doesn't know about this place. He wouldn't know what a bookshop looks like.'

They spent the remainder of the afternoon exploring the possibility that man is neither heterosexual or homosexual but plurisexual. Walter had rummaged through the shelves and located a copy of Kinsey. Heads locked together, they had analyzed how Kinsey defined homosexuality. Walter had asked why homosexual feelings should stand in the way of self-acceptance; no one should be made to feel he was going to be a bad priest because he was homosexual. The church was full of hard-working homosexuals, healthy in every way and this fact should be recognized and accepted. Philippe had suggested they write a letter to their Congressman urging him to raise the matter in Washington. Not a good idea, Walter had said.

A few Saturdays later they were seated side-by-side on the floor, talking quietly about the difficulty of accepting the virginity of Mary. Walter felt the problem was not whether Matthew or Luke were accurate; it was that the entire question must be seen in a wider concept. 'Nobody would have been interested in the details of Jesus' conception had he not risen from the dead,' Walter said.

'If Christ had not dramatically rolled back the stone and walked out of his tomb, there would be no church,' Philippe said.

'The problem is that if the church continues to look upon Mary's virginity as a historical fact, it will go on getting attacked,' insisted Walter. It was not important whether or not Mary was a virgin, only that everything she did was directed towards the will of God. Philippe developed the notion, saying that at the core of Mary's response to the Archangel Gabriel was the totality of her religious belief, her fidelity to God. Her faith, not her virginity, was important.

Walter had an idea. 'We should start a movement to drop "Virgin Mary". Just call her "Holy Mary".' He impulsively kissed Philippe. 'Man, just think of it. If we pulled it off and they asked us where we thought of the idea, we'll just say sitting on the floor! But we gotta get out of this seminary first.'

'You're on your way, mister. Both of you! Get to your feet!'

The Snot was standing over them. By nightfall they had both been expelled without a chance to say goodbye to each other.

Father Philippe moved to the next point of his lecture without breaking the fluency of his argument. He reminded his audience that allowing a person to be spawned by a deity was neither unusual nor as ingenious as the Gospels proclaimed.

Perseus, hero of all the Greeks, was fathered by Zeus. Mars created

Romulus. Aristotle, Alexander the Great and the Emperor Augustus who ruled when Mary conceived, were all said to be of divine origin. Buddha the Enlightened was conceived by a god who appeared in the form of a cloud. Centuries later Montezuma, the emperor of Mexico at the time of the Spanish conquest, was worshipped as the son of Tlaloc, the Aztec God of Rain.

He had acquired all this knowledge as a result of those Saturdays spent with Walter. He had tried to contact him once, calling his home from a pay-phone, but Walter's father said his son had gone to South America. There was no point in calling again.

Father Philippe explained that the birth of Krishna the Redeemer was remarkably similar to that of Jesus; there was the same angelic announcement to his mother, a similar adoration of the shepherds, and an almost identical persecution by the rajahs who ordered the execution of every male child in their domains on the night of Krishna's nativity.

'The story of Mary has survived in one form or another for one single and inescapable reason. The Lord wishes it to remain incomprehensible in order that our faith be more worthy.'

Life at home after being expelled was traumatic. His mother required increased medication. Her lucid spells grew shorter between the plunges back into despair. Once more Sister Helen intervened. She persuaded the bishop to give him a final chance at yet another seminary.

Again his life was no different from the previous two institutions. Bells governed his life; sensuality was all the more potent because everyone tip-toed around it. He sublimated in work; the endless grind of class. But the food at this one was not just badly cooked, it seemed tainted before it even reached the kitchen. He ate little, existed mainly on cheese, crackers and coffee. He lost weight and became nervous and irritable. He prayed a great deal including asking God to improve the supplies. He finally called the health department. An inspector impounded much of the food and recommended the seminary president give Philippe a reward for his vigilance. Instead, the dean ordered Philippe's immediate expulsion.

He was almost twenty-six and the past nine years had been spent trying to become a priest. Hour after hour he went over his arguments to be given yet another chance. Each time he reached for the telephone to call the bishop's office, a new thought entered his head to bolster his case. On the third day he made the call.

'Yes? What do you want from me?' The biting words accentuated the gap between them, one created by rank and class.

'Your Grace, I want another chance. To explain.'

'What is there to explain?' The voice kept him at a distance.

He began again. 'Your Grace, I want to be a priest. I know Jesus Christ is in me. I want to serve him.'

'Did you think you were serving him by trying to get a seminary closed?'

'They found tainted meat, your Grace.'

'Then perhaps God intended you to be a health inspector.'

The bishop was wrecking his thoroughly-crafted argument. Unable to defend himself, tears glazed his eyes.

'I'm sorry, your Grace. I thought you would give me another chance.'

'Why? Why should I?'

'I want to serve Christ. I want to be useful to him.'

It was, he knew, the absolute truth.

'You have still not told me why you did it.'

As the discussion continued, Philippe was gradually aware of the bishop's technique of grinding each of his points to dust before moving on. But the bishop was not trying to exact revenge or humiliation, only testing. Philippe had a sudden hope. They spoke for almost an hour more, the bishop questioning him closely. Finally the questions came down to one.

'Can you be trusted not to do it again?'

Philippe did not hesitate. 'God will give me the strength to serve him properly if you give me the chance.'

'Very well. You shall have your chance.'

The parish ran between two state highways. The church had walls of grey stucco. Inside it was narrow and lofty, bathed in diffused hues from the stained glass windows behind the altar. The air was redolent with burnt incense and varnished pews.

Philippe quickly came to love the place, as much as he loved and respected Father Franciscus. From the very first day he allowed Philippe to call him Frank, while at the same time establishing their situation.

'Okay, you got drafted here. I didn't ask for you. You didn't ask for me. They told me the score. You flunk here and you're out. O-U-T.'

He had a western twang when he spoke English, although his native tongue was Italian. There was an extraordinary briskness about Frank. Whether it was distributing Communion with Philippe as his server, or conducting a baptism, wedding or burial, he always gave an impression of frenetic activity. He said it was his way of handling the sexual compulsions of middle age.

Increasingly Philippe saw that Frank was a genuine holy man who understood what the church needed from him, who Christ was, and what he wanted to give in return. He taught Philippe about prayer, about giving and receiving love, and understanding and believing. Sometimes, because Philippe was a deacon, Frank let him preach, afterwards analyzing the sermon over a meal.

Their relationship was synthesized in Frank's words, 'What a man thinks is less than he knows; what he knows is less than he loves; what he loves is less than there is to give.' Sometimes he would smile and add that a man was wrong to see himself as less than he was.

A year later Philippe was ordained. At his first Mass, under Frank's watchful eye, he preached on the meaning of hyperdulia, the special veneration due to the Madonna.

Father Philippe told his audience that until the Council of Ephesus, Mary had no special place in the church. The Council had granted Mary divinity. In part, it was an act of expediency at a time when the church was under attack from barbarians.

Attila was ready to sweep the church into the Tiber. When he heard Mary had been raised to be the Mother of God, Attila hesitated. Instead, in the oppressive summer heat of AD452, he agreed to meet with Pope Leo on the muddy banks of the River Po in Northern Italy.

The papal entourage arrived to find Attila camped out with a vast army. Leo had 200 monks equipped only with their psalm books. While they chanted in the background Leo explained to Attila the terrible fate he would suffer if he made any move which would harm the Mother of God.

While the precise words have escaped record, Attila, the son of Mundzuk, who could trace his lineage back to Schongar, ruler of the air, had listened as Leo told him that he, too, could claim a divine lineage. His empire was even greater than that of Attila's and not of this world, but part of the invisible and supernatural one where salvation came through Christ's church. That the church claimed the Mother of God as its own and invested in her special powers of redemption. Leo had said he would pray for Mary to redeem Attila if he turned back.

Attila broke camp that night and marched home, his thundered promise echoing in Leo's ear. *I will leave the Mother of God in peace.*

When Attila was slain in battle, his last reported words were to ask Mary 'the great goddess of Rome', to ensure his redemption.

A wave of applause swept the hall. He let it roll on before once more waving them to silence. 'It is my contention that the only way to properly understand Mary's virginity was to see it in the context of prayer, faith and holiness. Mary teaches us what prayer is, how to pray, to realize that our very faith is irrevocably linked to that power to pray. It is nothing to do with whether she was a virgin or not.'

He noticed Simone was looking at him carefully.

'If it helps to believe that Mary was a virgin, that's fine. But it is not important. I think she should primarily be looked upon as holy. I believe that the essence of virginity is unison with God. Mary is the perfect example of a life given to the service of Our Father. Virginity today does not mean the same as it did at the time of Mary. Nor does it gain value by being defined in biological terms. Like marriage it is only because of the role it plays in the life of a particular person. I look at you and wonder if you are virgins in the sense I mean.'

There were murmurs of surprise. Simone was smiling. 'You may look at me and wonder if I am a virgin in the sense I mean! But our physical state is not the issue. The important thing is to recognize that virginity is meaningful only if it is part of a definite system of values. Just as with Mary, so it is with us. It is our interior selves, not our physical condition that matters. I believe it can be summarized in two words. Holy Mary!'

He stepped back from the lectern.

With the moon rising over the starboard wing, Philippe's plane cruised towards Dallas. Daniel Watts, the father of the bride, Blanche, had sent Father Philippe a first class round ticket. They had never met and only spoken twice on the telephone. The first occasion was when he was Frank's deacon.

Mr Watts had called to enquire about the times of Sunday Mass. Frank was out on a sick call and when he learned Philippe was Frank's assistant, Mr Watts wished him luck. Later, Frank told him that Mr Watts was a good man to have on your side.

The second time he had called, Mr Watts wanted to know about local fishing. Father Philippe was surprised at the question but had replied that the fishing was as good as always. Mr Watts enquired how he was liking parish work. He told him he had never been happier. Mr Watts said he would be in touch. Nevertheless, Father Philippe thought the wedding invitation was a mistake. But his name was on the appropriate space on the card and with it came the airline ticket and a slip informing him a room had been reserved at the Fairmont Hotel, all expenses to be charged to Mr Watts' account.

He had called to thank Mr Watts and spoken to his daughter, Blanche. She said how glad she was he was coming, adding a number of people at the reception were eager to meet him.

In his case, buried beneath the suit he would wear at the wedding, were his Roman collar, Bible, black shirt and trousers. He did not expect he would need them, but nowadays he saw himself like a police officer who went everywhere with his badge and gun.

The clothes, like his luggage, were gifts from a haberdasher, a parishioner. Every six months he provided Father Philippe with $1000 worth of clothes. The man called it his insurance policy to heaven.

In Father Philippe's pocket was the pendant. He still could not decide whether to give it to Blanche or not.

CHAPTER EIGHT

Proposals

As the blare of trumpets swung into *The Age of Aquarius*, Father Philippe realized Lauralene was content to cling in his arms. Tin badges were pinned to her dress. Over her left breast one urged, 'Make Love Not War'. Another, in purple lettering asked 'Had Any Lately?' On a shocking yellow background a third announced, 'God is on a Trip'. Among the few questions she had asked was his age. He'd told her he was almost thirty. She squinted her eyes and said she liked older men.

In their first minutes together she said everybody called her Lolo. She was nineteen years old and knew Blanche from college. They'd worked together in the Poor People's Campaign in 1968. Their efforts made no difference. President Nixon still won by a landslide. Lolo insisted the President was devious, he was even changing the flowerbeds outside the Oval Office, using his own gardeners from California to do so.

Father Philippe found it hard to keep track of her conversation, yet being with Lolo also made him feel as if the clamps bolted on his senses had been pried loose. The feeling had been there since he was picked up at the airport by limousine and driven to the Fairmont. His room was twice the size of his entire living space at the rectory. There was a bottle of champagne and a bowl of fruit on a table, compliments of Mr Watts. Father Philippe had swum in the hotel pool and breakfasted in its Pyramid Restaurant before visiting the shops in the lobby. He had decided the pendant was unsuitable. In the Neiman Marcus boutique he bought two napkin holders which he had engraved with the initials 'B' and 'G', Blanche and Greg, bride and groom. He charged the gift to his American Express Card, knowing he had expended almost a quarter of his monthly salary. On a card he wrote: '"We are one, after all, you and I. Together we suffer, together we exist. And forever remember each other." When Teilard de Chandin wrote that he was thinking of you. Affectionately, Father Philippe.'

Dressed in a tan lightweight suit he went to the wedding, the package in one pocket. Impulsively, he slipped the box with the pendant into another. An usher directed him to a pew on the bride's side of the church. Standing there, surrounded by couples, he was reminded of what Frank had once said. A priest stood out because he was set apart. He must always remember that he was part of a higher life and a nobler love. That was why he must remain detached. That was the only way to spare himself a great many crosses. That was Christ's way.

After the Nuptial Mass he returned to the Fairmont where a banqueting room was reserved for the reception. He placed his gift on a table already piled high with presents. Blanche turned out to be what he expected and Greg looked like a banker. The couple greeted him quickly, moving on up the reception line. Mr Watts' welcome was warm and genuine and included an explanation of why Father Philippe was present. He made it a rule to always have a priest along to any function, it was his way of reminding them how much he admired their strength. Mr Watts released him with the injunction to have a good time and he drifted over to one of the bars. Ordering champagne, he asked the barman if he knew what Chesterton said when he had been converted to Catholicism.

'No, sir, I don't.'

'He said it was to get rid of his sins.'

The barman looked at him carefully. Lolo, standing next to Father Philippe, turned and said no one should want to be rid of all their sins. The band came to life and she led him onto the floor. He felt a sense of panic. It was not because he hadn't danced for almost thirteen years – the last time was at his sister's wedding, and then only to move awkwardly around the livingroom with a cousin in his arms – it was the proximity of Lolo.

When the band stopped, she told a waiter to give them a bottle of champagne and two glasses. She led him to one of the couches along the wall, pouring drinks and talking all the time. She had been to Woodstock and when she asked if he liked acid rock, he felt almost middle-aged. But she was already talking about the murder of actress Sharon Tate. Had he heard that Charles Manson may be crazy, but he was also a bedroom jock? Father Philippe said he had not been following the case.

The band began a new set and he wondered what decibel level they'd reached. Lolo reached across and kissed him and said she liked him. He replied he liked her too. Lolo said she was glad and poured more champagne. He drank, racking his mind to know what to say. Then she was on her feet, saying she was bored. He was aware she was challenging him.

'Let's go some place,' she said.

He suddenly felt awkward. 'We can't just walk out.'

'Who'd notice? Half of Texas is here. They wouldn't miss us.'

He still hesitated. 'Where would we go?'

'Your room.'

'We can't do that.' He felt foolish.

'You're not scared, are you?'

'Just surprised.' He hoped his voice was steady.

Lolo took his hand and he allowed her to lead him towards the exit clutching a new bottle of champagne.

Her room was on the seventh floor. As they stepped from the elevator, she paused. He wondered if she had changed her mind.

'A bucket,' she sang out. 'I see a bucket.'

She hurried to a service trolley, removed an ice bucket and planted the bottle in the ice. Bearing it aloft like a trophy, she led him to her door.

'You strong enough to carry me over the threshold?'

'Sure.'

She opened the door and put down the bucket. He picked her up, carrying her into the room, his hand under her knees, her arms around his neck. Lolo giggled a she gave him a love-bite on the neck.

'Don't do that.' He lowered her to the floor, his voice sharp, thinking what his parishioners would say if they saw the mark.

Lolo said she would like to eat him.

He went back to the corridor for the bucket remembering another piece of advice from Frank. *None of us have absolute control over our physical and emotional feelings. But we do have control over the consequences they bring. That doesn't mean we have to play at being angels. We just need to be humble about thinking it was ever going to be easy.*

Lolo was drawing the drapes. He put the champagne on a table, watching Lolo turn down one of the two double beds. She told him to open the bottle.

'We need glasses.'

'Try the bathroom.'

She sat on the edge of the bed as he filled the glasses and put the bottle back into the ice. She motioned for him to sit beside her, touching her glass against his. The sound was flat, plastic clinking against plastic. She rose to her feet and began to undress. He watched as she refilled her glass, standing only in her bra and panties. She asked him if he liked her. He said he did, very much. She told him to take his clothes off.

He would have no clear recollection if she helped him. A swirl of blood was racing through his body, pounding in his ears, catching in his throat. Years of fantasy and frustration, of wondering what it would be like, was swept away. One moment she was under him, the next on top, her body hot and damp against his as she begged, moaning for him to take her.

That was the moment he knew he could not make love. He cried out he wanted her too, that she had the most beautiful body he had ever seen. The more he pretended, the more an awful deadness spread over him. She continued to urge him, yet the more she pleaded and the more urgent her demands grew, the greater his impotence became. *What was wrong with him?* He realized he was pounding the mattress with his fists in frustration.

Lolo suddenly pushed her hands against his shoulders and slid away, her body soaked with his sweat. She began to cry. He buried his head in a pillow, wishing he could die. Suddenly she was shouting. What was the matter with him? Why had he come if he didn't want her? His sense of abject failure deepened.

'I'm a priest.'

'What the hell's that gotta do with it? You think priests don't screw? Well, they do. Women, men and probably dogs for all I know! But you! You can't do anything,' she shouted.

He half-rose from the bed, turning so that he shielded himself from her. He knew what he wanted to say. *Look, you are the first girl I've ever*

130

been this close to – ever. Give me time. Let's talk about it. Don't rush me. It's not your fault. I think all those years in seminary killed everything I am as a man. But you've given me a chance. Please give me time. It'll be okay. I just need time.

'Get out! Just get out! Just get out of here, now!' Lolo screamed.

He dressed, avoiding her eyes and walked to the door. He paused, feeling for the little package in his pocket. He returned to the bed and placed it on the headboard shelf, opening the box to display the pendant. He let himself out of the room. Even in the air-conditioned corridor he was sweating.

An hour later he entered the church where Blanche and Greg had been married. A cassocked priest turned from the altar and asked if he could be of help.

'I want you to hear my confession.'

The old priest led him to one of the boxes off the central nave. Father Philippe closed the door behind him.

'Bless me, Father, for I have sinned. My last confession was a week ago but today I...' Father Philippe stopped.

'Take your time,' came the gentle voice from the other side of the grille.

'I'm in big trouble.'

'That is why you have come. Just start where you want.'

'I don't know where.'

'Wherever you like.'

Father Philippe wished the priest would stop trying to be encouraging.

'I would like to...'

'Just to talk? That's fine. You go ahead. I'm here to listen.'

Father Philippe shifted on his knees. He could hear the priest's breathing.

'Is it a mortal sin?' asked the voice.

'I'm a priest. And I've been to bed with a woman.'

In the silence, the confessor's breathing became irregular.

'Tell me exactly what happened,' the voice demanded.

Philippe did so. There was a longer silence when he finished. He remained kneeling, his face buried in his hands.

'Was there volition?'

'Yes. And I wish to place before God my sin of rejection.'

'Rejection?' The voice couldn't contain its surprise. 'Who have you rejected?'

'God. His Son. Our Lady. All of them.'

'Aren't you being too hard on yourself? You were genuinely tempted. You'd drunk quite a bit. The volition would not have been clear to you, would it?'

Father Philippe realized the confessor was trying to minimize what had happened.

'But I feel I have rejected them,' he said.

'That's natural. But it is after all only your *feeling*. Like being depressed is a feeling. But God doesn't say depression is a sin. You really must not be so hard on yourself.'

Father Philippe wondered why the voice on the other side of this stifling box didn't understand. *I feel dirty.*

'Father.' The voice was gentle. 'You are truly repentant, aren't you? For all you have done? For even those sins you may not have remembered?'

'Yes.' He wanted to get it over with.

'Then we shall make an act of contrition. Are you ready?'

'Yes.'

'Oh my God, I am truly sorry for having offended thee...', began Father Philippe.

He received his penance.

'Go in peace, Father.'

Father Philippe unlatched the door of the box and left the church. He was still sweating.

It was early evening. He had showered and dressed in his priest's suit, relieved the love bite was below his Roman collar. He had written a thank-you note to Mr Watts, clock-watching, waiting for the bus to the airport. He had rebooked on the first available flight home.

Waiting in his hotel bedroom he remembered what Frank had said. *For a celibate, the conflict will always come down to one between God or another person.*

The door chimes startled him. Lolo stood there, holding the pendant box.

'Hi.'

'Hi.'

'You going to work?' She indicated his clothes.

'Not at once. I'm going home.'

'I thought you might take me to dinner.'

'I'm sorry. I don't think I would be much fun.'

'Take a later flight.'

'I'm sorry.'

'You're not really.'

He said nothing.

'You going to ask me in?'

'I don't think that would be a good idea.'

'Father,' she said pleasantly, 'go screw yourself. And use this.'

She thrust the box at him and walked down the corridor. He opened the box. Where the pendant had been was one of her badges. 'Had Any Lately?'

After his return from Dallas, he had immersed himself in the routine of parish life. He took care to hide the bite mark until the bruise faded.

He had managed to rationalize what had happened with Lolo as an aberration. His behaviour with her was as out of character as he had now come to see all those Saturday afternoons he had spent with Walter. Every night he prayed for there to be no repetition. Frank was right. Each celibate had to face and overcome temptation. There was no other way. Nevertheless, the wider issue of celibacy continued to preoccupy him.

He was disturbed there had been no guidance on how to handle the deepening crisis over celibacy affecting the American church. In the past year almost four per cent of all its priests had left – nearly four times as many as in the previous ten years. Overwhelmingly, it was because they no longer felt able to subscribe to the vow of celibacy. The chancellor circulated a reminder to the diocesan priests. 'Through prayer we can always find the correct solution. Through prayer we will always find the appropriate truth of how the Father, Son and Holy Spirit wish us to behave. Through prayer we know we can love them and our neighbours in a proper way, one which will always allow for a faithful concept of our calling.'

Father Philippe thought that, typically, the chancellor had dodged, or perhaps was unaware of, the central question. Could celibacy be compatible with human intimacy? How far could that intimacy properly go? How far did culture have a part to play in redefining celibacy? Where did humanism fit into a rethinking of the traditional understanding of sexuality?

He had been surprised to receive a note from the chancellor saying his lecture to the ladies of the Sodality of Our Lady had been well received; he should repeat the talk to other groups.

One Sunday he dropped in to watch Simone teach. She had a clear style, making her points with a simplicity he admired. She had not interrupted her class when he arrived, merely motioning him to a seat at the back of the hall, then continuing with her account of how Pope Gregory VII had laid down the principle that the Pope could be judged by no-one. Now the pontiff presided over a church riven by moral and ideological schism. Hardliners continued to protest over Pope Paul VI's removal of the Index of Prohibited Books which had forbidden Catholics to read Voltaire or Victor Hugo, or allowing Mass to be celebrated in as many languages as there were people to speak them. That, Simone said, was only a start. The Pope needed to reinforce many more of the recommendations of the Second Vatican Council.

Later, he told Simone that on his way back from Israel he would visit Rome and try to judge for himself what was happening.

Clearing formalities at Tel Aviv airport under the watchful stare of Israeli soldiers, Father Philippe wondered how many of them realized their presence was striking proof that miracles do happen, that they were here because of the biblical prophecy of returning to the Promised Land.

A customs official tipped out his bag, thumbed through his Bible and missal and fingered his Roman collar. Father Philippe explained, being a priest, he was travelling light. The official said terrorists used all sorts of disguise. It was Father Philippe's first reminder this was a land under siege.

That had been ten days ago and he had still not become used to the rudeness, the sharp Hebrew words, the jostling, the indifference to polite requests. The food was often inedible, the wines sickly sweet, the beer weak and tepid. The humidity was draining. His cotton shirt and slacks clung to him in the heat. At night his sheets felt like thick blankets.

To compensate there was that unforgettable moment he climbed the hills of Jerusalem, realizing the truth of the repeated phrase in the Bible, 'going up to Jerusalem'. It was both a physical and religious experience. History was not just something he had been absorbing from books in preparation for this pilgrimage, it was *here*. He walked through the Old City marvelling that Jesus and his apostles had trodden the same cobbles beneath the shadow of Suleiman's walls. He went to the Mount of Olives and stared from its summit at the Wilderness.

He took a bus to Nazareth, discovering that where Jesus grew up had changed little in 2000 years, he wrote on a postcard to Frank. On one to Simone he said that, just as in the days of Mary, the men idled while the women worked. He signed hers: 'I wish I could show you all this. Very affectionately, Philippe.'

He visited Bethlehem and stood at the mouth of the cave where Jesus was born. Had Joseph hurried from this spot when Mary was seized by labour pains, seeking a midwife? Did that midwife, bearing the historic name of Salome, express understandable amazement that, even at the moment of giving birth, Mary preserved her virginity? Had those shepherds sat on the hills behind the cave, watching over their flocks by night? Had, as the apostle Luke reports, an angel appeared who praised God and expressed glory in the highest and peace and goodwill to all men on earth?

The tale of the shepherds had nagged at him through his seminary studies. Was it only a story? Now he could satisfy himself on the issue. He asked, and was told, that during the winter the temperature in the hills around Bethlehem falls to well below freezing and the rainy season lasts into March. Animals are not left outside. Therefore how could those shepherds have been watching over their sheep on the night Mary gave birth?

In the records in Bethlehem's library, he discovered that once the birth of Jesus was widely accepted as falling on a day between March 28 and May 29. Then, in the wake of the Council of Nicea which had first raised the issue of clerical celibacy, the birth date was recalculated.

Leo the Great – who had confronted Attila on the banks of the River

Po – became convinced that Jesus had lived for thirty-three years. That meant he had spent over thirty-two years living on earth, the remaining months in the womb of Mary. Working backwards from the date Leo gave for Christ's death, April 6, his theologians calculated that the nativity fell on January 6, the day of Epiphany in the Western Rites Church. Leo was not satisfied. He wanted and obtained a further revision which placed the birth of Jesus on December 25.

That was the day the pagan cult of *Sol Invictus* celebrated the annual ascendance of the astrological sign of the virgin over the horizon. It symbolized the powerful goddess giving birth to her son-god, the most awesome of all the deities in the entire Mediterranean basin. The son-god was the bearer of all good things: the end of winter, the sowing of crops, the harvest.

Leo the Great managed to have the attributes of the son-god imbued in Jesus, and that of the pagan virgin assumed by the Madonna. A simple change of a birthday thus helped to ensure the ultimate triumph of Christianity. Father Philippe not only marvelled at Leo's sleight of hand, but wondered what else had been changed.

In Jerusalem the Jewish quarter was as quiet as Father Philippe imagined the day of judgement would be. It was the Jewish sabbath. It reminded him of Sundays at his seminaries when he used to think God had come and gone, taking his chosen with him and leaving Philippe to fend for himself. On this Saturday he sat in his hotel room and contemplated a subject he realized had never been out of his mind. He tried to formulate his new thoughts on celibacy, based on what he had learned in Israel.

First he assembled all the information of the past two weeks, laying it on his bed and the floor, moving the material around so it was easier to follow in chronological order. He then divided it under separate headings. It took most of the morning.

In the lunch hour he had taken another walk to the Via Dolorosa through which the crusaders said Christ entered the city on Palm Sunday and later dragged his cross to Calvary.

Beyond, in the Arab sector, the streets were crowded, the shops open, the air raucous with sounds of trade. He had been warned not to buy from the street vendors for fear of amoebic dysentery. He crossed Christ's Street of Sorrows and was back in the virtual solitude of the

Jewish sector. He knew where he wanted to go. He had been there before and it drew him back like a magnet. The Wailing Wall was reached by a descending flight of steps carved into the limestone. Somewhere close to the wall, all that remained of the Temple, a Jewish priest had written a clear-cut statement on sexuality. 'And the Lord God said it is not good that man should be alone.'

Father Philippe formulated his first point. 'God does not want man to be lonely. That is why he created woman, a sexually different person. Sexuality is not primarily associated with propagation. It is shown as a gift from God to man so that man would not be lonely. A woman is God's way of showing his creative solution to end that loneliness. Sexuality was given to that first man in paradise because God wished him to possess it. From the very outset God was saying that man must associate sexuality within the fellowship of his contact with woman.'

It took him longer to make the next point, based on the Old Testament's the Song of Solomon, an anthology of lyrical love poems. At his seminaries he had immersed himself in this celebrative literature, attracted by the mystical beauty of the relationship between two lovers, the way it suggested the sacredness of love-making.

Every night before going to bed in Israel, he had read a portion of the Song. The priests who wrote the words were clearly familiar with sexual experience and enjoyed it. Their explicit message was that physical love and spiritual giving were closely related. He was convinced that abstaining from sex did not place a person, in the sense of meaningful Christian values, on a higher plane.

He had a sudden longing for home: to say Mass again, to administer the holy Eucharist – and to see Simone. He had thought about her a lot these past two weeks: after that first postcard from Nazareth he had sent her six more and two letters. All contained vivid descriptions of his impressions of the Holy Land. He had reminded himself that was all they must contain. He flew from Tel Aviv to Rome.

The Pope was physically small, Father Philippe said, lowering his fork and bringing his hand a little above the candles on the table, indicating the pontiff's height. Small, with a sad, wizened face.

Even more, Pope Paul seemed mentally shrunken. The abiding impression of his stay in Rome was of a supreme pontiff turning away from the opportunities of the Second Vatican Council to set the church on an exciting course towards the next millennium.

Father Philippe paused, eyeing Simone, aware the *maître d'* was watching them. The man had hardly taken his eyes off the corner table which Simone had reserved, and which he had led them to with the same stately gait with which he brought his family down the aisle every Sunday to receive Holy Communion at Sacred Heart.

The waiter had kissed Simone's hand, murmuring in French how well she looked and asked how her father was. When he greeted Father Philippe, his face was suavely blank. After they were seated he retreated and Simone explained she taught his children eighth grade catechism. She laughed unselfconsciously, the way she had when he called her a few hours earlier and asked her to dinner, saying he wanted to tell her all about his trip. He had sent her postcards from the Vatican Post Office in St Peter's Square describing his impressions. On one he had also written: 'If I had the money I'd send you a ticket to come here. This is the most romantic place in the world. Rome is full of lonely priests and nuns. It should only be filled with lovers.'

Glancing at Simone's hand, he noticed that Brad's engagement ring was missing. She said quickly, as if the topic was not to be pursued, that she and Brad were no longer engaged. He thought again how hope can be raised by a few words.

'Now, Father Philippe, I want you to tell me everything. About Rome, about Israel. *Everything.*'

He smiled and said only if she would stop calling him 'Father'. She hesitated and looked suddenly serious.

'In our family we were brought up to show respect. "A priest is always a priest", my Dad says. It's hard to forget that.'

'Try. Calling me Philippe doesn't actually change anything.' He tried to keep his voice light.

'Alright. Philippe. But only between us. You're still "Father" in front of everyone else.'

The *maître d'* returned and suggested cocktails. She ordered Kir for them both. Sipping, she listened without interruption.

He began by saying there had been a hardening of the Pope's attitude to celibacy in the priesthood. To even suggest optional celibacy appeared to him a threat which could lead to the dismantling of the church. The reedy voice echoing over the loudspeakers in St Peter's Square had reaffirmed a priest was the crucial link between God and man, and man and God.

From his pocket Father Philippe produced the notes he had made at the time and read: 'The Pope says the chain must be perfectly forged for man to climb towards heaven. The weakest and strongest link is the one upon which the strain is greatest – the priesthood. But a priest must continue to represent stability in an unstable world, fidelity in an unfaithful world, the supernatural in a natural world, the bringer of immortality and eternity in a temporal and transient world.' He put down the paper.

The waiter returned and listed the house specialities, addressing Simone. Father Philippe wished the man would go away so that he could reclaim her undivided attention. She continued to order for them in fluent French. The waiter finally bowed and retreated.

Again he asked her about Brad.

'He was obviously very much in love with you,' he said.

'I suppose so.'

'Of course he was! He'd be crazy not to be!'

She made no response, sitting perfectly still, her eyes on him.

'Did you love him?'

'I don't know.'

'That means you probably didn't.'

'Probably.'

'Is this embarrassing?' He asked.

'No.'

'I don't want to embarrass you.'

'You're not. Honest,' Simone said.

'The thing is, you see, I think I've been in love with you for weeks.'

Simone reached across the table and held his hand. 'I know.'

The seminar was a success. It formed part of a life within a life for them both. Twice a week up to thirty young people, either married or engaged, gathered in Simone's newly rented apartment. They sat on the long couch before the TV set, or on the floor. He would perch on a window ledge in his priest's suit and Roman collar. She always addressed him as Father Philippe.

His lectures covered every reason for reform in the church. At first he was cautious, fearing one of them might report him to his superiors. Simone reassured him. She had chosen carefully: they were intelligent and well-informed Catholics, concerned only to get a better insight into the complex issues facing the church and challenging their faith. He had relaxed and argued the full promise of the Second Vatican Council was being sabotaged by powerful voices in the College of Cardinals. He attacked *Humanae Vitae* and expressed the fear that Pope Paul was failing as a teacher. They questioned him for hours.

He would always leave with them, bidding a formal goodnight to Simone. He would drive away, then park his car in a side street and slip back to her apartment by the service elevator. She would always have a glass of chilled Kir waiting. Simone had told him she had rented the apartment while he was in Israel after receiving his postcards; even then she knew what was going to happen. In that first week they only talked. But on the Monday night of the second week she said quietly, as if she did not wish to frighten him, she wanted to make love.

He told her about Lolo and Walter. She assured him everything would be fine. As she led him to the bedroom he suddenly felt like a schoolboy. She carefully pulled off her blue sweater and then stepped out of her skirt and placed it over the back of a chair. Clad only in her panties she motioned him to the bed.

'Is the way I am behaving so terrible?' she asked him.

'No. Oh no,' he said softly.

She helped him to undress. His shirt came off, his Roman collar with it, then his pants. Lying flat on the bed, she removed her panties and pulled him towards her. He told her how beautiful she was; so beautiful he could cry. She told him tenderly not to cry. She removed his shorts. Naked, he felt neither awkward or embarrassed. Suddenly he wanted to make love and enjoy it, and he did.

Since then they had made love every day, some days as often as three or four times. He would hurry from the confessional to the apartment at lunch hour. He would visit before saying early Mass, returning to her once his priestly duties were over. On evenings when there was no seminar, they drove to a neighbouring town to see a movie. Afterwards he would cook her a meal, serving it with a flourish, uncorking the wine and sampling it as if he were a sommelier and not a priest. They made love on the couch and on the floor. They experimented and came to know how to arouse each other in new ways, discovering the many joys of sex. But he continued to resist her pleas to sleep over. He explained that his fellow priests would become suspicious. He could not tell her he often rose in the small hours and crept down to the darkened church. There he would pray to be forgiven.

Father Philippe gave the man penance and released him from the confessional. He wondered again if his absolution was valid since he himself was no longer in the state of grace. He had not been to confession since first making love to Simone. Sitting on the hard bench he pondered what he would do.

In the diary in the breast pocket of the shirt he wore beneath his cassock, he had written he felt he was 'adrift on a river in flood, being carried towards a waterfall and certain death', or 'in a rocket hurling out of control through space'. At other times he wrote he no longer wanted to flee from himself, from his feelings, as he had done all his life.

> *The marvellous thing about my love for her is that it is spontaneous. When I touch her I know I am alive. I need that affirmation and existentialists say we have to commit suicide to show we have lived in the first place. I don't believe that any more and when Simone holds me, I am affirming I am alive. She has shown me the easiest thing in the world is to be what you are, how to love.*

But now, in the confessional, he experienced old doubts. Was it true what Frank had said: that love was a curse as well as a gift, if it destroys what God intended.

He heard footsteps outside the box. He placed an eye against the small priest's spyhole. Simone was in a pew on the far side of the nave. He left the confessional, pausing quickly to genuflect before the altar. He knelt beside Simone. She was smiling.

'It's going to be okay. We love each other. I want us to get married,' Simone whispered.

They had gotten into the habit of giving each other little gifts: paperbacks, a handkerchief with his initials on it, a key ring formed in the shape of an 'S'. One day she surprised him when he arrived at the apartment. He had come straight from a funeral and there was a trace of incense on his cassock. She led him into the bedroom. Laid out on the bed were a new shirt, tie and trousers.

'What's this? You come into a fortune?'

'You're going calling,' she told him matter-of-factly. 'My parents have invited us for dinner. I thought you'd feel more comfortable in these.'

He kissed her and asked how much time they had.

She smiled. 'Enough.'

Afterwards, when she had hung his soutane in a closet, they showered, soaping each other, washing away the last traces of their love-making. They dressed slowly, eyes constantly on one another.

'I've told them,' she said as they left the apartment.

'What did they say?'

'It's going to be fine. I've told them we love each other.'

She pressed the elevator button and kissed him, pulling away only when the door opened. It was one of the games they played, seeing what intimacies they could risk in public without being discovered. Dining out she would kick her shoe off to stroke his leg with her toes, or he might reach across the table and quietly place a hand on her breast. She told him their love would not be imprisoned; it would wriggle free of any bonds.

Driving to her parent's home, Simone once more expressed her feelings. 'Being in love with you I've learned more about myself than I ever thought possible. How to trust. How to give. How to realize that love is faith and it needs to be strong.'

He wished he could put it so succinctly, just as he wanted to stop feeling he was on that river heading for the waterfall, powerless to save himself.

Father Philippe thought Simone was like her father. She had his voice, his directness and his smile. Judge Dupois led him to the back terrace while Simone and her sisters helped their mother in the kitchen. The judge sat on a rocker opposite Father Philippe.

'Simone says you want to marry?'

'Yes.'

'You realize what that means, for you, for her, and for us?'

'I do.'

'How will you live?'

'I'll get work.'

'What can an ex-priest do?' His questions were polite but firmly framed.

'I'll try anything.'

'Trying is one thing, succeeding is another. What qualifications do you have, Father?'

'Call me Philippe. I guess we had both better get used to the idea.'

'Fine. Have you any money, Philippe?'

'Only what I have saved out of my salary.'

'Where will you live?'

'I'll move in with Simone.'

Judge Dupois rocked back and forth, his eyes fixed on him.

'How long have you been a priest?'

Father Philippe told him: four years.

'And before that, all those years of study. A long time. A lot to give up. Are you certain?'

'I love her.'

'Love is not always enough.'

'It's all that matters to us both.'

'Now, yes. But what about later. You know how the church feels about priests who take off with parishioners. Unless you get a dispensation, you'll not be able to marry our daughter in the church. I've always wanted my girls to have that blessing.'

Simone had joined them. 'Papa! We love each other. That's all that matters.'

Father Philippe looked at Simone. The word 'Papa' made her seem suddenly young. He felt strangely uneasy, wondering what her father would say if he knew the extent of their relationship.

'I can wait for dispensation before we marry.'

'Philippe, no! Why should we wait? We love each other.'

Judge Dupois looked at them both for a long moment before he spoke.

'Simone is under your protection from now on. Always try and remember that.'

'Yes, sir. I will.'

Frank's questions echoed those of Simone's father. Did he really mean to give up fourteen years of a vocation to marry a girl he had only known six weeks? Why not wait? Go away for a few months? Something could be worked out with the bishop. Then, if he really still wanted to marry, Frank would do everything to help.

Father Philippe held the cassette recorder close to the telephone. He had asked Frank's permission to record their conversation so that he could play it over later. So that he could be in no doubt what his priest-mentor was telling him.

'You make it sound so easy, Frank.'

'No. You're the one who makes it sound easy. Turning your back on all you've struggled for, just like that. Where's all the discipline that kept you going?'

'I've told you, Frank. I'm in love.'

Father Philippe could imagine Frank seated at his office desk in the rectory, surrounded by papers of all kinds. Frank was the untidiest man he knew. He was also the only priest he had ever been close to. Frank began again.

'Your personal history has no doubt played a big part in what's happened. Your unhappy home, your mother, your battles at those seminaries. Struggle and rejection at every turn. You've come through more than probably any other young priest I've known. Why not see this as another test of your faith?'

'It's not, Frank. It really isn't.'

'How do you know? How do you know that God doesn't mean this to be something that can bring you even closer to him?'

'I'll still be close to him when I get married, Frank. Don't you see that?'

'It won't be the same. It can't be. You have a vocation. You're one of the best preachers I know. I hear great things about your ministry. Folk love you. Are you going to walk out on them? They need you. And you think you're alone in your dilemma? Listen. For years I have wondered at times about my celibacy. Is it really worth all the struggle? The loneliness? The hassle of doing everything myself? Going to the laundry, shopping. Of not having someone to talk to. Then I come back to what my celibacy really is. Something positive. I didn't choose it. It chose me, part of the package we call a vocation. When I see it like that, my doubts go away. I know God wants me. He really does. That's why I don't mind working all the hours he gives me, and some more. Doing the housework, making the bed, making sure I eat. It's no sweat because God wants me. I know he wants you too. He really does. Are you going to say no to God? Are you going to turn your back on all those values that he first saw in you? Are you?'

Father Philippe was silent.

'Frank?'

'Yes?'

'I'm sorry, Frank.'

'Come and see me. Come and spend a few days.'

'No, Frank. It won't help.'

'Let me talk to the young lady. At least let me do that.'

'Why, Frank?'

'Why? Dammit, Philippe, does she know what she's asking of you? Does she understand that you just can't say to a priest that you love him and he's got to give up everything else for you? Does she *understand* that?'

'We've talked, Frank, believe me. We've talked. She's a fine person. We pray together.'

'What do you pray for? That's the question. What do you pray *for*?'

'Frank, I'm sorry. I really am. I don't want to hurt you.'

'It's not me you're hurting. It's yourself. You need help. If I can't give it to you, go and talk to somebody. The priesthood is not just a part of your life to be picked up and put down. It is your *whole* life. You eat and breathe it. And celibacy is part of it. That doesn't mean it isn't something you don't have to work at. You've got to do that every day. Every single hour you've got to remember that your vow is really a declaration made before God and the church for life. That's what it's all about.'

'That's the ideal, Frank.'

'It's the reality, Philippe. Let me talk to her. If she's a good Catholic girl she'll not make you do this.'

'You'd rather I stay and be unhappy?'

'No. I'd rather you stay. And be happy. Period. Listen, you think you're the first priest to fall in love? It happens all the time. But falling in love is one thing. Being able to handle it is the real test. You *can* handle it. You've got to see that.'

145

'Thanks, Frank. You've been terrific.'

'You've made up your mind?'

'I guess so.'

'I guess you probably had it all figured out before you called. You just wanted my rubber stamp. To say it's okay to throw it all away. Everything God gave you. The church gave you.'

'That's not so, Frank. It really isn't.'

'Well... I can't convince you, can I?'

'It's not you, Frank. It's me.'

'Good luck, Philippe. I'll pray for you.'

'So long, Frank. And thanks.'

The bishop's office was modern and expensively appointed. The bishop and the chancellor were seated beneath a portrait of Pope Paul. They questioned him in turn to establish that he had only come to his decision after prayer, that he had not been coerced, that he was leaving on his own volition. Father Philippe said he was. The chancellor stared bleakly and said it was customary for a priest who resigned to move out of the area.

'No, monsignor. I intend to remain in the parish.'

The bishop urged him to think of the effect this would have on his former parishioners. 'And think of the girl and her family. Start elsewhere. You owe us all that much.'

'I don't see it like that, your Grace.'

The bishop sighed.

The chancellor motioned Father Philippe to a side table. On it was a single sheet of paper on which were the words: 'Request for Dispensation from Holy Orders'.

'Sign where your name is.'

Father Philippe did as the chancellor commanded. He turned and faced his superiors. 'Is that it? What happens now?'

'Go back to the rectory and remove your belongings before nightfall.'

The bishop rose to his feet and continued to address Father Philippe.

'You are not yet dispensed. You are only suspended from your priestly functions. You cannot say Mass or hear confession, nor can you receive the holy Eucharist. But you are still a priest and will remain one until Rome releases you.'

In the darkness, disembodied voices spoke to Father Philippe again, like the whispers of madness. Simone had turned over in her sleep and lay with her back to him. He continued to stare at the ceiling listening to the voices in his head. The same two, one cavilling and uncompromising, the other pleading.

They had appeared on his wedding night, offering him two very different explanations for his failure then to make love to Simone. The pleading voice suggested he was only emotionally and physically exhausted by the sheer speed of events. He had completed moving out of the rectory only hours before the wedding ceremony in the Dupois livingroom. His mother had come and offered her congratulations. She had not stayed long, abruptly asking his father to drive them back home.

The other voice said he had failed to consummate the marriage because of his guilt. The more he realized the enormity of betraying his vocation and, in the end, God, the greater his guilt would become.

Two hundred and thirty-four nights later, he realized how complete the destruction had become. For months he had taken tranquillizers to try and cope with the life he now led. He hated the ladies hair salon, the only place he had found work. He had been taken on because the owner said an ex-priest could attract business. *You're a bit of a celebrity, Father. All those you once confessed will want to go on sharing their secrets with you.*

He was paid a minimum wage, standing for hours shampooing their hair and hearing about their lives. At first he thought it would be like listening to them as a priest. And indeed many of them still called him 'Father'. But they didn't want his advice any more. They just wanted to probe his own life. He hated that most of all.

The doctor had said he shouldn't take himself so seriously and Simone kept reassuring him: 'It's going to be fine. I love you.'

She said it all the time. It made no difference.

'Oh God, please help me,' Father Philippe whispered, reaching for the bottles on the night table. He looked at his watch. It was too soon to take more medication. All he could do was to lie here beside the woman he knew he was also destroying.

From the outset he had competed with her – and won. He was a better cook and housekeeper. The more she had tried to please him, the more he had been goaded by that commanding voice to destroy her confidence. It made no difference that the other voice – pleading and patient – would try and appeal to his good nature, to say what he was doing was deeply hurtful to them both.

After two months his body began to be covered with a painful rash. It spread from his scrotum over his trunk and arms, red and unsightly. The more he scratched and drew blood, the worse it became. The doctor prescribed antihistamine tablets and said he must stop making love.

Simone had bitten back her tears and it had made him angry. Didn't she understand what he was going through? And the voice, when he could not sleep, had answered. *Of course she doesn't understand. She can't because she has never given up what you have. She is just a woman.*

Every work day he passed the Sacred Heart. He would stand across the street staring at the church but could never enter the building.

His former parishioners had been distantly polite, though a hard core remained hostile, crossing the street when he approached or ignoring him when they passed. Priests were embarrassed when they met him, exchanging only a few words before hurrying away. On Sundays he read the Bible and watched the preachers on television.

Staring at the ceiling, he counted. They had not made love for forty-seven days. He knew because Simone was keeping count. A few mornings ago he had found her putting a tiny check mark on the calendar in the kitchen. Blushing, she said she was keeping track of her period. He had gone to work that morning filled with new guilt. Why should he no longer experience the joys of sex and celebrate the mystery of creation? But all he felt was a sense of overpowering guilt.

He stared towards the window. He could make out the furniture in the dawn light. The room was filled with his belongings: cases of clothes and boxes of books. Beyond, in the livingroom, it was the same. The furniture had been rearranged, brought closer together, to make room for his possessions. Simone had not complained.

He knew something was beginning to jell inside him. As he silently repeated the words, the thought turned to resolve. One voice was pleading with him to try once more. *Remember she loves you. She really does.* The other voice insisted. *It is possible to escape.*

He looked at Simone. *Please don't be angry. It's not that I don't love you. But it's not enough, loving you. I don't want to be hurt any more. I have no other choice, don't you see?*

Father Philippe could not remember when he had been so calm. He rose from the bed and tip-toed to the kitchen. He dialled Frank's number. They spoke for a short time. Afterwards he held the receiver against his chest, his arms folded over it. He began to cry. Finally he put the telephone back in its cradle.

CHAPTER NINE

A State of Perfection

A robed figure insistently shook Clare from sleep and left the bedroom as silently as she had entered. It was ten minutes to midnight. Clare rubbed her eyes. In her full-length nightdress she slid out of bed, doused her face with cold water from the hand-basin and dressed for the death vigil. The stained floorboards were warm under her feet because of pipes running beneath the radiators. Central heating was one of the many innovations introduced in the aftermath of the Second Vatican Council. Others included the abolition of flagellation at the Chapter of Faults and the freedom to modify habits. But the permanence of other aspects of religious life still had an abiding appeal to her after seven years in the sisterhood. One was the ritual surrounding an impending death in the Community.

Clare had encountered few problems in adjusting to the new religious world the Council envisaged. She had attended all the Community discussions which had followed its deliberations. But her voice had been one for moderation, consistently suggesting that the independence, freedom and liberty the Council had indicated was now possible, must be handled sensibly. She had stated her position as she did everything else, with a minimum of fuss.

Within the Mother House the broad pattern of life continued as it had for centuries: academic work, manual labour, prayer and meditation. Reverend Mother had spoken of a need to remember tradition, that change must be considered in a historical context.

The reminder had preceded the first of many Community discussions on what length the Order's skirts should now be. The Council had left that to the sisterhood. Each Order could decide how far to raise their hems. There had been astonishment in the Mother House over a report that some US sisters had hoisted theirs to knee length.

Clare had little patience with the general behaviour of many nuns across the Atlantic. They had become openly resentful of their priests. Here, she was glad to see, the convent's chaplain was still treated with reverence. Only the Reverend Mother, her Deputy and the Superior General conversed with him freely; all others must wait to be spoken to. Yet, in the United States, nuns were campaigning to be ordained. Each time the subject was raised, Reverend Mother shook her coifed head disbelievingly.

Clare had tried to excuse the behaviour of those US nuns by suggesting they were only overreacting to their new-found freedom. Within living memory was the time when nuns travelled only at night, in cars with drawn blinds, ate off bare wooden tables, or walked through chilly corridors. Those days, said Reverend Mother firmly, had been hard, but they helped a nun to know her identity.

A nun had asked how being cold could make someone pray better? In a frigid voice, the one she had once used when doling out penance at the Chapter of Faults, the Mother Superior had replied: 'God, through prayer, should warm you. If he does not, Sister, you should consider whether or not you have the necessary spiritual voltage to pray properly.'

Reverend Mother had abruptly risen to her feet, delivered a benediction with quick, stabbing motions of the hand, and left the community room, her back ramrod straight, supported only by her anger. Yet she had also been the first to approve the proposal that each nun could decorate her own room as she chose.

Clare had adorned the plain white walls of hers with scenic posters of Ireland and quotations from the Bible scotch-taped in place, each excerpt printed in her bold hand on drawing paper. On the shelf over the radiator were photographs of her parents and sisters. The most recent showed her father in a wheelchair. Grave though his illness was, she had learned to cope. The possibility of her father dying was not something she even thought about. But she was uncertain how she would face the death vigil. She only hoped Sister Breda would not die during Clare's turn to watch at the old nun's bedside in the infirmary near the chapel.

Twenty-four nuns had been chosen by the Mother Superior for the task. She had assembled them in her office and explained how, for once, they need not measure time by the tolling of the great iron bell in the chapel campanile, but by their watches. Each would sit for six hours at the bedside. Then Reverend Mother had sombrely reminded them that Sister Breda was a special case. Many years ago she was Mistress of Novices, strong in her faith, a sister whom a visiting bishop in the 1930s had commended as a living example of what a nun should be. He had spoken of Sister Breda's love of God being unhampered by theological arguments. Afterwards she had gone to work in South America. Reverend Mother had stared for a moment at the nuns grouped before her.

In a hushed voice she had explained: 'Our beloved Sister has lost her faith. She has a fearful reluctance to accept her time has come, that Our Lord is calling her home. She fights a struggle she cannot win, refusing to surrender to the sleep which comes to us all. She will tell you she no longer believes in God or his church. That is her fear speaking. It will be your duty to try and help her regain her faith. You must show our dear Sister by your own belief that death is not to be feared. The love and companionship you can offer will help her to be composed to meet her end on earth. Do not, above all, withdraw the hope of eternal life. Make her again aware of the glory of the resurrection. Convince our dear Sister her death is the start of a new and glorious journey.'

Clare made her bed, covering the sheets with a gold coverlet which matched the curtains and the paint on the back of the door. She had read that gold and white was a restful combination. Space in the room had been cleverly maximized to allow for a desk, a wardrobe and a cupboard to hold her underwear and toiletries. Her lace-up shoes fitted under the bed. A bookshelf contained several interpretative lives of Jesus and the scriptures. There was also a well-thumbed copy of Cardinal Suenens' *The Nun in the Modern World*, and a paperback edition of the documents of the Second Vatican Council.

The Community was equally divided on the contents of both books. Reverend Mother was steadfast in not going beyond the documents, but calmly defended the cardinal's right to advocate change which went far beyond what the council recommended. Her Deputy had said the pope should dismiss his eminence for publishing such revolutionary ideas as nuns removing their veils in public, wearing make-up, panty-hose and fashionable shoes. If nuns wanted to dress like that they should leave.

The Deputy had looked aggressively around the Community room. In the embarrassed silence, Reverend Mother surprised Clare by gently asking what Freud would have made of a patriarchal church that continued to call itself the Holy Mother Church. Everyone except the Deputy laughed.

Clare switched off the bedroom light and walked through the dimly-lit corridors filled with religious statues. As a postulant, Clare had counted them as a punishment from the Deputy who had caught her running down a corridor. There were seventeen baby Jesus' in the arms of his mother; nineteen Blessed Virgins, and forty-one separate replicas of Christ on the cross. There were also statues of St Joseph and other saints; all told there were almost a hundred monuments. The walls were covered with an even greater number of religious paintings.

A former nun who had abandoned her calling in the wake of the Council had recently written to a newspaper suggesting the Order should sell its art collection to help feed the poor of the Third World. The letter upset Clare because it clearly gave the impression the convent was a treasure trove of useless wealth. In fact there was barely enough money to keep the building heated and to feed the women who lived within its walls. Generations of nuns had watched history sweep past: the Great Famine, the Fenian Rebellion, the foundation of Sinn Fein, the bloody conflict of the Easter Uprising in 1916.

On that Sunday, sixty years ago, Clare realized Sister Breda was her own age when British soldiers arrived at the convent looking for Irish rebels. Sister Breda had met them at the front door. She had asked all those who were Catholic to raise their hands. Some of the troops did. She had lectured them on the mortal sin they had already committed by carrying weapons onto consecrated ground. The shame-faced soldiers had galloped back down the driveway. Sister Breda had returned to the chapel and knelt beside the two terrified youths who had sought sanctuary. She had made them place their rifles in the convent furnace. Later she accompanied them to the docks where they boarded a mailboat to America.

Clare walked past the parlours, different in size but uniformly furnished. In each there were comfortable chairs for visitors and hard-backed ones for the nuns; the space between callers and a Sister was formalized by a table.

For the past week, while Sister Breda was dying, the parlours had remained closed. During that time Clare had increasingly felt the presence of death as something tangible. At meal times everyone was careful not to make a clatter with their knife, fork or spoon. Clearing away and washing up was conducted with whispered speed. At recreation no one switched on the gramophone. It was a gift from a relative of Sister Breda. The Deputy had covered the stack of records with a purple cloth, hiding the bright laminated covers.

Tradesmen left their deliveries outside instead of carrying them into the cold-storage rooms below ground. Burdened under the weight of the sacks and boxes, the nuns on kitchen duty brought in the supplies.

Impending death had made the Community draw away from the outside world so that each of its members could remind herself of the positive attributes of dying: it was merely a stepping-stone to an eternal and glorious life. Apart from the doctor no visitors were admitted through the massive front door. He had seen Reverend Mother in her office. Shortly afterwards, Declan, the groundsman went to the graveyard beyond the main house with the Superior and agreed upon a burial plot. By tradition Declan would dig the grave immediately the campanile bell began its sonorous toll. That would also be the signal for Sister Dualta to go to her workshop and carve in stone the figures 93. It was the number assigned to Sister Breda when she was registered as a postulant in the reign of King Edward at the turn of the century.

Clare's route to the infirmary took her past the chapel where the nuns assembled for prayers seven times each day. She pulled open its door. Inside it was dark except for the vigil light burning at the altar and the shaded lamp which illuminated the statue of Our Lady. Clare came here often, outside appointed times, to kneel and pray for her father.

The bond between them was close. Growing up she was the one who had always accompanied him to daily Mass; she was still the one to whom he turned to discuss all religious questions. She had often thought he would have made a fine priest and a handsome one too, with his shock of dark hair and his spare frame; an athlete's body before his crippling illness misshaped it. His presence seemed, as it often did nowadays, to slip into the pew beside her as she quickly knelt and said a prayer for Sister Breda.

She hurried from the chapel, the swish of her habit the only noise to break the silence. There was a junction in the corridor. To her right a passage led to the kitchen and laundry. Clare had often marvelled at the contentment of those who dedicated their lives to Christ by stirring pots and folding sheets. They accepted without question that this was what God intended for them. In spite of her own serenity she knew she had an ambition to serve him on a higher level, to have her intellectual capacity fully extended.

Clare was no feminist. She was concerned about the radicalism manifesting itself throughout the sisterhood. She did not think it mattered that men, canon lawyers in Rome, must approve any constitutional change in the Order's Rule, and therefore her life. That they decided when she should now get up in the morning, when she would eat and what she could wear. These were small matters to her. Nor did she yearn, as some still did, for a return to the days when women in religious life had wielded tremendous influence, both within their convents and in the world beyond.

In the Middle Ages nuns had been consulted by the kings and queens of Europe on many matters of ecclesiastical importance. The Council of Trent in 1545 stripped them of such power and ordered all nuns to remain in their enclosures. Even now the rule of enclosure remained strict. Clare knew that if she was to leave the Mother House without permission, she would face exclaustration – expulsion from the Order. Yet, she hoped that one day soon, with the blessing of Reverend Mother, she would join that select band of sisters who left every morning to receive the finest education the Order could provide so that they could become senior teachers in one of the Community's schools. A chance to improve herself further and use her knowledge to improve others would put a seal on a lifestyle Clare saw as already close to perfection.

She was aware of her body, but its sexual function had no part in her life. She totally accepted that forsaking marriage and the possibility of motherhood were more than compensated for by the realization she was living as God ordained she should. She doubted if anyone – except her father – would understand her day began and ended with the call 'Praise be to Jesus Christ.'

She took the left fork, climbing the stairs. Silence continued to envelop her. The period from midnight to dawn, Reverend Mother had warned, was an especially lonely and difficult time for both the dying and the sister keeping vigil at her bedside.

Outside Sister Breda's room the table for the dead was already in place. On a white cloth stood two white candles in solid silver holders, a bowl of holy water and a vial of anointing chrism. There was also a crucifix and a small vase of flowers from the convent garden. As Clare entered, the nun on duty rose from her chair and whispered, 'She's still worried that she's not ready. She's back at the "why me" stage.'

The infirmary was still the only place where it was permitted to break the Grand Silence.

Clare looked at the frail figure in the bed. She remembered the wisdom of her father. *Everybody bargains with God*. He had said it after he came out of hospital after tests to establish the course his own illness would take. He was in a ward where several of the patients prayed, promising to be good Catholics in exchange for an extension of their lives. Her father had smiled. *It's not like playing cards. You can't deal with God*.

Clare sat down on the chair, taking stock of the room. It was painted white from skirting board to ceiling. There were no curtains on the window. The floor was covered with grey linoleum. Apart from the bed and chair, the only furnishings were several small tables. On each one was a lighted candle. There was a box of unlit candles on the floor beside the chair.

'Have you ever seen anyone die?' Sister Breda's voice was barely audible.

'No, Sister Breda. I have not seen anybody die.'

'I've seen a lot of death. You do in South America. I was in one of our schools out there.'

She paused, lost in some secret reverie.

'Have you travelled?'

'No, Sister Breda. But maybe if God wills it…'

Clare searched for words to create, in the short time available, rapport.

'I'm full of cancer.' The luminous eyes set deep in their sockets continued to watch Clare.

'I know,' Clare said. If I can get her to talk it may become easier for her.

'They told me when it was too late.'

Clare was aware of the odour in the room.

'They didn't give me time to prepare for death. Everybody needs time,' Sister Breda whispered.

'In that sense there is never time. But God understands that. Would you like me to read to you?' Clare asked.

There was a Bible on the table nearest the bed.

'No, hold my hand.'

Clare did so.

'I had warm hands like yours once. You feel how cold they are now?'

'Would you like a hot water bottle?'

'You can't help me. Nobody can help me except God, and I'm not certain about him now.'

'If you stop believing now, it will all have been wasted.'

'Have you always believed?'

'Yes. Always.' And Clare began to tell her.

Her Catholicism was handed down to her as a birthright instilled by her parents as the only practical way to live because among other things it would help her practice self-reliance. Her mother was self-sufficient out of necessity and belief. Home-grown vegetables and home-made bread were cheaper and more nutritious than those bought from the local store. The concept of a consumer society had still to reach the Dublin suburb where they lived.

Her father was employed on the production staff of a national newspaper: away five nights a week, back with the early dawn bus, sleeping until lunch, then another night of supervising the presses. His had been a painstaking rung-by-rung climb and he was determined his daughters would have a better life.

Clare grew up with an acceptance that when she left school she would work for a while, meet a boy, go steady, accept his proposal of marriage, settle down close to home and raise her own family. Her husband would have the same strong religious beliefs as her father. There would be an identical picture of the Sacred Heart on the living-room wall as there was at home. The same ritual of saying the rosary before going to bed, the same strict observance of Mass on Sunday and on every feast day. It was the story of Clare's mother. It was still the expectation of thousands of Irish girls in the 1960s.

Nuns fitted naturally into the landscape. Clare's first impression of a nun was of a person who gave herself to God; who always knelt longer at Mass and even when walking had her hands clasped as if in prayer. Nuns were people who seemed to have no legs and moved with no visible means of support. She was too young to wonder why God wanted them to wear black; in any case it would have been incomprehensible to a nine-year-old that black symbolized a nun's commitment to die to the world. Later, in the sixth grade, it was Sister Imelda who explained that her habit was an outward sign of renunciation of self. The words planted a seed in Clare.

When Clare had reached the age of seventeen the nun said, in her no-nonsense way, she must think about her future. With her interest in scripture, her consistently good marks in English, history and geography, there were definite openings. Those words nurtured the seed.

She began to talk to Sister Imelda about the scriptures, marvelling at the way the nun was never stumped for an answer. On Sundays Clare listened carefully to Father Dolan's sermons. The Christ he preached about was someone who demanded the very highest standards from all those who wanted to accept his invitation: Follow me. Clare realized on her eighteenth birthday she had come to a cross-roads and chosen her path. Sister Imelda was the first to be told outside the family. She was her usual forthright self. 'Are you certain?'

Clare nodded. 'Yes. I know I want to be a nun. I want to be like you.'

The nun was insistent. 'You must not use me as your model. God would not want that. The start and end of a vocation is following Christ. He is your model. No one else. And that means you must be ready to say yes to the way of the cross. No one else must come between you and Jesus.'

The nun had other questions.

'What about your family? Your father is sick. It will not be easy for your mother to manage. You'll have no money to give her. You'll have nothing except the clothes you stand in. How do your parents feel?'

A few weeks before, the doctors had finally diagnosed her father's illness as incurable. He took the news stoically. Her parents seemed, if anything, to draw closer together.

'My father says he always knew I would be a nun. He even quoted what Jeremiah said.'

'What was that?' Sister Imelda smiled. 'Can you remember? If you're going to be a nun you'll have to be able to quote the Bible accurately.'

'I think so. "Before I formed you in the womb I knew you, before you were born I dedicated you."'

'But remember too what God also said to Jeremiah. "You know not how to speak. You are too young."'

'I'm eighteen, Sister. Girls get married at eighteen.'

Sister Imelda had explained there would be no more going to the cinema, or rocking to the music of the Rolling Stones. Even Clare's books – which included Amis' *Lucky Jim* and Kerouac's *On the Road* – would have to be given up. Could she really do all this?

'Yes. I am certain.'

'I think you are.' Sister Imelda smiled. 'I think God is calling you.'

Now, seven years later, Christ had brought Clare to this death-bed.

'Would you like me to read to you?' Clare asked.

Sister Breda stared at her. 'Isaiah. Thirty-eight, twelve.' The words rattled in her throat. 'Can you find it?'

'I think we both learned it in the noviciate. Reverend Mother said it used to hang on the wall outside the door.'

'She's wrong. It was above the door. I put it there myself.' For a moment Sister Breda's eyes were no longer grey and remote. 'Nineteen twenty-eight, the year they made me Novice Mistress I had it put up.' She stared at Clare. 'Do you remember the words?'

'I think so.'

Clare was glad the old nun couldn't see her tears. She began to recite. '"Mine age is departed and is removed from me; from day even to night wilt thou make an end of me."' She watched Sister Breda's hands compose and recompose themselves. 'My mother taught me that.'

'They are beautiful words, Sister Breda.'

The silence in the room was broken by the old nun's question. 'What time is it?'

'Four o'clock.'

Clare sensed the elemental fear grasping Sister Breda.

'My mother died at this hour. Four in the morning with no one with her. No one. Not the priest. Nor my brothers. Nobody.' She struggled up from her pillow. 'I was a postulant, seven months in. They wouldn't let me go home. They said... I should... be glad. Sacrifice. They kept saying, sacrifice...'

Clare cradled her, letting her whisper. She felt she had a very old child in her arms.

'I don't want to die,' whispered Sister Breda.

Clare rocked her gently, listening to the little wailing cries and thinking she had never realized how painful it was to let go of life.

'God wants us all back at some time. We should be glad to go, to renounce this life for a far better one,' Clare murmured.

Sister Breda suddenly stretched out a hand. Her lips moved but there was no sound, just a terrible rattling in her throat. For a moment there was a look of puzzlement and despair in her eyes. Then it was gone and she folded her hands in prayer. She was smiling as she died.

Clare dropped to her knees and prayed. Then she rose and fetched the table for the dead, carrying it to the side of the bed. Using one of the already burning candles she lit the two other candles on the table. Next she placed the crucifix in Sister Breda's hands, folding her fingers around the figurine. Finally, she closed the old nun's eyes using a thumb to gently press shut the lids. Then Clare fell once more to her knees and resumed praying until the Reverend Mother, accompanied by the priest, arrived to take over.

After the undertakers completed their work and placed the body in a plain white deal coffin, it was wheeled on a trolley into the chapel. Members of the death vigil escorted it to the altar. The priest received the remains. Candles were lit and positioned around the coffin. The priest recited prayers for the soul of the dead sister before he left. Only the nuns remained, kneeling in silent vigil on either side of the coffin.

While Clare slept, the Superior informed first the Community and then the archbishop's office of the death. Next the papal nuncio's office was told, so that it could be included in his next report to the Vatican. There a priest-clerk would record the passing of Sister Breda in the ledger for the dead.

That evening the chapel was crowded. Every member of the Mother House was present except those too ill to be brought down from the infirmary. Sisters had come from other houses in the diocese. Row upon row of black-robed figures knelt in the carved stalls.

During the day the casket had remained open exposing Sister Breda in her full habit, dressed exactly as she had been on the day she took her vows. Her face had a rested appearance and her hands clasped a rosary, its wooden crucifix facing upwards.

Nuns knelt beside the coffin after placing their posy among the many other floral tributes on the chapel floor around the bier.

Clare arrived late in the afternoon thinking how the flames from the candles gave Sister Breda's face a rosy glow. Early in the evening the dead nun's relatives, escorted by Reverend Mother, paid their respects before leaving again. Afterwards Declan prayed with Sister Dualta before they replaced the casket lid and tightened the nuts. Everyone then left the chapel.

The Requiem Mass was on the third day. Once more the chapel was crowded. The archbishop sent a representative. The nuncio's letter of condolence mentioned that in this time of grief they must remember that the church does not weep for death; it is merely the narrow gate which leads to everlasting life. The theme was central to the Mass in the homilies and the voices rising and falling in supple harmony. Afterwards, Declan and the undertakers carried the coffin to the graveyard. The nuns followed in procession, paired in seniority, heads upright, eyes shiny. A little distance behind walked the visitors. The only sound was the crunching of feet on gravel and the mournful tolling of the campanile bell. The Community formed a loose circle around the head of the grave. As the coffin was slowly lowered into the earth, the nuns chanted the final dirge: All things are alive in the sight of their King.

Reverend Mother escorted the visitors from the graveyard. Then she returned to stand at the foot of the grave while Declan filled it, finally mounding it into shape with the back of his shovel, striking the earth in time to the tolling. Sister Dualta stepped forward and placed the stone she had carved at the head of the grave. When she stepped back, the sound of the bell stopped. It was over.

Walking out of the graveyard, Clare noticed the grave near the footpath. The stone at its head had tilted with the subsidence of the soil. But she could still make out the figures: 136. It was now her number, given to her on the day she had been admitted. It had been handed on from that sister buried there, a nun she had never known. When Clare died, or for any reason left the Order, the number would be assigned to another postulant. It was another of the timeless things about religious life that so appealed to Clare.

After supper she returned to the chapel. Kneeling in prayer, she again felt the peace and stillness. The tiny living flame of the vigil lamp was visible proof of his presence. She could feel him all around her as once more she asked: *Dear Lord, if I am worthy of your trust, please tell Mother.*

CHAPTER TEN

An Attitude of Mind

Clare knew Declan, the convent groundsman, only drove like this, at such speed, when he brought the choir to sing at a Nuptial Mass. The Order rented out the choir for these occasions to help pay the Community's housekeeping bills.

Usually Declan drove the aged convent bus like a hearse when he transferred a nun from the Mother House to one of the outer houses or the airport, knowing he would probably only see that sister again after she left one of the Order's mission stations in Africa and Asia. Those times he wore blue coveralls and was morose.

Today he was dressed in a green tweed three-piece suit with a rose in his buttonhole, plucked from one of the convent's flower beds. He handled the bus like a racing car, crashing through the gears, whistling and singing and bellowing happily at startled passers-by.

Its twenty-six passengers sat bolt upright, knees braced against the seat in front. Clare was certain Declan had already taken more than his share of nips from the flask in his jacket pocket. Not even the protests of the Deputy Superior, seated immediately behind, could make him slow down. Bent over the steering wheel, he shouted over his shoulder, 'Don't worry, Mother. God is with us.'

He burst into another song. Clare felt a sudden lump in her throat. The song was one of her father's favourites.

As the bus cleared the last of the city traffic lights and headed into the countryside, she thought of him on the bed in the sitting-room her mother had converted after ill-health had finally forced him into early retirement. Now his wasted legs could no longer carry him upstairs. In her mind's eye she could see him propped up on pillows, combing the newspapers. There were stories about the collapse of Rolls-Royce, the dismaying spread of venereal disease and the discovery that one of

America's largest soup manufacturers had been marketing canned botulism. There had been another homosexual march in New York, another student riot in Paris, another demonstration at the Berlin Wall. And, of course, the church itself was once more in the news, this time over the closure of nine seminaries in the United States and Europe. An editorial asked: 'Where are tomorrow's priests and nuns?'

She wondered again why Pope Paul VI did not rally the church instead of dividing it by his actions. He looked benignly on Castro's Cuba and turned a blind eye to the arrest of Lithuanian Catholics by the Russians. He had spoken about the need for 'a people's church where everyone would have an equal voice', yet he had failed to allow priests to marry, while at the same time not dealing with bishops who wanted the status of regional popes, theologians who wished to rewrite doctrine into Marxism liberation theology and homosexuals of the Catholic Gay Liberation Movement.

As the bus sped through the countryside, Clare thought how these past months since the death of Sister Breda, change had entered her.

Clare could pinpoint its onset from one evening before the Grand Silence, the time assigned for Final Meditation. Then each member of the Community re-dedicated herself to God, choosing a text from scripture to ponder on. She had selected the words of the apostle John. 'If the world hateth you, ye know that it hateth me before it hateth you. If ye are of the world, the world would love its own. But because I have chosen you out of the world, therefore the world hateth you.'

She had always found John's words demanded the most study but were the most rewarding. Spare and unyielding, the way she liked to think the apostle himself had been, they had thrilled her with their unfolding of a divine plan.

Yet, kneeling in her stall in chapel, the text which had seemed such an inspired choice had the opposite effect. She began to reject the words. Why would the world hate her because she had chosen to follow Christ? John made the decision sound so selective. The kind of behaviour he was describing had an inverted possessiveness. It was directed inwards, not outwards. Jesus wanted those who followed him to love the world, not have the world hate them. She realized she had lost her concentration totally. She felt tired and on edge. For the remainder of Final Meditation she knelt, her mind blank.

That night, when the campanile bell rang three times – one sonorous clang for each member of the holy Trinity – Clare found it difficult to sleep. She thought of her mother and father and, though they had never mentioned it, she knew they would, in their reduced circumstances, welcome any financial support she could have provided if she were in a job instead of religious life. She wondered what type of work she would have chosen; one of the banks or the civil service? Nowadays many women went on working after marriage, delaying having families. Until recently, she had only a vague idea of how this was possible. Then, on a parlour visit, a cousin had worn a pretty, close-fitting hat, and she had said it reminded her of one of those Dutch caps in a Renaissance painting. Her visitor had laughed and whispered a Dutch cap was a contraceptive. She had listened as her relative explained that was how many women managed when the only family planning allowed by the church was the natural rhythm method.

Next morning the new electric alarm – another Vatican Council innovation – dragged Clare awake. The great bell in the tower was nowadays only rung to herald the Grand Silence, and on Sundays and feast days. For the first time in years Clare was almost late for chapel.

A few days later she again tried to meditate on John's words. Once more she found herself asking the question – *what is wrong in wanting someone to love me, and for me to love that person in return?*

At her weekly visit to the confessional, she knelt, one hand entwined in her rosary, the other caressing the crucifix suspended from the beads, and hesitantly explained her feelings. The priest whispered to her, his voice so low she could hardly hear the words. 'The Gospel speaks of loving your neighbour as yourself. Ponder the greater meaning of love. You must pray, Sister. Ask God to lift this heaviness. He will deliver you.'

She prayed and, in a way, had been delivered. The lethargy lifted. Yet something remained. She could not define it but it was there, a vague, unsettling feeling which still woke her in the night reminding her of words the Mistress said when she first lectured on Preparation. 'You will symbolically put your flesh to death so that your love becomes absolutely focused on God's will. You are being prepared to wait on God. To serve him and his Son here on earth.'

Clare knew she still wanted nothing more. Yet this troubling feeling persisted. What was so unsettling was that she could think of no reason for it.

As Declan parked the bus in a lane beside the village church, Clare once again felt a restlessness. She was aware the Deputy was watching her.

Might she end up like the older nun, a woman whose prayer-life seemed to have soured, who, even on a superficial level, seemed genuinely afraid of any meaningful relationship with anyone else. Did the Deputy's behaviour suggest that loving was a doomed process, drained of energy, no more than the emptiness of a chore?

The church was completely full. The sanctuary was banked with flowers and the choir occupied two stalls, listening to the organist play Bach. When the music stopped, the choir united in psalmody. As they ended, the organist swung into the wedding march, the anthem swelling as the bridal party entered the nave, the sun catching the dazzling white of the bride and the gauzy pink of her bridesmaids' dresses.

Suddenly Clare felt tears forming and blinked her eyes rapidly. She felt faint. She tried to focus, her eyes darting from the altar candles to the crucifix above, from the sanctuary lamp to the priest. She gripped the ledge of the stall to steady herself. *I must not, I must not faint.*

The dizzy feeling passed and, staring at the bride, Clare thought: *I accept this is not for me.*

Two days had passed since Declan drove them back to the Mother House. Sister Imelda was waiting for her in a parlour. Clare was delighted and surprised to see her old teacher whom she had not seen since her Clothing. Without a word Sister Imelda closed and door and leaned against it.

'How are you, Clare?'

'Great, of course. Why shouldn't I be?'

'I heard you nearly fainted at the wedding the other day.'

'Who told you that?'

Sister Imelda smiled. 'Don't worry, it wasn't Deputy Mother. She's tough, Clare. But that's what the job calls for. She was Novice Mistress when I was here. We used to call her "God's Warden", behind her back, of course. No. It wasn't her. It was a guest. She mentioned a nun had started to sway as the bride came up the aisle. The description could only fit you. She thought you were going to fall. What happened?'

Clare gave a little shrug. 'It was nothing. Probably I was a bit light-headed from the journey. You know the way Declan drives to weddings!'

166

'I do. But it's never happened before, has it? And you've been to a lot of weddings.'

Clare forced a smile. 'It was nothing, really. Anyway, I'm fine now.'

Sister Imelda moved away from the door and gently put her hands on Clare's shoulders. 'Would you like to talk about it, Clare? I just want to help.'

'I know.'

Apart from her family, no one now called her Clare. She felt an undertow of sudden emotion.

'This is just between you and me. If I can help, don't push me away,' Sister Imelda said quietly. 'We all have to go through this, Clare. It's part of celibate living. What you are experiencing is very natural.'

Late afternoon sun filtered through a high, gabled window into the parlour, enriching the dark wood.

'Natural? How do you know? How do you know what I am feeling?' Clare wished she did not sound so defensive. But she was being driven by some inner force to tell Sister Imelda everything: her doubts, her fears, her struggles. *Everything.*

'What we must do is to try and find a proper place for your feelings within the framework of your sacred vows. But first you must tell me what you are feeling,' Sister Imelda said.

Clare finally allowed the past weeks to surface. She could not accept the way of the cross was only suffering, that to follow him meant endless pain and being emotionally racked. She stumbled into silence, uncertain how to continue.

Sister Imelda finally spoke. Sexuality and spirituality could live in the same body. Developing one did not mean denying the other. Both were powerful forces. It was not a matter of choosing one and pretending the other did not exist, but integrating them.

'To live "in Christ" does not mean you have to deny being a woman. What it means is that you must have a proper awareness of the dangers. We both know what they are. We have known from the day God called us that we didn't expect to live like the Corinthians. But I don't think anybody expects you not to be troubled from time to time.'

'I don't know what is happening, Sister Imelda. All I know is that I keep thinking if I feel like this, I can't be loving God in the way he wants.'

Sister Imelda smiled. 'You're being too hard on yourself, Clare. Everybody has felt like this, from Reverend Mother down. It's part of what makes a good nun, having to go through this. But the important thing to remember is that you go *through* this. You don't *stay* with it. What matters is not that you have these feelings, but that in spite of them, you have never stopped loving God. That's what's important. Everything else will fall into place as long as you don't lose sight of that.'

'I wish I had your confidence.'

'You haven't lost your confidence, Clare. You've just buried it for the moment under all this soul-searching.'

Clare laughed. She had not felt so calm and secure for months. She felt able to put the questions she had been unable to ask until now.

'Why do I feel so lonely? I used to sleep so well. I used to feel so certain where I was going, what the church represents, where the challenges and promises are. Now I wonder. I wake up feeling so alone.'

Sister Imelda looked at her thoughtfully.

'Clare, the very fact that you can even identify what bothers you is a sign you are coping. We have all woken up feeling alone. Just because we were told to distinguish between aloneness and loneliness does not make it any easier. We have all got to find our own way forward.'

'But how? *How?* Sometimes, like at the wedding, I just wanted to love some person and have that person love me.'

'That's natural. But we have both also learned that we must strip ourselves of such feelings because that is what God wants of us,' Sister Imelda said quietly.

'I want to, but I don't seem to know how.'

'You will. You have in the past and you will in the future, Clare. I promise you. Reverend Mother tells me you have more than lived up to her expectations. There are high hopes for you.'

She knew Sister Imelda was watching her carefully. Clare smiled. Everything was going to be alright.

Once more Lent empurpled the convent. Statues and paintings were draped in puce cloth while personal sacrifices were silently made on knees in chapel. Clare gave up all other reading for the Bible. For hours she silently meditated on various passages which stated temptation was essential to test the strength of commitment. A great peace filled her. She felt renewed.

When her turn came, Clare stood at the foot of the main staircase and gripped two wooden shapes which resembled butter pats. She clapped them together, creating a sharp report, like a hunter's rifle. Throughout Holy Week the clappers marked the passage of time. Both the electric alarm and the campanile had been silent because the Rule decreed they were symbolic of joy in this period of mourning.

There were no recreation periods and talking was restricted to essential commands in the infirmary. Meals were cooked and served in complete silence; all domestic duties were performed in the same way. It was as if the entire Community had been struck dumb. Only at chapel was its collective voice heard, when the choir led the Community through the liturgies, the lamenting psalms and chants.

On Good Friday the convent seemed to completely die. Corridors were empty and the Community room deserted. The silence had a life of its own: watchful and enveloping like death itself over everything and everyone. In the chapel, row after row of motionless bodies knelt, precisely separated as if they had been positioned by a straight edge, so many inches between each inert figure.

A wooden cross lay before the altar. For hour upon hour the Community considered his agony, symbolized by the empty tabernacle. The host had been removed and its doors left asunder as a mute reminder of the violation Jesus had endured. Face buried deep into her hands, Clare meditated upon the Last Supper. The occasion reminded her of the importance of remaining unswerving in faith. Encompassed in the Last Supper was the spirit of poverty, obedience and chastity.

Holy Saturday stretched from the first crack of the clappers, and was spent kneeling in chapel waiting for hope, just as on that first Saturday after the crucifixion the apostles waited for a similar sense of purpose to enter their lives. While the Vatican Council had dispensed with the imagery of a bride of Christ, Clare nevertheless felt, kneeling before the cross at the altar, that her responses of grief and sadness for his death, were essentially no different from what a widow must feel on losing a husband. Gradually, as the long day drew to a close, her mood lightened as she silently told herself: *He is the resurrection. That is all that matters.*

Then, at last, the miracle of Easter Sunday: the host was returned to its rightful sanctuary, the altar clothed in fresh white linen, the paschal candle relit, its steady flame illuminating the scene of the resurrection carved into its wax. Renewal and joy were heralded in words and song as the choir swept the Community along through the *Gloria*.

Yet, watching the priest celebrate Mass, thoughts, new and disturbing, once more flickered through Clare's mind. A year ago she would have been shocked to discover she could think them. But, waiting to go to the altar rail to receive his body, she wondered again how Christ, who always stressed the role of women, would feel over the way the power of the church remained firmly clasped by men.

The Vatican Council, the Pope had said, acted in his name, and the Council had come out clearly in favour of a greater role for women in the church. But, male domination remained paramount. Even the devotion to Our Lady was designed to remind nuns of their duty to be meek and compliant. Clare wondered again whether such thoughts were a precursor to the return of her restlessness. When it was her turn to receive Communion, dissolving a piece of unleavened bread on her tongue did little to remove a feeling of being caught up in an irrevocably changing world, one in which her own future was both deeply troubling and uncertain.

Reverend Mother had attended all the discussions on modification held in the Community room, seating herself among other nuns, novices and postulants, listening carefully to the excited comments about the various design sketches produced by the Order's art teachers. Drawings were scathingly criticized, discarded or sent back for redesigning. Some suggestions involved no more than lopping-off a few inches from existing habits and shortening veils. Others would not have disgraced a high-fashion house with their sculpted bodices, pleated skirts, tucked-in waists and ruffled sleeves and collars. Designs which passed the drawing-board stage were stitched together by seamstress nuns. Other sisters took turns modelling. Prototype habits drew more intense discussion.

'How can I cook in such a fancy dress?' demanded the sister in charge of the kitchen.

'How would I manage in a thing like that? It's not much bigger than a duster,' protested a stout nun.

'I can't possibly wear that. I'd look like a Christian Brother!' yet another nun said about a habit styled like a monk's robe.

The models swept in and out with increasing aplomb, pirouetting and turning in gentle parody of the way professional mannequins move. The cheers and laughter at times were deafening.

It was left to the Deputy to dampen the mood. A young nun swirled into the room in an elegant creation: white lace collar and cuffs, a scalloped blouse-top and a straight skirt. As she spun around, the line of her pants was clearly visible. The Deputy rose to her feet, trembling with anger.

'Sisters, how could anyone go to chapel in that? How could we be close to God when we would be dressed to tempt the Devil? Sisters, I veto this on the grounds of immodesty.'

Reverend Mother said nothing. Next day she appeared at Mass in a perfectly tailored habit, its skirt exactly two inches below the knee, her legs covered in black panty-hose, her veil shortened and neatly clipped to the back of her head, the exposed hair brushed off her forehead. It was a sign for the Community to stop debating; the Superior's choice of modified habit was the acceptable option.

Almost every month there were instructions from the Vatican on how a Vatican Council document should be interpreted. The Sacred Congregation for Religious had sent word the Community could speak during supper, but for breakfast and lunch they must still maintain the silence of centuries, using precisely-defined gestures. For salt and pepper, a pinch of the fingers; for bread, a cutting motion; for the water pitcher, a pouring gesture.

Another order announced the abolition of many Latin prayers. A further edict revised the form of the Divine Office itself; some prayers were dropped. The bowing which accompanied the Confiteor could be abandoned.

There was guidance on 'pocket money'. Nuns who taught in the Order's schools and who did not journey there in Declan's bus would be allowed bus fares instead of depending on the bus to allow them to travel free. Some sisters found the idea of being doled out money the last straw and left the Order. The majority were of an age where they could marry and still bear children. The older nuns had responded calmly to all the changes in their lifestyle. Opposition came from those who were middle-aged, led by the Deputy. She challenged every liberalizing word and disputed every relaxation of the Rule.

At each meeting to discuss a proposal to abolish or alter something, the Deputy produced new evidence to support her argument there was too much frivolity. A hundred Italian Daughters of St Paul had been the latest to resign in protest over changes in their habits not going far enough. The Glenmary Sisters were in disarray over proposals to revise their Rule. The Sisters of the Immaculate Heart of Mary were racked with uncertainty over plans to rearrange their daily routine. There was not an Order, the Deputy claimed, which was not fearful of the future that would follow change.

The younger nuns countered that women were leaving religious life because the promises of the Vatican Council were not being implemented fully, or fast enough. The Community room rang with charge and counter-charge and tempers came close to fraying.

Clare had kept her own counsel. But, increasingly she feared that, in spite of Reverend Mother's leadership, the Deputy was an effective cork to bottle up the sweeping reform many of the younger nuns wanted.

A week after Easter, Clare made her way to Reverend Mother's office. She knocked and counted to five under her breath. The habit went back to her days as a postulant when the Mistress warned that Reverend Mother must never be surprised. Clare opened the door and entered. She waited for permission to advance.

'Benedicte.' Reverend Mother's voice was modulated and controlled.

'Dominus.'

'Come in. Sit down, Sister Mary Luke.'

Clare raised her eyes. Walking across the room, she was reminded again of how the crucifix on the wall behind the Superior somehow heightened the impression that she was more than a woman well into middle-age, but someone who, for a quarter of a century, had carried greater responsibility than many company directors. Only the lines around her eyes suggested the demands of combining the role of spiritual leader with a wide range of administrative duties.

As usual, the Superior sat bolt upright on her hard wooden chair, behind a desk whose surface was covered with paperwork. On each visit, Clare had been confronted by piles of bills, receipts, invoices and reports; the mound of paper never seemed to diminish.

Reverend Mother motioned for her to sit on a straight-backed wooden chair and located the paper she wanted. She held the sheet at a distance, her reading glasses at the tip of her nose.

'You have done well, Sister Mary Luke. The time has come when we must make fuller use of you.'

Clare felt her heart begin to race. She willed herself to sit perfectly still.

The Superior's voice was decisive.

'There is a place at Catholic College. You will fill it. You will get a further grounding in theology and scripture. God has given you a special gift, a brain able to understand his words better than many. You have a future in his work.'

The Superior rose to her feet. Clare bowed her head for the blessing. After leaving the office, she went to the chapel and knelt. Her prayer was short and heartfelt. *Thank you Lord for choosing me.*

Reverend Mother had arranged for a clinical psychologist, a nun from another Order, to address them. When the notice appeared in the Community room, the Deputy had stared in glazed disbelief and walked away. The notice read: 'Chastity – A Reassessment'.

The psychologist was in her forties and dressed in a dark grey two-piece suit. Above her eyebrows was an indentation, a reminder that, until recently, she had worn a constricting headband beneath a wimple. She invited anyone to make notes, then began with a quotation from Graham Greene: 'The church knows all about rules. But it does not know what goes on in a single human head.'

Clare jotted down the reference. The lecturer said that abandoning her own habit had not been an emotional experience.

'It has always been claimed our habits proclaim we have been called. More even than a priest's garb, they single us out as belonging to Christ. But that is an idea perpetuated by men who, down the centuries, have ruled our lives. Saint Ignatius said "no man should look into the eyes of a woman in a habit". What would happen if one of us wanted to look into the eyes of a man? No saint has ever laid down a rule about that! What Ignatius laid down was a rule to imprison us.'

The first murmurs of agreement came from behind Clare. The psychologist continued, her voice calm and controlled.

'Many of us here remember our Clothing, the day we wore a wedding dress. But it was also the day we were shorn and draped in black. Have you ever thought of the potential psychological damage for a bride to become a widow in the space of the same Mass? Those customs were designed by men. They have nothing at all to do with Our Lord. Think of the psychological trauma the Poor Clares still endure on their Clothing. Each novice must stand before a skeleton who represents Sister Death. What possible motive can there be for such an outlandish practice – except to reinforce the idea we die in our bodies when taking our vows? As a doctor I can tell you that is dangerous. It can cause permanent psychological harm and distort our view of religious life. As a nun I find that totally unacceptable. As a woman, I say it is disgusting.'

There was murmured agreement from the audience. The psychologist made her next point. 'We all look the same in habits because, until Vatican II, they fitted the concept that, upon entering religious life, we must renounce every thought about our sexuality. For centuries it has been an act of blind faith that we find it easier to cope with chastity than men do with celibacy. This is an arrogance once more perpetuated by men, based in part on the premise that if we are shrouded in habits, it will stifle all our emotional feeling.'

In the silence that followed, Clare made a further note. 'Ten years ago she would have been thrown out of here. Fifty years ago she would have been excommunicated. A hundred years ago she would have been imprisoned for heresy. Two hundred years ago she would have been burnt at the stake. She is the most exciting speaker I have ever heard.'

The psychologist quoted Saint Ambrose: 'A virgin is purity's immolation, the victim of chastity.'

She paused while several sisters wrote down the reference.

'The word "victim" expresses clearly what I object to. Our chastity, as such, is indeed important. It separates us from all other women. But we should not allow ourselves to be seen as victims. Chastity is a grace, not a penance. It is a virtue, not a sacrifice. But, above all, it is a voluntary condition, not something we must be coerced into by clothes and rules designed to exclude our femininity.'

A burst of applause greeted the words. The Deputy looked askance.

'Celibate bodies are still feminine bodies. We get periods. We go through menopause. And we are all capable of sexual urges that can bring us into direct conflict with our vow of chastity. Yet, most Orders prefer not even to consider such a possibility, let alone allow it to be discussed openly as we are doing here.'

The psychologist paused and smiled at Reverend Mother, sitting as erect as always, knees together, hands folded in her lap.

'But that does not mean that friendship is not possible. It is a matter of balance. There is nothing wrong in two nuns walking together. Indeed, it is clinically healthy to have contact, provided it does not get in the way of our relationship with God.'

She looked again at Reverend Mother.

'I am sure there are some of us who remember the days when a Superior said it was somehow ungodly to cross our legs in case it broke the vow of chastity.'

In the roar of laughter, Clare noted: *Reverend Mother seems delighted. She must have been very attractive when she was young. How did she manage?*

The lecturer continued. 'We are still women. The more feminine we are, the better we can serve our Order and Our Lord. God doesn't want people who are dried out in their feelings. Those sort of people have no love to give. And that is what chastity is all about – giving love in its purest form.'

She looked challengingly at her audience. 'Suppression breeds fanaticism. Following him takes on a dangerous distortion when sublimation leads to a misuse of power. No one who has never come to terms with their own emotions should have power over other people's.'

Clare noted the Deputy's response. *She looks as if she could spit.*

The lecturer developed another theme. Physical virginity was no longer an essential requirement for admission to religious life because many Orders now recognized that the act of consecration ensures spiritual virginity. 'Our chastity begins and ends with our hearts. What we must do is to place our sexual feeling into the framework of love.'

She said there was an urgent need for every religious woman to face certain questions. Did she accept that sexual drive was the most powerful single force in nature? That it could be destructive unless handled properly? That to forgo sexuality was a constant struggle? That to deny the struggle was to deny the right to live?

'If you can honestly answer "yes" to these questions, you have done rather better than the apostle Thomas who said the only way to cope with chastity is to steep yourself in a hot bath. In some quarters, that view prevails today. There is a mistaken idea that everybody can discipline themselves to withstand natural inclination. The theory is, if we say "go away", it will go away. Saints may be able to do so. For us, if we are honest, it is a daily battle. Unlike any other emotion, sexuality can surface at any time. A pretty painting. A scenic view. A passage in a book. Words and pictures. These are some of the potent forces which play upon our imagination and arouse our feelings.'

She reminded them that theology still neatly packaged chastity as a virtue. There was only one thing missing. A sense of reality.

The psychologist posed further questions. Were there any lessons to be learned from the world outside? From the widowed? From the divorced? From all those forcibly separated from loved ones?

Clare flexed her fingers, cramped from writing. The psychologist moved on, reminding them that chastity was a binding of their lives to Christ. But, just as in any relationship, the one they had with him was a continuous effort. A life of chastity involved a problem no theological text taught: how to handle risk.

'There is the risk of unhappiness and the risk of suffering. And there is the greatest risk of all. That, at the very end, all the struggles mean nothing because you may still fail before the finishing post.'

Clare sensed the sudden tension in the room.

'Each one of us here, if we are honest, if we stop and think, knows how high the stakes are. On the one hand, we are seeking human fulfilment in his name. On the other, we can be staring into the face of failure.'

She reminded them that religious life was based on the concept that satisfaction came from determination, that internal resources were always strong enough to grapple successfully with external forces.

'That is almost certainly not true with chastity. There are no guarantees that we will not fail. Awareness is the best guarantee of all. Be aware of your desires. To deny them is never a good thing. They must be faced. What is temptation for one is not for another. But how do you achieve what you want – living in Christ and living with your body?'

She took a sheet of paper from her pocket. 'Let me read you a letter. It's from a sister who until recently never doubted she couldn't cope. This is what she writes… "It hit me last Christmas, a time when all families are together. I have my family, of course, the Community. But I still felt alone. I got up alone. I ate in silence. I opened my presents in silence. I prayed alone. And I ended the day going to bed alone. I would give anything to take away this feeling of being alone…"'

Clare found her hand was shaking as she wrote her final note: 'It could be me. That's exactly how I feel.'

The Deputy's office was on the ground floor, close to the chapel. It was small and its walls lined with shelves of leather books. Clare wondered how a room could take on a person's personality. This one was stuffy and imbued with the Deputy's own sense of permanent disapproval. She sat behind her desk, the cross on its heavy chain dangling below the desk-top.

'Come forward and sit down, Sister Mary Luke.' The Deputy's voice was cold and impersonal.

'Thank you, Mother.' Clare walked to the chair, identical in shape and position to the one in Reverend Mother's office. The symmetry of convent life, she had often thought, knew no limits. Table settings and altar candles, kitchen pots and boxes of communion wafers: everything was aligned.

'You start at college next week.'

'Oh, Mother! I'm so excited.' Clare could not contain her joy. 'Oh, thank you, Mother!'

'You have nothing to thank me for. You might as well know that I did not approve of you going on to further study. In my view you would have been better used elsewhere.'

The bulky figure behind the desk was closing and opening her hands, making and breaking fists. It was a motion the Deputy used when trying to control her anger.

'Mother, I believe God wants me to be a teacher.'

'I am glad you are so certain what God wants of you. But may I remind you what I expect from you.' Her voice was even more chilled.

'You are going into the outside world to learn. The Order is paying for you to have this privilege. I need hardly remind you of the cost.'

Clare tried to keep her voice steady. 'I know, Mother, that it's expensive.'

'It is not just the cost I am talking about, Sister, as you know full well. I'm speaking of the Rule. Just because you are among seculars, you must not think you can behave as they do. Do you understand?'

'Mother, I'm not certain...'

'Then I will tell you precisely, Sister! You will limit your contact with them to the minimum. To the absolute minimum. You will not start a conversation. If they engage you in one, do not prolong it. You will confine any discussion to work. You will discuss absolutely nothing else. You will remember at all times that you are there to study and not fritter away your time. Do you understand now?'

'Yes, Mother.'

'Very well.'

The Deputy opened a drawer and took out a box which she unlocked and opened. She carefully counted out a number of coins and some notes, then passed them across to Clare.

'This is your bus-fare and lunch money for one week. Every Sunday evening, before Compline, you will come here and receive your allowance for the next week. If, for any reason, you have to miss college, then you will bring the unused money back here. You will not use it to buy sweets or anything else. Is that clear?'

'Yes, Mother. It's perfectly clear.'

Clare thought: *Why does she treat me like a child? I'm almost twenty-six years of age.*

The Deputy was reluctant to end the interview.

'I could not help noticing how approving you seemed of that dreadful woman's lecture. I cannot imagine what she thinks she is doing in religious life. It was disgusting. And I think it is disgusting for anyone to even think she represents what our life is all about. If it's still in your mind, Sister Mary Luke, put such rubbish out of it. Every word of it.'

Clare stared at her, horrified. Could this still be the voice of the church? In spite of everything, was this how little religious life had progressed?

'Thank you, Mother. I'll remember what you have said.'

The Deputy stared at her. 'You do that, Sister, you do that. And do it with humility. That's what you need, humility.'

'I will try, Mother. I will try to be more humble.'

'Do that.'

Seated in the tiered lecture hall, Clare listened to the monsignor building his argument that the apostle John's authorship of the book of Revelation was supported by the independent evidence of Justin Martyr, Irenaeus, Tertullian and others. The discourse not only covered familiar ground, but the lecturer's dusty-dry delivery was her first disappointment of the morning. She felt her concentration fading.

Outside the convent she had caught a bus crowded with rush-hour commuters, elbowing their way on and off at stops. She had instinctively tried to stand aside, remembering the lessons on self-effacement she had been given in the postulancy. Nobody had taken any notice, let alone thanked her for such courtesy.

Until the monsignor, she had found her lecturers stimulating. A theologian had spent an hour discussing the creation from the stance of how it effectively destroyed the argument for evolution: the choice was either to believe God's revelation or human theorizing, and that the inherent weakness of the latter was that evolution merely sent the idea of the origin of humanity back into oblivion but did not provide the original source from which it sprang. Another tutor had devoted his time to discussing the three stages of death: physical, spiritual and eternal, and how all were linked by the resurrection. A third concentrated upon the significant unnamed women of scripture: John's adultress, The great harlot of Revelation, Matthew's woman with seven husbands. All symbolized punishment and repentance, divine wrath and forgiveness. She had filled page after page, excited and stimulated by what she heard.

With a start she realized the monsignor's lecture was over. He asked the class to write an essay on the position of the preterist method of interpreting the gospel in conjunction with the continuous historical method.

She sat, frantically writing, wishing she had paid more attention.

'It's okay. You can borrow my notes.'

Clare looked up, startled. Standing over her was a tall, spare-framed man, wearing a white shirt, black tie and trousers. Stuffed into the pockets of his sports jacket were papers and he had a pile of books in his hands. He smiled down at her.

'The monsignor will give the same lecture in one form or another right through the whole term. He's hooked on Revelation. He drags it into everything.'

'I see.' She thought: *Do not encourage this. Do not get involved. Remember the Rule. Remember Deputy-Mother. She could have sent him to test you.*

'You're not one of those nuns who spend their time sitting in an empty classroom during lunch, are you?'

'What?' She started to pack her briefcase. 'Sorry, I wasn't listening.' She wished she didn't sound so distracted.

'We get a lot of Sisters here who don't eat. They just sit in class waiting for the break to end. You can always tell them. They're the ones who wear full habits to try and hide their thinness. Nobody's fooled, of course. We all know convents are a breeding ground for anorexia.'

'Really? Do they teach you that here?' Her voice was edgy, but she suddenly didn't care.

'Sorry. I didn't mean to offend you.'

'You didn't. It's just that I dislike...'

'People who invite you to lunch and never take you!'

She felt herself shrinking away, wondering how she could escape.

'Tom, are you coming?' The voice came from a group going through the door.

He addressed her again. 'Would you like me to show you where the restaurant is? I'm Tom by the way.'

She knew he was trying to reassure her with his smile.

'It's okay if you don't want to come. It was stupid of me to say what I did.'

'No. I'd like to come.' She hoped her voice sounded nonchalant. She rose to her feet and closed her briefcase.

Tom stepped back, smiling gently. The group in the doorway had gone.

'The first day's always the worst. After a week or so, you'll get used to it.'

'How long have you been here?' she asked, thinking: *Stop this. You must stop this now.*

'A year. I'm coming up to my deaconate.'

'Oh.' She wished she didn't have this urge to know more.

'What's your name?'

'Sister.'

Tom laughed. 'Not what they all call you. Your real name.'

'I'm not sure if…'

'Of course you can! What do you think Vatican II was all about?'

'Certainly not about nuns giving their names to anybody who asks.' She hoped her smile took the sting out of the words.

Tom looked serious. 'I know about the Rule. Here we try and put that aside. But nobody's going to push you. If you want to be "Sister", that's okay. Only you'll miss a lot, and that would be a shame.'

She was staring at him, at the texture of his male skin, at the small nick on his chin, at his thick eyebrows, his nose, his eyes, at the way his lips curved when he smiled. She was shocked to find herself in such proximity to his alien masculine world.

'My name is Clare.'

'And you'll be a poor starving Clare if you don't get something to eat!'

He led the way out of the lecture room. She was glad he could not see her face crimsoning, or detect the panic he had created in her. She had come here determined to attain intellectual excellence. Yet suddenly, emotions and passions which had troubled her for months had become sharply focused on the back of this tall man striding ahead of her.

Tom led her with easy assurance into the restaurant, through the wall of noise, to a table. He dumped his books on a chair and held another out for her. No man, she thought, had ever treated her like this.

Clare felt both stunned by his warmth and dismayed at her response.

CHAPTER ELEVEN

Recollections

The girl on the Pirelli calendar was kneeling in the sand, legs slightly apart, one hand casually dropped between her thighs, the other reaching for her long blonde hair streaming in the wind.

Andrew forced himself to concentrate. In his memory time was melded, some details obscured, others highlighted. Long ago he had realized his subconscious was highly selective and had wondered if that was how he coped with his introspection. He continued seeking, a lesson learned, an experience undergone, to help him decide.

It was late in the evening and he was in the snug of a bar in an English village.

That his father was a staunch Protestant, as devoted to his faith as his mother was to her Catholicism had made it that much harder for Andrew to decide. He continued slotting each memory into place. Family. School. University. The Army. Jane. Always Jane.

Once more he looked at the calendar pinned over the bar. The nude seemed to have arrived on her deserted beach in some mysterious way. There were no footprints in the sand, no horizon, nothing to distract his attention from her.

His reverie was interrupted by sudden laughter from another part of the bar. He'd already recognized them by their haircuts, the cavalry-twill trousers and the leather patches on their tweed jackets: the off-duty uniform of Sandhurst cadets, as distinctive as the shine on their shoes and the way they ordered pink gins. That tradition died hard in the Army was one of the reasons he hadn't wanted to remain. But not the main one. Once more his mind began to drift.

When Andrew was seven years old and about to enter preparatory school, his mother explained being a Catholic was 'special'. Catholicism in England was still a minority religion, its places of worship vastly outnumbered by those of the established church. His mother had a collective label for them. The Tory party at prayer. She used it as the ultimate weapon to silence his father when he went 'too far'. She would sigh and interject, with just the faintest undertone, 'Dear, that really sounds like something you heard in that Tory party at prayer place of yours.'

It was another round of verbal punches meant to score, not scar. It was one reason the marriage had survived: both understood the rules of engagement.

Andrew liked his prep school, not so much because of a total absence of religious bias, but for its uniform: battleship grey, with red piping around the jacket and stocking tops and a red cap worn squarely on the head. For the first time he was conscious of liking to dress up.

Uniforms, said Father Patrick in his custom-made clerical suit ordered from the Pope's tailor in Rome, made a person stand out. Every Thursday afternoon, except during Holy Week, the parish priest took tea with Andrew's mother. During Lent he refused sugar and her home-baked cakes. Father Patrick had a shock of hair almost as white as his collar, and fingernails bitten to the quick. His every word and gesture contained its own sense of drama; the most trivial of incidents retold with a sense of urgency, delivered in a soft lisp. Andrew's father said that Father Patrick should have been an actor.

When he was small, Andrew used to sit on Father Patrick's knee. When he was older, he sat at the priest's feet, marvelling at the buckles on his shoes. Before leaving, Father Patrick would stoop down and unfailingly ask Andrew how he was coming along with his catechism and remind him to say his prayers every night, otherwise God would be sad and perhaps even angry. In Andrew's impressionable mind, the Almighty took on a definite shape. Someone capable of sorrow and rage, but who also exacted all sorts of punishments that God had appointed Father Patrick to administer. It was Andrew's first realization of the importance of a priest.

One night, as his mother tucked him in, he murmured that when he grew up, he would like to have Father Patrick's job. His mother bent over him and whispered words which, from time to time, had surfaced in his mind. 'Darling, if that's what God decides, I will be very happy.' She had kissed him on the forehead and asked God to keep him safe.

The following Thursday Father Patrick had patted Andrew on the head and said it would be wonderful if he were to receive a call from God. Andrew sat there for the rest of the afternoon wondering how God would do this. More than likely, he decided, he would use the telephone; God would be too busy to write. That was what Father Patrick must have meant by a call. The telephone would ring in the hall and either his mother or father would answer it, and they would stand there, awed, and call out: 'Andrew, it's for you – God is calling.' It seemed the most natural explanation to a young boy.

Father Patrick was the only person who could literally drive Andrew's father out of his favourite chair in the drawing-room. On Thursday afternoons, his father would not return to the office after lunch, but sit in the chair reading the latest bestseller. The moment Father Patrick's car arrived, he rose from his chair saying he had work to do and would remain closeted in his study until the priest drove away. Afterwards Andrew's father prepared for the cocktail hour.

Changing into an old sweater and slacks, he poured drinks in the dining-room, a double gin for himself, a smaller one for his wife, a lemonade for Andrew and any of the other children who happened to be at home. His father would reoccupy his chair and listen to a recounting of Father Patrick's latest problems with the parish funds, the bell-ringers, the grave-diggers, or the sacristan: all faithfully reported by his wife in a voice very similar to Father Patrick's. His father invariably interrupted at some point, 'Now what is it he wants? How much this time?'

His mother would suggest a figure. His father would hum and haw before agreeing. That was the signal for her to serve dinner.

On Sundays when Andrew's mother took the children to Mass, she placed a sealed envelope on the collection plate containing a cheque drawn on his father's account.

When his mother gave dinner parties the mere possession of money, particularly through trade, was not a guarantee of a place at her table. Andrew's parents were extremely careful never, by so much as a gesture, to emphasize their own wealth and social position. His father spoke calmly of a new Elizabethan age of British supremacy having arrived with the election of Mrs Thatcher. He was not, he would add, anti-German or even anti-Japanese, he was just pro-British.

Each parent had clearly defined responsibilities. Andrew's father supervised homework and acted as a liaison with school. He wrote the occasional sick notes and asked the questions at the parent–teacher meetings. He handed out pocket-money and checked how it was spent. His mother instilled the ideal that children did not speak out of turn, carried the shopping from the supermarket to the car on Saturdays, saved their pocket-money to buy Christmas presents, helped the elderly to cross the road, and never, ever, discussed family matters outside the home. Honour and respect for their parents was more than taught: it was embedded in the bone-marrow of each child.

His mother was in charge of religion. Offering herself as an example, she made sure the children never forgot they were Catholics. Their lives followed the church calendar. There was Mass every Sunday, Lent was a time of renouncing, of giving up sweets, television or going to the cinema, and reciting the rosary every evening.

The ancient names and rituals reached far into Andrew's developing mind and stayed there. Early on, his faith started to burn as steadily as altar candles. When he understood the act of contrition, he began to fret over the fate of non-Catholic friends. Father Patrick had made it clear that, outside the church, there was no salvation. The thought of his pals being consigned to hell merely because they were non-Catholic was an unsettling one for Andrew. He offered to teach especially close friends the act because Father Patrick had also said that, if it was made even by a non-Catholic at the moment of dying, the repentance would miraculously wipe away all past sins. Andrew saw this as one of the many benefits of Catholicism. It offered hope to everyone.

It was his mother who explained to him that her family was old Catholic, in the same way people were described by her as being old rich, like his father's family. His maternal great-grandparents had crossed to England when the Great Famine swept Ireland in the mid-1880s. They had money enough to establish themselves on the fringes of Victorian society, suppressing their effusive Irishness for a low-key English profile. By the time Andrew's parents married, ethnic identity had been reduced to his father's solemn promise that all the children would be raised as Catholic and encouraged to remain loyal to the true church.

The family tree on his father's side went back five centuries to the days of the Stuart kings: one ancestor had fought at Culloden, another went with Cromwell to brutalize Catholic Ireland. Since then, in time of war, it had provided officers and gentlemen to serve king and country, and women to act as nurses in field hospitals in the Crimea and Gallipoli, and abroad in the hospital ships of World War II, and later in Korea.

Its sons and daughters also continued to stock the Church of England with vicars and rectors, and provided wives for Anglican clergymen. Many, like Andrew's father, had reached the upper echelons of law, medicine, merchant banking, underwriting at Lloyds.

When they met at family weddings and funerals, his father's relatives sang lusty Protestant hymns and recited prayers. Andrew noticed his mother never joined in. He was twelve when she explained that each time she took the children to a Protestant church, she needed Father Patrick's permission, always granted, but only on condition that none of them participated in the worship and prayer. Since then he had always thought of Protestant churches as lacking in something.

Father Patrick had pointed out further differences. Other faiths did not have a red light burning on the altar as a constant reminder Jesus was present. Nor did they use incense and bells to signify reverence. Often the cross on a Protestant altar was empty as though the agony of his suffering was an embarrassment. Protestants had changed the Our Father and interpreted the Bible differently. In doing so they were denied the true basis of faith on whose living experience the church was founded. Only to Catholics, insisted Father Patrick, did God reveal himself totally.

Andrew's years at home had given him a good grounding in many things but, at his Protestant public school, he realized there had been a total absence of any form of sexual discussion. He had never heard his mother or father express a single sexual thought or seen either of them naked and it had never occurred to him whether or not they even made love.

At school sex was discussed among pupils with a frankness that Andrew found both shocking and exciting. Boys went out of their way to catch a glimpse of matron or one of the domestic help bending or reaching up, revealing a glimpse of a petticoat. These sightings fostered further speculations about the sexual behaviour of that particular member of staff. On visiting days, the potential of older sisters and the younger-looking of the mothers was also coolly considered. Andrew's initial confusion and uncertainty gave way to stimulation under the stirrings in his body.

At school he had been encouraged to place a high value on self-reliance, to recognize that, while there was a time and place for critical analysis and discussion, there must first be a proper bedrock of self-awareness. He was taught the process of how to acquire knowledge: for instance, that scientific truth and poetic truth did not need to be pursued along separate paths, but could be approached on a common front. His English tutor had summarized the search for truth by quoting Pasternak: Facts do not exist until man has put them into something of his own.

Andrew used the approach to explore his religion. He enjoyed discovering more of its ancient truths and the reassurance of its fundamental ideals, along with the clear-cut way it distinguished between good and evil, not relatively, but absolutely. No other institution in history, he believed, put such emphasis on continuity and authority as did the church, and the tone of its voice, the comforting institutional cadence, was steadfast down through the centuries. No other faith could say that; this was what made the security of being a Catholic so reassuring.

His five years at school provided him not only with an excellent education, but also enhanced his belief that Catholicism was the only faith by which he would really live. It was realistic in its understanding of the human predicament while never losing its optimism; its concept of original sin and salvation was an honest acceptance of human imperfection, coupled with a belief in rehabilitation through the grace of God. The redemption of entire communities, even the whole world, was possible.

His faith made sense of history because it went beyond history: faith was the only way to understand the endless struggle of the human spirit and the continuous frustration of its hopes. Faith was the answer to those who argued that, after 6000 years of civilization, humanity was as far as ever from creating a perfect human society. By using faith as a measurement, the failure of history not only became intelligible, it was essential and to be expected.

In the snuggery, raised, clipped voices interrupted his reverie. The Sandhurst cadets were arranging themselves before the bar for a photograph but could not persuade the barman to take it. Andrew offered to do so. Focusing, he stepped back a pace to include enough of the bar in the background to give the photograph a perspective. He held the cadets in frozen cheer for a moment, then snapped the shutter.

Smiling now, he waved them back into position and rewound the camera. He knelt on one knee and tilted the lens up, filling the viewfinder with only the tops of their heads and centred on the Pirelli calendar girl. As he pressed the button he remembered how, in his last term at school and captain of the house, he had smuggled nude photographs into his room.

He reached his room and closed the door, feeling mounting excitement. He was finally alone. By tradition no one, not even the housemaster, would enter uninvited. As house captain his room was furnished with a comfortable chair and bed, a desk, shelves filled with books and a closet. He had a hand basin, and carpet on the floor. He put his squash racquet in its plastic cover on the bed and removed his clothes. Next he washed his hands and dried them. He unzipped the racquet cover, removing the small flat package he had hidden there. He placed it on the bedside table and quickly slid the racquet and cover under his bed. Outside, dusk gathered.

The photographs were of the same naked girl. She was big and tanned, with heavy black hair hanging over one shoulder in a thick braid. Andrew raised his knees under the blankets, forming a slope on which he could display the prints. He felt himself become aroused thinking this was awful, just awful. He gathered up the photographs, put them back in their wrapping and hid them behind a row of books. Then he climbed back between the sheets feeling guilty over what he had done. He was still undecided whether to admit his action at his next visit to confession when he felt sleep claim him.

The barman shouted for last orders. Andrew edged himself through the throng remembering another night in another bar when he had told Jane about the photographs. She'd laughed and said teasingly he shouldn't be such a prude, that there was nothing wrong in achieving solitary fulfilment. She had quoted a Kinsey statistic, that more than half the American student population masturbated, adding she regularly took care of herself.

Until then he had always thought of masturbation as sinful. She had laughed and quoted Wilhelm Reich, the Austrian psychiatrist, who had argued the church more than any other organization, was guilty of perpetuating dangerous nonsense about sex among the young.

He had not been able to think of a rebuttal and had listened, fascinated, as Jane expounded Reich's theory that sexual pleasure was positively healthy.

Finally she had looked at him and said: 'Take me to bed. It'll be good.' He had, and it was.

Jane had introduced him to the writings of Kerouac, Burroughs and Ginsburgh and made him read Karen Horney. She had surprised him in other ways during their first months together. He had never thought it possible to have a totally open sexual relationship where anything could be discussed. She had shown him how to be free about everything, with their bodies as well as their words. She taught him more about love than anyone else: how to make it, how to express it, how to recognize it. She was not merely sensual, but used each sexual episode to initiate him into new experiences. Afterwards, she would discuss the experience openly, oblivious even of who was listening or where she was.

Jane was taking a degree in psychology and English literature and had been captivated by D.H. Lawrence's masterpiece, *Lady Chatterley's Lover*. They had sat in pubs all over town and later, when they closed, in all-night cafes, and still later in her bed while she analyzed the symbolism of the story of the frustrated wife of an impotent aristocrat who bore her gamekeeper's child and endured the stigma of society. Lawrence, she asserted, was concerned to end unhealthy sexual puritanism.

She told him there had been other men and he probed for details, saying there must be no secrets between them. He tried to convince himself that once he knew all of her past, it could be excised from his mind. It was, of course, impossible: he would often look at her and imagine other men enjoying the feel of her skin, the taste of her lips, the sounds of her love-making, and only too well he remembered the night when, while lying beside her in the darkness, he began to question her once more about her past.

Her hand had tightened on his. 'You really should stop this. Just because I've been honest with you, it doesn't mean you have to go on grilling and judging me. I'm tired of it. My past is mine and nothing to do with you. My body was mine to give then, and I wanted to give it, as I am happy to give it to you. But you don't own me and I don't owe you anything. You'll either have to live with our jealousy or we can't go on.'

He had held her close and whispered. 'You do really love me, don't you?' She said she did over and over again as they made love and, for the moment, he had believed her totally. Just as he believed he should not feel guilt over what had happened to him in Hong Kong.

As Andrew walked with Tim through Kowloon, he continued to explain to his cousin why he disliked Australia. 'It's impossible to find a church that's open when you want it. It's rather like their drinking hours. Religion is crammed into a few hours each day. A funny place.'

Tim shrugged. 'I wouldn't know, old boy. I never go to church.'

Andrew had tried not to show his shock.

His trip was a gift from his father for leaving public school with enough marks to enter university. Several had immediately offered him a place. Instead he had accepted one from the Army. It would pay for his university education in return for a promise to go on to Sandhurst for a short-service commission.

Before entering university his father said he should travel. Family connections had been mobilized to provide a series of havens around the Pacific Rim in the homes of bankers, lawyers, brokers: solid, dependable men like his father.

Andrew had thought Tim was a similar example of rectitude until he suggested a visit to Madame Kwok's.

After dinner Tim's chauffeur had driven them there. The entrance to Madame Kwok's was brightly painted and festooned with photographs of the occupants; women of all ages and nationalities.

Madame Kwok pointed to Andrew. 'He first time. Pay membership.' Tim pulled out his wallet and handed over Hong Kong dollar bills. Madame Kwok motioned them to a couch, addressing Tim again. 'He must buy drink. All new members buy drink.' Tim handed over more money. Madame Kwok shuffled to the bar returning with two open bottles of beer and glasses. She poured the drinks, continuing to only address Tim. The house had a new attraction: Korean and barely out of school. Would Tim like her? No, he wanted his usual girl, Susie. He indicated Andrew, lapsing into the crone's pidgin language, 'New girl for him.' Tim handed over more money.

'New girl cost muchee more. New girl always cost muchee more, Tim-san.' Her tone was reproachful, as if Tim should not need to be told. 'Ten dollar more.'

It's like buying cattle, thought Andrew, watching as Tim gave her a further bill and Madame Kwok shambled from the room. There was the sound of giggling in the corridor. He wondered if he could leave now without offending Tim. Madame Kwok returned with two girls and Tim approached the taller and older one. The second girl, wearing a blouse and skirt, stood smiling, eyes averted, beside Madame Kwok. 'Girls like drink,' pronounced the old woman. Tim ignored her. 'You like drink now – or later, Susie?' Susie smiled. 'Whatever Tim-san likes.'

'Tim-san like drinkee later.' He grinned at Andrew and took Susie's hand.

Madame Kwok pushed the other girl towards Andrew.

'This Miki. Very fine girl.'

Miki stood before Andrew.

'Do you speak English?' he asked.

She giggled.

'Koreans all speak English,' interrupted Susie. 'Americans teach them all sexy words.'

Tim laughed. 'Not as many as I taught you, Susie.' He slid his hand inside her blouse.

'You teach good sexy words.' Susie laid her head against his shoulder, allowing one hand to brush across the front of his trousers. Andrew was shocked at the display. He looked at Miki and asked how old she was.

'For God's sake, Andrew, you're only going to screw her – not marry her!'

Susie guided Tim out of the room whispering in his ear.

Andrew turned and faced Miki. 'You like a drink?'

'You like drink?' She giggled and sat beside him, placing a hand on his thigh. 'Or maybe you like makey love first?'

Suddenly he wanted it over with. He wanted to end this business, not because of a physical need – he felt even less excited than he had staring at the photographs in his room at school. Just to end it.

Miki stood up, holding his hand. He felt powerless to resist. The room was at the end of the corridor. Miki closed the door behind them and gently pushed him onto the bed. She poured water from a pitcher into a bowl and washed her hands. Smiling at Andrew, she started to undress, unbuttoning and removing her blouse to reveal small firm breasts. Andrew looked away as she wriggled out of the skirt and stood before him naked, smiling and waiting.

He struggled to his feet and plunged into the corridor. Madame Kwok stood there. Miki was in the bedroom door, naked, finger in her mouth, looking more vulnerable and childlike than ever. Andrew fished in his pocket, handed Madame Kwok a wad of dollars, pulled open the door and ran down the stairs.

At nineteen, Andrew had been older than most of the first-year university students and his six months in the Far East had given him poise. Within his first weeks he made a sizeable circle of friends. One evening Rose drifted into his group while he was recounting his experience at Madame Kwok's, giving it an allure it never possessed. Rose sat, transfixed. Finally she asked him if he had not been frightened. He didn't understand and she explained.

'You know, frightened of catching something; the clap, you know!' Her flat Midland vowels gave the words an aggressive edge. He smiled and shook his head. Afterwards they strolled back to the halls of residence and discovered they lived in the same building. Her room was on the floor above his.

It took three more days before she invited him up. She asked him to tell her what really happened at Madame Kwok's and when he did, she looked at him with a triumphant little smile. She reached for him and pulled him to her.

They regularly made love for a whole year, sometimes in his room, more often in hers. But when they were not in bed, she seemed bored with him. Gradually he became aware she was seeing other students. When he confronted her, she admitted she had slept with several, adding that part of the fun of being at university was to be sexually adventurous.

Soon afterwards Jane had entered his life. He had been returning from delivering an essay to his tutor when he saw her standing by the notice-board outside the cafeteria. It was festooned with the endless trade of campus life. She said she was looking for a bicycle. He carefully scanned the board. There were none on offer. He said he had a car and would be happy to drive her anywhere. She laughed. He noticed she had perfect teeth and a dimple in her left cheek. Her eyes were the darkest of blue, almost black, in vivid contrast to her fair eyebrows and hair. He asked her name.

She looked at him, hesitating. 'Jane.'

'How about going for a coffee?'

She shook her head. 'Sorry. I never touch coffee or tea.' She started to walk away.

He called out. 'How about beer?'

She turned, looking at him. 'Beer's fine.'

'How about tonight?'

'Sure, pick me up at seven.'

Jane gave him her address.

One of the first things she had said was that she could not stand anyone who wasn't able to hold their drink. That night she matched him pint for pint and insisted on paying her share. After driving her home he parked outside her flat. She turned to him.

'Andrew, I think we should both understand something.'

He tried to sound nonchalant. 'You're married. Your husband's a millionaire indulging a whim to put you through university. If you flunk he'll buy the place for you. The story of my life – filled with beautiful women with rich husbands.'

'Be serious.'

'I am, believe me, I am. You've got that married look all over you.' He was determined to be flippant.

'Please, listen. If what I think is going to happen, does happen, I want you to understand certain things.'

'Like what?'

'Like not prolonging something beyond its natural span.'

'That sounds a trifle premeditated.'

'Maybe. But it's easier to be honest. I'd like to go to bed with you. I suspect you'd like to go to bed with me. But if it doesn't work for me, I don't want to go on. Sex is very important to me. I enjoy it. That's the way I am. If I'm not satisfied, I don't want you to feel bad, just accept that my needs are different.'

She led him from the car directly to her room, closing the curtains and lighting candles. Then she went to the bathroom, telling him to undress. He sat naked on the double bed wondering which side she slept on, and trying not to think who had previously occupied the other side. She stood in the doorway, her body even darker in the candlelight. She walked across to him, bent and asked him to kiss her breasts. Then she gently guided his head down to her stomach, all the time softly telling him what she felt. Night after night they expended their passions on the bed.

Six weeks to the day after they met, he vacated his room and moved in with her. The flat was overflowing but she didn't mind. A month later he came back from a tutorial to find her in the throes of packing. She paused long enough to tell him they were moving to a new apartment. She had spotted it on the notice-board only that lunch-hour.

The new apartment covered the entire ground floor of what had been a Victorian merchant's mansion. It took them one week to clean the place and another to give it the stamp of their own personalities.

The bedroom was the focal point of their lives. Not only did they consummate their relationship every day in the bed, but they frequently ate there, propping pillows against the wall, with plates of buttered toast and mugs of warm milk. On Sundays they studied in bed, scattering their books on its surface. After a few weeks Jane found a pair of square Indian brass trays which became ideal writing tables while in bed.

At first he secretly counted the weeks they were together, then the months. After a year he finally stopped, believing it would go on forever. Their families knew of their liaison and, if they did not openly approve of their living arrangements, they raised no objections. They went on holiday together to France and Italy, returning to the apartment ready for a new term, displaying mementoes from their vacation: posters, sea-shells and figurines for the fireplace mantle and alcove shelves. Every day he thought the place took on a deeper feeling of permanence.

The letter changed everything. It came in an envelope officially franked with a Whitehall postmark. It was waiting when he returned from a tutorial. She handed him the envelope as soon as he walked in. Then, without a word, she turned and went to the bedroom, closing the door behind her. He read the letter quickly, then more slowly. There was no doubt. At the end of this term, his last, the Army wanted him to report to Sandhurst.

That night they had gone out and gotten slightly drunk. In bed he asked her to marry him. She looked at him thoughtfully and replied, in the gentlest of voices, that she didn't want to marry anyone just yet. He said he would wait until she finished her studies; they could marry then. Jane said nothing. He tried again. could he hope that she would let him propose to her when she felt ready? She laughed and said he sounded positively Victorian. He would not let go, saying he really meant it. She switched on her bedside light and sat up in bed, hugging her knees.

'Andy, you're going to be away for quite a while. I'm still young. I said at the beginning I didn't want there to be any misunderstanding. I need a man around me. I just wish it could go on being you.'

'What are you saying?'

She patted his face. 'Only not to be so pushy. Let's just wait and see.'

Next morning he left at dawn. Jane had been cool and almost distant. He had offered to call her as soon as he arrived at Sandhurst, and she said he could try but she might not be in. He'd finally reached her at midnight and she said she had just come in from visiting friends and was too tired to talk.

Andrew saw the barman staring at the snuggery door, irritated. The cadets had returned, one of them calling loudly. 'Cigarettes, old boy. Out of cigarettes.' They propped themselves against the bar, plonking coins on the counter.

The barman said he was closed.

'That's all right, old boy. We won't tell anybody.' The cadet's voice was slurred.

'Sorry. It's after hours.'

The tallest of the cadets leaned across the bar, his voice aggressive. 'Barman, we've just asked for cigarettes. There's no law against selling cigarettes outside licensing hours. Now make up your mind. Sell them to us – or send for your boss. Don't just stand there, do something. Move, man! Move!'

Andrew was on his feet and walking to the bar. He tapped the tall cadet on the shoulder. 'Stop throwing your weight around, soldier.'

The cadet turned and stared at him. 'Who asked you to butt in, old chap?'

Andrew looked at him carefully. 'I'm not your old chap. And nobody asked me to butt in. But just stop throwing your weight around. All right?'

Another cadet spoke. 'You can't talk to officers and gentlemen…'

'Then behave like officers and gentlemen.' Andrew turned to the barman. 'Can they have cigarettes?'

'Sure. They've only got to be polite.'

Andrew addressed the tall cadet. 'I believe that's clear.' Then he turned and walked back to his seat wondering if they thought he was still in the Army.

'You're doing what?' his father gasped.

'I'm getting out. I can't stand all the pointless rigmarole.'

It was his mother who broke the stunned silence. 'But, my dear, what will you do?'

His father interrupted. 'None of our family have ever bought themselves out of anywhere.'

'I'm sorry, Dad. I guess there always has to be a first.'

'Sorry! It's not a damned matter of being sorry, you know! The Army's paid for your degree. Surely you owe it something?'

'Lots of students change their minds. The Army accepts it's a high-risk business, investing in education.'

'Oh, really.' His father poured himself another double gin. Fortified, he returned to the issue. 'You just can't resign after three weeks. Good God, people have been shot for less in war.'

His mother tried to be placatory. 'Nobody's going to shoot Andrew because he wants to give up the Army.'

His father searched for a culprit. 'It's Jane, isn't it? She's behind this?'

'No, Dad. She's not. She doesn't even know.'

'Jane's in Mexico, dear,' said his mother.

'Mexico! Good God, whatever for?'

Andrew didn't know.

Before leaving she had sent him a short note with her itinerary. Beside each entry was a hotel address and a telephone number. At the bottom of the note she had scrawled. 'Call me if you like.'

He called her twice, in Mexico City and Panama City, and each time the flat voice of the operator said she was not available. On the third occasion he had spoken to the hotel receptionist in Caracas who had promised to leave a message to say he telephoned.

'I suppose you're going to join her?' his father mixed a third drink.

'No. When I leave the Army I'm going to do some voluntary work.'

'Voluntary work? Good God, what on earth have you in mind?' His father stared at him in disbelief.

'Well, something in the Third World. Working with the poor. I'm sure Father Patrick will know of something.'

There was another lengthy silence. 'I'm not against charity. Far from it. But do you think it is the best use of your years at university, to bury yourself in some desert or jungle? Do you really?' asked his father.

'Albert Schweitzer did, dear,' said Andrew's mother.

'Andrew is not Schweitzer. I think even he will accept that.'

'It won't be forever, Dad. Lots of young men do it.'

His mother made her final point. 'Only the other day the Pope said more are needed to help.' She looked at Andrew. 'I think that's a very selfless idea, giving yourself to the service of Christ.'

Later he had spoken to his mother alone and for a long time. She had sent for Father Patrick who, in turn, had listened carefully before arranging for him to see the bishop. He had asked searching questions before coming to a decision.

The barman turned to Andrew after they watched the cadets leave.

'Snotty bastards.'

'It's the system. It makes them like that,' Andrew said.

The barman shrugged. 'Time the system was changed.'

'Yes.'

196

'I hated the Army. Two years on the Rhine. Best thing was the beer.' He looked at his watch. 'Like another pint?'

'Thanks.'

The barman walked back to the bar and began to draw a beer.

Suddenly Andrew understood what was happening to him.

He asked the barman for something on which he could write. The man brought him an old menu with his beer. On the back of the menu Andrew scribbled rapidly.

'10.40 p.m. Sunday. Heart beating furiously. In my head a sudden refrain. God wants me. God wants me to become a priest. I've found him. He wants me to become a priest. Very strong feeling. Very positive. Very clear. I've been called.'

Clutching the menu, Andrew rose to his feet and hurried from the bar ignoring the barman calling him back to drink his beer.

CHAPTER TWELVE

Goodbyes

The rectory Father Patrick shared with a curate stood in the church grounds. The widowed middle-aged housekeeper, who lived in a self-contained flat at the back, opened the front door to Andrew.

He had never expected the process of deciding if he was suitable to become a priest would be so thorough. 'It's worse than positive vetting in Whitehall,' his father had said after a month. 'Barmy, if you ask me, all this checking-up just to wear a dog-collar for the rest of your life!'

The housekeeper showed him into the same room as before, filled with over-stuffed furniture and shelves crammed with books with titles such as *The Religious Experience*, *The Individual and His Religion*, and *The Two Sources of Morality*. On a sideboard were copies of *The Journal for the Scientific Study of Religion*, *The Universe*, and *The Tablet*. On a side table a tray was set with cups, sugar-bowl and a creamer. Andrew was struck again by the faint but unmistakable aroma of burnt incense and candle-wax. For the past six weeks the cloying odour had greeted him as he arrived to answer questions, fill in forms and, finally, to collect a sealed letter to take with him to the bishop's palace.

The bishop hummed and hawed, cleared his throat and peered over his glasses, hesitant and distant.

'You had this *feeling*? Something had happened to you? This feeling of wanting to become a priest? You are certain that is what you felt? Can you tell me again, exactly, what you think you felt? Perhaps your surroundings might have played a part? Tell me exactly – what were you doing and thinking when you had this... this feeling?'

He leaned back in his chair and carefully inspected Andrew. Over the credenza along one wall hung a life-size colour photograph of the bishop greeting the Pope. Behind the desk, in a massive carved gilt frame, was a painting of Our Lady signed by the artist. The questions about what happened in the bar continued to be pressed.

'Why did you write it down? Is that what you normally do... write things down? Do you... perhaps fear you cannot remember exactly? How can you be certain what you wrote down was what you felt? Have you ever had a similar experience?'

The bishop's stubby fingers stuffed flakes of tobacco into his pipe. Father Patrick had warned that the smoke from the pipe was a sign of his Grace's feelings. When it rose steadily, the bishop was prepared to accept something. When it escaped in rapid bursts, he did not. He drew the flame into the bowl, sucking noisily, and the smoke rose in an uncertain spiral, wreathing his cropped grey hair.

'Tell me once more... everything. What you were doing and thinking about when you had this... what do you call it?'

'I suppose some kind of supernatural experience, Your Grace. I don't really know what else to call it.'

The smoke from the bishop's pipe spread, filling the air space between them with a pungent smell.

'Perhaps not supernatural. No... certainly not that. That would never do. But... interesting. Take me over it again, step by step.'

Andrew did.

A week later came another summons to the bishop's palace. This time he was shown into a small room, bare of furnishings except for two armchairs, a strip of carpet between them and a photograph of the Pope on the wall.

The monsignor was middle-aged, bespectacled and portly. He explained he was also a clinical psychologist. His eyes were bloodshot and he needed a haircut. He invited Andrew to sit down.

'Now, Andrew, let me tell you that I'm not unfamiliar with the sort of experience you have described. My task is to try and make linkage. To put what you say happened into the framework of a vocation. So let's go right back to the beginning.'

He had listened without interruption while Andrew once more described the incident. Then came the first questions.

'Do you think you could be striving too hard, Andrew, to connect what happened with your wish to be a priest? It's quite common, you know. And there's nothing wrong, as such, with that. Everybody has to have a motive, don't you agree? All I'm wondering is whether you've placed what happened into a rather over-dramatic framework? It happens to lots of people. They undergo something and say that it is responsible for something else. But the linkage isn't always there. That's the problem.'

Andrew watched the monsignor clasp his hands as if to restrain himself from saying more.

'It really did happen the way I said. Although I know that the mind can play all sorts of tricks.'

The monsignor nodded. 'Quite right, Andrew. But you don't seem to have left anything out.' He was smiling and reassuring. 'I have seen your medical history. Nothing to worry us there. You're physically as fit as a fiddle.'

Andrew sensed he had come through another test. Nevertheless, the monsignor's next words surprised him. 'I see history is your subject. I must say, your thesis on the correlation between faith and historical truth is intriguing.'

Father Patrick had asked to read it, but had not even hinted he had passed it to the monsignor. He began to ask questions about Andrew's views on Nietzsche, contrasting the Apollonian kind of religious belief with the ecstasy and excitement of the Dionysian. He wondered whether Andrew would accept that very often a specific religious experience was based upon mental conflict and a feeling of inadequacy.

'It's a bit like falling in love. Remember how Faust, before he meets Gretchen, and Romeo before he encounters Juliet, are both filled with discontent? Love for them is not a crisis but the way out of a crisis,' said the monsignor.

Andrew sensed that beneath the priest's gentleness was a toughness which could be unbending and uncompromising. His questions, often oblique on the surface, had a pattern. Each one was carefully placed in counterpoint to a previous one, the overall method designed to verify Andrew's responses and motivation.

'There is respectable evidence, Andrew, that sudden religious experiences often happen at a time when a person's personal life is disturbed. They frequently occur after a bereavement or when a relationship breaks down. We don't exactly know what causes this phenomenon, but it is definitely associated with an upset in the normal living pattern.'

He paused to give Andrew time to consider.

'I don't really think that applies to me. I've never felt a need to use religion as a substitute.'

The monsignor raised the question of religious experiences emerging from intellectual reasons.

'It's really far more common than most people believe. You'd be surprised how many people suddenly have what you could call a blinding flash. Something hits them and they say it's God. Many people have sat where you are now and insisted they have undergone a religious experience and want to throw out the window all their previous intellectualism. It's very dramatic. They believe something special has happened to them. It may well have, but it is not the basis for entering the priesthood.'

He peered at Andrew and asked if he thought it possible to classify his religious experience in the bar in a similar way?

Andrew said he did not think so, adding he was certain his experience had nothing to do with trying to find a creative solution to his life.

The monsignor asked Andrew to accept there are only two ways in which it was possible to eliminate anger, fear, despair and other undesirable feelings.

'One is to oppose them with an even more powerful opposite affection, an example being turning the other cheek. The other is to give up the struggle so that you don't care anymore. That part of the brain which deals with emotions goes on strike, creating a feeling of apathy.'

He paused, measuring his words, his eyes never leaving Andrew's face.

'There is ample proof that when that takes place, happily usually only temporarily, people can undergo a sudden religious experience.'

Andrew quietly rejected the possibility in his case.

The monsignor probed into his relationship with his family, his life at school and university, and gradually focused on his affair with Jane. St Augustine, he murmured, prior to entering the priesthood, had been pressed by his mother to give up his mistress. Had Andrew's parents opposed his relationship with Jane?

Andrew answered unhesitatingly. 'No, not at all. They were very good about it.'

The monsignor continued with a reminder that Pascal was hopelessly in love with a woman until he was drawn to the celibate life by what is now accepted as a highly emotional conversion. St Catherine of Genoa and Madame Guyon had both been insecure in their relationships with men before they claimed mystical experiences had led them to the church.

'Man's extremity, you could say, is God's opportunity. The question is, do you think your experience is in any way a response to Jane?'

Andrew finally admitted to the physical emphasis she had set on their relationship.

The monsignor silently considered this before asking if Andrew now felt a sense of guilt about his sex life with Jane.

Andrew replied that, truthfully, he did not know.

'What exactly does that mean?'

'Well, I still love her. But it's different now. I don't feel possessive anymore. I know she is part of something that has gone.'

'How can you be so sure?'

'I see her from a different perspective. I've thought about it. I've probably thought of nothing else. But I still have this overwhelming conviction I have a vocation.'

The monsignor pondered.

'You really mean that? In my experience there's always an element of the repenting sinner about so many of those who have a sudden religious experience. The attitude that they're going to give up something for God. It's very human. The danger is that they actually want everybody else to give up what they're giving up. Are you familiar with the story of St Bernard?'

Andrew shook his head and the priest explained that the fervour of the saint's religiosity had been so overpowering that when he preached, mothers had hidden their sons and wives their husbands in case they were lured away into new-found celibacy.

'He broke up so many homes that the abandoned women formed themselves into a sort of nunnery.' He smiled. 'I'm not suggesting you're another St Bernard, or that Jane will go into a convent. All I'm trying to explore is your emotional responses. It's a difficult life being a priest, probably more so today than ever before. And it's expensive to train someone and then lose them afterwards. We try to be certain, as far as possible, from the outset.'

The monsignor probed him about his attitude towards guilt, anxiety and suggestability and what created emotional turmoil in him. Andrew explained about his visit to Madame Kwok's and the sadness he felt that his father did not embrace the Catholic Church.

The priest spoke about Walpole's detachment from religion before returning to the central theme of the discussion, this time musing whether Arthur Koestler, daily awaiting death in a Spanish prison during the Civil War, was right to believe he underwent a religious experience.

'And what do you make of Tolstoy's experience? His call to God being preceded by suicidal impulses and other trauma. How do you see that?' asked the monsignor.

Andrew responded by saying he had no reason to doubt the validity of Koestler's claims, and that while Tolstoy's conversion to Christianity was highly unorthodox, he had, nevertheless, been sufficiently strong to allow him to embrace the life of Soviet peasants as a lasting cause.

The monsignor put a final question. 'If you are accepted, are you prepared to also accept that old ties, where they exist, must be severed? That, in effect, you must pass a sentence of death upon everything which is of this life? Can you do that?'

Andrew had replied. 'I can't be certain. That would be arrogant. But I will try with all my power because I really feel God has asked me to serve him.'

A few days later he had been summoned again to see Father Patrick to answer more questions. What did God mean to him? How did he see the Christian humanism of the Holy Father? Did he agree that the celestial manifestations of faith were evidence of a growing presence of God in the world? What did he say to the argument that respecting truth meant respecting and fearing God? Did he accept that infallibility was a truth of last resort, the ultimate deterrent to error? Could he recognize that conception, birth, marriage, procreation and death, were all contingent upon each other, impossible to isolate, and that to desacrilize one would mean doing the same to all? What role did he think the church had to play in political commitment? How did he see the real perspective of Jesus' mission, and how would he interpret it?

Andrew had discussed them from the standpoint that this was the age of perplexity, that many religions and theologies offered different ways to escape from the real necessity of thinking about the meaning of life and how it should be lived. The Pope's humanism was uncompromising in his affirmation of mariology as a restatement of a fundamental truth of the church; that papal infallibility was in danger of being excluded by the manipulation of faith; that birth, marriage, procreation and death were given a vicarious glamour which, in itself, was symbolic of the untidiness of living. The message of Jesus was as true as ever: Baal was alive and well and the church must use every means, political and spiritual, to combat these influences.

'For me, Father Patrick, the mission of Jesus is to end the dilemma of all those who do not know how to live. The words of Jesus are not interpretation of "a truth". They are the truth. They are not to be thrown away when we think we have achieved some goal. They are our goal. We should try to live by them, just as Jesus lived by his words.'

Father Patrick stared, silently and fixedly, at Andrew for a long, long moment. When he spoke, his voice was devoid of any theatricals.

'My boy, this is quite remarkable. Please go home and write it down for me.'

Then, finally, there was another meeting. Andrew turned towards the door as Father Patrick walked in, holding a coffee pot.

'Make yourself comfortable, Andrew. We've lots to talk about.'

Carefully putting down the pot, the priest went to the desk and raised its roll-top. It was stuffed with papers. Father Patrick rifled through them, calling over his shoulder.

'Be patient! Drink your coffee! I have news!'

He finally turned, two pieces of paper in his hand, waving them dramatically at Andrew.

'My Lord Bishop has written. And his Eminence.'

He pulled down the roll-top and walked stiff-legged from the desk, reading to himself. He stopped before the couch and tapped the letters almost with a reverence.

'They have both written to say you have secured a place at the Gregorian University in Rome, one of the most prestigious in the Catholic world.'

Father Patrick watched Andrew's every reaction. Satisfied, he continued.

'I still have a few questions of my own.'

Some invisible fist buried itself in Andrew's stomach, the unexpected always produced this feeling.

'Yes, Father.'

Father Patrick scanned one of the letters.

'My Lord Bishop is still concerned about the validity of your experience in the bar, my boy. His Grace feels, and I must agree with him, that no one who is totally honest with himself can ever pinpoint the exact moment he experiences the call to God. No one is given a vocation in a moment. I think you should see what happened as the final extension of a growing awareness of what you want to do.'

'Maybe, but that was the moment I really felt I needed to serve him.' Andrew plunged on. 'I'm quite sure that what I felt, I wrote down. It was a very clear feeling. God called me.'

Father Patrick raised a hand dramatically.

'But, my boy, you've clearly been thinking of this all your life. It isn't something sudden. It's been there all the time.' His eyes stared unblinkingly. 'Creation, in a sense, is vocation's first moment. God leads us into the world. He chooses our path in life. If you see it like this, what happened in the bar can take on a proper perspective.'

'I understand what you're saying but I can't find a logical way to fit it into my experience.'

Father Patrick's voice quickened. 'I don't think it serves any useful purpose to say your whole life from now on is going to be based on some blinding revelation in a pub.'

'Why not, Father? It's what I think did happen.'

The priest sighed. 'In recommending you, both his Grace and his Eminence would like to think that there is a more solid foundation to your vocation. It's always better to know, my boy, that God's been there from the outset, steadily nudging you along. That's the way the church likes to see its priests. Just because Saul was transformed into Paul, does not mean we all need such psychodrama. I'm sure you can see that.'

That evening, Andrew sat in his father's study and was again reminded how the furnishings complimented the man: they had the same solid, dependable look, built for comfort rather than elegance.

The wall-space not filled with books was covered with the memorabilia of his father's life. A faded print in the arms of his nanny. A group photograph of his school's Cricket First XI; his father, unmistakable in the front row, staring solemnly into the camera, bat between his knees. He had been a fine player and Andrew had acquired his skill. A formal portrait of him, dressed in mortar-board and gown, on the day he qualified. A picture taken when he was commissioned into his regiment, stiffly erect, a swagger stick under his arm. His father had commanded an artillery unit in North Africa, Italy, and across the Rhine, collecting a Military Cross and bar for valour under fire in 1944.

Between the photographs were trophies: stuffed pike and perch in display cases, and a shotgun, its hammer long removed. Beneath was a framed inscription: '1937: bagged 280 pairs of grouse and 127 pairs of pheasant.'

His father stood beside a drinks trolley, crammed with bottles of vintage whiskys and liqueurs.

'What'll it be?'

Andrew asked for a port.

'Pack a bottle or two to take with you. You can't buy this stuff in Rome.'

'Thanks, Dad.'

His father poured the drinks, handed one to Andrew and motioned for him to sit down opposite him.

'Long ago, Andrew, I learned that attempts to change the opinions of others are older than the development of speech. Well, I'm not going to make a speech.'

'Dad, I know it isn't easy for you.'

'It isn't.' He sipped his gin. 'It isn't, and it hasn't been. I still think this is a fad.'

'Dad! I don't think…'

'No, no. Let me finish. I said no speeches. But at least let me have no interruption. I thought at the beginning it was a fad. I still think so. Nothing you have said or done can convince me otherwise. I'm personally very sad about that. In a way I wish I could be convinced that you know what you are doing.'

'I do, Dad. I really do!'

'You think you do. That's the problem. That's what's so especially sad about you going off like this –'

'Dad –!'

'Please, Andrew. Let me *finish*. I've tried, but I can't really buy this idea about giving a son to God.'

At university he had gone with Jane to listen to an experimental psychologist lecture on attitude changes. There had been a lot of talk about unconscious mental mechanisms, responses to frustration and reactions to adversity. He had thought then, as he did now, that neither Freud nor anyone else could have made headway with his father.

Andrew tried again. 'Rome's not the end of the world, Dad.'

'It's the end of my world, Andrew.' His father pointed vaguely towards the desk and high-back chair. 'I always had in mind these would be yours one day. It would have made me very proud to see you come into the business.' He shifted in his chair. 'To marry and have a family.'

'Dad, I know it's hard to see, but God has a definite plan for each one of us. He wanted you to become a broker…'

'I do wish you'd try not to sound like Father Patrick! This whole idea of some divine planning authority is just too Catholic for me. It really is. I'm afraid I can't take on board the idea of God being up there with a list, ticking off what he wants you all to be. Really, Andrew, that's a bit much.'

Andrew sat staring at his glass, thinking: *He's hurting. I'm hurting him. But I can't turn back, not now.*

'Dad, nobody's talked me into this. Quite the opposite. They checked me out very carefully.'

'I'm sure. It can't be every day they get a priest from a mixed marriage. I bet someone was a little worried that you could still have a touch of good old Protestant England in your genes…'

Andrew knew his father saw his Protestant faith as a kind of armour against all sorts of external pressures. And, just as he abhorred Communism for its ideological effectiveness, so his father suspected Catholicism for similar reasons. He believed both systems operated through carefully structured hierarchies.

'Don't try and tell me it's no different from doing another university course, Andrew. The priesthood…' His father's voice trembled slightly. 'Where do you expect to end? There's only one Pope and a handful of cardinals. Pretty limited chance of getting promoted from the ranks, if you follow my meaning. You'll probably begin and end as a foot-soldier.'

His father downed his drink and poured himself another. He indicated Andrew's glass. Andrew nodded and his father refilled it, smiling thinly.

'You'll get used to having drinks poured for you. Look at Father Patrick. Your mother has waited on him hand and foot for years. Can't think why, unless she hopes it will give her a pass to heaven.'

'Dad! Please don't go on like this. It really doesn't help, you know.'

'It's purging. My version of your confession. You're off in a couple of days, and I want you to know how I feel. You think I won't miss you? You think it's easy to accept that I'll never get to meet your wife or hold your children?' His voice was suddenly husky. 'You think that's easy, Andrew? You'll never know the pain I feel now. You've chosen a life that excludes my hopes.'

Andrew blinked back the wetness in his eyes.

'Have you told Jane?'

'Not yet. I missed her in El Salvador. I've booked a call to her in Bogota.'

His father grunted. 'It wouldn't have worked, you know. You and her. She's much too independent. But she's going to miss you, too. We're all going to miss you.'

'I'm only a couple of hours away by plane.' Andrew tried to sound reassuring.

'That's not the point, Andrew. Can't you see? Going off to be a priest is not like joining the Army or going abroad to work. It's supposed to be forever. Do you really know what you're giving up? Not just a chance to make a real go of things in this world, but a lot more.'

He stared moodily at the trophies on the wall.

'Listen, you're twenty-four. For the last three years you've been living with Jane. Your mother and I weren't exactly wild at the idea, but we said, this is the age we live in. You've had a full relationship with Jane. How do you think you're going to cope with the rest of your life? Have you really thought of that? Wouldn't you think it is the sort of matter Father Patrick would talk to you about, though I bet he didn't.'

His father had never before discussed any aspect of sexuality with him.

'You're wrong, Dad. He spent a whole morning explaining that the call to Christ does not magically negate a person's sexuality.'

'Without wishing to lower the level of this conversation, I think both of us are aware of the regularity with which priests fall by the wayside. Just because the Pope says you have to become celibate, you don't become a celibate.'

'That's absolutely right. But it isn't the Pope who says I have to be celibate. It's my choice. That's the difference. I make the choice voluntarily. Because I want to.'

Andrew paused, remembering Father Patrick explaining how insistent Pope John Paul was over the matter of sexuality and the priesthood, saying the pontiff had no patience with the old teachings that the body was merely a housing for the soul. John Paul believed the body had its own special importance and all its functions, especially those in the sexual area, were part of God's plan. For a priest, that involved recognizing there could be no half-measures on the issue. Celibacy was total. To fulfil his function, a priest must undertake sacrifice, complete and unconditional. Just as marriage was a gift of the spirit, demanding its own indication and devotion, so celibacy demanded a similar response. For those who accepted that it did not infringe on their humanity, it was a reminder that they were ready to follow him. Having that clearly in his mind, all else had fallen into place.

'Dad, the church doesn't want supermen. It wants men to understand what the struggle is all about, yet have the strength to face and overcome it. Men who recognize why they must be free from personal commitment, and who see celibacy not as some sort of restriction, but as a wider freedom.'

His father remained still and expressionless, his hands gripping his glass tightly.

'You would make a fine lawyer, Andrew.'

Andrew smiled. 'But, Dad, I could still be a lawyer. The church has trained lots of canon lawyers…'

His father looked weary and defeated.

'It won't be the same, Andrew. It won't be the same at all. We both know that.'

A knock on the door ended another painful silence. Andrew's mother said his call to Jane was on the line. He strode rapidly from the room.

'Hello, Jane.'

'Andy? How are you?'

'Fine. I tried to call you in Panama. They said you'd left for the airport.'

'The place was awful. Full of bugs and lecherous men.'

The telephone was in an alcove in the hall, with a bench-seat and ledge, beside it was a pad and pencil. Andrew jotted down: 'J. had bad time getting to Bogota.'

'I miss you, Jane.'

'I'm okay.'

He tried to translate the hesitation.

'Are you alone?'

'Of course, silly. In my room, lying on the bed. You dragged me from the shower.'

He tried to imagine her, 6000 miles away, to put flesh to the voice. There was static on the line.

'Jane?'

'I can still hear you.'

'Jane, I've got something to tell you.'

There was silence.

'Jane, can you hear me?'

'Yes.'

This time the hesitation was more definite.

'Jane, I'm going to be a priest.'

The only sound was a faint crackle on the line.

'Is that why you called?' Her voice was distant.

'I wanted you to know.'

'I already did. Giles dropped me a card a week ago.'

Giles worked in the university administration office. He would have known after the bishop's secretary wrote asking for information.

'I'm sorry I didn't write.'

'That's alright, Andy. I suppose it has been very hectic for you, getting everything fixed up.'

'Rather, yes.'

'Yes, well. I must say it is a surprise.'

'But you do understand?'

'Understand? That's a funny word. What is there to understand? I mean, you've made your decision. What more is there to say?'

'Will you come to Rome to see me?'

'To see you? I don't quite see why.'

'Jane. I still love you. Don't you understand that? It's just, well...'

He closed his eyes.

'I'm sure you've thought things through very carefully, Andy. I'm sure you have.'

The formality of her words hammered in his head. 'Jane...?'

'Yes?'

'I'm sorry.'

'What for? About us? There's no need to be. Not at all. You'll be a terrific priest. You really will.'

'I miss you, Jane.'

'Please don't say that. Please don't.' She laughed. 'You're lucky in a way, having settled your future.'

'What about you?'

'Oh, I'll be okay. Remember, I'm a survivor. I'll manage.'

'Come and see me in Rome. Please.'

The silence stretched. He wrote: 'Rome and J.'

'I'm not sure. I don't think it would be a good idea. It could be very unsettling. Remember what Milton said?'

He remembered the night they had sat in bed and read Milton. *Of man's first disobedience and the fruit of that forbidden tree.*

'I still want you to come.'

'We'll see, Andy. Listen. This must be costing your father a fortune. Why don't you drop me a line when you've settled in? Tell me what a seminary is like.'

'Will you write back?'

'Sure. I always answer letters. Have you forgotten?'

He had not. In their apartment, every Sunday afternoon without fail, she would answer all her correspondence, writing to her mother and friends long detailed accounts of what she called her week's adventures, enclosing snippets from newspapers and magazines which might amuse or interest them.

'Jane?'

'Yes?'

'I love you.'

'I'm glad, Andy. I really am glad for you. I know you won't believe this, but when I got Giles' card, I went into a church and said a prayer for you.'

'Oh, Jane. I feel awful. I just wish…'

'Andy, I think we should hang up now. I really do.'

'Jane…'

'Take care, Andy. I'll be thinking of you. I really will.'

He heard the click of her receiver being replaced and felt the tears on his cheeks.

The traffic was heavy as they drove to the airport. Andrew sat in the back of the Bentley, watching his father grip the wheel tightly, easing the car past another truck, constantly checking the mirror, staying exactly on the speed limit. His mother sat in the passenger seat, a light autumn coat over her dress and a hat on her head. His father looked at him in the mirror.

'Will they let you out for Christmas?'

'I don't know, Dad.'

'You make it sound as if Andrew's going into prison, dear. Father Patrick showed me pictures of the university. It's a lovely place.' His mother's voice was brave.

After checking in, they strolled to the bar, his father once more drifting towards sharpness, complaining about the poor service. His mother sat in forlorn dignity. Andrew felt close to tears for them both. Each in their own way seemed lost. He was relieved when the flight was called. His mother clutched Andrew by the arm and looked suddenly broken.

'Andrew, you really can come home any time. I'll keep your room for you. And write, won't you?'

'Of course, mother.' He bent down and kissed her on the cheek.

His father continued to stare woodenly at the line filing past passport control.

'Goodbye, Dad.' Andrew thrust out a hand.

'Goodbye, Andrew.' His father's grip was still strong for a man of his age.

CHAPTER THIRTEEN

Discussions

Andrew's room was on the top floor of the seminary and provided a breathtaking vista of the Roman skyline. But even here he had almost been deafened by the ringing of bells, peeling in mysterious discord, marking the canonical hours and calling the faithful to Mass. Only with dusk had the sonorous clanging ceased.

His first impression remained of his room. It could be a prison cell. The walls were dingy white and bare and the floorboards scarred. There was a wardrobe with a faulty lock and a desk, a hardback chair and shelves above the narrow bed. The mattress was lumpy and the bedsprings sagged. He wondered how many seminarians had tossed and turned on them before him. As soon as possible he would replace the mattress. He continued to unpack.

There was a knock on the door. A soutaned priest stood there. He introduced himself as Father William, Andrew's spiritual director.

'Just popped along to see how you're settling in. May I come in?'

'Of course.' Andrew stood aside.

Father William nodded approvingly. 'It takes some people a week to get sorted out. It looks like you've been here for ages.'

He walked over to the books Andrew had placed on the shelves.

'An interesting selection. Sheen's a bit simplistic, don't you think?' He indicated a copy of *Life of Christ*. 'I'm not sure he's got it absolutely right about Christ's attitude towards property.'

Beyond the open window the night sounds of the city had started: a renewed blare of scooters and car horns, the clamour of radios and television sets, street calls, raucous and repetitive. Father William closed the window.

He noticed Jane's photograph. 'Your sister?'

'A friend. We were at university together.'

'A pretty girl.' He continued to study the picture. 'I always encourage friendships with the opposite sex. It's a healthy way to remind ourselves about resilience.'

He turned and faced Andrew. 'I expect you know John Paul's vocation came late in life. He had girlfriends and knew all about the life any virile young man leads. But when he recognized his vocation, he embraced celibacy. I've always thought that because he had such a full life beforehand, it made it that much easier for him to stay in touch.'

Andrew wondered briefly what Jane would make of this priest. Perhaps she would find him too cool and casual in manner to be easily pinned down.

Father William sat on the chair, his hands on his knees.

'Andrew, these first weeks are going to be tough. For you. For us. But there's one area where, from the outset, neither you or we can afford to fail, and that is over the question of celibacy. There are no "ifs" or "buts". The Pope has made it clear to each of us he will enforce it with all the authority at his command. And he's right to do so.'

Andrew suspected the spiritual director had delivered the warning to each new student. Father William returned to the window, peering down into the seminary courtyard. He turned and leaned against the window-ledge.

'This place has seen a lot of changes, most for the good. But the one thing which has not changed is the rule of celibacy. Obeying it totally is the only way for us to have total stability and certitude in our lives. I always say our celibacy is a symbol, plain for everyone to see, telling the world our church has not lost its way. The standard of conduct and self-sacrifice we expect from our priests is not going to be lowered and never will be. I want you to always remember that. Our celibacy is a fixed point in an increasingly unstable world.'

Smiling, the director returned to sit on the chair. It was a quizzical smile, a Father Patrick smile. A priest's smile.

'You will be encouraged to debate everything. Liberation theology, moral theology, philosophy, objective values, what Socrates should have said to Thrasymachus. The ethics, rationalism and empiricism. You'll have them for breakfast, lunch and dinner. You'll get a dozen different interpretations to any point because we want you to have the broadest possible spectrum. I need not remind you our faith is designed to offer the best possible opportunity for salvation. Remember what Matthew said about the narrow gate which leads to eternity? In a sense we are the gatekeepers. And the only way we can keep the gate open for millions of others is to show them we will not fail them. That's why we don't debate celibacy here. We know it works. It goes with being a good gatekeeper.'

Father William stood in front of Jane's photograph. After a while he turned and bade Andrew goodnight.

Over the following weeks Andrew's diary continued to record his transition to religious life. He wrote it up every night before he went to bed. He made no pretence at style, concentrating on simply recording what he saw, thought, felt and experienced during the day.

The early entries described his exploration of the vast building that was now his new home. Its foundations had been laid when the Popes were in exile in Avignon. For centuries, apart for World War II, when it had served as a hospital, nothing had disturbed the monastic calm of its chapels, libraries, study rooms, refectory, and the majestic Corridor of Cardinals, its walls lined with portraits of the seminary's cardinal-protectors, some of whom had eventually become popes. At one end of the corridor was the office of the rector who ruled over the building and its occupants.

The seminary, for all its size and brooding presence, drew Andrew to comment: 'I expected it to be much holier than it is, much more Christian. Instead, it's somewhere between a residence hall and a barrack-room.' He had been equally candid about his fellow-seminarians. 'Some are straight from school, and rather provincial in their outlook. This is the first time most of them have been away from home and it shows. I don't feel I have much in common with them.'

He also felt uncomfortable at the way some of them fawned on their tutors and always seemed to spend hours on their knees in the main chapel, alternately bowing their heads or staring at the massive portrait of the Martyrs behind the altar, and almost swaying in rapture at the fresco of the Assumption covering the entire ceiling. At mealtimes they talked endlessly about how the Pope should solve the continuing crisis in Catholic theology.

Another entry recorded. 'An interesting question raised at lunch.

How is it possible for the church to accept much of Vatican II when Christ made it quite clear his kingdom is not of this world.'

And: 'Over dinner everyone was involved in a lively discussion on why there were no women apostles. I mentioned that Luke lists a group of women standing behind the apostles assisting in Jesus' ministry. That led to a wider discussion on the Pope's view that being a housewife is not a humiliation but a consecration. It strikes me as rather amusing to have such intense discussion without a woman present.'

Andrew had been enrolled in the Pontifical Gregorian University, the most influential seat of Catholic higher learning. Its Centre for Marxist Studies was rated among the best in the world. Its Bible Institute regularly sent graduates to the Hebrew University in Jerusalem for further scriptural research. Its department for the study of non-Christian religions was unrivalled. The faculty's professors included the world's leading authorities on philosophy, metaphysics, nicomachean ethics, monadology and pure reason. There were academics on the campus who spent their lives considering the words of St Thomas Aquinas, the meditations of Descartes and Locke's essays on human understanding.

Founded by the father of the Jesuits, St Ignatius of Loyola in 1551, the university had seen no fewer than sixteen of its students acclaimed Pope, almost 1000 become cardinals and close to 10,000 go on to wear the mitres of archbishops and bishops. Nine former graduates had eventually been canonized.

After his first day he wrote: 'Everybody calls it "The Greg". It's a few minutes from the seminary. It's built to last and massively ugly. There are 3000 students from all over the world. I have a Kenyan on one side and a Thai on the other. There are nuns too. Only a few of the tutors wear clerical garb. Most just have crosses in their lapels. Those who do dress formally, stand out; the Scots with their fancy cassocks and red sashes, Americans with blue braid on their soutanes. Many of the students are also casually dressed, lots of Levis and open necks. The exception is the Germans. They all turn up in crimson cassocks and round hats. An Italian told me they call them "*gambari*", crayfish. I was astonished to see how many students walk around openly with books by Kung, Schillebeeckx and other forbidden theologians. All lessons are in Latin or Italian.'

Andrew learned his tutors regularly travelled to scholarly conferences, spent their vacations in the deserts of the Middle East, searching for further evidence of the life and times of Jesus, or travelled deep into the Soviet Bloc to make further contact with Communist scholars and leaders of the Russian Orthodox Church. They had gone in search of Noah's Ark in Turkey and travelled to Portugal to ponder anew the miracle of Fatima. They had flown to Canada and the United States to see for themselves the stress on the church within the North American continent. They regularly visited Central and South America to debate with the exponents of liberation theology. They turned up in the bush of Southern Africa and the jungles of Asia seeking answers to complex questions of faith. When they returned to Rome their discoveries were often of sufficient importance for a faculty member to be called to the Vatican to brief a member of the Secretariat of State, or even on occasion, the Pope.

In his second week at the university Andrew made a judgement.

'The Greg is, in religious terms, mainstream liberal. But everybody says that the Pope is tightening the reins and his influence is very clear.'

His first encounter with papal thinking was the lecture which dealt with the concept that violence was the antithesis of truth and love. The lecturer emphasized the pontiff's belief that the anti-truth was as great an enemy as the anti-Christ, and that there was a direct connection between violence and verbal or written distortion. He offered the Lebanon and Northern Ireland as examples, saying that in both places violence had been allowed to establish its own immoral authority because of anti-truth. He told the class to write an essay on the subject.

Back in his room with a new mattress purchased from his monthly allowance from home, Andrew fashioned his arguments, frequently consulting a dictionary to check the precise meaning of a word in Italian. He had started to devote a part of each day to improving his fluency in the language.

He began his essay by quoting the Pope. 'Murder must be called by its proper name. Murder is murder. Political and ideological ideas do not change its nature. On the contrary, they are degraded by it.'

He launched into an assessment of the role the church could play in bringing peace to Belfast and Beirut. The substance of his argument was that the church should make clear that to relinquish violence did not mean having to remain silent against injustice. Any form of injustice must be challenged without fear of the consequences.

His essay was one the lecturer chose to criticize before the class. He said Andrew's views were far too absolute and failed to take account that very often direct challenge was self-defeating. He reminded them of another papal pronouncement. 'Injustice must never be exposed in a way which can provoke further violence.'

Part of Andrew's general studies were directed to understanding why the church was the only religious body which engaged in global diplomatic relations. He began to realize that, under the present pope, ecclesiastical diplomacy was now more active than probably ever before in its 400-year-old history.

His letters home reflected the developing pattern of his life. Descriptions of Rome were interspersed with copious references to his studies. The daily rituals of the Italians – their endless visits to espresso bars and siestas – were interspersed with thoughts about 'secularization being the dogma of defiance'.

He recounted how his professors discussed such abstract ideas as how to resist evil through good, Catholicism as a faith of choice, God as love, how the entire mystery of Jesus is summed up in two words: gentleness and humility. Throughout his letters a number of themes recurred: the meaning of life, the total authority of Christ, the need for personal faith, the benefit of silent meditation. He described how his tutors regularly warned about Satan. 'We were told again today that he is never more deadly than when he waits for those of us travelling the road into religious life.'

As the weeks passed, his observations became more acute. Theology generated its own special kind of emotionalism; one that a tutor had called *rabies theologorum*. In the view of that tutor, its victims now included Hans Kung, Jacques Pohier and the Flemish scholar, Edward Schillebeeckx. His tutor, who from time to time personally advised the Pope, had encouraged Andrew to judge for himself the extent of the errors committed by these theologians to see how far they had moved from the church's own theology.

For the next week, Andrew read far into the night about Schillebeeckx's view that existentialism, phenomenology and philosophical inspiration all blended together. Intellectually, Andrew saw its attractions.

The following Monday he sat in class, spellbound, as the professor demolished the Flemish theologian's arguments. He pointed out how far modernists including Schillebeeckx had departed from the theological essentials Thomas Aquinas had insisted upon by their refusal to make a complete submission of mind and heart to divine revelation. Instead they had launched an assault on the church's interpretation of the Gospels and on St John in particular, the apostle who most emphatically pressed the divinity of Jesus. In doing so, they challenged the sacred authority of the Pope.

The tutor paced before the class a slight figure with wispy hair and nervous darting eyes, quoting Schillebeeckx's words: '"I do not deny that Jesus is God, but I want to assert that he is also man, something that has been overlooked. It is precisely as man that he is important to us. But when you say that you are suspect."'

The tutor paused, his eyes glinting as he asked them to write an essay explaining why Schillebeeckx was wrong.

Andrew spent another week reading before he wrote that Schillebeeckx grounded his argument solely in systematic theology and took little account of traditional Catholic doctrine, and in particular, left no room for the role of the magisterium, the very heart of that doctrine. The scholar's thinking, for all its intellectual brilliance, in the end was a flawed fact because he presented an irresponsible dilution and simplification, bordering at times on a heretical one-sidedness that took no account of the teaching of the early fathers of the church. 'The modernists seem to be proposing we each become our own Christologist and, ignoring the fundamentals of revelation around which our faith revolves, allow Christ to become what we might wish him to be.'

Trained to think for himself by his teachers at school and university, and influenced by Jane's fascination with psychological development, Andrew began to structure rules for his new commitment to celibacy. Living in an all-male Community had already produced effects on his emotional life.

He was more aware of women. In the street he discovered some of the younger ones stared at him, and he stared back, forcing them to lower their gaze. He enjoyed the satisfaction this gave him. Sometimes he sat in sidewalk cafés, sipping a beer, watching them go by, often thinking that a passing girl resembled Jane. But none were as beautiful. He could recall entire conversations with Jane.

His rules insisted he set the scene with total accuracy, and that he remember exactly what she wore. Almost always his memories ended with them making love.

He wrote her a long letter about these experiences. She responded with a short friendly note, suggesting he should read Schonfeld's *Normal Sexuality in Adolescence*. He had been slightly hurt by her response and had not mentioned his fantasies again, though he wrote to her regularly.

Andrew continued to probe his inner feelings, trying to place them within the framework of what he read and felt. He began to realize that self-control was the high ground between self-destruction and self-repression. In the Greg's medical library he discovered the writings of the American psychologist, Nathaniel Branden, and came to accept that a positive way to handle both his sexuality and his celibacy was neither to repress his feelings nor allow them to make him act impulsively. He must always try and identify his emotions calmly and to justify them without feeling fear and guilt.

In his diary he wrote: 'What is love? It is to give everything to another person – complete generosity. Is the only true love, the love of God? Do all other loves fade into pale insignificance when compared with the love of God? If a man is to give himself he must first possess himself completely; to be in complete possession of his inner being, completely open and available.'

He continued to think of Jane.

Late one night, he tip-toed down the main staircase to the pay-phone near the massive front door; he resisted the impulse to call her, thinking how he wanted to be a gatekeeper. Returning to his room he felt relieved that the irritable, depressed feeling which had filled him for most of the day had gone.

He fell asleep thinking of that passage in Isaiah about the man singled out by God and whom God keeps in obscurity. Was that why he was here? Suddenly he awakened, grinding his teeth and sweating.

Jane had been here, standing at the foot of the bed staring at him. She said his name, over and over again, the way she used to when they made love. *Andy, Andy, oh yes, Andy.*

In the weeks that followed Andrew constantly told himself he must develop a new way of loving. It would be the only way to handle his sudden bouts of intense anxiety and dissatisfaction. Why did he feel so intolerant of others? Above all, how could he, a committed witness to Christ, live with the strong sexual feelings which gripped him? In his diary he wrote: 'The saints of old had been able to go into the deserts, having nothing except the wild animals to tempt them. But here in Rome, temptation is at every turn.'

Every day, in one way or another, in his mind's eye, Jane confronted him. Once more he tried to rationalize the situation on paper. 'Is it psychologically healthy for me to be so focused on her? Is there some meeting place in which both my sensuality and spirituality can rest easy? Perhaps, after all, accepting celibacy is a slow process, not something to be achieved in a few months, but requiring years of practice, maturing in one like a wine ages in a cask?'

At night he wandered alone through the streets of the neighbourhood and afterwards he would sit in his room staring out the window. He made another diary entry. 'I feel alone. But do I really understand I am always going to be alone until I die?'

He stopped writing and stood at his window, staring into the night sky, feeling his senses drifting. Jane floated before him, naked, her hands beckoning him. Then she was gone.

Andrew returned to his desk, shivering, reminded of what Father William said at their last meeting. 'Each one of us from time to time experiences a moment when we are happy to be impaled by the spirit of the church and accept the limitations she asks of us. But there are also those moments when we no longer clearly feel the spiritual superiority God has seen in us. Those are the times dark thoughts enter our minds. Don't run from them. That's what the Devil wants. They must be faced. They are our old enemies, the Devil and the flesh. See them for what they are: temptation. Face them squarely and without fear.'

He remembered the searching eyes of the spiritual director. 'Andrew,

God doesn't think you are a superman. He just believes you can do what he wants. So do I.'

He had left Father Williams' study, his mind filled with new certainty.

The feeling was there now as he wrote another long letter to Jane, filled with another incident of Roman life. He had been to Trastevere, the raffish district on the right bank of the Tiber. Two policemen had tried to apprehend a purse-snatcher on a motorcycle. The thief's machine had skidded out of control and his body had been hurled, broken, onto the steps of the Church of Sancta Maria. He ended by promising that when Jane came to Rome he would show her how to carry her purse properly.

All his letters to her contained an invitation she should visit him.

Two days later the Greg was agog. A Spanish Jesuit had privately published a booklet on the spiritual and moral travails he had faced. He admitted to masturbating to cope with his bodily demands, but argued this was not a breach of his vow of celibacy. No one could recall a precedent for not only a priest, but a Jesuit, making such a public admission. Copies of the booklet circulated like wildfire.

That night Andrew wrote in his diary: 'The church expects many things. Because I am a very passionate person and because there are times when I do want sexual satisfaction, there is no doubt my faith will fail me. I have this feeling that there is a good chance I could fail because I am a sinner and because I am a man.'

Somewhere a clock struck the hour.

What would Jane be doing now? Surely she would be home. Andrew was half-way down the great staircase, dark and deserted at this hour, before he realized what he was going to do. He stopped before the phone and began to feed coins into its slot. When he had inserted the required number, he began to dial the number they had once shared.

A man answered.

Andrew almost slammed the receiver back into the cradle. By the time he returned to his room his eyes were filled with tears. Then, through his desperation, he began to reason. Why had he felt so angry and jealous? It was perfectly natural she should find someone else. Why should she remain beautiful and alone?

This, he reminded himself, was what renunciation was; it was a sign of his spiritual maturing to show such selfless love. He only wished he could have told her.

Next day a letter from Jane announced she was coming to Rome to see him.

CHAPTER FOURTEEN

Into the Twilight

By the time Father Breslin arrived, the four bodies had been removed to the city morgue. The police sergeant in charge of the accident said: 'No need for the oil tonight, Father. They died before they knew it.' He resumed measuring skid marks of the fatal road accident.

Father Breslin stared at the carnage, holding his vial of holy oil, feeling useless among the rescue workers. He wondered if the victims had been drunk or caught up in some mindless race with time? So many were, nowadays. He offered a silent prayer for the dead and another for their relatives. On impulse he added a prayer for his own father.

Six months ago, stone-cold sober, Liam Breslin had stepped into the path of a car in broad daylight. Everyone agreed the driver had been blameless. His father's sight and hearing had been deteriorating since the day they had both stood together at the graveside of his mother, fifteen years previously, at last united through grief. His father's injuries had included brain damage. The doctors said he would never leave the hospital but would eventually recover his speech. It was a dubious blessing. His father used his restored voice to cry out his terror about impending death. That, too, had helped to bring them closer together as Father Breslin tried to assuage the old man's fears.

Shortly after the accident, he had accepted the post of a curate in a country parish. He had been warned before doing so that Father McKenna, the parish priest, was cantankerous, which turned out to be true.

On occasions Father McKenna's portly figure would shake and his voice thicken. A newspaper item about the church could provoke his ire, but most times it was something Miss Maddox said or did.

From the beginning he had enlisted Father Breslin as his ally against their housekeeper. 'A vixen in tweeds. That's what she is. A vixen in tweeds. Nags non-stop,' Father McKenna would fulminate. 'She'll have to go.'

But Miss Maddox remained entrenched, the sharp end of a triangle of lives in the large rambling parish house. On that first day she had spoken to Father Breslin with blunt familiarity.

'I've seen curates come and go for all sorts of reasons, Father. But I've said to them all: I run this place my way. The way Father McKenna likes it run. Three good meals a day. If you're not going to be in, you tell me. If it's an emergency I'll keep something warm in the oven. You keep a record of all your private telephone calls and settle up once a month. Visitors into the sitting-room, but only if Father McKenna is not requiring it. Then you see them in the back parlour. I change the beds once a week, Thursdays, after breakfast. I collect all your washing at the same time. I try to run a happy house and I hope you'll be happy here, Father.'

She had escorted him to his bedroom at the back of the house and explained he had one bucket of coal a week to heat it. Winter or summer the room was like an ice box.

In spite of the turbulent changes affecting the church, these past four years had been the happiest and most rewarding of Father Breslin's ministry. He enjoyed the routine of a country parish with its rotation of baptisms, weddings, funerals, school meetings and house visits. His parishioners were always willing to allow him into their lives, though they never went beyond strictly defined limits. Even at the most informal gathering, he was still Father.

He had once asked Father McKenna, 'Who do they really think we are? Robots in cassocks?'

The old priest thought for some time. 'Best let them think that. People are always more comfortable with their fantasies.'

In the privacy of his own cheerless room, he had continued to conjure up his own fantasies. In his mind Mary had not aged a day. Her skin was as tanned and free of make-up as in those last months of the war. At first he had tried to send her away, whispering fiercely that she had no place in his life, only to imagine Mary laughing the soft, beguiling laugh he had last heard almost twenty years ago. And, finally, he allowed her to encourage him, and he had obeyed her, doing exactly what she told him to do to himself.

Afterwards he had felt consumed with guilt. But time and again it had happened. He had tried to pray away his behaviour and, for a while, that had worked. But the image of Mary, of what might have been, had returned stronger than before.

That, finally, was what had brought him, every Wednesday afternoon, to a consulting room in Dublin. The psychiatrist had questioned him carefully about his childhood, his lack of girlfriends, his early commitment to a vocation, his first nocturnal emissions at Clonliffe, what occurred with Brigid and then with Mary. The doctor had said it would be more comfortable if they both agreed the dreams occurred in what could be termed "the twilight zone", a place somewhere between drowsiness and sleep. Later the doctor had suggested it would help if Father Breslin began to keep an audio-diary of his thoughts.

He began doing so in the winter of 1966.

At first he found it difficult to speak into a cassette recorder. He did not recognize his voice on play-back, and his words sounded stiff and premeditated. But, over weeks, he mastered the skill of putting on tape his innermost feelings to better understand what happened to him in the twilight zone.

On one tape he admitted he loved Father McKenna and felt his love in return.

It is the sort of affection that defies description. It is certainly not physical, but neither can it be defined as mere friendship. It is subtly more. It is what a good son feels for his father!

On another tape he had expressed his views on his vocation.

Commitment is a denial of sexual pleasure, of having a loving wife and the pleasure that must come from that. I have often thought about what it would be like to have my own children. Now all the children of the parish are mine, and I love them as a father, although I don't have the same responsibilities.

On another tape he had recorded his sexual feelings.

My sexual feelings still rise from the depths of my twilight zone. I'm walking down a country lane with Mary. She says, 'Let's go home', and we make love... joyous love... No guilt is involved. Guilt involved the will, and if there's no will, there's no fault. If I'm asleep, there's no will, so I can't be guilty. My only bother is at what stage of consciousness I am at. Am I semi-conscious, or am I totally conscious? Or am I fooling myself, trying to pretend to be asleep when I am not? As far as the church goes, sin involves clear knowledge of the intellect and full consent of the will. Passion outside that, is not a sin.

Later he had tried to intellectualize his behaviour.

First of all there is the objective act. I can say, objectively, that murder, blasphemy and masturbation are all wrong. But when I ask the question, 'Is it a sin to masturbate?' I can't answer 'yes' or 'no'.

How difficult it had been to express that statement so it held the exact meaning he wanted. Sometimes he could talk into the recorder without any special thought as to what he was saying, the way the psychiatrist had encouraged him to do. But on the matter of objectivity he could sense his uncertainty.

I cannot live my life if I continue to look back. I have to be free of guilt. Coping with my sexuality is the same as handling my other passions. My anger. I can't just get mad because I feel like it. I have to learn to control a feeling I used to have, to do others down which was quite strong... if I can do that, I suppose I can control the sexual thing. I'm not sure this is very clear.

On another tape was the revelation.

Seventeen years... no, seventeen years, seven months and five days precisely, this very day, I was ordained a priest. I feel strong and healthy and vigorous enough at forty-one. I am a celibate still. It is still the most worthwhile challenge I know.

Nevertheless, there were still those moments with Mary, and they continued to trouble him deeply, he had told the psychiatrist.

The doctor had asked him questions.

'In his mind did Mary persecute him? Did she ask him to do anything he found unpleasant or degrading? Did she revile him afterwards? Had his willpower been weakened by her presence? Or his faith?'

He answered each time: 'No'.

At the end of six weeks in therapy, the psychiatrist's conclusions were reassuring.

'Father, you came here full of anxiety, almost obsessional anxiety. But there's nothing psychologically wrong with you. Quite the reverse. You're an impressive example of a person able to function in the twilight zone. We all have lived part of our lives in that zone. But you have managed to remain there, perhaps for considerable lengths of time. Certainly long enough for you to fantasize satisfactorily. While you are in the twilight zone you are not guilty of any volition. Rest assured you have not committed the mortal sin of co-operation. You are not in breach of our vow of celibacy. You should not feel any guilt, the cause of your obsessional anxiety.'

He had memorized the words and put them on tape.

Wrapped against the cold, Father Breslin left his bedroom, pulling the door quietly behind him and avoiding the squeaking floorboard at the top of the stairs. In the hall he put on his topcoat and scarf and his black priest's hat. He quietly drew the bolts and chains on the front door, barriers placed there by Miss Maddox as a defence against the world. He had often thought it would require a team of burglar-locksmiths to break through these defences which every morning required him to perform a slow glissando of openings before he could swing the door open to the world.

The snow swirled in his face. He quickly pulled the door behind him and walked to the church. Ian, the altar boy, was waiting, his face as white as his surplice. He had walked a mile to get here.

Father Breslin smiled sympathetically, thinking it needed real dedication to turn out on a morning like this. He began to robe thinking, too, how comfortingly timeless was the act, a reminder for him that the church still stood alone and certain in all it did, its record of survival no other could match. It had fought off persecution, exile, intemperance, rebellion, syncretism, hate, ostracism, scorn, calumny, war, corruption, greed, weakness, cruelty, heresy and hypocrisy. On the issue of its authority it had never given ground. Neither Attila and his Huns, or Luther and his reformers, or the modernists of a century ago, had been able to make Rome yield a single sentence in its interpretation of all it held to be true and holy.

Yet, once more the religious arsonists had begun to stoke their bonfires. They had worked methodically, the vanguard of a secret army, eager to launch new discussions and concepts, introduce revolution into theology, turn the Sacred Congregations into politicking caucuses.

That was all still to come when he had taken his place on the lowest ladder of the church, a priest without a regular job. Graduation from Clonliffe had not automatically guaranteed work. He had survived in that first year on Mass stipends, receiving modest sums in return for celebrating Mass in various churches around the diocese. Later he had been appointed chaplain to a Catholic college. Then followed a lengthy spell doing youth work among Dublin's docks. From there he had been appointed to the staff of the Pro-Cathedral, the diocese's imposing centre of worship.

He had still been on the Cathedral staff when Pius XII died and a new and altogether more robust and compassionate successor, John XXIII, had taken his place. The change in papal direction became noticeable at once. Visibly mortal, with his belly-laugh and passion for jokes, Pope John displayed a determination to shake the very foundations of the church by calling a Vatican Council, the second in history.

The men with matches sensed their moment had come. The fires were well out of control when, at the age of eighty-one, John, after one of the longest death agonies on papal record, finally succumbed. Cancer had wasted his body but left his mind contemplating the failure of his brave gamble to introduce change, which had allowed the arsonists a free hand.

His successor, Pope Paul VI, from the outset had shown himself to be a timid pontiff. For a while he successfully hid his weakness behind a call for unity; his charisma disguised his inability to control, let alone stamp out, the raging inferno consuming the church on every major issue. He was a pigmy-pope who had allowed his divine-invested authority to slip and fall.

Now, standing here in this cold sacristy with a seventeen-year-old boy glancing at him curiously, and no doubt wondering why he had hesitated so long after robing, was neither the time nor place to continue pondering such matters. All Father Breslin could be certain of was that despair was the first and most dangerous sin, the one which leads to all others. He had admitted this on part of his taped record.

He smiled at Ian and motioned him forward. Together they stepped into the sanctuary, genuflected to the altar covered in a starched white cloth, the lights from the candles shimmering before their eyes, bathing the sacristy in a soft glow, and the faces of the holy family etched into the stain-glass window had a life of their own.

Some things, indeed, did not change.

Father McKenna sat on the sofa, thinking hard. The snow had stopped but the wind had risen. Father Breslin sat to one side sweltering, wondering how the old priest, directly in front of the hearth, stood the heat.

Some of his most rewarding moments had been spent contemplating in this room something Father McKenna had said. It was here, for example, that the parish priest had pinpointed that the church's way out of humanity's moral distress was not the Greek way of knowledge based on redemption from ignorance. Nor did it echo ancient Egypt's escape from mortality with its elaborate ritual centred on the embalmed mummy. Nor, again, did it embrace Buddhism's doctrine on self-elimination set out in the doctrine of nirvana. Father McKenna had said that, after a life of ministry, he remained as certain as he had been on the day of his ordination, that the church's doctrine of redemption was that God was gracious. No more – no less.

Miss Maddox was dusting on the far side of the room. Father Breslin was reminded again of how she resembled a tree which had grown in the permanent shade: she looked undernourished, gnarled and pale. Her hair was unnaturally black, as if she dyed it, a half-completed vanity, perhaps? Her expression now was, as always, fixed and frozen as if by some terrible moment of long ago. It had aged with her, deepening the lines on her face. Hers was a suspicious and resigned face.

Father Breslin wondered why Miss Maddox behaved as she did. It was almost as if she derived some pleasure in hearing the anger surge in

Father McKenna's throat, his face darken and his temples throb. She could drive him, in moments, to almost speechless fury. And yet she was happy when his anger abated, and they could be once more reunited in a silent, strongly-bonded union, each aware of the value of his or her space, never physically encroaching upon it. The sofa was undeniably Father McKenna's territory.

On Sundays, after breakfast, Father Breslin went through his sermon point-by-point with the parish priest and every time without fail Miss Maddox contrived to be present, listening, indicating approval or rejection through facial movements as distinctive as any semaphore.

'I thought I'd base it on the text "needs must I carry my life in my hands", to show the meaning of this Sunday, a new coming, a new call from God to us. Time for a renewal, a new time for decision,' said Father Breslin.

Miss Maddox's lips, by the slightest fraction, parted. Approval.

Encouraged, he continued to expound upon the sermon.

'I thought I would tell them about the feasts of the new year of salvation.'

'A good phrase. Perfect for the Pro-Cathedral. But a mite high-falutin' for here, don't you think?'

'Fair enough.' Father Breslin scored out the words.

'Remember, Seamus, our faith has never confessed the ineffable mystery of God's eternal being. It implies it. As priests we must never forget to preach that man may only worship something which cannot be conceived as being greater. To worship anything less is idolatory. They taught us both that at Clonliffe. We have to show the true and wider meaning of faith to those who would never really understand what I have just said. Always keep it simple, Seamus.'

Miss Maddox's nose twitched. Disapproval.

Father Breslin continued reading from his notes, explaining how he wanted to remind the congregation that Advent was the first great liturgical vision, a reminder of the longing for salvation.

'"Man cannot achieve it alone. God must come to him. God's eternal love, drawn by the poverty of man, gives him the pledge of salvation. That, we must see, as the first meaning of Advent."'

'Excellent. Really quite excellent, Seamus.'

They continued to go through the sermon until the housekeeper reminded them, as she did every Sunday, of the time. Father Breslin went to his room and typed up the notes, reducing them to a series of headings on a single sheet of paper. He put it in his cassock pocket.

It had started to snow again. It was not only, he reminded himself, another liturgical year which was ending and a new one starting. He was about to begin a further twelve months of struggle within himself. The fact must be recorded as well as additions made to previous explanations. He set up the recorder on his desk and began to speak.

What I am trying to say is that I must be perfectly truthful to myself, and to God, when I say afterwards there has been no volition. That is the whole key to living a sexual life within this framework, which I fully accept. What I want to do here is to put down a few thoughts. I think there should be a proper course for every seminarian and for every priest, given by a psychiatrist, not a theologian. All about the twilight zone.

He stopped. Long ago he had learned there was no sin so subtly dangerous as the self-sufficiency of the morally righteous man. Was this what he was doing in suggesting guidelines for his fantasies?

He pressed the button.

I do not know. Into my mind comes Browning's lines about the reality of our faith. ''Tis the faith that launched point-blank its dart, at the head of a lie; taught Original Sin, the corruption of man's heart.' There is a lot more in that than I had first realized... and all the great thinkers of modern times... I'm thinking especially of Montaigne and Pascal, Kierkegaard, Nietzsche and Freud... not all, by any means, in the church's good books... well, they have probed the human heart and told the truth about its strength. But we, as priests, we need to know about how to handle its weakness. It is. the submerged rock on which our complacency will be shipwrecked. Sin... that is what I am talking about.

He paused. He had recorded, in these past weeks, a great deal about his views on sin. Much of it was an intellectual reasoning that humanity's apostasy was not something which occurred at one single awful moment: it was always present. The symbolism of the creation complements the fall. Now he decided to personalize his argument.

232

There is a state of sinfulness... something that mysteriously forms the empirical side of my character. But if I commit a sin, it is not my business alone. My failure is a failure for all priests who are struggling with me. That is why we call it the priesthood... our lives are interlocked. That is what St Augustine meant when he spoke about 'each the work of all, in all the work of each'. And it was Dostoevsky who said that 'we are each responsible to all for all'. And yet, where does the church help us to understand that below not only our conscious, but also below the unconscious, there is another layer? There live my hidden inborn forces that are in all truth beyond the conscious control of my will.

There was a knock on the door. It was Miss Maddox reminding him it was time for the morning Mass.

CHAPTER FIFTEEN

The Road Less Travelled

The interior of the battered Ford smelled, as Victoria remembered the saying in this part of the country went, like a bachelor on Friday: a mixture of Sam's tobacco, his body sweat and his dog. The hound was curled up on the back seat asleep, his paws resting on top of the larger of her two suitcases, the one which contained her modified habit. The other was crammed with brochures extolling the glorious life the Order offered all those who joined.

Victoria wore a light grey two-piece suit and a blouse with a frilled front. Her make-up was expertly applied. These past ten years had been kind to her. She looked as vital and youthful as she did on the day she became a bride of Christ. Only she knew the differences; they were all inside her.

Sam had met her train, lifted his hat and grabbed her cases. A small hard-bodied man with old-fashioned manners, he was uneasy around a strange woman. He had not spoken a word since leaving the railway station, leaving her to her own thoughts.

Chicago, like Detroit and Minneapolis-St Paul, had been a depressing reminder that the church was no longer guaranteed respect even within its own ranks. In Chicago, priests and nuns had told her bluntly that their archbishop, Cardinal John Cody, who ruled over one of the richest dioceses in the Catholic world, was a racist, a financial cheat who used diocesan funds for his personal profit, a lecher who had his way with whichever woman he fancied. In every sense he behaved like a Borgia pope.

Though her own transgressions were very different from those of the cardinal's, they were, nevertheless, in the eyes of the church, sins. Yet she no longer felt a need to confess them. The church, not her, was out of step. It was no longer enough to forbid, to say it had always been so, and must remain so. There had to be a good reason. The Order had educated her to think, yet the church expected blind obedience to rules devised by men a long time ago.

She found masturbation a healthy relief and could cite some of the world's leading clinicians to support her view. In the suitcase in the back seat was a thick notebook containing the history of her psycho-sexual development in religious life. She brought the book with her on these long trips when she was away for a month at a time, so that she could continue to trace her journey into self-realization.

In this, her fourteenth year as a professed nun, Victoria was as fully committed to her faith as ever. But now she never felt a moment's guilt over her sexuality. Within the Order she was regarded as a good recruiter, able to make girls share her excitement over Christ's command: *Come. Follow me.*

This would be the fifth school in a week she had visited. In the next month she would call on a further eighteen, travelling by train and bus or flying in and out of small municipal airports. Across the country other recruiters were visiting other schools to give identical vocation talks.

Before departing, Reverend Mother had addressed them. She had grown more frail and distant with the passing years, remaining seated behind her desk, her lips bloodless and barely moving as she reminded the group:

'You have a heavy responsibility. Our ranks are far from as full as they should be. We need new girls to be trained to carry on our mission. We need them urgently. And we need a goodly number of them. The percentage, as you well know, is higher than ever before of those who leave during, or at the end of, their postulancy. I fear there is no longer the spiritual strength among the young there once was.'

She paused, gathering her thoughts. The nine nuns around Victoria were, like her, young and personable, each one hand-picked by the Order. Reverend Mother continued.

'Be careful in your assessment. We cannot afford this high level of wastage. It is a drain on our finances. You must make it clear to those you think are likely candidates that our way of understanding Jesus Christ the Saviour has not changed. At the same time, you must make it sound attractive as a lifelong commitment. Yet, please do not stress that they are coming for life.'

'The important thing is to persuade them to enter. Once they are here, we will endeavour to keep them, offering you, among other things, as examples. It is a great responsibility you have. But I am certain you will discharge it with love and care for what you represent in his name.'

The Order's treasurer had given them each $1000 to pay for motel bills and food.

Victoria had found it strange at first, handling money after years of being told it was one of the causes of sin. A Sister with a penny isn't worth a penny, the Mistress had once said. Though she was no longer called Mistress but the Director of Formation, she still remained the same doctrinaire teacher, her faith as flinty as her voice.

Victoria had twice as many schools to visit as her last tour. She had queried this with the Sister of Administration, a tall, bony woman, who had entered religious life rather late, after a career with IBM. 'You've got to do twice as much in half the time. If you believe you can do it, you will. Good luck, Sister.' The Administrator could have been still working for IBM.

Tomorrow Victoria had to be in Minnesota, almost 1000 miles away. There, she suspected, she would face not only competition from sisters from rival Orders, but also challenges from industrial recruiters and bemedalled officers from the armed services.

She began to question Sam. How large was the neighbourhood's Catholic community? Were they regular church-goers? What did the girls usually do after leaving school? She drew him out slowly, careful not to step on any small-town susceptibilities.

What would Sam make, she wondered, of a church in which so many of its priests and nuns were confused in their sex role. A month ago she had attended a lecture in Philadelphia on the role of androgyny in religious life. The statistical evidence had been shattering: over twice as many priests as laymen in one sample poll, admitted to feeling and wanting to behave like women.

Sam drove into a town that was like a hundred others she had visited these past two years: tacked-on porches, a drugstore, a handful of other shops, perhaps a hundred modest houses scattered on either side of the highway.

Sam pointed at a single-storey building with a playing area at the rear: the school.

'I have to change,' she explained.

'Well, seeing as who you are, I'd be honoured if you'd use my place.'

236

He swung the Ford across the road. The house was beside a garage. He carried her case, apologizing before he opened the front door.

'My wife died three years ago. I don't bother much.'

She still remembered when her own father had died. The pain had lasted long afterwards. During those first years in the Mother House she sometimes awoke, imagining his voice. That was before she had learned to call up other male voices, ones able to excite and dominate her fantasies, and finally to satisfy her.

Sam led her into a bedroom. The bed was unmade. He rushed forward, pulling up the coverlet. She smiled as he closed the door behind him. She opened her suitcase and took out her habit. It was made of crease-resistant material.

The Order's Director of Recruitment, a middle-aged nun, had explained. 'Modified it now is, but it is still a habit, the outward badge of your office. It is special. It's your badge of courage. It shows you have made sacrifices. These are the thoughts you must get across to a class. Courage. Victory. Positive ideas. They are the captivating images.'

Victoria changed out of her suit, standing in her bra and slip, and walked over to an old-fashioned mirror on a stand and used a tissue to remove her make-up. She stared for a moment, as she often did nowadays, at her reflection. It was, she knew, not that she was making up for all those years when she had been forbidden access to a mirror. She searched for something else, a confirmation of what she had written in her notebook.

'I want to be a good nun. But I want to be a fulfilled woman, allowed to behave as I want, openly, without having to hide and pretend. The more I learn, the more I see that it is a convenience for the church to stamp hard on all forms of sexuality. It is the most powerful way it has to control us. Sexuality is the force of life and all energy. God gave it to us. Why should men take it away from us?'

Just as she had dressed on that first day as a postulant, Sister Victoria now put on her habit, garment by garment, thinking again how indeed some things never changed.

Victoria waited while the religious teacher, her introduction complete, retired to a chair in a corner of the classroom. For a moment longer she surveyed the girls seated at their desks.

'I chew bubble gum, like French fries and bacon burgers. I also dated when I was your age,' Victoria said.

A shivery murmur, a mixture of surprise and delight, swept the class.

'I've also had a call from God. Not collect, but if you like, direct. He dialled into my soul one day when I was your age, and here I am. You get a lot of recruiters trying to convince you they hold the answer to your futures. Well, I'm not going to do that. Your future doesn't rest in my hands. Just as it doesn't rest in their hands. It is between you and God. I just want to spend this time explaining why I answered his call, what it means to do so, and why. His voice is deep inside me still. Then, when the going gets tough, he is always there. If anybody thinks this is not what they want to hear, then please feel free to leave.'

She paused. The Director of Recruitment had stressed the need for immediate identification, to be followed by an option. *Give them the chance to get up and walk out. They almost certainly won't – because they will not wish to miss anything. You've got their attention then. It's up to you to hold it.*

Nobody moved.

The Director had emphasized the need to be realistic. *Anything that can help them to identify will help you to get across your points. The important thing to stress is that being a nun is not doing something weird – that it is a very natural choice for living.*

Victoria continued. 'It's a tough life today for many of us. More nuns are being persecuted today than at any other time in history. This is the age of their martyrdom. In Czechoslovakia right now, there are over 10,000 nuns in prison.'

There were gulps from some of the girls. The idea of women going to prison for their faith always struck a chord.

'What keeps them going is the knowledge that Christ promised them his divine protection. No other job offers that. No other employer can, or would, dare say to you that he will guarantee to protect you twenty-four hours a day until you die. Christ does.'

Victoria defined a vocation and said that, from the beginning it had been ordinary boys and girls who had recognized a commitment. She explained that the core of a vocation was renunciation. She dropped in her first scriptural reference: St Paul's message to the Corinthians that Christ saw them as ambassadors for him and that they should renounce their licentious ways.

'For me, it meant giving up dating. But, you know, what surprised me was how quickly I came to see that worldly pleasures really aren't everything. I saw what St Augustine meant when he said he had felt something was still missing by only having a good time. He wanted more in his life. I guess I did.'

She paused, giving time for her words to settle.

When had she first missed all those physical joys she had promised to renounce forever, had she really believed she could? The question had drifted into her mind again last night as she lay awake in her motel room, blaming the softness of the bed and the strangeness of her surroundings for being unable to sleep. She had lain on her back, naked as she always now slept, her legs apart, her hands by her sides, listening to the roar of the trucks on the expressway, reminded of Art and that night in the car. She never tired of his memory, of the last time she had been physically touched. The roughness of his movements had again aroused her and afterwards, when it was over, and she had been able to assuage what she described in her notebook as 'this raging hunger that rushes up through me', she wondered if he was still as she remembered him. Or had marriage and three children calmed his passions?

He had never become a pilot, ending up instead as a salesman with a ball-bearings company. He used to send her postcards from all over the country, the words carefully innocuous, always signed 'love A', as if he suspected his first and only letter had never reached her. The cards helped to reinforce her fantasies; she imagined she was with him in the places he had posted them from. Then, abruptly, the cards stopped. She discovered he had become a desk-bound executive. It made no difference. In her twilight zone, he still made love to her in his office after the staff had gone home.

She wondered how many of the girls seated before her had experienced full sex. Victoria began to explain about choice.

'For most of you here today, it is already made. You will get married and raise a family. That's absolutely fine. But perhaps, for one or two of you, the idea of getting married and having children is not everything.'

The Director had been clear: *Always emphasize the concept of being special. That's always important. Always get across the idea that a vocation is something precious. And link it with family pride.*

'No one's locked away – like they show you in the old movies. Those days are gone. Your family get to visit you. You get vacations. If there has to be renunciation, there is also reward.'

She paused, expertly assessing the impact so far.

The girl with the faraway gaze was a possibility. So was the fair-haired teenager at the back who stared fixedly at her. Perhaps a third potential postulant was the young black in the middle of the class. It was more than she had expected.

Victoria explained the life of any nun was governed by vows. She began with poverty.

'Have you ever thought how much trouble possessions can cause? How many times have you fought with a brother or sister over things? And in the end it isn't worth it. And look how much emphasis everybody puts on possessions. People are measured by what model of car they have, where they go on vacation, which country club they belong to. In religious life we don't value such things. Our convent car is almost as old as Henry Ford himself! None of us every goes to a country club, except to collect gifts for a jumble sale. And yet we don't live like paupers.'

She explained that, since the Second Vatican Council, the church had dramatically reassessed its views on poverty. No longer were its ascetic values emphasized: now the emphasis was on seeing poverty as part of living a modest life in Holy Orders.

'The bottom line with poverty is forgetting our selfish needs. It is a turning away from our egos. St Luke put it very well. "Whoever puts his hand to the plough but keeps looking back is unfit for the reign of God." To look back is to cling to possessions. Someone very dear to me told me that.'

Once more Victoria paused, giving them time to think, for her to remember.

Sister Beverly Rose had been dead for three years, never regaining consciousness after being mugged. Her cross and chain, the only item of value on her body, had been torn from her neck. At her funeral, Reverend Mother had reminded them that if Satan had a plan, Jesus could work through it.

Standing at the graveside of her old teacher, Victoria recalled it was Sister Beverly Rose who had taught her, almost twenty years ago, that it had once been permissible for faith to use violence to spread its message because, as the

Gospel says, 'the kingdom of heaven suffers violence and the violent bear it away'.

Victoria felt the church still used this piece of scripture to continue to exercise control over all those who sought that most basic of freedoms – that of their body. She believed that by denying them such liberty, many nuns had been driven into socio-political activity and activism.

Victoria smiled at the class.

'Now for the vow that makes everybody say: "Thanks – but it's not for me." Chastity.'

When the murmurs had finally run their course, she asked a question: 'How many of you have seen *The Nun's Story*?'

Hands shot into the air.

'I bet you all remember Audrey Hepburn going through all that preparation and having it drilled into her that she had to cut herself off from the world forever in an emotional sense. Die to it. You all remember that?'

They did.

'Well, it is, and it isn't, like that any more. Do you remember how the doctor said to Miss Hepburn when they worked together in that mission hospital in Africa, "Do you know, Sister, what I most admire in you?" And she asked him, "What?" And he said "Your total faithfulness to Christ". That is what chastity comes down to in the end. Being faithful.'

In the beginning, when she was preparing and rehearsing her talk under the watchful eyes of the Director, it had taken her weeks to perfect chastity to that short statement. She had worried over every word, wondering how far what she had said actually reflected what she thought. But the Director had been satisfied, repeating her words as a model for the other vocation counsellors.

The final vow to be explained was the one which gave her least trouble.

'When I was at high school, I was probably the most disobedient in the whole class. I just bucked authority. I thought that was terrific. Later, I saw what my problem was. I just didn't have faith to be myself, so I was disobedient – trying to be somebody else. You have to be obedient to be a nun. You get asked to do some pretty hard things. Like going off to work with Mother Teresa of Calcutta. Or helping the poor in Africa. We send our people everywhere. It's a bit like being in the Army – except every nun is fighting the Devil. That's what it comes down to in the end. Good versus evil. If any one of you want to join in that fight, I'll be happy to see you afterwards.'

She stopped, hoping that in this room was one girl who would have made this long journey worthwhile.

Some 5000 miles away from where Victoria continued to the next stage of her recruiting drive for postulants, Father Breslin unlocked the door of his family home in Dublin. He instinctively stamped the snow off his shoes and wiped his feet on the doormat, the way his mother always insisted everyone should do before entering the kitchen. Even now, fifteen years later, he still thought of it as *her kitchen*. Right to the very end this had been her domain: his father could occupy it, but she owned it.

He closed the door behind him. There was still a faint smell of turf smoke, even though the oven had been converted to gas the year before she died. That was when she also agreed to move the eight-day clock from the sideboard to the front parlour. On a wall hung its replacement: an ugly battery-operated square-faced timepiece his father had bought in a pub off a crony. It had stopped after six months, at a quarter to four, and its battery had never been replaced.

Every Sunday afternoon, on his way to the hospital, he came here to check on the house to make sure it had not been damaged by the weather, or vandalized. It would have to be sold eventually; that would be the hardest part, disturbing all these memories. He moved around the kitchen, touching and remembering.

Only the week before she died, his mother had stood at the table and prepared a teacake for him, mixing the ingredients from a recipe which had been in her family for over a hundred years. He had driven over to collect it. She was wrapping it in greaseproof paper when she had winced and closed her eyes, squeezing back tears of pain. He had wanted to call the doctor or drive her to the hospital. She stopped him, saying very calmly there was no need to waste their time.

He glanced at the photographs on the sideboard top. Where once there had only been her children, there were now grandchildren: his sisters had married and produced families of their own. His mother had never missed a chance to photograph and frame any member of the family: at Christmas and Easter; inside and outside the house. There was only one snap of her, standing in the kitchen doorway, the pretty print dress hanging on her like a shroud. That was three months before the end.

He still firmly believed her faith had enabled her to survive so long. In her kitchen they had shared some of their most important conversations about the meaning of death. Her one wish had been she would pass over peacefully to a better world.

Father Breslin left the kitchen, walking through to the parlour, remembering the last time he had helped his mother along these few steps. The parlour was dark, the curtains drawn. He switched on a light. The room was furnished from another age: a shiny imitation-leather sofa, a coffee table, its top scuffed. His father would sometimes sleep-off his drinking bouts in an armchair, using the table top as a foot-rest. The clock was on the mantle, long stopped like its kitchen replacement. The grate was stuffed with old newspapers, the fire hadn't been lit for years. The plant-holders were empty; the plants had died with her.

Here they had explored another aspect of death, that it represented opportunities gone forever. Once more she had displayed, in her own modest way, that she had more instinctive insights than many theologians he knew, explaining that accepting death was the greatest of all thoughts except thinking of God. He had said that was very profound, and she smiled and said she had not meant it to be.

He turned off the light and closed the door. The wind was sighing through the letter box. After the break-in, his father had removed the key on its string. A thief had brazenly pulled it out through the letter box, opened the front door and made off with some loose change on the hall table. He might have got away with more if his father had not emerged from the kitchen. He had given chase, but lost the youth in a side street. His father had not bothered to report the incident to the police; long ago he had said they were incapable of providing the law and order he thought necessary.

Father Breslin checked the bedrooms. He could not recall ever seeing his mother in bed, except in hospital. Even then she had seemed well, able to take care of herself. She would wave the nurses away, whispering for them to tend to other patients, saying she wanted nothing. They had been sitting holding hands, not talking when she finally gave up the fight. She had been dead for some minutes before he realized it. He had wept, dried his tears and then anointed her. Later he conducted her funeral service. His mother was the first person in his ministry he had buried.

His father had come home from the cemetery trembling, already in fear of his own mortality.

Finally, Father Breslin carefully locked the kitchen door behind him and walked to Father McKenna's car to drive to the hospital, one of the oldest in a city of old hospitals. He parked in the forecourt, among the doctor's cars, still a priest's privilege. Entering the building, the porter at the desk told him the duty doctor would like to see him in his office.

Instinctively he walked faster, past the cafeteria where relatives sat smoking and drinking from styrofoam cups, waiting for news and decisions. The office was a cubbyhole with a dirty window and a single chair facing the desk. The doctor was young, but already equipped with the voice of professional kindness.

'I'm sorry to have to tell you your father died an hour ago. It happened suddenly. A total collapse. Heart. Lungs. All at once. Nothing could have saved him. Mercifully it was all over…'

'May I see him?'

'I'd really advise against that. Try and remember him as he was in life.'

'I'd like to see him. Please.'

'Of course, Father. I'm sorry, of course you can.'

His father had the mortuary to himself, laid out on a trolley in the pyjamas he gave him last Christmas. It was here, at last, that Father Breslin felt a grief, raw and lacerating.

The priest whose name he did not know commanded Father Philippe to remain silent.

Not by so much as a whispered syllable must he offer a word of defence: none was open to him. One black-gloved hand held the cowl across the priest's face so that only his eyes were visible, bloodshot and filled with an intensity he found even more terrifying than the man's spectral voice.

For months he had been incarcerated in one of the dungeons of the Apostolic Palace in the Vatican. How, or who had brought him there was a blurred memory. Simone, with the connivance of his doctor, he suspected, must have drugged him. She had, he knew, co-operated in other ways, giving evidence against him, describing the most intimate moments of their life. She had lied, of course; it was her fault, all of it. But his judges had not listened.

Now he was being brought from the depths of this stronghold to hear sentence pronounced. The hooded priest urged him forward up another flight of stone steps, icy cold to his bare feet. They reached a great inner courtyard, cobbled and open to the elements. A blistering merciless wind howled around the piazza, chilling the blood in his veins. He was naked under the high-buttoning cassock which hid the absence of his Roman collar. Before leaving his cell he had been made to burn the collar in the presence of his priest escort.

The windows of the buildings around the square were filled with faces; stone-faced men in the red, black, purple and white vestments of the church. In one window was Frank, peering down at him, talking on the telephone, dressed in medieval clerical garb. Before he could attract Frank's attention the priest once more pushed him forward, past another window. In it, jewelled and bewigged but nevertheless recognizable, stood his mother. She was shouting at him in a language he did not understand.

A few windows beyond was Walter, dressed in one of the most splendid of all the church's uniforms, the full regalia of a Knight of Malta. One of Walter's hands was extended accusingly towards him.

At an adjoining window stood Lolo, naked, as she had been when he left her in the hotel bedroom. Suddenly she opened her mouth and he saw she had no teeth.

Waiting for him in a massive doorway, spanned by a lintel of hewn marble, was a priest who wore the armour of a crusader. He turned and marched into the building, leading the way, shouting this was the time of repentance, that penance was justice and pardon only possible after punishment.

He led the way down a short corridor ending in two doors. The crusader rapped on them with his sword. They silently swung open.

At the far end of a vast hall was a raised platform covered with candelabra and tall, free-standing crucifixes on white starched cloth. It resembled an altar, stretching from wall to wall of this hall.

The judges seated behind it were dressed in purple. Mr Watts was there, as imposing and ascetic-looking as he had been in the banqueting room in Dallas. Close by sat Blanche, her cloak trimmed with gold coins. Beside her sat the priest to whom he had confessed about Lolo.

The majestic figure in the centre of the tableau towards whom he was finally approaching, wore on the index finger of his right hand a ring surmounted by a perfectly carved crucifix – the Fisherman's Ring. On his head was the towering conical mitre of the supreme pontiff. The Pope nodded for him to kneel.

At first he could not see Simone, only hear her chanting. Then she emerged from behind the Pope's throne. She was taller and more beautiful than when he had last seen her, dressed in a full habit. He still could not make out the words of her chant. His tutors had often warned him to pay more attention to his Latin. Then, with a shock that made him tremble, he realized that each long divided syllable was an account of his failure to live a celibate life. The Pope finally raised his hand. His Holiness' voice stunned him. It was that of Judge Dupois.

Father Philippe once more awoke from his nightmare and began to tear at his skin, drawing blood, spotting the sheets of his bed. Night after night he had experienced the same nightmare, always identical to the last detail.

He had been ordered into this monastery in Georgia by the Prefect for the Sacred Congregation for the Faith, formerly known as the Holy Office, while Pope Paul VI considered his future.

The previous evening Father Philippe had learned that a letter, its envelope embossed with the Pope's heraldic coat-of-arms, had been hand-delivered to the abbot. After reading it the monk had gone to the monastery's chapel to pray.

It was the terrible uncertainty over what had been decided would be his fate that had jerked Father Philippe out of his recurring nightmare. After tearing at his flesh, he fell to his knees and begged God, through his Holiness the supreme pontiff, Pontifex Maximus of the Universal Church, Patriarch of the West, Primate of Italy, Archbishop and Metropolitan of the Province of Rome, State Sovereign of Vatican City, Servant of the Servants of God: Father Philippe had begged the man who possessed more titles than any other man on earth to give him another chance.

CHAPTER SIXTEEN

Beyond the Dawn

Inhaling slowly, the way he had learned to calm himself after the nightmare, Father Philippe stood at the window of his monastery cell. These past four months in therapy had been the most painful of his life.

His psychological needs and deficiencies had been located one by one, a process so hurtful, at times he had just sat in the church-appointed doctor's office and wept copiously. The analyst had pinpointed his obsession with possessions, position and power, explaining they represented his desperate search to seek selfhood from without, using *things* to serve as a measure of his ego. Walter had, in that sense, been a *thing*. So had Lolo, and marriage to Simone. His adulation of Frank fitted the same pattern. Even his vocation could be seen as a *thing*.

The doctor said therapy would be designed to give him a new and dependable sense of maturity. It would be a long and demanding process, one in which all the implications of a recurring nightmare, would be thoroughly explored.

Father Philippe had asked what the chances of success were. The doctor had been honest. 'There is no way of knowing. There never is. But let's both be always positive.'

His journey to the monastery had begun after he had telephoned Frank and begged him for help to return to the priesthood. Frank had arranged for him to see the bishop. At the interview the chancellor had also been present and had said there could be no question of him returning to his old parish. 'I'm sure you understand it would be difficult for those ladies whose hair you have been shampooing to have you resume ministering to their souls,' the chancellor had said icily.

The bishop had been more sympathetic. 'An aberration. That's what you experienced. A genuine aberration. That's why I never forwarded your dispensation to Rome. I just wrote the Holy Office a report. The bare facts. They agreed to wait. We both hoped you would come to your senses.'

However, he must agree to be confined in the Georgia monastery while the Holy Office considered his future role in the church.

'Use the time valuably. Think upon your experiences. See the lessons. Put them on paper. It often helps, you know,' the bishop had said, not unkindly.

Father Philippe had at first found it difficult. When he tried to record his feelings about his mother, he had felt nauseated and would walk away from the desk and stand at his cell window. But slowly, over weeks, he became no longer afraid to search the deeper recesses of his mind and commit his discoveries to paper. He had written, among other things, how the wind so often reminded him of a child crying for its mother.

Shortly after he had arrived, the wind had suddenly become a howling fury and he sat on his bed scribbling how it reminded him of how his mother would croon 'When the wind blows, the children will cry.' He used to hate her singing it. The therapist had said his reaction was further proof of trauma.

Father Philippe was puzzled the analyst had not immediately zeroed in on celibacy; he had always seen his inability to live within the vow as the root of his failure. He had raised the matter several times in those first sessions until the doctor patiently explained: 'Celibacy is only a symptom. We have to find the cause of its failure in you before we can get some perspective on how you can handle it in the future – or indeed whether you should.'

That thought stuck in Father Philippe's mind. Later he had given the doctor a full account of the incident they had both come to realize had a special significance.

Father Philippe's divorce lawyer had been adamant. 'Stay away from Simone. No contact at all. The fastest way to end this business is to show grounds for incompatibility. Just because you shared a bed with her doesn't mean you forgot your vocation. But no contact with your wife. None at all.'

The lawyer added he had a reputation for getting priests divorced faster than any other attorney in the state. He had not elaborated. But the thought that he was not the first to need such help had also stuck in Father Philippe's mind.

The day the divorce papers were filed, Simone called him at the monastery. He was pleasantly surprised to find her voice was free of the bathos of their last weeks together. How was he? Doing fine. How was she? Coping, she said laughing, adding she was going back to teach Sunday school class. He had thought for a moment before agreeing. It was a good idea. She'd hung up after telling him he could always call her.

A few days later he did. It was after a day of crop-spraying with only a monk as company who spoke endlessly of the joys of contemplative life. Father Philippe wanted to hear her voice. They had spoken for a long time, until the campanile bell for the Grand Silence tolled.

Soon the calls had become their secret. She would phone him one night, he would call the next. In one conversation he had explained he had asked his lawyer not to press for the return of his possessions, she could keep his pair of solid silver candlesticks, pieces of antique furniture and paintings, all gifts from his former parishioners.

In the weeks that followed, they both enjoyed the sensation of fooling their respective lawyers with those phone calls. For Father Philippe there was the additional pleasure of hoodwinking the abbot. The elderly monk had struck him as being supercilious and condescending.

When Simone finally suggested they could meet, Father Philippe felt no compunction about lying to the abbot that he was going to visit his mother.

Parking the monastery's car outside the motel, he had an unsettling moment when Sister Helen came into his thoughts telling him to turn back. Instead he had gone to the room she had reserved in her name.

Simone had already bathed and put on a nightdress he'd once told her was his favourite – purple and clingy. She was sitting on the edge of the bed. She embraced him eagerly, as if trying to kiss away the weeks they had been apart. She made him feel wanted and attractive and aroused feelings he thought were dead. She undressed him slowly, the way she had always liked to do, caressing and touching, exploring him.

They had reached new heights that weekend. Then, on the Sunday night, as he dressed to return to the monastery, Simone had looked at him steadily and said, 'Let's go home.'

'Simone, it would not work on a day-to-day basis. I have to go back.'

She stared at him. Finally, she asked with a bitterness he had never heard before: 'What sort of man are you? You think you can just take me and dump me?'

He had thrown his things together into his overnight bag and driven back to the monastery. Only in its keep did he feel calm and able to control his raging panic.

The abbot sent for Father Philippe after supper, saying he had called his mother who said her son had not been there. Where had he been?

The monk's voice was suddenly gentle and compassionate. 'You can say anything to me and only you will know if it is the truth. Only you and God. It is not me you will be speaking to him, but him. Please, tell him the truth. However much it pains you, be assured he will understand.'

Father Philippe made a complete confession.

The abbot pondered. After some time he came to a decision.

'There will be no more phone calls. I am sure your wife will feel the same. You must also tell your therapist. It is most important you do. And from now on you will never leave here again, except to see him or your lawyer, until a decision is made in Rome. Is that absolutely clear?'

Father Philippe said it was.

A few days later Father Philippe recounted the episode to the therapist. After he finished, the doctor remained silent. Suddenly, Father Philippe began to shout. 'I've been talking to you for an hour. Talking, talking, talking, week after week. What good is it all doing me? I'm tired of it, sick and tired of the whole business.'

The doctor let him continue for a while, then asked, 'Doesn't your outburst remind you of someone?'

'Who? What are you getting at?'

'You used to say your mother and Simone browbeat you. Now you're trying to do the same to me. It's time you saw yourself for who you still are. You lie to your abbot, go to Simone, then leave her dangling. In everything you do, you cut and run. Always. Until you understand that, you're right. There is no point in talking. I only want to see you again when you are ready to accept your own responsibilities.'

It took Father Philippe two weeks of brooding before he telephoned the analyst and said he was prepared to do so. He had taken the first all-important step to recovery.

In subsequent sessions he gained insights into his behaviour. His craving for affection went all the way back to his mother not maternally fondling or caressing him. This had further contributed to his anxiety, creating a feeling of being unable to fully trust himself with a woman. In later years this had created an unhealthy fear in him about sex itself. That was why he had failed with Lolo in spite of the initial pleasure she had provided. The same had happened with

Simone. The visit to the motel was another desperate attempt to deny that truth.

The doctor continued to question him carefully about the episode. Each time after he had made love to Simone had he gone to the bathroom? He had, why? Had he examined himself? Father Philippe nodded. Had he been thinking his penis was still whole and unharmed? Father Philippe nodded again. Then he began to sob and said he was glad somebody finally understood.

It was another step forward.

After two months the analyst asked Father Philippe whether he felt that the holy Trinity was a model for a religious celibate who felt lonely and alienated, even though deeply committed? The question had so excited Father Philippe that he had expounded that, indeed, the Father, Son and Holy Ghost formed a union in which each remains autonomous and unique.

The analyst finally interposed, 'In your case the church seems to have overemphasized a priest should focus on his intimate relationship with God to the exclusion of all others.'

At the end of the session he handed Father Philippe a book, explaining a priest, not a doctor, had written it.

That night, Father Philippe sat up until dawn reading *Mystical Passion*. For the first time he saw it was possible to live a life in Christ without enduring an everyday emotionally barren existence, that the whole purpose of loving God was to develop along healthy spiritual and psychological lines. For a priest, that meant taking a realistic approach to his sexuality. There was one sentence that captured exactly how he wanted to be, 'If as sexual beings we love not only God, but human persons, we become living witnesses, passionate witnesses to him, and alive and joyous to others.'

At their next session, the therapist explained that sexuality and spirituality were not incompatible. The tragedy was nobody had shown Father Philippe how both were at the very core of his vocation. Instead of encouraging him to integrate them, his seminar tutors had faced him with an impossible choice. He could either be holy or sensual, but not both. Some priests were able to cope with this ultimatum. He had not been one of them. Over the years it had stretched him to psychological breaking point because no one had told him it was healthy for a priest to be sexual.

The analyst had summed up, 'Though you are a priest, you are also a man. You cannot split your sexuality from your faith. You have to see them as one unifying force which makes it possible for you to live your vow and be a human being. See celibacy not as something mysterious, consecrating yourself only to God, but also as an intensely human condition. That's part of the reason why you lost touch with your own feelings. Your training as a priest repressed them. Your every word and action warned others to keep a distance. It is a psychologically unhealthy thing for a priest to be on a pedestal. You are always "Father". You are encouraged to see yourself as "special" and "separate". That worried you from the beginning. The more you tried to integrate, the more isolated you felt.'

At the next session Father Philippe had admitted how, for all its trappings, his own life had been 'an empty and cold one, filled with thoughts about feelings as opposed to feelings about thoughts. I became a workaholic who had plunged into a marriage because of the emotional emptiness of my life as a priest. Anything was better than waking up alone. Only when I had shared Simone's bed did I realize I had changed one emotional prison for another.'

In the gentlest of voices, the analyst had responded to this outburst.

'Too many *mea culpas*. Far too many. And, you're labelling yourself. Failure, failure, failure. There's no shading in your self-preservation. You were almost certainly never quite as bad as you have painted. And that is another reason why you have had a problem in coping with celibacy. You still only understand it on an intellectual level, not on the emotional plane. Separate them. You still live by the dangerous principle of dividing yourself into compartments. Faith in one. Suppressed sex in another. Vocation in a third. A fourth holds your fantasies. That was fine until the boxes all popped open at once. You did not know which way to turn. So, after running into a marriage you never wanted, you had to blame something. Celibacy seemed the most obvious. You could convincingly blame it because it was something you genuinely did not understand how to handle. Hopefully, that can be changed. But it is going to be you, not me, that works out how to live with a new set of values. I'll lay them out for you. But only pick those you know you can be genuinely comfortable with.'

Father Philippe said he could no longer pretend to be comfortable with the existing view of the church, that the only effective way of living his vow was to suppress his sexual drive. The analyst raised the issue of guilt.

'You will have to learn how not to feel guilty over how you handle your celibacy. Assuming, of course, you want to go on being a priest.'

Father Philippe said he did. The analyst made no comment.

Four months and twenty-three days after the papers were filed, Father Philippe's divorce was granted. The certificate of dissolution was on the shelf-desk beside his bed. A week later his mother called to say that Simone was going to marry another man.

In session with the therapist the news had been examined, along with every aspect of Father Philippe's nightmare. Each part had been teased out and examined in detail and the role of each commander in the fantasy examined. The analyst suggested the crusader figure represented Father Philippe's resentment of authority. The presence of Walter was the fear in every man of his own latent homosexuality. They had explored pain and pleasure, the meaning of loneliness, both physical and spiritual. They had examined love in relation to forgiveness. Time and again they had returned to sin.

At their final session the therapist had summed up their months together.

'The important thing you have learned is not to justify. You have been doing that all your life – deluding yourself with explanations. A lot of your defences were installed before the age when you could intellectualize. You have now learned to explain away tensions that are natural to feel and not to place a burden of guilt upon yourself that is quite unnecessary. For instance, now that you see your mother's reference to premature ejaculation in those terms, you have also seen how those words further impressed upon you the idea that sex is something dirty and bound to end in failure. But you now understand it is not. That is the single most important thing you must not forget. All the other answers will come from that to enable you to live a healthy, normal life.'

Beyond Father Philippe's cell window was the dawn of a cloudless sky. He had dressed in black pants and open-necked white shirt, said his Divine Office, joined the Brothers celebrating Mass in the chapel, eaten a light breakfast and returned to his room. Normally he would be out in the fields at this hour. But he had been told he must wait indoors until the abbot was ready to see him.

The abbot's office, like its occupant, once more struck Father Philippe as deceptive. Both were less austere than they appeared: he had discovered when he returned form his weekend with Simone that the abbot was a gentle, kindly man who exercised his authority benevolently.

'Let us be seated by the window.' The abbot motioned towards the armchairs overlooking part of the gardens. 'Being inside so much, I never miss an opportunity to gaze upon nature.'

The abbot had a curious way of speaking as if his elocution had been acquired far from here. For a moment he remained staring out of the window, then settled himself in his armchair, hands on his knees.

'So, we have come to this. I will not hold you in suspense any longer. The Holy Office have agreed to have you back.'

'I'm very glad...'

The abbot raised his hand. 'There is no objection from Rome, provided I am satisfied you are fit to resume your priestly duties. That is why I have asked you here.'

Father Philippe realized how the apparatus of power and discipline magnified a man's presence.

'They tell me you haunt the library.' The abbot steepled his fingers. 'Have you ever read Sam Keen's *To a Dancing God*.'

'Yes. My analyst recommended the book.'

'Then you will perfectly understand why I ask.'

Keen had written feelingly that he himself had discovered the road to maturity was only possible after he had understood the prejudices of his personal history.

'Would you not concede, Father Philippe, that Keen is dealing with the truism that self-discipline can only lead to an enlarging of self in spiritual terms?'

'I accept that completely.'

'Why are you so positive?'

'I think I've learned more about being honest with myself since I've been here than I have over the past twenty years.'

The abbot weighed the response. 'That, of course, is commendable.'

'I've also learned not to expect an answer for everything.'

The abbot smiled. 'So you have learned that any worthwhile living involves a risk, and the more worthwhile your life is, the greater the risk. Do you accept that?'

'I do.'

'And your former wife? How do you see her now?'

Father Philippe said that he regarded his decision to end the marriage and return to Holy Orders as the first really independent step he had ever taken. He now accepted his dependency on Simone had been a living death for them both.

'Could you ever envisage repeating the experience again?'

'No one but God would dare to answer with absolute certainty. But I honestly believe I will not. I could have gone anywhere when I left her. But I came back to the church because I felt this is where I belong. I believe I have a place within it. I would go anywhere and do anything to serve it. I'm saying that, not because you have told me what Rome has decided, but because this is what I truly feel. I now see my vocation differently. I understand its deeper meaning. I want to serve. It's as simple as that.'

'Ten months ago you were crashing out of control. A danger to yourself and the church.'

'I just want another chance to take up my vocation. A new beginning.'

'Labels. You're using labels.' The abbot's voice was gentle but firm.

'I'm sorry.'

'Try not to use labels. I want you to convince me.'

'I'm not certain I can.'

'Why not? Why do you think I can't be convinced?'

'I'm not sure it is important that I do convince you,' Father Philippe said calmly.

'What makes you say that?'

'The real world is out there. That's where I have to make it. Not here.'

'That is perfectly true.'

It was the first sign of encouragement.

Father Philippe asked questions. 'How will you ever know when I am ready? How will I ever know? I just have to take a chance. Three months ago I wouldn't have risked saying that. Now I feel able to because I feel strong. Not blindly strong, but quietly strong. And it's not just my strength, but my limitations. I hope I know them. But I'll never really know until I go out there and try. I have to face the challenge. The responsibilities. And the risks. If I don't, I'll never know. But I do know I'm not the same person. I've got a feeling of self-worth. I'm more mature now.'

The abbot considered. 'But maturity and weakness are two sides of the same coin. How are you going to cope with the inconsistency, Father Philippe.'

'Prayer for a start. That's the most powerful tool I have.'

For a while there was silence in the room.

'Supposing you start to feel the pressures simply do not allow you to live up to your obligations as a priest?'

'I'm going to try and unite myself with God through my work.'

The abbot leaned forward, staring intently at Father Philippe.

'The world is full of Lolos and Simones. They'll be waiting, you know.'

'But I've a new perception of reality about them I never had before.'

'Are you certain? No doubt at all about what you are saying?'

'I've learned not to treat celibacy as a precious pearl or an abstract, but more as an ideal to try and live up to.'

The abbot continued to probe. 'What happens if you fail?'

'I'll try again. And keep on trying. That's really all I can do.'

'The church won't like that.'

'No.'

Once more the silence stretched. 'You seem to be very certain. That worries me a little. Growth is not something that generally happens overnight.'

'I'm not going back with any expectation of being Super Priest. I just want to pray together with parishioners again. I want to serve in a healthy way. I don't feel blocked any more. I'm now aware of the emotional experiences going on inside of me.'

The abbot was silent. Finally, he walked over to a wall of books and found the title he wanted and rifled through the pages.

'Let me read you this. "The crucifixion hurt his feelings very much; the carved nails; the unfeeling spear. If God had been there, he would not have let them do this."' The abbot snapped shut the book. 'What do you make of that?'

Father Philippe had read Richard Jeffries' book *Bevis: The Story of a Boy*, on Walter's recommendation. They had spent an entire Saturday afternoon discussing the drama of the words. Father Philippe told the abbot now what he had said then to Walter.

'The whole point is that God was there. The whole of Christianity, the very existence of the church, depends on the fact that God was there when his Son was crucified.'

'Please go on.' The abbot placed the book back on the shelf.

'I think the first important point to consider is that Jesus was a man, in the full psychological sense. He ate and drank. He knew thirst, hunger and what it was like to be tired. He had a sense of humour, yet could be severe.'

'What about sin?'

Father Philippe did not hesitate. 'I think it is impossible to accept that Jesus was not capable of sin. But the important thing is that he was without sin. You could argue that Jesus may have been tempted to succumb, such as when he was in the wilderness. But he did not.'

'Indeed. He did not. But, please, I did not mean to interrupt. Please continue.' The abbot remained leaning against the shelves, his arms folded, completely still, his eyes intent upon Father Philippe.

He began to explain how, through the human Jesus – Christ the man – came the loving God. To bring them together was the only way to fully comprehend the incarnation. Jesus was the amazing grace of God. To reject this fundamental is the very meaning of sin. 'To see Jesus in this way is the only critical attitude possible. Without accepting that Christ is the Son of God who gave his life as a ransom – there is little else of value in the Gospels. Without total acceptance of this one central fact, they become mythological fiction.'

The abbot broke the lengthy silence. 'I am much reminded, listening to you, of what Calvin said about the Nicene Creed. "Out of abundance of the heart the mouth speaketh".'

'I appreciate the compliment.' Father Philippe felt, at last, completely relaxed, as he had been caught up in an old and abiding enthusiasm for theological speculation. He spoke without interruption for a time, restating the evangelical truth that God and Christ are one.

The abbot gripped Father Philippe's hand. 'I am glad to be the first to welcome you back into your ministry.'

Two days later, Father Philippe left the monastery and headed eastwards in a rented car which held all his possessions. In his jacket pocket was a business card the therapist had given him. Written on the back was the name and telephone number of another psychoanalyst in the diocese he was going to. Father Philippe had been tempted to throw it away but something stopped him.

Andrew watched Jane inhale and thought her smoking marijuana was symbolic of the gap between them.

A week ago she had arrived in Rome and, over dinner that first night, produced a tin crammed with hand-rolled joints. Giles, she said casually in response to his question, had introduced her to the habit.

In the past seven days they had regularly lunched and dined in a trattoria near the Pantheon, chosen by him because it was off the beaten track for anyone from the seminary. They had quickly established territorial rights to a table in the rear, sitting beneath an enlarged still photo from Fellini's *Satryicon*. The owner said he had been an extra in the film. Jane, slightly tipsy from wine, had offered to share her joint with him. Inhaling, the man murmured he enjoyed the taste of her lipstick as much as the drug.

Jane had smiled across the table. 'Andy, don't look so severe. You're beginning to look like a priest, sitting there so stiff and disapproving.'

She and the owner had finished the joint between them. When they left, the man had kissed Jane on each cheek, and Andrew was shocked to see her response, pressing herself close to the restauranteur.

Strolling back to her hotel, she had asked him what he was thinking.

'Oh, lots of things.'

'Want to share?'

He smiled. The words reminded him of when they had lived together, and would curl up reading in the apartment, and he would suddenly look up, struck by something he had just read. And she would put aside her book and ask, 'Want to share?'

'This time tomorrow you'll be back home,' he said.

'It's really flown, Andy. I never thought we'd cram in so much. You're a great guide.'

They had walked the length of the Corso, gazed upon the Trevi Fountain, stared in awe at the ceiling of the Sistine Chapel, attended Mass in St Peter's, wandered around the Colosseum, strolled along the Via Veneto, visited the Pantheon, bought fresh fruit at the great market in the Campodei Furi, sipped coffee in espresso bars. He had shown her the Greg, the seminary, and even his room. She had, he knew, noted her photo on the wall, but said nothing. She did, however, comment that the pay-phone by the front door was a very public place for any private conversation. He wanted, then, to kiss her on the mouth, to pull her to him, to say he still loved her. Instead, he turned away, trying to hide his feelings.

'I'll miss you, Jane. I really will.'

'You've settled in very well, Andy. Giles said you would.'

'I wish you would stop talking about him.'

She looked surprised. 'Why? He's been a great help to me this last term. He got me into the Debating Society and the Dining Club. He's very good on his French wines…'

'I'm jealous.'

'But, Andy, that makes no sense. Why should you be jealous?'

'Because I am. And I wish you were too.'

'But that's totally irrational. Why should I be jealous? What is there to be jealous about?'

She looked at him quizzically.

'Jane, I'm sorry. I suppose it doesn't make sense.'

What would she say, he wondered again, if she could see what he had written in his diary these past nights. There, on paper, he had fought with himself.

I'm glad she has come. I know I have a lot of qualities as a man that can help me to be a priest. I love very strongly and I can commit that love to Christ. I love Our Lord. Like him, I have a passion for people. It is this ability though, to feel, that makes it so hard to be with her. I can feel her closeness. I can feel myself thinking, 'Oh, God, if only, if only.' But having her here is a very strange and unsettling experience. I keep on thinking what would happen if she made a move. How would I cope? Would I run away – or to her? I just don't know. I know that I am still a very sexual person. I can't help my feelings.

'Andy, don't be sad.'

'It's difficult at times not to be.'

'Try and remember we had a good time. We can still be friends.'

'I'd like that, Jane. I really would.'

He thought how impossible it was to exorcize his love for her.

'Andy, about Giles…'

He knew she was looking at him carefully.

'We're very close,' Jane said.

She reached for his hand, resting her fingers lightly on his knuckles. He could still remember the first time she had done this, in that pub, when she said she did not like a man who couldn't hold his drink. Giles, he recalled, had a limitless capacity for beer.

'Andy, did you hear what I said? We're very close, Giles and myself.'

His hand tightened over hers. 'Please, Jane. Don't. It hurts too much. I still want you.'

She pulled her hand away. 'Andy, you must understand. That's all over between us. It has to be. You made that choice. And it is the right one. You really are cut out for the priesthood. They need people like you. Vibrant and aware.'

'That's the point, Jane. I am aware – of you!'

She stroked his hand gently, murmuring. 'Andy. Poor Andy. I think it was a mistake to have come. Giles said it wouldn't help...'

'To hell with him! I still love you!'

Jane stared into his eyes. There was understanding but no hope there.

'Andy, you have to be realistic. You're going to be a priest.'

'Jane, who knows what the position will be when I'm ordained!' He realized he sounded desperate. 'Priests may be able to marry. There could be optional celibacy!'

'Oh, Andy! You know nothing will change. If it did the whole church would collapse. It's what makes priests special – their celibacy. We both know that.'

She pulled her hand away.

'Andy. I think you had better know that Giles has asked me to marry him.'

'Marry? That's just incredible. Marry? I've never heard anything so unbelievable!'

'No, it isn't. It happens all the time. My God, Andy!'

'Have you accepted?'

'Not yet.'

'Well, maybe...'

'He is certain it would work.' She looked thoughtful. 'We do have a lot in common. He's not the possessive type. I told him about us, and he said that was all in the past. I think that's very healthy.'

'He sounds like a budding psychologist.'

'Don't be bitchy! Actually he's now got his own business.'

'Well, good for Giles.'

'Oh, Andy, don't be like this.'

'How do you expect me to be? You come to Rome. We spend a week together. I mean, how do you expect me to be?'

She started to walk faster.

'You haven't changed, have you? You still think you can have everything. Snap your fingers and it's all yours. Life isn't like that, Andy. It really isn't.'

'So... you'll get married?'

'Yes. I think being in Rome has made me realize how much I miss him.'

He nodded, unable to think of anything to say.

'I'm sorry, Andy. I couldn't think of any other way of telling you.'

'Is that why you came?'

She nodded. 'I wanted to tell you myself. I felt that was important.'

He nodded, not able to speak, close to tears.

'Please, Andy, don't spoil our last evening together. Please don't do that.'

He pulled himself together. 'What did Oscar Wilde say about the past? That no one can buy it back?'

'But think of your future.' She smiled brightly. 'You know, maybe in forty years time I'll be able to tell my grandchildren that I had one of the best weeks of my life being shown around Rome by a future Pope!'

The gulf, he finally realized, was unbridgeable.

CHAPTER SEVENTEEN

Revelations and Responses

Huddled among the Christmas shoppers waiting for a bus, Clare continued to formulate in her mind the answer to the question set by the lecturer in mystical theology on how the church should evaluate the role of married saints. She wondered whether Tom would take the same approach as she planned.

Not for the first time he had suggested a list of references. The first time he had done so, she had hesitated. Later, when she read the books and magazine articles, she had seen how right he was in his choice. She began to see much of what she read reflected revolutionary ideas coming into the church.

The Second Vatican Council had produced a crisis that had profoundly affected traditional values. Now the traditionalists were fighting back. The church she still loved was like a great ship heading for the rocks, out of control, unable to keep pace with events.

Tom had revealed a further development could be about to happen. The latest news from Rome was that the Pope was dying. His successor would undoubtedly want to assert his authority and the present crisis would deepen. In the meantime, they should enjoy what they had: who knew how the church would look upon friendships like theirs in the future.

Months ago they had discussed what Jesus meant by friendship and Tom had said, 'A complete giving. Not being possessive or secretive. People fall in love. You and I know marriage is out. But we can still be friends. I think that's much more important. Don't you agree?'

She had.

Another time Tom defined friendship as described by Aelred de Rievaulx, a twelfth-century Cistercian monk, and Tom had applied it to their relationship. '"A friend must be chosen, then tried before being accepted forever as a friend." That's us.'

She had felt compelled to say, 'Tom, don't forget what de Rievaulx also said. "If a friendship has to end, it should be done gently, so as not to cause pain".'

He had looked at Clare and said very quietly. 'I hope this won't end. Friendships are very important for us celibates.'

She had begun for the first time to seriously read and think about celibacy. Along with everything else, there was a full-scale sexual revolution sweeping the church, led by the United States, Holland and West Germany. In those countries the most frequent reason given by priests and nuns for abandoning their vocations was celibacy. Those who remained were engaging increasingly in heated and public debate on such issues as how intimate a friendship could be for a nun or priest, what were the limitations on tactility, how could celibates cling to their sacred vows and yet have meaningful sexual identities? There was talk about an entirely new theology of sexuality based on a reinterpretation of teachings going back to the Yahwist, the Song of Songs, St Augustine and the Gospels of the New Testament. There were even those who claimed that Jesus could be called a sexual celibate.

Clare knew she still could never accept the more outspoken American demands for a full sexual life within a vocation. But she also realized she had moved a long way from her original perception that chastity was something natural for a nun, and therefore easy to handle.

Tom finally convinced her that sexual desires were not 'wrong' for either of them. It was how they were interpreted that mattered. The capacity to love, he stressed, not making love, was what was ultimately important. He argued that to be a celibate did not mean having to be asexual; it only meant never having physical intimacy.

Yet, when she asked if he wanted to redraw the rules of their own relationship, he had grinned and refused to be drawn. That was one of his defences when he didn't want to be pursued. He retreated behind his grin.

Her father had liked Tom from the day he dropped in with a pile of magazines and stayed for an hour to talk. He had done this several times since. It was one of the qualities that would make Tom a good priest, his caring. When she first told him about her father's illness, Tom went to the city's medical school and collected everything available in its library on the disease. The paperwork made it clear there was no cure

263

for her father. All his family could do was give him as much loving care as possible.

Every time she visited home her father seemed physically weaker, but his mind remained clear and alert. And Tom continued to treat him with kindness and affection. He was like another son to her father.

It had helped make her even more comfortable with Tom to talk about the reasons she became a nun. In turn he had made his life equally accessible to her. His parents had indoctrinated strong religious values, including the popular belief in Ireland at the time that to rear a son for the priesthood was a matter of pride. When the time had come, the decision for Tom was clear-cut. 'God loved me. It seemed the most natural thing to work for somebody who loves you totally. I just wanted to love like that.'

He had been at Clonliffe six years and in a few weeks would be ordained a deacon.

Clare was still wondering how Tom would tackle his essay on mystical theology when she boarded the bus.

The wind was blowing off the sea as Clare hurried along the long darkened drive towards the Mother House. She opened a side door and entered the kitchens. She could see her meal under a warming cover on top of the stool. She put down her books and briefcase on a table and lifted up the cover, savouring the plate of stew.

The warmth of the kitchen and the smell of food made her realize how tired she was. Putting the plate back on the stove she removed her topcoat and laid it across the back of a chair, oblivious to the water puddling the floor. She turned to pick up her meal.

'Sister Mary Luke, what are you doing?'

The Deputy stood in the kitchen doorway. Draped around her neck were yards of electric cord and coloured lights.

'You know perfectly well no one brings wet clothes into the kitchen! Have you forgotten there's a drying room?' The Deputy grabbed Clare's coat and carried it out of the kitchen. She returned with a mop and pail. 'Now, sister, clear this mess up!'

'Why are you treating me like this, Mother? You never seem to be satisfied...'

'How dare you, Sister Mary Luke! How dare you speak to me like that! First you're thoughtless, making such an unholy mess. Now you're insolent!' The Deputy's lower lip trembled with fury.

Clare's eyes filled with tears. 'I'm sorry, Mother. I didn't mean to make a mess. I was just so glad to get inside.' Clare mopped up the water, took the mop and bucket to their cupboard, and returned to the kitchen.

The Deputy was waiting. 'Why have you come back?'

'I was about to have dinner, Mother.'

'Dinner? At this hour?' The Deputy glared at her. 'Where have you been until now?'

'It's the weather, Mother. And the Christmas rush. The buses are all full.'

'Sister Mary Luke, stop making excuses. You are *late*. You should have been here an hour ago. Now come with me. There's work to be done.'

Clare glanced towards the stove.

'But, Mother. It won't take me a moment to eat this.'

Anger once more convulsed the Deputy. 'How dare you continue to argue with me! Is that what they teach you at college? To be insolent to your superiors? How dare you stand there and answer back. Now, come with me. This instant!'

She turned on her heels.

With a last look at the plate, Clare followed her into the main entrance hall where Declan and the kitchen nuns were busy erecting the convent's Christmas tree. The Deputy removed the lights festooning her neck and thrust them at Clare.

'You know how these go. Or at least you should.'

Clare felt the hunger rumbling in her stomach.

'Mother, couldn't I just have a quick bite first. Please! It won't take a minute. Then I'll be glad to get…'

'Up that ladder now! Do you hear, sister? Now!' The Deputy was shaking with renewed anger.

Clare responded in a voice which seemed to come from someone she did not know. 'You're not being fair! I do my share. I always have! But you go on goading me. On and on. You seem to hate me going to college! You go on and on trying to make me lose my temper! You've done it to others. They couldn't stick it, so they left. Well, I'm not going to leave, but I'm sick and tired of your meanness. Leave me alone! Just leave me alone!'

There was a stunned silence around the tree.

'Do you know what you have just said, Sister Mary Luke?'

The Deputy's voice was cold and unemotional. Something about her reminded Clare of an unexploded bomb in a Belfast street: danger embedded in a familiar landmark. She was suddenly too scared to cry.

'I'm sorry, Mother. I really am. I lost my temper. That is unforgivable.' She pressed her hand against her mouth.

The Deputy's heavy breathing filled the silence.

'You must also apologize to all your sisters for causing them to feel such embarrassment.'

'Yes, Mother.' After doing so Clare climbed the ladder and began to hang the lights on the tree, her eyes shiny with tears.

Below her the Deputy ordered how the lights should be arranged. Finally, she handed Clare the large, silver-painted tin star Sister Dualta had fashioned in her workshop. Clare placed it at the top of the tree. After the Deputy stood back to admire the effect, Clare was allowed to climb down.

She moved towards the kitchen.

'Sister Mary Luke! Where are you going?' called the Deputy.

'To eat my supper.'

'Really, sister! You and your stomach. Have you so lost touch with life here that you've forgotten silent meditation? What are they teaching you at college?'

Clare followed the others into the chapel.

Kneeling in her stall, Clare felt an old restlessness had returned and, with it, familiar questions. How could anyone stop her being a woman? How could she be true to her vows and yet be honest to herself? For weeks now this had become a time when her mind raced instead of being still; when it drifted instead of being focused.

She remembered Tom's words. 'You look the same, but you're different. You don't have convent tunnel vision anymore.'

That had prompted a discussion about women and power in the church. Tom had insisted only men – priests – could properly exercise that power. She had countered women were not seeking personal power, only the right to better serve the church.

Clare opened her eyes. She felt utterly miserable. Tears streamed down her face. She never imagined this could be happening to her. She had seen others cry in chapel but that had always been shortly before they had left the Community forever. She knew she did not want to leave. Yet she was filled with a terrible dread that she was no longer so certain of her future.

Leaving chapel, Clare slipped through a narrow door between two of the parlours. On visiting days it was normally used by the kitchen nuns bringing tea and cakes to guests. The passage was long, narrow, winding and pitch-black. She felt her way along the walls and had gone some distance when she realized she was not alone. She could hear breathing. She hesitated, not knowing what to do, remembering there were several alcoves on either side of the passage used for storing supplies. Someone was hiding in one of them.

Clare crept forward towards the sound. She looked behind her and could no longer see the crack of light under the narrow door. Peering ahead, the door leading to the kitchen was also not visible. She began to feel frightened.

In the back of an alcove she could make out a vague shape.

'Who's there?' Her voice was unnaturally loud.

The shape shrank back.

'Who's there? Come on out,' she repeated.

The shape moved towards her.

'Sister Mary Luke.'

'Declan.'

Clare leaned back against the wall, relieved. 'What on earth are you doing here?'

Declan whispered, 'It's my nip hole. Every time you're all in chapel of an evening, I come in here for a quiet tot.'

He struck a match, lighting up the alcove. He had a whisky bottle in his hand.

'But what if Deputy Mother caught you?'

The groundsman cackled. 'No chance of that, sister. She's scared of the dark! Won't come down here once the light goes!' He smiled his slightly tipsy smile, the one he had whenever he returned from a wedding.

Clare led the way into the kitchen. Her meal was a congealed mess. Declan picked a key from a ring hanging on a hook and unlocked a pantry. Its shelves were laden with food Clare had never seen served in the refectory.

'Deputy's private store. For impressing priests and the like who come visiting her.' He grinned. 'I don't think she'll miss anything.'

Clare hesitated.

'No, you just sit down, sister. Leave it all to me.'

He motioned her towards the table. Clare looked at the dried-up stew on the range and her stomach gave another rumble. That decided her. She sat at the table.

Declan removed a tin of salmon from a shelf and in no time had provided Clare with a substantial supper. He leaned against the sink, watching her eat, taking nips from his bottle. 'Sister, if you ask me, you don't look well.'

'I'm fine, really.' She smiled. 'A little tired, that's all. And you scared me back there.'

He shook his head. 'No, that's not it. You have that uncertain look, if you don't mind my saying so.'

'Uncertain?' She was alert. 'I don't feel uncertain about anything.'

'I hope not, sister. I really hope not. But I've seen that look in nuns before they even knew they felt uncertain. I always can tell, you know.'

'Well, you're wrong this time, Declan.' Clare wished she hadn't sounded so sharp. She gathered up her books and briefcase.

'Don't worry about the washing-up, sister. I'll take care of that. You be off now.'

He gave her another lop-sided smile.

Going to her room, she thought, *has it become so obvious that I love Tom?*

The amplified metallic voice in the airport concourse once more announced that all flights out of Harrisburg were delayed indefinitely due to severe weather conditions. Victoria had heard a ticket agent say it was one of the worst blizzards he could recall. The snowstorm had begun as she left her last high-school appointment, and, by the time she reached the airport, the snowploughs were fighting a losing battle to keep the runways clear.

Victoria glanced at her watch. There was no way she could reach the Mother House before the Grand Silence. She decided to stay overnight in one of the nearby motels. She walked towards the courtesy telephones where lines were already forming. She chose the shortest one and put down her suitcases. One was empty. She had distributed the last of her brochures at the school. It had been a deeply disappointing tour. Not one girl had given a firm commitment, only eight had given uncertain promises to consider the matter further. She should not, she told herself, be really surprised. Religious life was losing its appeal for America's youth. Many of them had become as cynical about God as they were about the Watergate revelations which had started to surface.

Matters had not been helped, she knew, by reports that in Europe the church had discreetly trafficked in young Asian girls. They had been brought from Vietnam and Cambodia to supplement the falling numbers of vocations, particularly among the teaching and nursing Orders of France, Germany and Holland. They were put to work in convent kitchens, and on the land for little money and housed in spartan conditions. The scandal had forced the Vatican to order the matter to stop.

Victoria was suddenly aware a man was watching her. He smiled, making him look almost too young for the chest full of ribbons on his air force colonel's uniform. She wondered briefly if he was also on the pitching circuit. He had the steady gaze and trim figure that would attract students into the military.

'Hi.'

'Hullo,' she replied.

He edged his tote bag forward towards the bank of motel courtesy phones. 'I guess we both made it in time.'

He had a pleasant voice; West Coast and well-bred, Art would have said. She had used him again last night. He looked like Art too: that same determination, same fixing look.

In front of her a man was shouting into the telephone, 'What do you mean you have no rooms? How is this possible?'

The colonel had reached his courtesy phone.

The man was still yelling. Suddenly he slammed down the phone and stormed away.

Victoria picked up the telephone and a bored voice told her there were no vacancies.

'Are you absolutely certain there isn't just one single…'

The voice disconnected her before she could complete her question.

The colonel was looking across at her and speaking into his telephone. He was smiling again, a smile, she decided, with no hooks in it. She nodded. The colonel spoke into the phone just as the loudspeakers paged a passenger. He replaced the receiver, saying he had booked her a room.

'Thank you.' She smiled. 'But can I afford it?'

'They're all at the same rate, ma'am.' He picked up his tote bag. 'Here, let me take one of these.' He motioned towards her cases.

He introduced himself. 'Frank Rivers. United States Air Force, ma'am.'

She hesitated. 'Victoria John. Actually, Victoria Sarah John.'

Waiting for the motel bus, the snow swirled around them. She was glad now she was wearing a trenchcoat and fur hat. He seemed indifferent to the weather.

'You get used to it in Alaska.' He had Art's way of cutting out anything superfluous.

'Are you based there, colonel?'

'Frank, ma'am.' He smiled. 'Was based there, Victoria. Posted now to Manila.'

She noticed his left shoulder was slightly hunched.

'Are you a flier?'

'Used to be.' He tapped his left shoulder. 'Baled out the wrong side of 30,000 feet. Wrecked a plane and my shoulder blade. Now I fly a desk. Anchorage, Manila. It's the same desk. What line are you in?'

A snow plough roared past. Suddenly she did not want to say she was a nun. That would only lead to more questions. Why, she often wondered, was it always open season on nuns? Strangers asked her questions they would never put to even their closest friends. Is it really possible to live without sex? Do some nuns make out with priests? Is it true that nuns still whip each other? People still associate nuns with all kinds of covert sexuality.

'Oh, I travel.'

She had long ago decided to keep part of herself private; she supposed it had a lot to do with there still being so little privacy in the Mother House. The really hard thing was the age gap. What could she possibly say on infirmary duty to an eighty-year-old whose last lucid memories were of the Depression?

'You like travelling?'

'You can get to dislike anything on a day like this,' she said.

'You work for a big company?'

'Big enough.' She smiled, switching roles. 'Are you looking forward to Manila?'

'My second tour. A wild place. You can't beat it.'

She let the remark pass.

He was still talking about the attractions of Manila when they arrived at the motel. He marched towards the desk and gave his rank and name.

'Yes, sir. Here we are. Colonel and Mrs Rivers.'

Victoria stepped forward. 'I think there's a mistake.'

The clerk consulted his list. 'No. I have it here. One double with bath. Forty…'

'A double? There is a mistake. Definitely.'

The clerk and the colonel looked at each other. Victoria sensed something move between them, short and swift. It was gone in a moment.

'It's the only room right now.'

'Then I'll take it.' She smiled at the colonel. 'I'm sure you won't mind giving up your room.'

He hesitated, crestfallen.

'Well, not at all, Victoria.' He turned back to the clerk. 'Would you check again, please?' He slipped a five dollar bill across the counter. 'I believe I did reserve two singles.'

The clerk shrugged, pocketed the bill, and ran his finger down a list.

'Okay. I have it. Two singles.'

The colonel turned to Victoria. 'I'm really sorry about this.'

'I'm sure it doesn't happen very often to you.' She smiled sweetly.

'Will you at least let me buy you dinner?'

'There's no need to, really.'

The clerk asked them to register. Victoria leaned forward so he could not see over her shoulder. She slid the form across to the clerk. He looked at it and blinked. He handed the keys over to their adjoining rooms.

'Look, about dinner…'

'Please, Victoria. I'd really like you to have dinner with me.'

'Well… okay. I'll need about fifteen minutes to freshen up.'

'Wonderful. That's just wonderful.'

She caught him glance triumphantly at the clerk and then look momentarily puzzled when the hotel employee gave him a quick shrug.

Victoria gave herself a final check in the mirror and went down to the bar. The colonel was leaning back against a banquette, sipping a cocktail.

She advanced into his stunned expression, explaining, 'I didn't want there to be any more… misunderstandings.' She smiled. 'Now, I'd like a glass of red wine followed by a steak, medium rare. And I want to hear more about how wild the Philippines are.'

The colonel could only nod, dumbfounded, at Victoria standing there in her modified habit and veil.

CHAPTER EIGHTEEN

Journey into Madness

Andrew sat opposite the spiritual director counting the minutes until he could escape from Father William's good intentions. The silence between them had stretched after the priest had said that, from time to time, everyone felt 'out of sorts'. Andrew thought those words came nowhere near describing the real truth of what he felt.

Fifty-six days had passed since Jane's letter had arrived. He had read it several times before finally crying himself to sleep. When he awoke next morning, he was filled with a despair he had never experienced before. He lay in bed, silent and inactive, his mind alternating between bouts of pain and guilt. And the punitive, unrelenting voice of his conscience would only say: this you deserved. The knowledge absorbed all his vitality, leaving him exhausted. Jane's letter had left no hope. She *was* going to marry Giles.

For an entire week, he missed his seminary duties and classes, pleading a summer cold. His depression had deepened and had remained. Yet some instinct told him he must share the reason with no one, never even admit he was depressed. His inner mourning – torpor, despair, failure and self-rage – were his alone to bear.

After a week, to the outside world he was once more someone busy with his daily tasks. His feelings were bottled inside him, his self-reproach unsuspected. It had taken root in the form of a threatening, devouring, object he called *The Thing*.

It told him nothing could fill the vast void Jane had left in his life. That living itself was pointless.

In the past two months, *The Thing* had encouraged him to keep his ever-deepening sense of loss secret. His sadness and tears, along with a deep feeling of inner emptiness, were for the privacy of his room. He spent an ever-increasing amount of time there, and he knew his tutors and seminary staff assumed he was studying or meditating. In chapel, at the Greg, and during mealtimes, he still managed to conceal what was consuming him.

He continued to do so now from Father William. *The Thing* had warned that someone like the spiritual director would try and find another answer to the question increasingly uppermost in Andrew's mind. *What was the point of living?*

At first the stark directness of the question had frightened him. But its continued presence in his mind had taken away its initial fear.

He could be going to class and the idea would occur to him how easy it would be to step in front of a bus or car. He would be leaning out of the window of his room and it would cross his mind what little effort was needed to jump. Death would be a relief from the constant reminder it was his loss, his bereavement, caused by her betrayal.

Father William looked at him through tented fingers. 'I can't think of anyone who has not felt out of sorts in their first year here. The feeling everything is getting on top of them. That little doubts are becoming big ones. The important thing is not to let them grow. You can see that, can't you?'

'Yes.' Andrew felt the hopelessness curdling his stomach.

Once more feelings of suicide had surfaced. His death would be his ultimate triumph. It would show Jane he had not lost his sense of self-purpose, that he was not half-hearted about matters, that he was not lacking in judgement, that in taking his life he was displaying a higher form of courage few possess. His brave action would make Jane realize what she had done to him.

Once more Father William's voice intruded.

'As I was saying, Andrew, the human spirit is a powerful force. I've seen young men sit where you are, filled with all the woes of life. They weren't getting on with their studies. They felt all the distractions of Rome. Their prayer life seemed to be up the creek. They couldn't relate to their situation. Life, they felt, was a real mess.'

The spiritual director paused, reflecting and remembering.

'Sometimes they couldn't talk to me. So I suggested they should go to chapel. Find a place in a corner and kneel and pray and have direct contact with God. I can't think of one student it didn't help. I really can't. I think it would help you. Open yourself to Christ fully. Tell him that things are a bit difficult right now and that you want him to guide you through a bit of a bad patch. That's what it is, you know, Andrew. A bit of a choppy sea. There you were sailing along, everything as smooth as the Med in August, and then something probably said "what am I doing here?" We all think, can it really be that God has called us to his service? But he has, that's why we are here. Why you are here!'

'I'm sure you're right.'

Andrew now knew no amount of praying would help. For weeks he had been awakening exhausted in the small hours, filled with intolerable restlessness. He would get up and pace his room, composing in his mind letters to Jane and his parents, explaining why he had no alternative but to take his life. He never managed to complete a letter before once more he would lie on his bed, desperately trying to sleep. Each morning he had lain, waiting for dawn, utterly alone, filled with a deepening conviction that *The Thing* was right. There was no point in living.

It was after one of these mornings that Andrew had crept downstairs to the seminary's store room. He brought back a length of rope and hid it under his bed.

Father William was smiling at him.

'I realize that when the novelty wears off, the food isn't quite what you are used to at home.'

'The food's fine. Really.'

Andrew had developed a dislike for eating. Food reminded him of Jane.

'I hear you've cut back a bit. Not quite filling your plate the way you used to.'

Andrew forced a smile. 'I find I don't need so much now that I like to study alone. I picked up the habit in my last year at university.'

'But don't let it take you over. Study is important, I grant you. But a priest, you know...' The spiritual director hesitated, framing his thought. 'A priest needs to be a bit of an all-rounder. Good on the theoretical stuff, but also able to make contact. One of the things the rector is very keen on here is having everybody integrate. He puts great store on that. So, for that matter, does the cardinal. His secretary was on the phone the other day. He asked how you were getting on.'

'That's my mother again.'

The director smiled, understanding about the importance of family connections. Andrew risked a quick glance at the mantle clock. It would soon be over. 'I'm sorry if I've sounded like some homesick kid away from home for the first time. I'm really happy here. I'm certain about my vocation. The Greg is a challenge and it's really... well, all I'd hoped for.'

Once more Father William nodded approvingly. 'Good, that's very positive. The important thing is not to feel sorry for yourself. It's so easy to drift into...' He paused, once more searching for the right words. 'Once you are adrift, all sorts of things can go wrong.'

Father William peered at Andrew over the top of his fingers.

'From time to time seminarians have problems distinguishing between friendship of a non-sexual kind, what I would call a Christian friendship, and other feelings. Some of them find they cannot cope without affection. So, they turn to each other for comfort. There is nothing intrinsically wrong with this, providing it remains within a healthy dimension. The important thing is to distinguish between a close and loving relationship and one which contains sexual elements. Apart from the sinful, moral aspect involved in any kind of friendship other than a purely celibate one, there is the very real psychological problem of guilt which homosexuality can produce in people. The more balanced a person, the more is his guilt. Because we live in an all-male Community, friendships can take on a more intense meaning. And so the temptation to go that little bit further takes on a new attraction.'

Andrew could not contain himself. 'You don't think I'm turning gay, do you!'

Father William's voice was reassuring. 'No. I don't think you are. But if I may say so, you are turning into a bit of a sartorial mess.' The priest flexed his fingers and resteepled them. 'I'm sorry to be so blunt. But I've always found it best not to mince matters when it comes to self-neglect. There's something about one's outward appearance that's very important. It's one of the reasons a priest's cassock compels respect. No one can look untidy in a soutane.'

'I'm sorry. I hadn't realized I'd become scruffy.'

The director collapsed his tented fingers and placed his hands on his knees. In the past, these periods of silence had been reflective pauses, allowing each of them to consider what had been said, and what further needed to be stated. But now Andrew, in the numbing silence, was unable to concentrate. It was even an effort to remember how this conversation began.

'I gather you're still doing extremely well at the Greg. We're all very pleased. That's why I think this is no more than a passing mood. If it was more, it would show in your work,' Father William finally said.

'I'm sure you're right,' Andrew said.

There were spells when his mind suddenly raced from one idea to another on how he could persuade Jane to give up Giles. He would telephone her. Write to her. Have his mother visit her. No, have his mother call her mother and have them join forces to make Jane see reason. He could appeal to Giles, man to man, to give up Jane. No, not appeal, explain: that Giles had only caught her on the rebound. As the impracticability of each idea became clear, the awful feeling of hopelessness grew.

'The important thing, Andrew, is to keep a sense of balance between your studies and your prayer life. Knowing what is important to take from each.'

'I hope I do that.'

Father William was on his feet, his voice mellifluous and sympathetic. 'You know, when I first came out here, I imagined I would never settle. Those first couple of years were, to put it bluntly, hell. Suddenly it all fell into place. I accepted I belonged here. I think that's what we all have to do. Accept.'

'Yes. I suppose so.'

The spiritual director put his hands behind his back, rocking gently on the balls of his feet – a signal he was running late. It meant, thought Andrew, suddenly relieved, that he could leave this sanctum of books and platitudes. *The Thing* had just silently whispered in his mind that he really shouldn't waste any more time.

Father William opened the door. There was a certainty in his eyes and voice. 'Remember. Prayer. See you in a fortnight. But drop by any time you feel the need for a chat.'

Andrew felt drained, yet triumphant. He had achieved what *The Thing* had commanded. He had kept their secret.

Andrew reached his room, buried his face in his pillow. After a while, the tears subsided and the pain turned to resolve. He sat at his desk and began to compose another farewell letter to Jane.

After an hour, he was still unable to find the right words. He finally retreated, defeated, to his bed, watching the sky lose its hard blueness and take on the softer paleness of dusk. A while later an abyss of blackness filled the windowspace, then the stars appeared all at once. And, after them, the moon, bright enough for him to see the crumpled sheets of paper scattered on the floor around his desk.

The thunderstorm jerked Andrew upright. The clap of thunder appeared to be directly overhead, like artillery fire, then an enormous cataract of water descended from the sky. He rushed to close the window, and turned to the desk. The words began to swirl once more in his head, faster and faster. *I love her. I hate her. Love. Hate.* He held his hands over his ears to try and blot out the silent, inner voice. *You need to rest. You need to put an end to this pain. You can't take any more. You must stop now.*

The storm passed as quickly as it started. Tomorrow, the sky would be blue, a new day. It would be like being reborn. But not for him.

He lay in the darkness, somewhere between sleep and wakefulness, his twilight zone. The stars were out. The street sounds had returned: shrill voices, an interminable blaring of horns, radios and televisions. But it was all so far away. He closed his eyes.

Instantly, *The Thing* was back inside his head. *Put an end to this. Take the rope. Do it now.* Andrew silently pleaded he was not ready. *The Thing* reiterated. *To use the rope is not a sign of weakness. It requires a special strength. Stop resisting.*

Beyond the window, the blare of traffic faded. Rome was going to sleep. 'No. Please. No,' whispered Andrew aloud this time.

It is time for you to rest. You are very, very tired. You deserve to sleep.

Andrew continued to plead to the persuasive voice inside his head. 'I must write Jane a farewell note. I must. You must let me do that.' Andrew stumbled to the desk and started to write. 'I love you. Goodbye. I love you. Goodbye. I love you. Goodbye.'

He filled a page with repetition.

The Thing was consoling. *You have done everything. There is no more to be done. You are making the right decision. You really are.*

'Jane.' Andrew called out her name, as if she would appear and unlock the doors closing in his mind. 'Jane. Please understand. I love you. Goodbye. I love you.'

As he walked towards the door, there was a tightening feeling in his throat, as if he was being choked. The secret voice commanded him to stop. *Have you forgotten? The rope. Take the rope.*

The tears welled up behind Andrew's eyes. 'Please,' he pleaded, 'not just yet.'

Now. There is no time to waste.

'No!' The shout burst from Andrew. 'No! No! No!'

Immediately *The Thing* was gone. It hated to be shouted at.

'Go away! Damn you. Go away!' Andrew continued to shout.

Tears spilled down his cheeks. He was so weary that he could barely stagger back to bed. He lay in the darkness, looking at the rectangle of moonlit sky framed in the window. *The Thing* was back.

Slowly Andrew rose from the bed. He walked to the window. His parents would be asleep. He wanted so much for them to understand. But would they? How would they live with the stigma? People would point them out as the parents of the boy who committed suicide in Rome. What would Father Patrick say? What would his mother say to the cardinal? How would anyone ever begin to understand? *The Thing* promised: *they will understand. They will reserve all their anger for Jane. She will be the outcast, not you. She will bear the stigma, the one person who has driven you to this. She will suffer eternal damnation, not you.*

Andrew knelt before the bed and pulled out the rope. He fed it through his hands, foot by foot, feeling its thickness and the roughness of the hemp, silently counting as he had done before. It was eleven feet long. He would need two of those feet to fashion a noose. That would leave him nine feet. A beam or hook ten feet clear of the ground would be ideal. He recoiled the rope. *The Thing* was silent. But he could sense its approval.

Andrew turned and descended the staircase to the ground floor. He paused near the chapel thinking there was no loneliness as great as that of utter silence and complete darkness. Standing there, perfectly still, sweat on his skin, his bare feet cold on the tiled floor, his mind was filled with a feeling he was somewhere between purgatory and hell. Then, overriding all else, came the thought that, at last, he could discover for himself the greatest mystery of life. What lay beyond it.

He pushed open the chapel door, the rope in his hand.

CHAPTER NINETEEN

Ministering

Father Philippe's study window provided an uninterrupted view into the ghetto where he did most of his ministering. Forty years ago the ramshackle suburb across the street had been farmland until the post-World War II boom enticed the developers. By the early 1950s, a community had been established, comprised exclusively of young, white, professional families whose children went to one of three local schools, one Catholic. Later, when they grew up, they were married in St Mark's where Father Philippe now worked. When they died they were buried in the neighbourhood's Catholic cemetery, segregated even in death from non-Catholics.

Then came Freedom Summer, 1964. The Civil Rights Act which followed saw street by street, house by house being bought by Afro-American families. Within a year there wasn't a white person left in the neighbourhood. Gardens became less well-tended, and houses needed repainting. The pews of St Mark's were overwhelmingly filled with black Catholics who gave thanks to the church which, during the decade of civil unrest, had supported their cause.

In Father Philippe's six months at St Mark's, he had become a familiar figure in the ghetto. Yet he still managed to retain a friendly relationship with his handful of white parishioners. The bishop had said how pleased he was about this.

From the beginning Father Philippe had liked the gentle, soft-voiced leader of the diocese of 30,000 Catholics scattered through ten parishes, each with a solidly-built church and rectory, schools, counselling centres and a hospital, the General. The bishop was a paternal figure, unlike the chancellor, who Father Philippe had found distant. The Monsignor was proud of being FBI – foreign-born Irish – and, in his soft Galway brogue, made it clear he knew all about Father

Philippe's past. But Father Ray Nolan, the parish priest at St Mark's, had welcomed him warmly.

Father Nolan was a born worrier and completely unable to delegate. He also never allowed a woman inside the parochial house except Marcia, the Mexican who cleaned. All other women conducted their business with Father Nolan on the doorstep.

Nevertheless, Father Philippe found his superior was no stick-in-the-mud and, when he had suggested the old-fashioned confessional should be replaced by a confession room, Father Nolan accepted Father Philippe's argument that parishioners would feel more relaxed admitting their sins in comfortable surroundings instead of having to crouch in the darkness of a stuffy box.

The confession room had a silver carpet, pale blue walls and two overstuffed armchairs covered in crimson velvet facing each other, with a low table in between. The colour scheme was Father Philippe's, just as he was responsible for the decor of his own five-roomed apartment in the rectory.

His study had a pale pink carpet and lime-coloured walls. The living room was richly red from floor to ceiling, the way he imagined a Renaissance baronial chamber might look. His bedroom was the softest of cream: carpet, walls and ceiling. The kitchen was predominantly dark green with solid oak panelling. The bathroom tiles were covered with exotic birds and flowers, hand-painted on ceramics; it reminded him of a picture he once saw of the Garden of Eden. The wall-coverings and furnishings had been gifts from parishioners. Another church member, a haberdasher, had provided him with an entire wardrobe of clothes.

Father Philippe's paperwork was once more interrupted on this summer's morning by another telephone call from Father Nolan who was making his weekly visit to the chancellery down town.

'When you get to the Schiff house, remember to check on Beth. Her mother says she's always asleep when I call. Try and see her, Philippe.'

He had never visited the Schiff's. They had always been Father Nolan's responsibility. All he knew was that Beth Schiff had been bedridden for some weeks.

'Oh, and make sure the church is locked before you go.'

'I already have.'

A month ago Father Nolan had spotted a youth about to prise off the gold-plated door of the tabernacle. He had chased him out into the street, but the teenager escaped. Since then, the church had been locked whenever one of them was not on duty.

'Did Fern East drop off that money?'

'No. But I can go and ask her if you like. She's just gone by.'

'No, no. Don't do that,' Father Nolan said hastily.

Father Philippe watched Fern complete another lap of the jogging track next door to the church. She ran every morning. Fern had told him keeping her body fit was helping her recover from the shock of losing her husband from cancer a year previously.

A couple of months ago Fern had asked him, on her way out of the confession room, if he would like to join her. Next morning he turned up, and Fern approved his sky-blue suit but rejected the sneakers saying his feet would soon be a mass of blisters. She had driven him to a sports store and bought him a pair of jogging shoes. Since then, he had regularly run beside her.

He learned that Fern was past fifty, loyal to the memory of her husband and devoted to her children, all of whom, except Margot, were married. Her eldest daughter was a concern to her. Margot was taking an unusually long time to get over a broken engagement. Perhaps one day, Fern suggested, he could drop by the house and explain she must stop feeling sorry for herself. Perhaps he would, he said.

Their morning work-outs had become occasions when he was able to speak increasingly freely about his own past. Fern listened sympathetically, occasionally interjecting to remind him his secrets were safe and she felt privileged he should share them with her. In so many ways, he realized, Fern was the mother he wished he had.

In every way he knew this was the life for which he had been ordained. Parishioners told him his sermons were some of the best they had heard. He knew his off-the-cuff speeches at weddings were widely quoted. Parents said they had never known a priest who could baptize an infant without causing tears and everyone agreed there was no better priest in the diocese to conduct a funeral.

Father Philippe felt he especially understood death and its effects on the bereaved, because he had come so close to his own spiritual death. It had helped him to always try to make sure people understood their grief was his, and that he shared their despair at the loss of a loved one.

He reminded himself on these occasions what it was like to feel broken and emotionally adrift. Faith, he resolutely believed, had been instrumental in bringing him back from his brink of despair. He offered it to others, using words which, for all their repetition, still retained a freshness. 'I know what you are enduring. I have a few suggestions that might help. I don't possess any secret knowledge or any special comforting skills. But I can try and show you how to survive.'

The proof of his success as a priest was in his diary.

Tuesday, October 30. The bishop introduced me at a deanery meeting. Said I had come to do missionary work. That's why he was giving me St Mark's. Spent rest of the day driving around the parish with Ray. He did not say much.

Saturday, November 7. Getting to know Ray. He's like the bishop. I feel they want to protect me from my past. They are good men and very generous to me. But the chancellor is a s.o.b. In his mind I am someone who has been allowed a second chance after doing the unforgivable.

Monday, November 16. Ray called me up to his office and read the riot act. He had a whole list of things. I'd left a light burning when I wasn't in a room. Had the radio playing too loud. Made me feel like a kid. Then, he said okay, don't do it again, and I'm doing a good job.

Monday, December 3. Sat with Mrs Woodstock all day. She knew she couldn't last until morning. I said to her, 'when you die it'll just be like the candle going out. It'll be very quiet. You'll just die like that.' She was saying her rosary when her candle went out. Her last words to me were 'Oh, my Jesus, save us.' Then she died in my arms.

Sunday, December 9. I realized again how much I love babies. Held the Lawrence baby for a long time when baptizing him and really felt he was mine. I told his mother. She understood. But big Dan Lawrence told Paul Kirwan that there's no way a priest can feel like I did. I just took Big Dan aside and told him he was a crock of b.s. if he didn't understand that the person inside the cassock was a man first and a priest second. He looked at me strangely and said that was being honest.

Saturday, December 16. First wedding here. Andy Newton and Jodi Bonham. I was very conscious of how fragile a relationship is. Marrying them I kept on thinking of a tiny plant that has just been put into the ground. If that sounds dramatic, it's the only way to say what I want to

say without being philosophical or theological. Told them they would,
like a tiny plant, be buffeted by the wind and pelted by the hail and
scorched by the sun, but somehow they should look upon their vows and
their prayer life as providing them with shelter and shade to survive.
Marriage, I said, was the most tremendous risk and if they could survive
they would have a miracle. Any marriage that survives is a miracle.

He waved to Fern as she completed another lap and decided to make
his first call on Beth Schiff and her mother.

An hour later he watched Ma Schiff shift from one foot to another, as
if her massive body was searching for a point of equilibrium. She had
several chins, a purpled goitre on her neck and her hair was matted,
greying and plaited like a child's. Her hands reminded him of ancient
tree roots, gnarled and twisted, leathery, like her skin. Standing on the
porch, she towered over him asking where Father Nolan was.

'He had a meeting, Mrs Schiff.'

'That so?' She dug her hands keep into the pockets of her shapeless
dress. It was stained down the front as if she spilled everything she
touched. 'He ain't missed a call before.'

'The bishop wanted him.'

She turned abruptly and resumed tugging at a mass of creeper curled
around one of the porch pillars. It snapped quite suddenly under her
strength and she tossed the clump of tendrils to one side. 'That so?'

He could see her looking at him, sceptical and suspicious. He knew
that gaze: it had sometimes come into his mother's eye before one of
her attacks. From somewhere inside the house came a strange croaking
sound, more animal than human.

'Is that Beth?' He tried to sound casual.

Ma Schiff did not answer.

'Sounds like she might need some help. Don't you think we should
go and see?' Father Philippe suggested.

Ma Schiff's eyes narrowed.

'What's the matter with Beth, Mrs Schiff?' he asked gently.

She tore away more of the creeper. He had a vision of her being able
to destroy anything with those hands.

'She's got problems.' Her voice was surprisingly high-pitched. 'Can't
think why you've come if you don't know the problems.'

She continued concentrating totally on her work, pulling away more ivy.

He wished Father Nolan had briefed him. Dogs were growling around his car. Across the street children stood, silent and wary, aware of him. Father Philippe concentrated on Ma Schiff.

'Why don't we go inside?'

She hesitated, then turned and led him into the house.

It took a few moments to adjust to his surrounds and the stale odours of cooking. The linoleum was torn in several places as if gnawed by rats. The furniture was oversized and from another age, too broken to have any antique value, too dirty to be even sold as junk. The only wall decorations in the living room were religious symbols: a wooden crucifix and a Madonna framed in plastic. There was a bunch of wax flowers on a table littered with dirty crockery.

'I've let things go since my husband died,' Ma Schiff said.

'When was that?'

'Ten years ago next May.'

'What happened, Mrs Schiff?'

Father Philippe stood in the centre of the room feeling her silent anger.

'Auto crash. Father Nolan went there, right in the middle of the night and gave him the Last Rites. He still died on the way to the General.'

She started to rub her face, working her hand hard back and forth across her big drooping jaw.

'And Beth? She your only child?'

'Yup. Never tried again after her. Saw no point in repeating the mistake.'

The animal sound came again from the adjoining room.

'What's the matter with Beth?'

She caught her lower lip in her teeth. 'Matter? Nothing's the matter. She was made like that. God made her like she is.'

Father Philippe waited a moment before he spoke. 'She has some congenital defect? Is that it?'

'Questions!' Ma Schiff uttered the word almost fiercely. 'Don't you come here and try and question me!' She resumed rubbing her face. 'Ain't nothing I can do for the child. Ain't nothing anyone can do.'

She walked heavily around the room, her foot catching a hole in the linoleum. She appeared not to notice. 'You know, best thing for Beth, she was dead.'

'Mrs Schiff, she's your daughter. Your flesh and blood.' Father Philippe had spoken softly.

'Still best she was dead.'

He looked at her uneasily. 'You told Father Nolan this?' He sensed her eyes, dark and accusing.

'Nope.'

He took a step back, watching her. 'Beth has got to be helped.'

'No one can do anything.'

'Yes they can.'

'No! Nobody can.'

'You've got to let them try, Mrs Schiff.'

Suddenly she was screaming for him to get out.

'You can get help, Mrs Schiff. I can get help. Welfare, medical…'

'I don't want no help! You hear, Father? I want no strangers coming in here. Poking around. Minding my business!'

'But, Mrs Schiff, it's for Beth. For you both…'

'No! Who's to say what I need? What she needs? You come in here and tell me I need help! Who's to say *you* can do that? Who's to say that, Father? You tell me. God? You think God says you can say that to me? I don't need help, do you hear? No help!'

He waited until she finished shouting.

'Mrs Schiff, when I go from here, I'm going to go straight down to City Hall to see what can be done.'

'No! Better she dies!'

'Take me to Beth.'

'No.'

'Why not?'

Suddenly Ma Schiff was on her knees before him, sobbing, the tears running down her jowls. 'Don't you understand, Father? Nobody cares. Nobody cares what happens.'

'I care. I promise you. I care. And God cares.' He kept his voice calm, stroking her head.

Ma Schiff looked up at him, suddenly fierce again. 'God! You think if he cared he'd let this happen.'

'God doesn't let things happen, Mrs Schiff. We make them happen. And then we turn to him and ask God to help put things right. Don't you see that? You can't shift the blame on to God. You can't do that.

God wants to help you. That's why he has sent me. Why Father Nolan comes. But if you won't let us do what God wants, to help you, then you can't start blaming him.'

Father Philippe placed both his hands on her head. 'Mrs Schiff, we're both of us in this together. Let me share the load with you. Let's try to remember that God gave us courage and strength. Let's try and make a new beginning.'

After a while she managed to control her sobs. She rose and fetched a candle from the kitchen, lighting it and placing it on the table.

'Don't you think we should see Beth first, before I give you Communion?'

'No. Afterwards.'

'Okay. Do you want to confess anything?'

'No.'

She lowered herself on to her knees again, staring up at him.

He removed the wafer from its gold case and made the sign of the cross before her face, placed the wafer on her tongue, watching while she closed her mouth and dissolved the host. Then she rose to her feet.

The sound came once more from the adjoining room.

'Mrs Schiff, let's go to Beth.'

'No! No, she's resting. She don't want a visit!'

'But you said...'

'What I said and what I mean are different!'

Suddenly she was giggling softly and shivering uncontrollably, pacing the room as if it were a cage. He had seen his mother do the same thing.

Father Philippe looked at her levelly. 'Mrs Schiff, you can't hide Beth away.'

'I'm not hiding her.'

'I think you are, Mrs Schiff.'

He started to move towards the door into the adjoining room.

'You don't go in there! You hear me? You don't! You don't go in there!'

Father Philippe turned and faced Ma Schiff. His voice was still gentle but firm. 'I only want to help. I'm not going to harm Beth.'

'You can't help.'

'But I can get help.'

'No. She's better off dead.'

'I just want to see her.'

'No!'

'She obviously needs help.'

'I've got no money to pay for that. Don't you understand, Father? I ain't got a cent to spare!'

'Help doesn't cost you money. I can arrange things.'

'I don't want your charity! Now leave. Get outta here!'

Father Philippe kept his voice steady. 'Mrs Schiff. Either I see your daughter or I come back here with the proper authority. But I am not leaving until I see her.' Without waiting, he walked into the adjoining room. The blinds were drawn but there was enough light for him to see the form curled up beneath the sheet.

'Beth? I am Father Philippe.'

He advanced towards the bed.

The form gave another strange sound.

He stood, staring down at the emaciated figure, her face yellow and skeletal.

'You satisfied, Father?' Ma Schiff was behind him, trembling. 'Father Nolan should have told you. She was born sick. She got sicker and sicker.'

'She should be in hospital.'

'She should be dead.'

Father Philippe whirled on her. 'God forgive you for that, Mrs Schiff. I don't know what is the matter with her, but she should be in hospital.'

He pushed past Ma Schiff.

'Where you going, Father?'

She started to follow, then stopped as he ran out of the house.

Father Philippe asked the children where was the nearest telephone. One of them pointed. He ran to a door. An elderly man opened it. When he explained, the man nodded. Father Philippe phoned the General and returned to Ma Schiff. She was standing in the living room, cradling Beth in her arms, crying.

Father Philippe put his arms around them, whispering, 'It's going to be alright. She'll get help. And so will you. I'll see to that.'

Three hours later, Father Philippe stood with Ma Schiff in the General's medical intensive care unit. Beth was surrounded by equipment attached to her body.

'Is my girl going to live?' Ma Schiff's words were muffled by her face mask.

'Mrs Schiff, they'll do all they can. But she is a very, very sick girl.'

A doctor had already taken Father Philippe aside to explain that Beth's pneumonia was bilateral, with a well of pus filling both her lungs.

'Let's go home,' Ma Schiff suddenly said. 'Nothing we can do here.' She had once more retreated into a world of her own.

'No. We'll wait.' Father Philippe's voice was gentle but insistent, as a nurse led them to a waiting area.

Another hour passed when the voice over the ceiling loudspeaker began to insistently repeat, 'Code 3! MICU 7! Code 3! MICU 7!'

Seven. That was the number on Beth's cubicle. Father Philippe was on his feet at once and out into the corridor.

'Get out of the way, Father! Get the hell out of the way!'

Two white-coated interns rushed past him, pushing a trolley painted red and stocked with equipment. Other doctors and nurses were running towards Beth's room as the loudspeaker continued its repetitive command.

Those around Beth's bed were working swiftly, unloading, opening, preparing. A nurse was standing to one side, stop-watch in hand, counting aloud. He remembered there were perhaps only four, never more than six minutes, to resuscitate a person. He looked at the monitor above the bed. The lines were almost horizontal. Beth, he suspected, was already close to death.

Father Philippe fingered the aspergillum in his pocket, filled with its measure of holy oils. He began to pray that the doctors would triumph, that Beth would be resuscitated, that he would not have to uncap the silver vial.

Another doctor arrived, taking command, bringing authority to the speed, knowledge and experience of the medical team.

Father Philippe could feel his heart hammering as he prayed that the feverish activity around Beth's bed would succeed.

A nurse disconnected the last of the electrodes attached to Beth's body. One of the interns whipped out the plastic prongs from her nose. The monitor above the bed went blank. Instantly, a smaller screen on the crash cart began to pulse. Father Philippe thanked God she was still alive.

An intern inserted a tube in a vein in Beth's arm. A nurse felt for a pulse in Beth's neck.

The senior doctor stood poised over Beth's bared chest, his fist raised and closed. He brought it down swiftly, delivering a hard blow to her breast-bone. Father Philippe winced. He had never known until this moment how primitive a precordial thump was.

The doctor delivered two more blows in rapid succession. The monitor on the trolley showed Beth's heart was still beating. The nurse with the stop-watch continued to count. The doctor gave new instructions. An intern removed from the trolley the defibrillator, a machine which could provide a more powerful shock than the doctor's punches. A nurse coated Beth's breast-bone with paste from a tube. The intern handed the doctor two paddle-shaped electrodes attached to the defibrillator. He pressed them to Beth's chest, one just above her left breast, the other above the right. The doctor glanced at the intern who adjusted a dial on the machine. Everyone stepped back from the bed.

The doctor pressed down hard on the paddles, touching a button on each. A measured electrical shock passed through Beth's heart.

Father Philippe closed her eyes as Beth went into spasm, her spine arching and her legs stiffening as the electricity pierced her body. He opened them as Beth slumped back on the mattress, inert as before. The nurse was still counting aloud. Father Philippe remembered it took nine seconds for the defibrillator to recharge.

All eyes were watching the monitor on the trolley. Beth was still alive. The doctor delivered a second powerful shock. Beth's body once more lifted clear of the bed. She dropped back, limp. Nine seconds later she received a third shock.

The doctor lifted the paddles from her chest, shaking his head. He put them back on the trolley. He bent over Beth and closed her eyes. The doctor shrugged and walked out of the cubicle. The team began to switch off the machines.

'She's all yours, Father,' the doctor said. 'If she had survived, she would have been a total vegetable. Sometimes God is merciful.'

'Amen to that.'

Father Philippe waited until the last nurse had left before entering the room. He used the holy oil to make the sign of the cross on Beth's forehead, and murmured the shortened form of absolution and extreme unction.

He spoke softly over the bed. 'God's called you home, Beth.'

Father Philippe left the room and walked towards where Ma Schiff was standing, slack-faced in the corridor. He began to formulate the first, all-important, words he would say to her.

That same evening, staring across Fern's dining table, with her and the rest of her family, daughters, sons and in-laws seated around him, Father Philippe realized something was about to happen.

Until then he had convinced himself that Fern's daughter, Margot, had been no more than a pair of willing hands in the kitchen while he had insisted on cooking dinner. He had stripped off his clerical collar, donned a butcher's apron and a chef's hat and began to turn the shopping list he had given Fern into a feast of French cuisine.

While the baking and roasting and basting had gone on, he had poured Margot and himself glasses from the remains of a bottle of champagne he had used in one of the sauces. They had sipped and talked.

Now, over the meal, his words continued to flow. Yet, something was happening. Something potent was being forged in this crucible of family-talk.

His eyes were riveted on Margot. As she raised her glass to him, he could feel her bare toes exploring inside his trouser leg under the table, rubbing against skin, working themselves up and down his calf.

CHAPTER TWENTY

New Beginnings

Father Breslin hesitated again over a paragraph in his sermon for the coming Sunday.

It was the 1,253rd one he had prepared since his Ordination Mass thirty-five years ago. He kept all his sermons in binders on a shelf beside his desk, consulting them regularly, seeking themes he had first expounded as a young priest and which, over the years, he had felt a need to restate. Most dealt with the consistent position of the church on marriage, sin, morality, social responsibility, hedonism, abortion, catechism, human dignity, fidelity, justice and the holy family.

The sermons marked the passing of his years more so than physical changes in him. Apart from his hair thinning and greying, and his spectacles needing stronger lenses, he was otherwise now, in late middle age, little different from the way he had looked when he first came to Father McKenna's parish thirteen years ago. His body weight had not varied by so much as a pound, his voice remained clear and expressive. There was a courtliness about him the years had not diminished. It was there in his shy smile, his old-fashioned good manners and a natural vibrancy. He knew women continued to find him attractive – just as he now better understood how to handle such danger.

His ever-growing library of tapes, neatly racked beneath the shelf of sermons, contained a great deal about coping at all levels. Like his sermons, the recordings revealed how far he had travelled along his own spiritual and emotional road.

Only he knew how hard he sometimes still found coming to terms with a church which had changed more since the election of Pope John Paul II than under the three previous pontiffs he had also served.

The Polish Pope had attempted to regain control the day he had assumed office, 22 October 1978. Through his own unyielding values, he was trying to haul a battered and bedraggled church back from the abyss. So many seminaries and convents were empty. Too often those who remained in them were lipsticked, short-skirted nuns, and priests and prelates who sounded more like revolutionary politicians with their Marxist-inspired diatribes.

Like the Pope, Father Breslin felt the battle lines were drawn. The church of Jesus was in deepening crisis, not least because of disastrous diplomatic failures in Ulster and Central America.

Everywhere the church was being dragged into open conflict. Priests and nuns whom he had known, had gone to the Third World and aligned themselves with political extremism of all kinds, and even armed revolution. He could not begin to understand them and, from time to time, he had roundly condemned from his pulpit their claims to subject historical Catholic revelation to revisionism. Some of his most powerful preaching had been against those who rewrote the Gospel message, using it to defend birth control and all kinds of sexual freedoms.

Their attitudes were a long way from those days when he had lived from Mass stipends; his time as a school chaplain; the years when he worked among the youth of Dublin's docks; his spell on the staff of the archdiocese cathedral; and his time as a curate in a fashionable mid-town Dublin parish; before he had become Father McKenna's assistant. Now it was time to move on again.

Father Breslin scratched through the paragraph which had caused him to ponder, and started again. 'One of the greatest and wisest things in Christian life consists of accepting all graces as they are revealed, and offering your own.'

He was genuinely surprised at his forthcoming elevation to parish priest. He had long believed he would end his days as a curate. On the day of the announcement, Miss Maddox had prepared a magnificent dinner served not in the kitchen, but in the dining room where Father McKenna and he normally only ate on Christmas Day and Easter Sunday.

Waiting until Miss Maddox had taken her place at table, her presence another sign of the importance of the occasion, Father McKenna had raised his glass and delivered a short toast. Then, eyes glistening, Miss Maddox rose to her feet and said, her voice unsteady, she had never had a finer curate in her house than Father Breslin.

Both had supported him through his spells of illness and the sorrow over the deaths of those he loved deeply. As well as his mother, he had lost in the past ten years a sister, a nephew and a niece. The experiences had affected him deeply, making that much clearer to him the importance of not resisting the natural tide of mourning, but also refusing to give in completely to it. Each death had been different, each a learning experience which made him that much better a priest.

He penned a fresh thought. 'What does it mean in practice to live as a member of Christ's body?'

He hesitated once more, thinking Father McKenna would say the thought was too erudite. After all these years he was still grateful for the guidance, encouragement and protection of the old priest.

Father Breslin reworded the thought: 'We must never forget that the glory of God's work will be born from the pain and terror of the body of Christ.'

The sentence would, perhaps, trigger another of Father McKenna's astounding recollections. He always seemed able to sketch with remarkable accuracy the small peculiarities and eccentricities of his parishioners, often forecasting their later character traits when they were still boys and girls.

The old priest, Father Breslin remembered, had been right about Betty Dolan and Mick Byrne. Betty, barely seventeen, was five months pregnant. Mick was close to nineteen. Tonight he would see them for the last time before they knelt before him in the morning, when he would pronounce them husband and wife.

There was still, after all those years, something about an impending wedding which produced a tension in him. Self-examination, he had found, was a powerful relaxant. He put aside his sermon and selected a tape recorded when he was recuperating from another bout of illness. He had lain in this room for five weeks receiving daily injections from the doctor, while Miss Maddox had fed him the most tempting of foods. He inserted the cassette in the recorder and listened, eyes closed.

It's taken a long time to realize that, in the end, all that matters is love. Love which is genuine and non-involved in any physical sense, but is established in the spiritual and supernatural. It is this kind of love that, hopefully, everyday allows me to look at, and judge the best in, a person.

That matters, especially in giving guidance on marriage. At first I had not found it easy to sit down with a young couple and talk about the practical side of intimate marital life as seen by the church. The only way to do so is to sound totally convinced that the teachings are right. But I am also certain that by being detached from physical sex, it does allow me to judge its rightful place in a person's full life. Because of my celibacy, I see sex in a clear and objective way. It is not part of my physical life. I am not ensnared in any of its physical aspects. But, being above it as a priest, I must never forget I am not beyond it as a man. While I must appear sexless, in the true spiritual sense of that word, I dare not for a moment pretend to myself I am outside the realm of mortal temptation.

This is particularly true of the emotions aroused in everyday human relationships like marriage, bringing up a family, paying the bills. Those involved are so close to the problems their own flesh brings, their passions and demands – so close they do not often have time to see the greater picture. That is where a priest can help. The one thing I have learned in life is to have an overview. Personal emotions do not allow for an objective judgement. Yet those are the judgements which matter. It is the true absolutes that make us all what we should try and be – strong in our faith, committed and sympathetic. It is never easy, even now, knowing that celibacy is not in one sense a normal condition. God, we all know, intended that a man and woman should be of one flesh. And it is perfectly true that for a priest that was once allowed within the church…

He wound forward the tape, hunting again for evidence of this struggle and acceptance.

I have come, and it has been a slow process, to realize that in a way my very celibacy can help protect the sacredness of marriage vows. From the day a child understands what a priest is, he also knows a priest is 'married' to God. Now, if a priest was to be permitted to break that contract with him, and marry a woman, then it would make it just that much easier for the advocates of divorce within the church to move closer to victory. It would open the gates to even more confusion. I have not met one person who, when the subject has come up, did not say that he or she felt my celibate state was even holier than marriage itself. Of course, there are those who will try and disrupt this situation. There are women who have almost an obsession with trying to seduce priests. There has been one in every parish I have been. To avoid them is to encourage them further. The only way to handle them is with firmness. I make it clear that, as a priest, I am the representative of Christ in the world, and that for her to behave as she does is to betray his teachings. There is no need to get angry or make a great issue of it, though it is not always easy to remain calm.

Mary drifted into his mind. He felt sleepy and relaxed, only half listening to the words.

There's a certain Eve in every parish. She has a partiality to forbidden fruit. A collar turns her on. It sort of excites and stimulates. I used to be concerned about the effects of my sexuality on my celibacy. I felt pulled and tugged until I began to really understand that love held the key. Loving myself, knowing myself, I could face my sexuality. God gave it to me. He had never meant it should be removed the moment I became ordained. He had intended for me to use my inner resources to face my sexuality. Until I could do so, I had that constant feeling of panic, that things could get out of control. I always felt a danger of letting emotional feelings dominate personal commitment. The important thing, and it took me a long time, was to understand where feelings and commitment can come together.

After Miss Maddox had shown in Betty and Mick, Father Breslin motioned them to the couch, while he sat in the fireside chair.

'All set? No backing out? You can still change your mind, you know.' He smiled, teasing. 'One, or both of you.'

Tonight he planned to remind them of some of the key issues he had raised previously.

'Love is a funny thing. It is not like anger or jealousy or any other emotion. And it changes direction as we go through life. But the one rule about love that never alters is one you must always remember: that to love each other, you must love yourself. That is the only way you can give your love to each other – when you have it in yourselves to give.'

They nodded, understanding.

'Catholic marriage is a lifelong contract in response to God's wishes. I cannot say that in all honesty about other forms of marriage where divorce seems to be a built-in option. But within the church, marriage demands integrity and a willingness to acquire a deep inner understanding of where God fits in. That's the key, of course: faith. If you have faith, marriage can work. Your faith may be tested, many times, but as long as it is there, you will survive all the risks.'

He turned to Betty thinking how, in these past weeks, her baby had visibly grown inside her.

'Loving yourself doesn't mean you have to be like the old witch in *Snow White* and look in the mirror all the time and ask who is the fairest one of all. That's *not* loving yourself.' He smiled at her. 'Mind you, Betty, you look very fair to me. I must say, having a baby does suit you.'

'Thank you, Father.'

'And you, Mick. You've planted a seed that's going to be part of you until you die. You must always see your child as your way of offering new hope in the world. Each baby is. When your first one comes, he or she will be starting a great journey. But what your baby discovers in life depends very much on you both as parents. In the end, your baby's growth will result from how good and loving, how feeling and caring, you are to each other. That's what I mean by loving yourself. If you can do that, love yourself properly, then you can really love each other, and your baby will thrive in that love. That's much more important than anything else you can give that child.'

He liked the way they sat relaxed, hands entwined. Not embarrassed by anything he said.

'The important thing is never to use love as a label. There's nothing wrong in saying to each other as often as you like, "I love you". But don't let it become an escape. God gave us language so that we could communicate in a different way than animals. Words were our great leap up the tree of evolution. The trouble is, down the centuries we have taken them for granted, used them as excuses to say what's so often convenient, not what should be meant. Nowhere is this more evident than when we speak of love, loving and being in love.'

At their last visit he had opened a copy of James Joyce's *Ulysses* – now no longer banned in Ireland – and pointed out how the book ends with Molly saying page after page of 'yes's'.

He reminded them of the word's significance. 'Saying "yes" is the greatest promise you can make to each other. You'll be saying it tomorrow in your vows. What you will be saying is "yes" to a life together. "Yes" to growing together. "Yes" to being realistic about your life together. "Yes" to understanding that having differences is natural. But, as long as you keep on saying "yes" to love, you will be able to handle any disagreement, squabble or cross words. As long as love is there, they will not cause you a problem.'

He reminded them about the practical realities they must incorporate into their love for each other. They should put aside a set sum each week for the baby's future. They should learn to shop wisely. He had told them how, whenever he organized a parish function, he went from one supermarket to another, pricing items before buying.

'From tomorrow each of you will have twice the responsibility – one to the other. It sounds very romantic, but it can soon sour if you don't know what is involved. I always say that after the candlelit dinner comes the stale taste of wine the following morning. It must be difficult to think of love when you have that taste in your mouth. Our mouth is the most public part of our body, simply because we speak through it. It's the surest way we can tell the world what we think and feel. So we tend to guard our mouths. And that, too, is a mistake. Another way to ruin a marriage is to be always on guard and never relaxed. That's the quickest way to destroy love before it has had time to take root. And it must have time.'

He thought how young and vulnerable they looked; yet there was also about them a strength which went back through the generations.

'Tomorrow you will start a journey that, to work, is going to take you back, each one into yourself. You are going to find in yourself that you really do have the faith to guide each other towards a permanent love. Both of you are going to discover the demands of marriage begin and end with one word – love. But also remember this. To make your marriage work, you have not only to go forward hand in hand, but you must also go forward at your own pace. I think it's one of the hardest things to realize that separation and togetherness, in a good marriage, are essential. You must live together, but separately. You must be as one, but remain two distinct individuals. You must grow in the same direction, but accept it will be through a different way. That, in the end, is what a good marriage is: being together – and understanding the importance of being separate.'

When he finished he made the sign of the cross before Betty's stomach murmuring as he did so for God to bless and protect her baby.

Four days after he had solemnized the wedding of Mick and Betty, Father Breslin raised the gold and silver chalice, knowing this one movement placed him gloriously at the centre of his faith. He was celebrating his last Mass in Father McKenna's parish. At that part of the service, the memento for the living, he included Father McKenna and Miss Maddox.

He had decided to keep his sermon short, taking as his text, Matthew 28:19. 'Go, therefore, make disciples of all the nations, baptize them in the name of the Father and of the Son and of the Holy Spirit.'

When he had said his goodbyes to the parishioners at the church door, he had walked back to the parochial house for Sunday lunch.

Five hours later, with the good wishes and blessing of Father McKenna ringing in his ears, and the chaste kiss of Miss Maddox long dried on his cheek, he turned a bend in the road. There, up on the hill, beyond the village in the Wicklow hills, he could see the building, steep-roofed and granite walled.

Throughout the long drive, he had been filled with expectation. Now, warm though the day was, he felt a sudden chill as he drove towards his very own church.

CHAPTER TWENTY-ONE

The Celibate Traveller

Walking with Sister Cornelia to chapel, Victoria reminded herself that this was her sixth election. Every four years the Order voted to reappoint either its present Mother Superior or elect a new one. In previous elections, Victoria had cast her vote for the Reverend Mother who had welcomed her into religious life twenty-two years ago. A month ago the aged nun had died from a brain haemorrhage and the Community was about to vote for a new Superior.

Sister Cornelia continued to fume. Another Catholic activist group had launched a campaign for women to celebrate Mass. Eyes flashing dangerously, the old nun snapped neither Catherine of Siena or St Theresa of Avila had wanted such a privilege.

Victoria thought how once more Sister Cornelia had magnificently missed the point. But then, any form of liberalism in her eyes was a direct challenge to ancient truths and fundamental values.

'This is my fourteenth election. But, if I died tomorrow, I'd want to go knowing the present Pope will exorcize all this liberal nonsense.'

Sister Cornelia was eighty, but she sounded as old as time itself as she continued.

'The first time I voted was in 1928. We put in a strong Mother that year. She used to hold regular all-night vigils. And we had to do a full day's work on top. We had discipline.'

'But, did it make you a better nun? I'm not sure if praying round the clock makes anyone holier,' Victoria said.

Sister Cornelia sniffed. 'It made us different. That was the whole point. We were different. We could do it. We could stay on our knees for a whole day or night with just short breaks to go to the bathroom or sip some water. This place has become a hotel. Soft beds. Talking at meals. The discipline's gone. We've got a good Pope in Rome at last, but he still probably can't do what Pope Pius did in the first year I voted. He spent a whole week in prayer. Never slept a wink. In those days we used to get news like that from Rome. Mother would read it out to us as encouragement. But now…'

The old nun fell silent once more, her mind locked into events over half a century earlier.

Nineteen twenty-eight was the year, Victoria realized, when Pope Pius XI had signed the Laternan Treaty with Benito Mussolini giving the Vatican guaranteed sovereign independence and 90 million US dollars compensation for the loss, in 1870, of the Papal States.

Art had once told her the church, in the wake of the 1929 Crash, had acquired a large financial portfolio in the United States, one which had eventually led to the burgeoning financial scandals currently rocking it. These included the disappearance of vast funds from the Chicago archdiocese under the stewardship of the late Cardinal Cody, the multi-million dollar machinations of Vatican Bank under its present governor, Archbishop Paul Marcinkus, an old friend of Cody's, and the links between Cody, Marcinkus and even Pope Paul VI to the convicted Sicilian swindler, Michele Sindona. Art had added, no one should be surprised, given the church's fiscal dealings these past fifty years.

After her last visit to his hospital paraplegic bed, the doctor had told her Art would remain totally paralyzed after his mountain climbing accident. The doctor had likened Art's survival to a miracle.

That night Victoria had written in her journal. 'A miracle that Art should be doomed to live the rest of his life like this? That his wife has left him and his children can't bear to visit. That, apart from me, no one ever comes. A miracle?'

She had lost count of the times since then she had prayed God would show Art mercy.

Sister Cornelia had returned to the attack. 'We must choose a strong person to lead the Community. Someone who can reflect the strong values of our Polish Pope.'

The fierce timbre of the old nun's voice and the absolute command in her words were like a sudden slap on Victoria's cheek.

'We must elect someone who can deal with our own dissidents! The church has always led from within. That's why this vote is so important!'

In Sister Cornelia's voice was the conviction that time could not only be arrested but actually turned back.

Her own puritanical rejection of consumerism, one of the Pope's own bête-noire's, was reflected in her dress. Sister Cornelia's habit was darned and patched in several places and she would go on repairing her shoes for as long as the leather survived. She judged all human relationships by the standards of her personal frugality.

Victoria was conciliatory. 'I think we have to recognize the tremendous pressures building up.'

Sister Cornelia sniffed again. 'Because we have allowed them to build! There have been too many unchecked challenges to authority! Too much compromise! Too much analysis! We've analyzed Vatican II until I'm sick and tired of hearing about it. No! We need a Superior who will see our vows upheld, now and forever. Freedom is one thing, recklessness another. There has been too much of that.'

Victoria wished she hadn't encouraged the conversation. She would rather have gone straight to chapel to spend another few minutes thinking of Art. She had told him she would be unable to visit any more because the Order was sending her to San Francisco to complete her course in counselling.

Four years ago, the Order had begun training Victoria to help nuns who were experiencing emotional trauma. Her academic achievements had been sufficiently good for the Order to send her to one of the nation's pre-eminent universities in the Bay Area.

On that last visit, she had held before Art the earrings she had worn at her profession and said she would always treasure them, just as in her heart she would always keep a place for him. He had looked at her and she had felt closer to him than ever before. Art, in his helplessness, was someone who had become uncorrupted and incorruptible. For all his terrible physical destruction, it had given him a spiritual strength.

All around them nuns converged on the chapel, taking last-minute soundings among themselves. Throughout the past month there had been discreet lobbying to advance the claims of candidates – the *consultation* allowed for under the Rule.

Sister Cornelia returned to the attack. 'You know the root of the trouble? Sex. There is too much emphasis on it nowadays.'

Victoria smiled. Her own spiritual happiness depended on achieving physical satisfaction. Yet, each time she emerged from her twilight zone, she sensed she had failed to experience what she had hoped for.

'You know why we don't get more girls coming in, Sister Victoria? We don't offer the same challenge. We should be more demanding. Better to have a few postulants with the right ideas about vocation, than all those who come and go. We need old-fashioned leadership to stop the rot.'

Leaning on her cane, hobbled by arthritis, Sister Cornelia was a matriarchal figure. Oblivious to the dust raised by the first swirls of autumn around the hem of her long black skirt, she continued to harangue Victoria on the sort of qualities the new Superior should have.

'In my experience, Sister Cornelia, the reason we don't get girls is because they don't want to live their lives in a system that's out of date.'

The old nun waved her stick.

'You're wrong, wrong, wrong! Look what happened when Pope John loosened his grip. Italy voted for divorce. The churches of France emptied. West Germany went secular!'

Victoria was filled with compassion, wondering what must have happened all those years ago to Sister Cornelia to make her as blinkered as her old-fashioned headgear. The harshness to which she had been subjected had instilled blind obedience, without understanding the only worthwhile discipline stems from self-imposition.

Sister Cornelia had been raised in a system that provided for her every material need, but did not care for her as a *person* – Victoria realized, any more than it had done for her. Sister Cornelia still clung to the belief that discipline was the answer to *everything*, still a small price to pay for safety and protection against a world beyond the Mother House, which she saw as a dangerous and frightening place. Victoria doubted if the old nun could even begin to comprehend that discipline was the only *possession* she had been allowed to retain.

She had seen this in so many other nuns unable to accept their concept of religious life was doomed, that the whole idea of a formal institutionalized life in Christ was on the verge of being swept away. The young did not wish to live in monolithic buildings like the Mother House. While their lives were still dedicated to God, there was an increasing belief they need not live, controlled by an outmoded Rule and figure of bleak authority.

Victoria was convinced the only way forward was for nuns to be allowed greater personal freedoms to live and work as they wished, and be able to dedicate themselves in a far more healthy way to keeping the church alive. For her, the vow of chastity was infinitely less important than having psychological stability. An awareness of the ways of the world would make her better equipped to deal with it.

Yet, constricted by a lifetime of misconceptions and illusions, Sister Cornelia was cut off from any chance of exploring the rewards this reality offered. Her last words as they entered the chapel sadly confirmed this.

'We must elect a disciplinarian.'

Two elections ago every pew had been crowded. Now there was often only a solitary nun occupying a stall. Where once there had been rows of postulants and novices, there were only a handful. They could not vote. Only the professed had that right. On the paper the names were divided by serrated lines, making it easier to remove them. Victoria's name was twenty-ninth on the list.

Joining in the chants and responses, she reminded herself that increasingly her religious life had become an endless and critical self-examination. She now knew no other way to live it. It was part of her own dedication to the truth. That was why, in many ways, living in the Mother House had become a stifling experience; it was like existing under a huge dome in which old ideas were continuously recycled until, like breathing fetid air, they created a stagnant atmosphere.

Unlike her, Victoria knew most of the Community was made up of women in whom avoiding challenge was ingrained. They continued to accept the church had total control over their lives. Indeed, the entire apparatus was designed to do so. A Pope as strong-minded as John Paul II controlled the Roman Curia, who controlled the bishops, who in turn controlled the clergy and the sisterhood through the Sacred Congregations and Secretariats, Pontifical Commissions and archdiocesan offices.

From the moment she was elected, the Superior's word would be absolute. There could be no appeal against her decisions. The only way to circumvent her commands would be to resign. It was the same in every Order. Yet, Victoria wondered whether the new Reverend Mother would understand that many women in religious life no longer wanted to be abused or taken for granted.

That was why she would not vote for Sister Bernadette, whose cause Sister Cornelia had been avidly promoting. Sister Bernadette was a thin little woman in her late sixties who bossed her kitchen staff mercilessly. For her obedience was everything.

In many ways Sister Monica, who worked in admissions, would be an ideal choice. She was close to fifty, a large raw-boned, cheerful woman who had been one of the first to modify her habit. But her presence was intimidating. She was physically intrusive, speaking loudly and standing uncomfortably close to someone when doing so. A person so unaware of the importance of personal space might well be insensitive in other ways. She would not win Victoria's vote either.

Sitting across the aisle, Sister Paula was an obvious choice, in spite of her age. At the last election she had forced a second ballot against Reverend Mother. A quiet women in her late sixties, and devoted to her duties, Sister Paula had given her whole life to supervising the Order's various links with the outside world: its schools, colleges, hospitals and remedial clinics. Although she had never said more than a few words to her in all those years, Victoria sensed that, behind her prim demeanour, was someone who recognized the need for change. Her only drawback was a tendency to over-agree, shaking her head up and down and making a continuous little clucking sound. A Superior like that could be very wearing.

Victoria's own choice would be Sister Joan who was seated beside her. She was in charge of the infirmary, a gracious woman who had entered five years before Victoria, and who had always shown a calm good humour. She, more than anyone else Victoria could think of, was aware of the need to exercise decision-making with compassion and dignity, dealing as she did with the aged and dying. That had given Sister Joan a level of understanding which Victoria felt many others in the Community lacked. Sister Joan would maintain her position against the more conservative forces in the Mother House without producing open conflict. She would understand the real challenges and, with her well-integrated perspective, ensure a harmonious relationship between all the various groupings, balancing the call for new ideas against some of the wilder rumblings of protest.

Sister Joan would be a marvellous Superior, charismatic in every sense of the word. Nevertheless, Victoria thought, there could be, all told, half a dozen possible contenders for the post. This might mean repeated balloting before a candidate emerged with the required 51 per cent of votes.

The bishop would not be pleased if it went beyond the lunch hour. Over the years Victoria had watched him grow bulkier and as purple-faced as his stole, while Father Lowell was now almost as pale and delicate-looking as the filigree of his vestments. The two men sat side-by-side, on identical thrones before the altar. In front of them was a table draped in white. On it was a silver chalice, gleaming in the candlelight. To their left, behind another table, also covered in white, sat two nuns. Before each was a silver plate. On the opposite side of the sanctuary was a vacant chair.

The bishop addressed the Community, asking for the roll to be called.

Each nun rose as her name was spoken by Father Lowell. When that task was completed, Sister Cornelia hobbled to the sanctuary, removed the Bible from the lectern and placed it before the bishop. The bishop rose and placed his right hand on it.

'I swear by Almighty God to conduct an election without fear or favour and in absolute conformity to holy Rule,' he intoned.

Father Lowell swore to do all in his power to observe there was no breach of the Rule. The two scrutineers left their seats and solemnly vowed to perform their function.

Sister Cornelia addressed the bishop.

'On behalf of this Community and by the power invested in me as its authorized representative, I swear on this Holy Bible, and before Almighty God, that each one of us will vote solely for the one considered the most suitable to hold the office of Superior and will do so without favour or personal bias, and in the knowledge that each one of us have not been offered, or engaged in, any pact or favour of any kind; that we are each conversant with the holy Rule and will follow it.'

The bishop remained seated as he spoke. 'Consult the list before you and choose your preference. May the Lord Jesus Christ guide your deliberations.'

He extended a hand in benediction.

All over the chapel there was the distinct sound of paper separating and being carefully folded. When each nun had made her choice, she dropped to her knees and silently prayed. Victoria was one of the first to kneel, her vote in her clasped hands.

Only when every sister was kneeling, did the bishop break the silence.

'I call upon the Mistress of Ceremonies to place her vote before me.'

Sister Cornelia rose slowly, her left hand clenched. She stood in front of the two men.

'I call to witness Christ the Lord who will be my judge that my vote is given to the one who before God I consider worthy of election.'

She dropped her tightly folded ballot into the chalice, paused for a moment, genuflected to the altar and retreated.

Father Lowell called the scrutineers forward, who repeated Sister Cornelia's actions. Then, answering to the sonorous voice of Father Lowell, each nun took her turn to cast her votes.

Victoria dropped her ballot into the chalice before walking quietly back to her place and kneeling. In a week's time, all this would be a thousand miles behind her. In the end, it would not really matter who became Superior. She would continue to lead her own life.

Victoria peered through her fingers at Father Lowell, thinking how this ceremony would better fit into a time when the supply of young girls willing to die to the world seemed endless. Now they were almost unobtainable.

There was now far more competition for any worthwhile position as the Order's own existence in the world demanded it provided only the very best teachers, nurses and administrators. Those who applied for such posts, and did not measure up, were relegated to menial posts inside the convent, increasing their feelings of failure and even abandonment.

Nuns were rising from their knees.

Once more Sister Cornelia picked up the chalice and placed it before the scrutineers, who commenced counting. She informed the bishop that the number of votes cast matched that of the electors. He ordered the scrutineers to move to the next stage.

The first teller tipped the slips back into the chalice. Sister Cornelia placed it in front of the second scrutineer. She removed a ballot, opened it, ticked the name on a tally card and refolded the paper and replaced it on Sister Cornelia's plate. She tilted it so that the vote fell on to the other teller's plate. The second scrutineer repeated what her companion had done.

Sister Cornelia returned to stand over the first teller while she removed another slip. The checking continued. Finally, the old nun took the two tally cards to the waiting men, handing one to each. They compared the results.

The bishop rose and, in a loud, measured tone, began to read.

'Sister Bernadette, thirty-three votes.'

There was a ripple of excitement.

'Sister Paula, twenty-six votes.'

Victoria remembered that at the last election she had collected the same number of votes in the first ballot.

'Sister Theresa, nineteen votes.'

The murmur turned to an incredulous gasp.

Victoria felt suddenly exultant. Sister Theresa taught in one of the Order's schools. Victoria had excluded her as a likely contender because she had gone to Chicago during Pope John Paul's American tour to join other nuns keeping a silent vigil outside the cathedral, protesting the pontiff's attitude over limiting the role of women in religious life. Sister Cornelia had been furious at seeing her on network television news.

'Sister Joan, nine votes.'

Victoria sighed. The chance of a dream come true had vanished. The opportunity to elect a moderate, centrist Superior had been rejected. The next round of voting would be critical.

The bishop ordered the tellers to collect the first ballot papers and distribute new ones.

Almost an hour later his redolent voice read the result of the second ballot.

'Sister Bernadette, thirty-five votes.'

She only needed nine votes for victory.

Victoria had hoped there would have been enough nuns willing to reject the sort of leadership Sister Bernadette would bring. But there had been profound forces at work, and probably still were, to enable a victory for conservatism.

Sister Bernadette would clamp down. She would rule through

condemnation and demotion. For the first time in religious life, Victoria silently prayed for someone's defeat.

'Sister Paula, thirty-four votes.'

A renewed concerted murmur swept the chapel. Victoria guessed, suddenly elated, that Sister Paula must be drawing votes not only from the other candidates but had also blocked Sister Bernadette's advance. There seemed to be a sudden mood for compromise.

'Sister Theresa, eleven votes.'

She had had her moment; the more extreme of the progressive liberals had made their point.

Victoria watched Sister Cornelia. She sat impassively, her cane tapping the floor just once at the end of each of the bishop's announcements.

'Sister Joan, seven votes.'

It was going to be a straight fight between Sister Bernadette and Sister Paula: reactionary versus compromise.

Victoria prayed once more as the bishop announced the third ballot. Forty minutes later he read its result.

'Sister Paula, forty-nine votes. Sister Bernadette, thirty-seven votes.'

Victoria smiled. Compromise was better than defeat.

Next morning at Mass, when the newly elected Reverend Mother asked the Community to pray for its departing sister, Victoria noticed how, in only a few hours, Sister Paula had assumed the distinct tone of her predecessor.

Victoria's suitcases were waiting by the main door. The Grand Silence was in force and those who had said goodbye had done so the night before. Reverend Mother gave her a final embrace.

As Victoria opened the door to go to the waiting taxi to the airport, she heard a familiar tip-tap behind her. She looked around. Sister Cornelia embraced her, and broke the Rule by whispering: 'Yesterday we had compromise but never live to regret it – or compromise yourself!'

She turned and hobbled away.

CHAPTER TWENTY-TWO

A New Journey

Clare sensed she was approaching the core of her crisis. It was past three in the morning and she was still in chapel. Yet it was not only exhaustion or the chill at this hour which made her tremble. It was an inner force, one she had named Jimminy, after the celebrated cartoon character who was Pinnochio's conscience. Jimminy – the calming voice of serendipity – was telling her again to accept that, after months of skirting the issue, she was ready to face reality.

Another part still told her to resist: that, in spite of all she had endured, to give up would be completely out of character, reminding her that the Order had given her a valued education, culminating in a degree. Though she had been severely tested, it was only because she had the strength to cope.

Once more Jimminy silently asked her to be more realistic. She had worked extraordinarily hard, studying well into the night because it was the only free time she had.

The questions that had brought her to the chapel in the first place returned. Did God really want her to continue the way things were? How could she grow the way he wanted when until recently she had not been aware of what she should be growing towards? What *did* God want of her?

Jimminy told her the way to grow closer to him was to have complete understanding of her responsibility to herself. Her sense of enlightenment had grown the more she came to understand her trauma and how it could be resolved.

It was not enough for her to set out the problems and hope that by honestly and painfully admitting each and every one of them, they would go away. Something more was required. She must accept that the greatest wisdom she could know had been placed deep within her by

God himself. It was the best reassurance she could have, knowing each decision she came to would be done in his name.

Accepting that, familiar words had taken on a new meaning. *Thy will be done.* What she was asking herself to do was not for herself – but for him. God was telling her what to do. *God was Jimminy.*

In these past weeks she had frequently sat alone in the chapel, often until dawn, trying to come to the one decision from which all others would naturally flow. Clare sensed she was close. Trembling, realizing what was at the core of her crisis, she knew she would only leave here when she had finally settled the matter.

Looking back, the signposts were clearly marked; the wedding when she had almost fainted, her defensive response to Sister Imelda's well-meant words, her reaction to the Deputy, her own silent anger and frustration. Through tears – she had wept many times on this lonely and difficult odyssey – she could once more see Tom clearly, sitting at their table in the college restaurant, making another of his points.

Their table. She still thought of it as *theirs*: the one in the corner near the doors leading to the kitchen. It was identical to all the others, the same four metal tubular legs, the same plastic surface. It was the table he led her to on that first day and became the one over which they had exchanged so many ideas about duties and obligations and much, much else. When Tom became especially intense about a subject he would curl his long legs around one of the metal supports. She had often wondered if that was how he had sat when he wrote her the letter.

On that morning five months ago her life had suddenly changed direction. She had as usual awoken to the shrill of the electric bell and risen in the dark knowing that, winter or summer, her day would always begin in the pre-dawn. After swiftly dressing and turning off the low wattage light in her room – the drive to save electricity was the Order's latest money-saving measure – she joined the silent procession to chapel.

Kneeling, she heard the familiar sighs accompanying weary bones being lowered on to stained wood. After silently meditating, she blended her voice with all the others offering the first salute to a new day. Rising at the end of her devotions, she had genuflected again to the altar and then filed through the corridors, keeping close to the walls, which was another way to demonstrate humility. Being Tuesday, breakfast had been a boiled egg, toast and tea, taken in complete silence. Afterwards, she had gone to her pigeon-hole in the long line of open-fronted boxes where mail was left by the Deputy. There was one envelope. Though the Deputy no longer had the right to open and censor letters, Clare knew she would have inspected the envelope carefully.

Clare had glanced at the envelope, her heart starting to thump. She had hurried to her room before opening the envelope. The letter had covered one sheet of the pad Tom used for note-taking.

My darling Clare

I have wanted to call you that for months. It is only an hour since we last saw each other, yet I miss you desperately. Though I have never dared to say so, I love you.

You must wonder why I have written it instead of telling you. But I did not want to embarrass you by saying this face to face. If it makes me an emotional coward, well yes, I suppose I am. Nobody has ever told me how to handle a situation like this, that is why I'm frightened of my own feelings and the way they pull me between what I feel for you and what I know is also true: I want to be a good priest. I know that. That, I suppose is why I hesitated over whether you should come to my ordination as a deacon. It seemed to me that having you there would only make matters worse. It would make the conflict that much harder for me. You came, and I was glad. When I stood before our bishop, I felt your eyes on my back. I really did. When I turned and walked back to my seat, I could see your face. I have never told you this, how could I? But at that moment I felt there was something there. Dare I say it – love. Right then I had an urge to go to you and say what I had felt and what I had seen. Yet, my calling is, like my love for you, a very real matter.

So there is my conflict. In spite of all we have spoken about these past months, I have not been able to discuss this with you. I have, I suppose, been frightened at how you would respond. I do love you. To pretend otherwise would be to deceive myself. But, at the same time, I want to go on living my life in the eyes of God, not on the edge but at the very centre of my vocation. I know you have a similar feeling about your calling. That is why I will understand if you wish to end our friendship.

In one way, as you know, it is already about to be physically separated. Soon I will be ordained. But I wished to share my feelings with you. In a way,

I suppose I want a reassurance that you understand them and why I can't walk away from what God has intended for me. Please don't be angry. God bless you, always.

Love Tom.

Clare closed her eyes. The letter had left her void of intelligent thought. She had abandoned all ideas of going to college and taken to her bed, convincing herself the pain in her stomach was food poisoning. All day she had read and reread every word, driven to distraction, filled with a dread and a strange feeling of excitement. That night, shortly before the Grand Silence, she had gone to the kitchen and had read the letter one last time before tearing it into pieces and throwing it into the furnace.

Returning to college next day, she had felt a mounting panic at what she would say to Tom. Waiting for the lecture to begin, she had frequently glanced across at his seat.

Tom had not shown up. He had gone on a retreat. Ten days later, in the great chapel at Clonliffe, he had been received into the priesthood.

For weeks she agonized over whether or not she should respond to his letter and, if she did, what she should say. She finally tried several times to put her thoughts on paper, to assure him she did understand and that she wished there had been proper guidance on how to handle their emotions, but that to deny they existed was only to create further problems.

Tom, she saw, was frightened because he knew where his feelings would lead. His love for her, their love for each other, would only have brought him to a situation totally incompatible with his vows. In writing as he had, Tom was really saying he would not change; that the risks were too high for him – but he wanted her to know he was aware of them.

Clare did not blame him. She had learned that a part of true love was being able to accept and respect. But she would go on loving him.

Six weeks after Tom's letter, Clare found a note in her box from Reverend Mother ordering her to report to her office that morning instead of going to college.

Clare sat on the chair before the desk and, for a long moment, the Superior simply stared at her. When she finally spoke, her voice was barely audible. In the past year Reverend Mother had aged markedly.

'There has been a change of plan. We are well satisfied with your degree. When your college term ends in three weeks, you will not be returning.

Instead, you will commence teaching in our local boarding school. You will sleep there but must return here every day for meals and to partake in the Divine Office. It will require abundant energy to cope, but you will, with God's help.'

Clare had been too dumbstruck to speak and merely nodded, her hopes of doing postgraduate studies over. After the Superior had given her benediction, she had immediately gone to the chapel and, in its solitude, wept and prayed for God to help her understand the meaning of the vow of obedience.

At the boarding school she rose an hour earlier than usual so as to arrive at the Mother House in time for first devotions. After breakfast she had hurried back to spend her morning in the classroom, returning to the convent for lunch, then once more back to the school for the afternoon. After class she marked homework before returning to the Mother House for supper and Compline. Then it was back to the school to supervise bed-time of the children for whom she was responsible. In her cubicle beside their dormitory, she would continue marking papers and preparing the next day's lessons. It was frequently midnight or later when she climbed exhausted into bed. Even so, she had often been unable to sleep. In three months she had lost twenty pounds in weight.

Her sense of frustration at what she was being made to endure had only been partially eased by prayer. Yet, the harder she prayed, the more elusive was the comfort the familiar words had always provided. God was there – but where? She had to find a way to him. But even St John, who had never failed to show her the value of living a humble religious life, could not replenish her spiritual exhaustion.

Gradually she had come to understand why. The Order was unable to function without squashing all feelings and individual wishes. Denial, not desire, was still at the core of all it represented. In spite of all the changes introduced by Vatican II, the Order failed to see that, for all the self-control and moderation she exercised, she was a passionate person who found it increasingly hard to identify with a system which relied on the destruction of self. There was something she found deeply unacceptable in a way of life which routinely used authority as its prime form of control.

At the first tinge of creeping grey light where night ended and a new day began, five o'clock by her wrist-watch, new thoughts dominated Clare's mind as she knelt in the chapel.

Her father was dying. The doctors had said he had a year left – maybe less. She and her mother had both agreed he need not be told. Each time she had gone home, his body appeared to have wasted a little more. While the cancer etched lines of pain deep into his face, her father's gaze remained clear. He had accepted, and was not troubled by, doubt. He understood himself. Her father had achieved his own inner grace.

He would be pleased she knew, when she told him of all she had experienced: that now, at last, she had braved the storm. She knew what she must do – and why she must do it. She rose to her feet, totally calm and certain, and walked from the chapel.

Through the Deputy, Clare had submitted a request for an interview with Reverend Mother. The first available time, she had been told, would be on a Thursday evening immediately after Compline. That was two days away. In that time Clare had spent every available moment in chapel, kneeling for hours, completely convinced God was still telling her this was the right decision.

On that Thursday evening, when Clare had finished her explanation to Reverend Mother, the Superior was gently probing.

'Why did you not come before?' The voice was old and faint. 'I would have prayed with you.'

'I wanted to be certain in my own mind first, Mother. I had to be absolutely certain.'

'We can never be certain. God called you. That is all you can be certain of. That he called you, just as he called each one of us.'

Clare leaned forward to catch the Superior's words.

'I really feel he understands, Mother. I really do have that feeling after praying.'

The Superior's lips moved wordlessly for a moment.

'If you are so convinced, will you at least put your certainty to a test?'

'A test, Mother?'

'Yes. Will you talk to somebody first?'

Clare hesitated.

'Not the chaplain, Mother.'

The convent's confessor, for all his good intentions, would not understand.

'No. Not him. A specialist. A priest trained in counselling. Will you see him for me? I will prepare a report. Will you be willing to talk to him?'

'I think it's too late, Mother.'

'It's never too late, Sister Mary Luke. Will you do this for me?'

Clare hesitated once more.

'Mother, I don't want to waste his time.'

The Superior shook her head. 'Never see it like that. You are a valued member of our Community. You have undertaken many arduous duties and responsibilities. It has not always been easy for you. But Our Lord is clearly in you. Do this, if not for me, for him.'

'Very well, Mother.'

The appointment was arranged for a week's time. In the intervening period, Clare continued to pray. At 4.30 on the appointed afternoon, she knocked and entered the parlour where, years before, Sister Imelda had sat with her.

The priest-counsellor invited her to be seated. She sensed his immediate warmth and kindness. He was, she was relieved to see, surprisingly young. He could be barely thirty. She liked the way he came straight to the point.

'Reverend Mother has told me of your feelings. I have read her report. She has great respect for you.'

'Thank you, Father.'

He smiled. 'Let me say at once that I completely sympathize with your decision. I am not here to try and change it. If there is to be change, it will be a matter for you. I merely wish to act as a catalyst. To see if you have really thought it all through.'

'I have, Father. I can assure you I have done more praying about this than anything else.'

'Well, that's good. Then you are very certain.'

Clare sat back in her chair relaxing. There was to be no inquisition, only a discussion based on acceptance.

She told him why she wanted to leave religious life. It took her almost an hour to describe her inner conflicts and how she had resolved them.

'I know that while I have changed my commitment to a life in religion, I have not changed my religious outlook. My parents gave me values. From the beginning they didn't force them. They just planted them and let them grow. I grew up believing it was the most natural thing for a girl to be a virgin when she married. That may have changed for others, but not for me. Marriage is still a sacred state for me. So are all the teachings of the church. It's people's attitudes towards them that have changed. It's a matter of adapting the church's teachings and modifying them here and there. But sin is sin. Right is right. That hasn't changed for me.'

The priest looked at her carefully.

'When do you want to leave?'

'As soon as possible, Father.'

'I'll ask Reverend Mother to see that all arrangements are made.'

They shook hands and Clare left the parlour.

Next day, Clare was told by the Deputy it would take two weeks to complete the arrangements for her dispensation. In the meantime, she would continue performing her normal duties.

A fortnight later the Deputy sent for her. 'You will go during the supper hour. We have arranged for a taxi to take you home. Reverend Mother will see you at 6.30.'

After she left her office, Clare realized the Deputy had not addressed her by her title in religion. It was as if she had already been divested of her links with the Order. The truth, as they both knew, was otherwise. Reverend Mother had offered her a teaching post at one of the Order's schools far from the Mother House.

'Even though you have chosen to leave, we do not wish to lose your experience, and remember, we are always here for you. Always.'

She had gratefully accepted. Few nuns returning to the outside world, she suspected, had any form of guaranteed employment.

Astonishingly, apart from the Reverend Mother and the Deputy, no one seemed to know she was leaving. Her name was still on the duty roster for next week. At lunch, instead of joining the Community for its midday meal, she went to chapel and knelt, knowing this would be the last time she would do so. She finally rose and bowed slowly towards the sanctuary lamp.

She spent the afternoon packing. The previous evening her mother had dropped off a suitcase containing her going-out clothes. By 6.15 she was dressed in the skirt, blouse and shoes she had worn a decade earlier. She sat on the edge of her bed, staring at her suitcase. It held everything she possessed: her posters, books, photographs. In the closet she had hung, for the last time, her habit and cape.

There was a knock on the door. She opened it to Declan.

'Sister Mary Luke. I've come to take your case down while you see Reverend Mother.'

He twisted his hands, suddenly embarrassed, the words coming in a rush. 'It's not going to be the same without you. I'm going to miss you. Good luck, sister.'

Clare had a sudden lump in her throat. She reached forward and impulsively kissed him on the cheek.

'Thank you, Declan.' She would miss him.

Clare left her room without a backward glance.

Reverend Mother and the Deputy stood behind the Superior's desk.

'Step forward, sister.'

Reverend Mother's voice seemed to grow fainter on each occasion she came here.

On top of the desk Clare saw the dispensation documents prepared in the archbishop's office.

The Deputy stared at Clare glacially.

Reverend Mother's question barely reached across the desk.

'You are certain, Sister Mary Luke, that this is what you wish? Even at this late moment you can reconsider.'

'Thank you for the opportunity, Mother. But I am sure. God wants this of me.'

The Deputy's harsh words filled the room.

'As I have remarked before, you are truly fortunate to be so definite about God's wishes for you.'

Reverend Mother sighed. She picked up the document.

'The moment you sign this paper you are released from your sacred vows. You are then no longer a sister in religion. You will notice the document is in triplicate. We will witness your signature on all three copies. You will receive one. One will be forwarded to the archbishop and one will remain in your file. After you sign, you will hand over your profession ring.'

The old nun paused, searching for the words which would complete her task.

'Finally, you must clearly understand that if at any future date you wish to re-enter religious life, your time here will count for nothing. You will have to begin at the very bottom again, as a postulant. Is that clear to you?'

'Yes it is, Mother.'

'Very well. I ask you now. Will you accept and sign this dispensation I hold in my hand?'

'Yes, Mother. I will.'

The Superior silently extended the paper, taking care that she did not in any way touch Clare's waiting hand. The Deputy passed her a pen, also avoiding any physical contact.

Without reading the words, Clare signed her name three times. Then she quickly worked loose her ring and placed it on top of the document. The Superior eased the paper and band back towards herself.

There was a lengthy silence before the Reverend Mother delivered her final whisper.

'May God protect you and keep you in his mercy, Clare.'

Apart from that time with Sister Imelda, it was the first time anyone in the Mother House had called her by her baptismal name.

The Deputy brusquely handed Clare her copy of the dispensation document.

'Your taxi is waiting. Goodbye.'

Clare addressed Reverend Mother.

'Thank you for all you have done for me. Goodbye, Reverend Mother.'

'Go in peace, my child.'

Clare walked towards the door. She could not help it, but tears started to well in her eyes.

At the door she turned and looked for the last time at the two nuns, as inert as statues staring at her. Then Reverend Mother raised her hand in benediction.

Instinctively, as she had always done at this moment, Clare bowed and the question crossed her mind whether she would always only be able to think and respond as a nun.

CHAPTER TWENTY-THREE

New Powers

In his mind's eye, Andrew could still summon Jane's voice and recall her skin and touch. But his depression had gone.

It had been replaced by a belief the rules he had designed would enable him to grow deeper in the love of God. While they were not based upon the church's teaching on celibacy, they still required from him considerable perseverance and determination.

He had achieved this through prayer, using its gift and mystery to love less selfishly and try and become a more sensitive person, yet one strong enough to handle those negative emotions which had come close to completely destroying him. He was now convinced that what Jane had really represented had paved the way to his salvation.

In his seminary room, Andrew continued to dress for the wedding of two strangers who had a role to play in his new attitude. As he carefully fixed in place his Roman collar, he remembered the morning he had finally seen the way forward. He wrote in his diary: 'I have sighted a landfall rising from the wastes of the spiritual wilderness which have all but claimed me.'

Six months later, his journey to the edge of hell and back had left him not only mentally, but physically, transformed. His hair shone, his fingernails were pared and his skin was tanned and glowed with vigour. The overall effect of a commanding presence was completed by the cassock he liked to wear, and he had confided to his diary, 'It sets a priest apart.'

Dressed, Andrew sat at his desk and once again dipped into pages in which he had tried to describe why he needed to attend a wedding here in Rome at the very hour Jane was getting married to Giles in London.

He turned to the entry where the idea began.

I don't know how long I stood in the chapel, feeling I was somehow looking at myself. My eyes were going everywhere: to the arches and the supporting marble columns; anywhere I could fix the rope. The spiritual director once said that if those ancient pillars could speak, what secrets they would reveal. But there was nowhere suitable. Yet I felt very set and determined, holding the rope.

It was quite extraordinary, standing there debating with myself: Did I or did I not, want to commit suicide? It was really a simple as that. I had somehow managed to reduce my entire life to one question. I remember thinking: if only I could do that in moral theology.

That person I was watching in the chapel, that other me, was quite detached. I really was so absorbed by what I was thinking, it made me feel quite giddy. I had to sit down. I wonder how many serious suicides go through this phase of rethinking? I sat in a pew and thought about that for a long time. I had always imagined being close to death I would feel calm and resigned. But I had the sick feeling which always happens when I'm badly frightened, that goes all the way back to when I was about nine and I'd missed altar boy duties two days in a row and Father Patrick said I should feel sick and ashamed.

When I next looked at my watch, I'd been sitting for an hour. If I did go ahead, my watch would be ticking for a whole year after my own heart stopped. I'd just put a new battery in it. I wondered why I thought about time in that way. Was it because I realized life would go on after me? That my suicide would not change anything? That Jane would still marry Giles. There would be no reason for her not to. My parents would be shattered. That was absolutely certain. They would be the helpless victims of my sin. I would be ruining their lives because I could not manage my own. Is that what I wanted?

Something said I should go back to my room. The Thing was very upset and kept saying I was a coward. I told it to shut up. I would have used stronger language but I was in chapel. Even so I said it quite loudly. Shut up. I suppose I should have realized the significance of this, but I didn't. For one thing, I was still on the edge. I could feel I was walking a tightrope in my mind. But I did get up at last.

Andrew paused and looked at his watch. He had often wondered what part it had played in that crucial decision to return to his room.

Nowadays, time as such had a new dimension, how long it took him to achieve goals. The time needed to understand that, while celibacy involved sublimation, it could create it own psychic energy. The time to work out how to handle his sexuality, understanding that it was not a matter of running away from it, but learning how to integrate it into his life. Time to recognize and accept that his body was always going to confront him with its physical demands and the time it had taken him to realize his fantasies were an essential part of his new-found mental health and human dignity.

But, in that predawn, returning from the chapel, he had precious little left of either. Coming up the stairs he had met Paul, a newly-arrived seminarian, going down to pray. Andrew didn't know who had been the more startled and he had wondered if Paul suspected why he was carrying a rope.

Months of despair passed before the renewal of his prayer life allowed him to explore what role love would play for him in the future. With Jane, he had seen it predominantly, and often exclusively, as a physical pleasure. Slowly, a deeper thought took root. Celibacy, to have any meaning at all, must be totally related to the right to enjoy genuine human affection, above all, he must love himself before he could love anybody else. Once he had built this ideal into his value system, he used it as a springboard to judge his emotional needs, and to understand how to satisfy them.

He came to see celibacy not as a solution, merely a means; by itself it was not a whole way of living, only an aspect. It could be woven into the fabric of commitment, but it must not assume a supreme importance. Above all, celibacy could not be rationalized but must retain some of its mystery. Consequently, it could have no hard and fast rules: it must always be a matter of individual interpretation, depending in the end on the quality and extent of his own imagination.

Andrew turned a page, written ten days after his intended suicide.

Been back to chapel every night, sitting for hours. Dark thoughts when The Thing was at its most powerful. Then it was gone. In its place a huge feeling of relief, even joy. I was kneeling, eyes closed and fingers so crushed together that they were really hurting each other, when the realization came. I realized I wanted to live.

I came back here and lay on my bed and I examined all those thoughts about Jane once more. What she had done and why she had done it. But there was this feeling of being able to go on. I went back to chapel and prayed and prayed. I spent a whole day on my knees. I came up around six in the evening and just dropped into bed. I slept for a straight twelve hours. When I awoke I felt hungry. I didn't realize how important this was. Hunger goes with a will to live.

But next morning the depression had returned and once more he had dropped to his knees and asked over and over again for God to show him how to survive. He had remained like that throughout the day. That night, exhausted, he had written –

A tiny seed stirred again from deep within me. It was as if God had personally spoken to me, saying I could never reach a state of well-being as long as my mind continued to drive me to extreme action. I must come to terms with the reality of Jane and live without her. God, I was certain, had suggested the solution. It was too awe-inspiring to have come from anywhere else. God would become my friend. Our relationship would transcend all others: through it, I would see my spirit grow, my ability to face and overcome problems, stronger than ever. That silent presence inside my head urged me not to fear pain; it was part of legitimate suffering. But I could deal with it in a healthy manner. And this time I would not be alone. God would be there.

Intellectually, he found theological objections to having God as a friend.

Friends are on a par, giving and receiving in equal measure. Such a relationship with God, at its highest value, suggested an equality – an impossibility – I could see what God could give me, but what could I offer in return? How could my finity match divine infinity? How could God come any closer than being a father to a child?

In the book of Romans, Andrew found a clue. 'God the Father, through his beloved Son, and the power of the Holy Spirit, makes me a son of God by adoption.'

The second book of Peter offered reinforcement. 'Ye might be a partaker of the divine nature.' Andrew turned to the Gospels. They too said it was possible to share an equal friendship with God because, through his grace, God, in the fulness of truth, goodness, beauty and spiritual strength had always been in him. He was, in its most humbling sense, the Trinity. God, Jesus and the Holy Spirit had never deserted their place inside him. All they were asking was that he should not turn his back on them. Then, and only then, did Andrew finally understand the fullest meaning of prayer.

Since then, Andrew had seen it work every day in this room, bringing him face to face with his past, stripping it away layer by layer and replacing it with legitimate suffering. The journey back was well documented.

This is my first entry for sixteen days. I don't really know what has happened to me this past month, but something happened. The power of something. There is no other way to describe it. I don't feel as if the strings are about to snap anymore. And the most extraordinary thing of all is that when I checked under the bed, the rope had gone. I went down this morning to the lumber room and there it was. I must have brought it back. But I have no recollection of doing so. It is God's doing.

Four days later he had written:

God never seems to be far away. Today was typical. I just could not get going. I had a whole stack of work from the Greg to catch up on. The workload is now formidable. I had three essays. I just sat there, staring at the paper, thinking what a mess life still was. I really got quite down in the dumps. Really low again. I must have plunged quite a bit before something seemed to steady inside me saying I had been down there before and had hated it. It was time to continue rebuilding. God is able to bring me back to a level of real emotional security. I suspect I will plunge again. But I know he will be there. That is a very good feeling.

He read C.S. Lewis' *The Four Loves*, an exploration of affection, and transposed Lewis' rather abstract ideas into the framework of his new life. Affection was really a question of shared values and ideas. He had never had that with Jane. But he could experience it here: seminary life was bound up in living and praying together. He could begin to explore the affection and friendship on offer, a kind largely lost to the outside world. Out there, little time was available for affection that was neither sentimental or physically sensuous. But the affection he had in mind could hold its own beauty and rewards. It would have no physical basis. It would be love in its noblest form. And he would still have his own private inner world intact, using it when required: a very necessary haven. Slowly, he began to feel that inner force, God, increasingly enriching him, allowing him to make calmer judgements, ones in many ways more profound. These, too, had been written down.

> I have also begun to realize that, for anything to be worthwhile, it has to be absorbed before it can be appreciated. It must go through the soul. In making that one decision, I have agreed to accept full responsibility for how I will live the rest of my life. I've stopped thinking life should be easy. It is only through the difficulties and the pain of resolving situations that I can ever hope to go on growing. It comes down to what Benjamin Franklin once said: 'things which hurt, instruct'. I've taken the first timid steps towards welcoming the problems of living and also looking forward to the happiness which comes from solving them.

He had cleaned his room and answered his letters. His clothes were once more pressed and his appetite had returned. Father William had said how pleased he was and Andrew had even heard that the spiritual director was using him as a model of the good life a student could have once he was fully integrated into seminary life.

But there had been one problem left to resolve.

> This compulsion to hear Jane's voice always comes at night. I try and con myself that I am really going to chapel but end up at the phone. Nothing can stop me from dialling her number. I hear the ringing tones and I think how a telephone is plugged into one's feelings. I can see her stretching to answer – see her face and the bedroom. I can anticipate the click as the instrument is picked up at her end. As the phone begins to ring, I put it back on the cradle, saying to myself I don't need to hear her voice just now. It is quite a moment.

He looked at his watch. It was time to go.

The church was in the Parti district of the city, behind Castel Sant' Angelo, a residential area close to the high walls of the Vatican. Andrew had come across it on one of his first post-depression walks. He had been back several times to sit in its nave, the gloomy silence only broken by footsteps coming and going to the confessionals. After a while Andrew had come to know the priest, who told him about the wedding, and had suggested he drop by: it would be another experience for him to remember after he left Rome to begin his ministry.

The priest had given Andrew the seat he requested, beside the choir stalls, on the bridegroom's side of the church. His cassocked presence would, he knew, go unremarked. To the congregation, he would be no more than another acolyte among those assembling before the altar. The priest was supervising the robed figures. Satisfied, he led them down the nave to the main doors which were open, waiting to receive the bride. Organ fugues filled the expectant silence.

The bridegroom and his best man were already standing at the sanctuary rail, nervous blue-suited young men, occasionally glancing over their shoulders towards the open doors.

Andrew was certain that in Jane's parish church, the atmosphere would be the same. He closed his eyes, as if in prayer, and in his mind he could see Giles in formal dress, standing, waiting with his brother, Tony; he was whispering nervously and Tony nodded reassuringly. He imagined his parents seated as close as possible to the places they would have occupied had he himself been the bridegroom.

Around Andrew the music swelled as the bridal procession slowly made its way up the nave. He opened his eyes and had his first glimpse of the bride. She was not as pretty as Jane or as tall, but she had, unusual for a Roman, Jane's fair hair.

In his mind's eye Jane, as she had once said she would, was wearing a gown with a train long enough to require the support of four bridesmaids. She wore the veil off her face and her eyes were shining with excitement.

Andrew watched the Italian bridegroom nudge his best man and give him a quick, relieved smile. The bride took her place beside her future husband and they, too, exchanged smiles.

Once more Andrew closed his eyes and Jane was smiling at him. He opened them at the point where the priest blessed the wedding rings.

Andrew's gaze was steady as he watched the man place the ring on the girl's finger, and the priest pronounced them man and wife. As they knelt in their first act of marital worship, he closed his eyes for a further moment, long enough for him to visualize Jane and Giles performing a similar action.

Then he opened his eyes again and murmured, 'Goodbye, Jane, goodbye.'

On a Sunday morning the dominant sound in the parochial hall was Father Breslin typing his sermon, and the rattle of window frames shaken by another gust of wind blowing in from the sea. The presbytery was over a century old, built in the days when the parish priest shared it with a couple of curates and a housekeeper. Father Breslin lived alone in the grey-walled and slate-roofed building.

There were five bedrooms, a dining room, a living room, a study and the large kitchen where he ate his meals. He slept in the smallest bedroom, leaving the remainder of the house almost undisturbed. A woman from the village came twice a week to dust and do his laundry.

It was little over three years since he had first sat in this study, still gripped by that strange chilly feeling that had taken hold as he drove towards the village, wondering how best he could serve his new parishioners.

He now knew each one of them by their Christian names: the tradesmen in the high street, the four publicans, the farmers with surnames that are part of the history of Ireland: Byrne, Kelly, O'Brien, O'Connor, Devlin, Duffy. He knew them as: Maeve, Pat, Sean, Joe, Paddy, Biddy. To them he was 'Father', or more formally, the 'P.P.', their parish priest.

He was pastor to them all; from old Ned Flynn, eighty-seven next birthday, to the latest Wilson baby, Louise, christened only a week ago. The tiny infant would be there this morning, in her mother's arms, crying no doubt, but he loved the sound of children. It reminded him there would always be a tomorrow.

He continued to type his sermon. The typewriter was a gift from his parishioners. They had also bought him a car and a television set.

He had never, by so much as a hint, told anybody there were periods these past three years when the burden of work had seemed too heavy to bear. Then the depression, dark and silent and dense, returned, leaving him filled with a dread of having lost faith in God and in the future. Realizing the gap he would leave in the lives of these people whom he loved as his only family if his ministry were to be continuously interrupted by these debilitating spells, he had returned to the psychiatrist.

He had suggested Father Breslin should go into hospital. Instead Father Breslin had contacted another psychiatrist who had explained the depression could be successfully treated by drugs. The tablets had indeed brought the melancholia under control and this past year he had become emotionally stronger than he had ever been.

The church was packed, pew after pew filled with freshly scrubbed faces, country faces – round and shiny. The men mostly wore blue or brown suits, the women frocks. This was a part of Ireland where the tradition of dressing for Sunday Mass persisted. Standing at the back were the late-comers, mostly young, who had slept until the last moment after a Saturday night up in Dublin.

Father Breslin ran his eyes over his flock to see who had returned from a holiday or from a bout of illness, who was absent, gone perhaps into hospital to have an operation, or a baby. Mass was another way of keeping track of developments within the parish.

He stood at the lectern to one side of the altar, rearranging his typed notes. He had allowed ten minutes for the sermon, remembering what Father McKenna had said about keeping it short.

Three months after he had come here, Miss Maddox had found the old priest dead in bed. A heart attack the doctor had said. She had herself died a few months later. He had continued to remember them both in his prayers.

Father Breslin began his sermon. 'Today, I want to speak to you about human love and sexuality. The first thing I want to emphasize is that it is God's wish that men and women should be united with each other through love, and that real love can only be truly experienced through the joy of marriage. This, we all know, does not always fit in with so-called modern thinking.'

He glanced at Paddy Dolan sitting with Marie O'Dwyer. They had been living together for two years and had told him they saw no point in getting married because their sense of commitment to each other was all that mattered. He had explained that while he could not accept this view, they were still welcome in his church. Marie was seven months pregnant and he hoped that, when the time came, he would baptize their child and receive it fully into the church. Then he would make renewed efforts to persuade them to marry.

'There are those of you today who will ask what gives me the right to stand here and speak about love and sex. I can feel the questions forming. "What does he know about either? How can he tell us? He's only a priest." Perfectly fair. But I am also a man. Jesus, too, was a man. In choosing to follow my life in Christ, I have had to make sense of what Jesus meant when he said: "it is never going to be easy for anyone to live life the way it is meant to be lived".

When I marry a couple, I do so in the hope that they will remain together until death. When I baptize their babies, I know what it is to see love. Marriage and parenthood are things I long ago chose to forgo. But I can share in them. So, yes, you may ask the questions, and I can say in all humility, that I can answer them.

The smallest deviation from what Christ intended for each of us matters. That's the first thing to understand about love. You can't sell it short.'

He told them the rules that must govern their sexual feelings were those based upon moral goodness and true Christian loving. Sex was not something to be treated casually, it was a powerful and potent force, one that could only be handled within the sanctity of Christian living. He was not talking only of marriage, but speaking of the benefits accruing from a loving relationship.

He hoped Molly Doyle would take note. She sat in the front pew, a buxom widow, fifty and full of vitality. In his first year she had emerged as his parish Eve. He had finally taken her aside and explained that he was perfectly happy to have her visit the parochial house and accept her invitations to a meal, but these occasions must be spaced out, otherwise the other ladies in the parish would feel he was neglecting them. They had both smiled: an understanding had been reached. The best way to deal with a problem, he knew, was to settle it before it developed.

'Human weakness is something we all experience. Each one of us.

But God's grace is powerful and helps us overcome it and grow in his love. We should be as tolerant as Christ himself was. No one except Jesus and his Mother has ever lived on this earth without sin. We all die with promises to be fulfilled. Healthy people are indeed those with a proper sexual awareness. But they must still look to God to see the conditions under which love may be expressed. The commandment: "thou shalt not commit adultery" is not a law against love. It is a law that protects love. It is not a law that restricts freedom. It is one that gives real freedom. Married love is shared, unique and untouchable. In that framework sex is a beautiful experience.'

He gazed at the silent, attentive faces. He had deliberately softened his voice.

'The only love which really works is the kind that can be given and expressed freely, without guilt. It is not something separate from you. It is part of each one of you. You are love. Love is you. There are not different kinds of love. Love is love. The only way it can vary is in how much of it you can give and how much you can receive. You can only do that in a truly loving and Christian relationship. Then, and only then, can you see love working as a trusting and accepted reality. The sort of love I am talking about does not need guarantees. Guarantees are what sex is all about. Will something guarantee to be a turn-on? Will something guarantee to titillate and excite? Real love is the Christian joy of mutual sharing in a Christian life. If you do not already have it, leave here and search for it. But don't look for it in your pasts. Or in your futures. Love is something that exists in the moment. Love, in the end, is this moment, in each one of us.'

He made the sign of the cross and walked slowly from the lectern to the altar.

CHAPTER TWENTY-FOUR

Unless the Spirit Dies

Victoria had a case-load of fourteen nuns. Nine were members of her own Order, the remainder came from three other Communities. Each sister required up to six months of counselling before deciding whether or not to remain in religious life. Victoria had told each of her patients that anyone who wished to leave should feel no guilt and she would do everything to help her successfully face that decision.

The emphasis in most church-sponsored counselling centres was only to get nuns and priests back into religious life. Victoria was glad this was not the policy of the unit to which she was attached. Its director had told her that if she was to make the best possible use of her long and expensive training, she must have a free hand, even to how she furnished her office in the guidance clinic.

At their first meeting the director, a priest who was a psychiatrist, had explained: 'For too long the church has avoided its responsibilities to its nuns and priests. Having brought them into religious life, it has, until the past decade, virtually ignored the plight of those who cannot live by the Rules. There are men close to the Pope who still insist there is no link between the increasing number of priests and nuns seeking our help, and vows that are more appropriate to the Middle Ages.'

He had smiled and said: 'The last thing I want to see is your office looking like some hospital room. Our patients are not sick – only the victims of unrealistic expectations.'

The desk at which Victoria wrote her case reports was against a wall in one corner. There were several plant-holders dotted about the room: ivy and ferns created an impression of a healthy, vigorous atmosphere. The curtains complimented the theme: sunflowers against a summer blue background.

A moment ago, Victoria had reminded Sister Catherine, who sat opposite in one of the room's two comfortable armchairs, that when she had first come here she had sobbed at the sight of the curtain pattern because the sunflowers reminded Catherine of the first time Eddie had driven her into the country and they had made love in a cornfield.

In the story that unfolded, Victoria had been deeply moved by the young nun's unhappiness, and something of this had come through in her questions until Catherine had once more sobbed, 'What do you know about love? You're just another one the system has sucked dry!'

In those first weeks, Catherine had vacillated between abject self-pity, lengthy periods of silence – for one meeting she had refused to say a word – and outbursts. Gradually, over the months, Victoria had brought some order to Catherine's torment. The nun's face had lost its strained look. The outbursts became less frequent. She had even started to smile as, together, they explored Catherine's relationship with Eddie, that had finally led him on a Sunday evening to drive up to the Mother House and Catherine to jump into his car with a suitcase of clothes and literally flee her commitment to religious life.

Within weeks the sense of freedom Catherine had craved, had been replaced by a deepening guilt and a sense of betraying her faith, and her Order. She had finally contacted her Mother Superior who had referred her to the unit. Victoria had been assigned the case.

She had remained virtually silent during Catherine's weeks of purging, only interrupting to ask an occasional question, but always careful never to comment on what Catherine persisted in calling her sins. Victoria had remained equally non-judgemental as Catherine described how she had finally blamed Eddie for all that had happened. If it had not been for him she had railed, she would still be a nun. Eddie was responsible for everything. Through a flood of new tears, Catherine had said she wanted to return to the Order.

That evening, over dinner with Jim, Victoria had unfolded her plan. As usual, he had listened most carefully.

Jim had resurfaced in Victoria's life as easily as he had left it almost thirty years ago. That had been the day she had cheered him on as he churned through the water to win the 100 yards crawl for their High School. He had lifted himself out of the pool, waved at her casually and loped off to the locker room. Later, over burgers and fries, he had told her he was going to be a

332

priest. She had blurted out that his decision would break the hearts of a lot of girls. He'd looked at her surprised, and she had added, only half-joking, that perhaps she would have fallen for him herself if Art hadn't been around. Jim was now one of the unit's therapists. He had ministered in Canada, served for a spell in Rome, then returned to the United States to work in church-run clinics in New York and Detroit before joining the unit.

At first their contact had been confined to discussions in the clinic's staff room or over lunch in the coffee shop across the street with other therapists. But one evening Jim had dropped by her office and suggested dinner. He had spent a particularly difficult hour with a young priest who had a fetish problem – he liked to wear women's underwear – and said he wanted a break from patients' problems.

Victoria had suggested over cocktails that he should refer the case to their superior. Jim had resisted; this was his case. His quiet determination impressed her.

Reaching the house in the suburbs she shared with three other sisters, he had leaned across and kissed her gently on the mouth. She had been too startled to resist. For a moment she looked at him carefully and then they had clung together in silent embrace. He had whispered that everything would be fine; that they could handle the situation.

The most surprising thing for her was how easy it had been to do so. It had, she was convinced, also helped her to resolve Catherine's dilemma.

She and Jim had gone to their favourite restaurant where she explained Catherine's situation.

'Will they have her back?' he asked.

'Of course. But that's not the point, Jim. Catherine is still fundamentally Catherine. This recent shift is no more than a variant of her overall behaviour pattern. Going back is the last thing she should be encouraged to do.'

'It may be she's also regained her commitment. It does happen, Victoria.'

Victoria shook her head. 'Her problem is that the church sold her a bill of goods, and she doesn't know how to cash it in.'

Jim looked thoughtful. 'You could still tell her to quit. You've done that before.'

Victoria nodded. 'Catherine's more complex. Deep down inside her she wants to challenge the authority of the church, or at least what she has experienced of it. But she knows she cannot do that. Nobody takes on the church on that level and wins. My fear is that the same guilt that drove her from Eddie will drive her back to the Order for all the wrong reasons.'

'The Order could simply refuse to have her back,' Jim said.

'It could, but it won't. It will simply see her as somebody who went off the rails, but is now ready to return to the fold. That's why they sent her to me. For them I'm supposed to work the miracle which gets her back into religious life.'

Jim was silent for a long moment. 'And you're saying you can't.'

'I'm saying that it would be wrong for me to even try. The only way to help Catherine is for me to make her see she's absolutely right to feel as she does about the church.'

'I'm not sure, Victoria. I mean, it's a hell of a thing to do.'

Victoria's voice contained a new certainty. 'I think it's the only way. I really do. It's the only way she will ever face herself – by accepting that much of what she has been told about God is wrong for her.'

'Victoria!'

'I'm serious, Jim. Her guilt, her anger, all her hang-ups go back to the fact that some smart nun or priest, anxious to score brownie points with a bishop, talked her into becoming a nun. They sold her a glossy package that was about as realistic as saying heaven is up and hell is down. That's the level Catherine psychologically operates at. She bought the package blindly, and the only way she saw how to unscramble it was by grabbing the first man who looked at her. She's got a strong sex drive, but her sexual fantasies are a childish hodge-podge. Eddie was a sort of sex toy for her, making up for all those lost years. Common enough, as we both know, but at the root of it, sex is not Catherine's problem. It's simply she should never have become a nun. The only way to help her is to make her see this.'

Once more Jim was silent for a long time. He looked across the table, sombre-faced. 'That's a big gamble you're taking. You could get yourself busted out of the unit.'

Victoria sighed, suddenly realizing how tired she was. 'I know that, Jim. But, in Catherine's case, it is the only way. It really is.'

So had begun the slow process of exploring Catherine's guilt which continued to draw her back into a life for which Victoria was convinced the nun was unsuited.

'Catherine, in every sense, this is a new start for both of us. As from now, I want to hear no more *mea culpas*. You have done enough confessing. You could probably spend the rest of your life searching for new evidence to support your guilt. But what I want you to think about first of all is this. All these recriminations of yours are only a mask. What we have to do is look behind that mask and see what is really there. To do that you need to have your ego in as good a shape as possible.'

Each session produced its small but significant victories as Catherine began to see herself differently. Victoria pried Catherine loose from her old beliefs. She explored Catherine's feelings for her parents, getting her to finally admit her entire family had been completely dominated by her father. It had been largely to escape him, and ironically, to earn his rare enough approbation, that Catherine had allowed herself to follow the advice of her catechism teacher and become a nun.

Catherine entered religious life at seventeen. Very quickly she began to see that the endless strictures and restrictions were how the church, like her father, held power.

She began to experience sexual fantasies and she enjoyed them. That was a double sin – having them and enjoying them. Her voice had shaken as she made the admission. The morning after she became fully professed, she awoke to find herself masturbating. The discovery distressed her deeply. She had gone to the communal bathroom and filled a tub with cold water and immersed herself until she could no longer bear it.

For a while the idea of numbing her body had been sufficient deterrent to keep her sexuality at bay. But a week later she had found herself masturbating again. From then on, she had regularly done so. The cold baths only stopped when she developed pneumonia, and lay for weeks seriously ill in the Mother House infirmary.

Restored to health, her sexual demands returned. Her guilt, already well established, became almost obsessive. She developed a compulsion to wash her hands; the more she did so, the dirtier she felt.

Victoria began to explore Catherine's concept of sin. Why did she believe masturbation was wrong? What made it so? Who had told her that? Why did she think it was wrong to fantasize? Who said so? When she had met Eddie and made love to him, why had she felt guilty? Where did she think was the guilt in responding to a normal human emotion? What was love? What was sin? What was the difference between good and evil?

The questions had been carefully spaced and Victoria had allowed Catherine all the time she needed to respond.

Gradually, Victoria had led Catherine to the point where she began to ask questions of herself. Why had she allowed herself to think she had a vocation? Did that even matter? Surely what mattered now was that she could see her mistake? Why hadn't she been able to see that the best thing to do would be to ask for dispensation instead of running away? But had she the strength to do so?

Victoria had for once interrupted.

'Yes, you have, knowing what you now know. This sort of life is wrong for you. But that doesn't mean you have behaved wrongly. It is what is being asked of you that is wrong. That is important for you to grasp.'

'But I'll still feel I've let God down.'

'Catherine, whatever you have done, you have not done that. None of us are big enough to let God down. Not one of us is clever enough to even begin to know his mind. All I can say to you is that the God you describe is not the God I know. You are talking of a punishing God. You are trying to make your God sound like your father, and perhaps even like the Order. But that is not the way I see him. God wants you to be happy. He knows you are not a bad person. You have to understand that and believe it from this moment. Okay?'

It had taken time to nurture the idea. But Catherine had, at last, been able to see her affair with Eddie only as a symptom. The root cause had begun with her father, and was compounded by the Order, and ultimately by the church and its doctrines, which she finally found impossible to live with.

Resolution, when it came, was dramatic. At first, Catherine had come to therapy in her habit. But, one morning at the start of her fifth month, she appeared in a new dress. It somehow completely transformed her personality. From then on, each time she came, she wore either a dress or casual clothes. Each month she somehow found enough money to add to her wardrobe. The effect of being able to dress as she liked became instantly noticeable.

'The clothes have made me change inside. I not only look different, but I feel different. I see God differently. He's still very important to me, but in a new way. And I don't need to worship him within a framework. You know what I mean, Victoria?'

Victoria had said she understood perfectly.

Two weeks later, Catherine announced that she had applied for formal dispensation. She also had a new man in her life, a buyer in a department store. While she would continue to date him, she would live alone in an apartment she could now afford to rent with the money from her new job as a sales clerk in a bookshop.

Victoria had asked how she felt about making the first independent decision of her new life?

'Good. Pretty damn good.'

On a cold January morning in 1984, Victoria rose from her chair and handed Catherine her copy of the dispensation she had arranged to be sent from the Mother House. Catherine stared at the sheet of paper thoughtfully. 'It seems strange, needing all this formality, all these Latin words to start living.'

She looked at the document with her name inked-in and the end of her religious life affirmed by the flourishing scrawl of the archbishop. 'It's impressive enough to be framed.'

Victoria smiled. 'We normally only frame things that matter. Today is the first day of your new life.'

Catherine thrust the paper at Victoria. 'You keep it. A reminder of a difficult patient.'

Victoria accepted the document. After Catherine had left, she picked up her large bag from beside the desk and took a cab to the airport, filled with a sense of mounting excitement.

For the first part of the flight from New York to Athens, Victoria and Jim had slept, holding hands beneath their blankets.

He wore jeans and an open neck shirt. Victoria had chosen a linen trouser suit. Each had packed a rosary and missal in their bags. Jim also packed his anointing oils and stole. Occasionally his fingers would stroke her profession ring; sometimes her hand would stray and touch his thigh. Both had discovered they were very tactile.

At Paris Orly Airport, while the jet refuelled, they mailed postcards to friends and colleagues at the unit. Victoria hesitated about signing her name next to Jim's.

He laughed. 'There's your guilt showing.'

She kept her voice level. 'I don't feel guilty. I just don't want to make people uncomfortable. Father James, for one.' He was the medical director of the unit.

'You're forgetting he's a psychiatrist. Anyway, he knows.'

She couldn't keep the surprise out of her voice. 'You told him?'

Jim shrugged. 'Sure. What's there to tell? We're going to spend ten days looking at the ruins of Greece. So?'

'We're also sharing a room. Remember?'

'I haven't forgotten.'

'I bet you didn't tell Father James that.'

Jim laughed. 'No. That would really have been pushing things a little too far.' There was a bantering tone to his next words. 'Of course, you can always switch the reservation.'

Victoria looked at him steadily. 'Now who's feeling guilty!'

She wished he would drop the subject. The idea for the vacation had come up on a cold night last November when they sat in his apartment watching a travelogue on TV about the Greek islands. Pouring more wine, Jim had said they should go. Not really taking him seriously, she had replied, why not? At lunch next day, he surprised her by saying he had made the reservations. She should have remembered. Jim was a person who followed through on his impulses.

A month before, she had moved out of the shared house in the suburbs and into a small comfortable apartment a few blocks from Jim. He had found it for her after she had called Reverend Mother and said she needed more privacy to work at home on her case notes. Her Superior at once agreed that the Order would furnish and pay the rental on the apartment.

Four nights a week Victoria reviewed her files, steeping herself in the crises of other nuns. The other three were invariably spent in Jim's company. On Fridays he cooked for her; on Saturdays they generally ate at the Chinese restaurant. On Sunday evenings, she cooked for him. A large portion of their salaries were remitted directly to their Orders who paid their living expenses. They saved out of their remaining income for extras such as this vacation.

By the time Jim suggested they should go to Greece, they both realized their relationship had few limitations. Walking through the Orly concourse, Victoria reminded him of the decisions they had agreed upon together before the vacation.

'Jim, I don't want to change anything. I don't see anything morally wrong with sharing a room. Or for that matter, a bed. Sleeping together in our case is just what it means. Sleeping. Together. It's really no different from sitting close together on your sofa or on my couch. The same emotions are engaged. The same temptations are there. You know that. I know that. We could just as easily made love on a couch as in a bed.'

She smiled, wanting to end the matter on a light note. 'Besides, it's cheaper. On our budget that's important.'

Jim stared at her. 'I don't think many people would believe we are doing this because we want to run a test-temptation experiment on the cheap.'

'Look, if you want to switch when we get there, fine. But let's not make a production out of this. We both said we want to try it. If you've changed your mind, it's no big deal.'

'No, Victoria. I haven't. It's just, well, a little scary.'

She looked at him. 'If it's any help, I'm also scared.'

He took her hand, and they walked silently towards the departure gate as their flight to Athens was called.

She had often thought their relationship was unpredictable, yet revealing as any case history. She had thought, in many ways, it was a love story no novelist would dare invent, how she and this vigorous-looking fifty-year-old priest had explored their passions.

The hotel was in the Kolonaki district of Athens with an unrivalled view of the Acropolis and Mount Lykabettus. They registered and handed the forms back to the clerk. He looked at them for a long time. Then he lifted his eyes and stared solemnly, first addressing Jim.

'You are a priest of religion?

'I don't know of any other kind.'

The clerk nodded to himself, glancing down at the form to make sure he had not misread what Jim had written alongside 'Occupation'.

He looked at Victoria. 'You are a sister of religion?'

She smiled. 'Yes.'

The man once more nodded slowly, murmuring to himself in Greek. He looked at them both. 'A nun. A priest.' He smiled. 'But why not? Nothing is impossible today.'

He turned and handed them the room key. 'Enjoy your stay.'

Jim took Victoria by the arm as they followed the bell-hop to the elevator. 'It's the only way to be, Victoria. If they'd found out, it would have made us seem furtive and dirty. If we behave up-front, people will see we've nothing to hide.'

Victoria looked at him. 'Jim, don't protest so much. It's no big deal, two adults sharing a room.'

They rode up in silence. The room was large, with twin beds several feet apart. The balcony looked across the rooftops of Athens. Victoria motioned towards the beds.

'Which one? Nearest the balcony or the bathroom?'

'I'll take the balcony side.'

She began to unpack, shaking out the creases in the new nightdress she had bought. She noticed that Jim had paused in his own unpacking and was looking at her.

'Something wrong?'

He shrugged. 'You know, I thought I'd got it all straight in my mind. But now, here…'

She walked over to him, unselfconsciously holding a pair of pants. 'Jim, the worst sin is pride. Don't forget that. I know you don't want to be the first to fail. I think I know how you feel.'

'Would you please mind not standing so close.'

She stepped back.

'We're still too close.'

'Jim! For goodness' sake, we can't start like this.' She looked at him seriously. 'Would you like me to take another room? Maybe next door or across the hall?'

'No. Don't do that. I'll be fine in a minute. It's just seeing you there with your nightie and those pants in your hand.'

'I'm sorry, Jim.'

340

'No. It's okay. Really. But try and keep a little distance until I get used to this.'

Victoria took another pace back. 'I can't spend every minute wondering if what I do or say is going to either arouse you or make you feel guilty.'

'Victoria...'

'Look Jim. Have you ever thought I might also need some space? You're not the only one under vows in this room. But we can't just stand here and calculate how much of a sin it is to unpack our clothes.'

'I'm sorry.'

Jim reached for Victoria, encircling her with his arms, and kissed her. She started to pull away, but he held her close, murmuring, 'Hey, I'm sorry. Kiss me. Kiss me.'

She did. 'Come on, Jim. It's going to be fine. Here, give me your hand.' She led him to the bed. For the first time she took the initiative.

The days slipped by. From Athens they had gone to Corfu, Rhodes and the Gulf of Corinth.

Now, late in the afternoon, a boat was bringing them to their final destination, the volcanic island of Santorini. Tomorrow they would return to Athens to begin the long journey home.

Jim pointed at the spectacular pumice and lava. 'Erupted in Minoan times. The whole island shot up in a day.'

She studied the towering cliff faces, with the white-housed town of Thira perched on the cliffs, usually reached either by mule or cable car.

'It's a climb of 800 steps from the harbour.'

'You're a mine of information.'

'I read it up while you were sleeping.'

'I wasn't sleeping. I heard you get up. I've heard you get up every night.'

'I'm sorry, Victoria. I thought I'd been quiet.'

'I guess, getting used to having you in my room, I notice when you've gone.'

Night after night, they had lain side-by-side, usually on her bed, kissing and cuddling. One night she had looked at him. 'Why don't you let me take care of you? I'd like to do that.'

From then on, she had.

He had brought her to orgasm, her entire body trembling as she sobbed her relief. Then he would give her a final goodnight kiss and return to his bed. After a while she would hear him sigh and begin to murmur a prayer.

At some point he would rise and sit on the balcony, smoking, the moon bright enough for him to read, staying there until dawn.

Just once, in Rhodes, she had risen and started to go to him. Then she turned back to bed. Next morning, while he used the bathroom, she jotted in her journal. 'Jim can't really cope because he doesn't understand that he can still be a priest while recognizing he's a man. He must find himself. It may come before this trip is over. It may take him longer to work it out. He knows a great deal about loving others, but he doesn't know how to love himself.'

Coming out of the bathroom, he asked her what she was writing. She smiled at him. 'Trying to put on paper something that can't easily be written down.'

Riding up in the cable car to Thira, Jim suddenly said that they should try and get a good night's sleep in preparation for the long flight.

'I agree. An early dinner and then bed.'

'Why don't we take separate rooms for tonight.'

She looked at him. 'Is this what you want?'

'I think so, yes.'

'Alright. It's no big deal.'

'Thank you, Victoria.'

Over dinner in a restaurant dug out of a cliff-face, he was already back at work, talking about his case-load.

She realized that already the holiday was over for Jim; that he could not wait to return to where he felt most comfortable: living his life on his terms, seeing her when he wanted to, able to come and go as he liked, free of any of the pressures he had felt on vacation. She understood perfectly.

They kissed outside her room.

'I think it went fine, don't you?'

'Same here. I think it went the way we expected it would.'

'Yes.' He kissed her once more.

CHAPTER TWENTY-FIVE

A State of Grace

Father Philippe lobbed the basketball into the net and resisted the urge to rush forward. Being able to restrain himself was a further indication of the new values instilled in him by Dr Stanway, the director of the Chronical Dependency Unit at the General.

Among much else, Dr Stanway had shown Father Philippe his impulses were not rationally related one to another, but often jostled side by side or even coalesced in paradox in a largely unknown part of the subconscious mind and the outside world. Dr Stanway had put it more graphically. 'It is the world before civilization, filled with the images of primitive creation and destruction. There is no logical structure, no social understanding, in that world. That only comes with awareness. And, in your case, that always leads to stress. And stress is no more than fear spread thin.'

For the past two months Father Philippe had seen the psychiatrist for an hour each day, six days a week, as an in-patient at the unit. On Sundays he had spent hours in the hospital's chapel, praying and meditating.

He now knew his impulsiveness, impatience and lack of forethought would always remain part of his make-up. Dr Stanway had said all he could do was to provide a self-understanding of how he could best live with them. This would not make him a bad priest. Quite the opposite: it made him human and someone more able to identify with the failings of others. But he would always be at risk.

At their final session earlier that day, Dr Stanway had explained that Father Philippe was being sent to a church-run counselling rehabilitation centre where he would be assessed as to his suitability to return to active ministry. Dr Stanway had risen from his desk, shaken him by the hand, and led him to the door. 'Go play ball, Father. It's still as good a therapy as any to understand what I mean. And remember the mantra I gave you. It synthesizes all I've been trying to say these past weeks.'

Father Philippe stood beneath the basketball net and recited. 'I know you. I created you. I have loved you from your mother's womb. You have fled – as you now know – from my love. But I love you nevertheless, and not-the-less, however far you flee.' The words had been written by another priest who imagined what God would say if they met. They fitted perfectly what Father Philippe would like the creator to say to him, and he had learned to quote them regularly.

He recited another portion of the mantra. 'Far beyond your understanding, when you suffer, I suffer. I also know all the little tricks by which you try and hide the ugliness you have made of your life for yourself and others. But you are beautiful. You are beautiful more deeply within than you can see.'

Dr Stanway had stressed at their first consultation that Father Philippe was not mentally ill. Confused, certainly; suffering, absolutely; anxious, fearful and hurting, no doubt. Calling his condition an illness was no more than a convenient label, one attached by those doctors he had seen in the past eighteen months before coming to the Chronical Dependency Unit.

They had prescribed drugs to make him sleep, to stop him scratching, to keep him calm, to give him energy, to take away his stomach pains and remove his headaches. But no tablet had eased that deep inner core of hurting, so agonizing it had continued to make him cry and tremble.

These past two months in Dr Stanway's care had been to make him accept that conquering his own inner pain by himself was the only way to achieve maturity. The time in the unit had passed in a swirl of sudden insights when the truth hurt so much he had wished he could continue to delude himself into believing he could resume a double life: the demands of Mother church and his craving for Margot.

From the very beginning she had insisted he must play the game by her rules: that he could still be her priest as well as her lover. He was honest enough to admit he still missed her but he could become strong enough to live without her. Margot had been wrong to say a priest could also be a man. A priest must always be a priest whose sexual drive must never get the better of him.

Dr Stanway had kept saying there was no drug available to cure soul-pain. Instead, Father Philippe must discover his own solution, accepting pain was a step towards not repeating it. Self-discipline was a prerequisite for self-love. Without that kind of love he would have no real chance in life; he would be reduced to chasing fleeting moments of pleasure which would never provide lasting satisfaction.

Father Philippe began to bounce the ball expertly, thinking how Margot still loved him, in spite of everything he had done. He wished she didn't. He started to dribble the ball, feinting around imaginary opponents, moving swiftly across the court, hands and legs working in perfect unison, his whole body committed – the way it had once been to Margot.

His time with her had been absorbed with the heady sensations her love-making evoked: the way she would look at him, the sensuous contact of her hands, the revelation of her nakedness, which made him draw breath. Her body was only a succession of proofs she had given him of her love: each one had its own special bouquet, heady enough for him to have become so helpless he forgot completely he was a priest.

Dr Stanway had explained that, with his powerful and unpredictable sexual drive, went an equally strong joy he derived from his ministry. Early on in therapy, they had spent an entire hour discussing the positive values of celibacy. Dr Stanway had suggested that celibacy was an ideal and a challenge. To be a celibate was the closest anyone could come to living the fullest possible life in Christ.

Dr Stanway had said that, even as a child, Father Philippe had known that: later, as a seminarian, the thought had been further inculcated. And it had been there throughout his priesthood. That was why he had begun to silently question his behaviour shortly after Margot started their affair. That was why Father Philippe's itching had returned, and with it the awesome nightmare – where once Simone had the starring role in his horrendous dream, Margot had taken over.

On the nights they had not slept together, he had lain in the darkness of his presbytery bedroom, twisting and turning, in spite of medication, his mind filled

345

with a longing for her. Unable to sleep, he would go to the church and kneel on his prie-dieu near the sanctuary lamp. His gaze would wander from the light to the statue of Our Lady and he would reach out and touch the cold marble folds of the Madonna's robes and, in the limitlessness of his imagination, would imagine she was Margot.

From early on in their affair, he had repeatedly torn at his thighs, drawing blood. Margot would wipe him clean and dust him with medicated powder. For a few nights, until the wounds began to heal, they did not make love, just lie on her bed, holding each other. She had always been comforting, ready to give of herself in any way he wished. When he pretended he wanted to sleep, she had curled up, her back to him. He would wait until her breathing steadied, then begin once more to scratch steadily.

Margot would awaken and go to the bathroom, returning with a cloth soaked in cold water and, after she cleaned him, she would hold him in her arms, rocking him gently back and forth. Lulled by the motion, a new thought entered his mind. Margot was his devil, his temptress, his downfall. While he could not do what the saints of old had done, plunging into the burning sands of the desert or seek the company of wild beasts, he could promise he would never return to her bed. He had made such a vow many times.

He had been driven to love her by turning to the Bible. It had been filled with interpretative comfort. The first Christian martyrs, the bedrock from which the church had risen, married one another in the Roman arenas before the lions tore them asunder. Even Jesus had not lived continuously in his impossible saintliness. In Bethany, he had created his own haven. Beneath the shade of the trees in the garden of his friend, Lazarus, Jesus had himself put his hand on the head of Martha, the woman he loved, who was sitting at his feet.

Father Philippe had asked himself where was the difference? He was guilty of no more than a breach of outmoded canon law. In the Gospels, Jesus had never mentioned celibacy. Each time this had been enough to allow him to return to Margot.

On the first anniversary of their affair, he spent an entire evening in his study composing a letter, pleading with her to understand why they must end it. He never posted it. Instead, he returned to Margot's bed.

One night, after making love, he had waited until she had drifted into sleep, eyes glued to Margot's bedside clock, counting the minutes until he could return to the rectory. He always left before dawn.

He found Father Nolan waiting, an embarrassed look on his face. The old priest said he did not wish to pry, but this was the third night that week Father Philippe had been out until this hour. The previous week it had been four nights and the same the week before that. Father Nolan asked what was going on?

Without mentioning Margot's name, Father Philippe said there was a woman. Father Nolan sighed and closed his eyes and remained like that for some minutes. Then he asked Father Philippe if he had tried to pray this away?

Father Philippe told him he had.

The older priest suggested they could pray together. They had knelt side by side before the altar for almost an hour.

For two nights Father Philippe managed to stay away from Margot. On the third, the desire to make love to her overcame everything else. He drove from the rectory at dusk and had once more returned in the early hours.

Father Nolan was waiting. He uttered just one word: 'Why?' They had stood together in embarrassed silence and he had felt the other priest's interminable sadness. Next day, Father Nolan said the chancellor had booked him a bed in the Chronical Dependency Unit. The bishop wanted him to know he was praying for him, as they all were. He had felt an overwhelming relief. Mother church had once more reached out to recover him.

He entered the unit without telling Margot. In their first session he had revealed her existence to Dr Stanway. The doctor told him to call her and say where he was, inviting him to use his own telephone. Margot pleaded with him to let her come to visit. Father Philippe firmly refused. She finally burst into tears and hung up. Dr Stanway suggested he should wait a few days before calling again and next time, he should try and explain he was in hospital because he wanted to return to being a good priest.

Since then, Father Philippe had spoken frequently on the telephone to Margot. Each time she begged to see him; each time he felt more able to resist. Sometimes Margot had hung up while he was trying to explain his feelings.

Leaving the basketball court, Father Philippe walked past the occupational therapy area where, as part of his rehabilitation, he had learned to work in ceramics. He continued down a hallway, known as Shrink Alley, because this was where the doctors had their offices. He pushed open the fire doors and entered another corridor. On either side were separate bedrooms for fifty patients.

The bank of pay-phones were in a recess beside the nurses' station. He chose the one farthest away and began to dial.

Margot answered the telephone.

''Lo.'

'It's me.'

'Hi, Phil! How are you?'

'Much better.' He hesitated. 'Margot, I have to talk to you.'

'Go ahead.'

'I'm sorry about the last time. I guess, well, I was still coming off drugs and I was jumpy.'

'That's all right, Phil.'

'I've thought things through. I've spent days thinking of nothing else, Margot.'

'Days? That's not a lot of thinking time.'

'Margot... could you pack up my things and have your mother drop them off here?'

In one of Margot's bedroom closets were his sports jackets and pants, some shirts and underwear. He'd brought them over from the rectory in the first month of their affair. The silence stretched.

'Is this why you called? For your clothes?'

'Margot, please don't get mad at me.'

Dr Stanway had explained Father Philippe had seen all the women in his life as punishers and providers. Beginning with his mother, they had shown themselves capable of taking personal offence and revenging themselves on him.

'I'm not mad at you.'

'Could you get your mother to bring them over?'

A new silence.

Fern, he was certain, was the only one in the family who had known about their affair. From the beginning she had tacitly approved. She had bought his ticket for a holiday in the Bahamas with Margot only a month after they had met, slipping him an envelope filled with dollar bills for spending money. Fern had spoken to them daily in their shared hotel room, and he was certain she had only pretended to be shocked when Margot told her they only needed one of its double beds.

It was Fern who had reminded them to travel back separately; for good measure Margot had disguised herself behind California-sized sun-glasses and a huge beach hat. Next morning, Fern had joined him on the jogging track and said she had come to see him more as a son than as a priest. He had come to think of her as the most remarkably open-minded mother he had ever known.

'I could bring them over,' Margot said.

'I don't think that would be a good idea.'

'Okay. I'll ask mother to drop them off. You want your toothbrush and your razor?'

'No, dump them. I've got new ones.'

He had left the toiletries on the shelf below the mirror in her bathroom.

'Margot, are you there?'

'I'm here.'

'Did you hear what I said?'

'What I hear is a small and frightened voice crying for help.' Her voice sounded as if she was dying and crying inside.

'You hear wrong, Margot. I'm fine. That's why I called. I want you to know I'm fine and I've made up my mind.'

Margot's voice was questioning. 'What have you decided?'

'Margot, I'm being discharged from here.'

'Phil, that's terrific!'

'I'm going to a sort of halfway house, out of state.'

'Do you have to go?' She could not contain her disappointment.

'I don't have to, but I want to. That's the point. I really want to try this time.'

'Phil, you've said all this before. Every time you've called, you've said it. Then changed your mind. You seem to be always shifting your centre of emotional gravity.'

'You're beginning to sound like Dr Stanway,' he said lightly.

Her sudden anger surged down the phone.

'Do you know what you sound like every time you call? Like a damn shrink! When you're not telling me what Stanway's saying to you and what you feel, you tell me what he says you should be feeling. It's the only conversation we seem to have!'

He could hear her sobbing, saying she could not understand why he was like this, turning inwards, away from the world, away from her.

'There has to be a limit, Phil. There just has to be!'

He had told Dr Stanway that Margot had said that the priesthood was the last harbour for primitive and unreal thinking. The analyst had smiled bleakly and said that the trouble with women like Margot was that facts that did not fit into their scheme of things were pushed aside. So many good priests had found that out to their cost.

He could imagine her gripping the phone until her knuckles were white, tears rolling down her cheeks.

'I love you. Don't you understand? I love you! Can't you understand that?'

He steeled himself not to respond.

Margot was pleading once more. 'Why are you doing this? Why don't you come here? I'll come and pick you up. Let me drive over. You could be out of there in an hour.'

He had believed she would accept why he had to return to his ministry. Instead, she was gouging into his resolve.

'Margot... please!'

'My mother will help. She wants to. We can find a good analyst. You don't need one with an in-built bias towards the church!'

'Dr Stanway's not biased.'

There was sudden silence.

Dr Stanway had said he should see the crucifixion as an act of unconditional forgiving. If he could regard his affair with Margot as his own crucifixion, then he would realize that the church was only anxious to show him a similar forgiveness. All it wanted was to see him safely returned to his calling.

'If you really love me, Margot, let me go. Please.'

'Is this what you really want?' The tension and anger had gone. Her voice was resigned.

'Yes. Margot... look...'

'Hang up. Just leave me alone.'

He whispered into the mouthpiece. 'Take care, Margot.' It took him a moment to realize she had already replaced her receiver.

Three weeks later, Father Philippe intoned the words of the promise and fulfilment of the holy Eucharist. The church was small and cold in the first chill of another winter. A handful of people had come to Mass.

He had been sent here after being discharged from the church-run counselling centre. A priest-therapist, Father John, had spent most of their time together assessing his readiness to return to a full life in religion. They had explored every aspect of his ministry. Father John had spoken about the need to recognize that spiritual health only came through suffering, in seeing Jesus as the ever-availing victim.

Father Philippe reminded the congregation of the timeless purpose of their presence.

'He that eateth my flesh and drinketh my blood, Christ promised, abideth in me, and I in him. As the living Father hath sent me and I live by the Father: so he that eateth me, the same also shall live by me. This is the bread that came down from heaven. Not as your fathers did eat manna and are dead. He that eateth this bread shall live forever.'

One by one the congregation came forward to receive the host. He felt a single-minded devotion to his calling and that being a priest was one of the greatest gifts given to man. Standing at the sanctuary rail, he was Alter Christus. Another Christ, his every word and action performed in the full knowledge he was again God's direct instrument.

As he returned the sacred vessels to the tabernacle, he knew that once more he had been given the power to bridge heaven with earth. Through him each member of the congregation had, for the moment at least, understood again the meaning of adoration and the need to yearn for their eternal home. For them he was not only the glory, but the true power.

That, he had told Father Nolan on the telephone last night, was why he was ready to come back to St Mark's. He said he had finally worked out who he was and what he wanted. Father Nolan had said how glad, how very glad, he was to hear that, and he wanted him to know how much he and his parishioners were looking forward to having him back. Father Nolan had added that the past was over: it would never be mentioned again by him.

Two days later Father Philippe returned to his old apartment in St Mark's presbytery.

For the next month, Father Philippe drove himself relentlessly. He had forgotten how demanding a parish like St Mark's could be. In between his regular duties, there were hospital calls, house visits and school meetings. There had been four funerals, three weddings and two baptisms.

Father Nolan's welcome had been touching; he had put flowers in the apartment and stocked up the refrigerator. A number of people called at the rectory to welcome him back. Nobody mentioned his spell in hospital.

Fern jogged past every morning, and when she saw him standing at his study window, she waved. That first morning he raised his hand and continued talking to Harry Turner. The haberdasher had discovered his eldest son was on drugs. Father Philippe arranged for the youth to see Dr Stanway.

He had spoken to the psychiatrist on the phone a few days after he returned to the rectory and told him he was completely at peace with himself. Dr Stanway asked if he was still practising with the basketball. He confessed he had not found the time. What about the mantra? Again he had pleaded pressure of work had made him forget to say it as often as he would have liked. The psychiatrist had grunted and told him to hang in there.

Next day, Fern passed and waved again. This time she had beckoned him down. She had kissed him on the cheek and said how delighted she was to see him around. Keeping his tone casual, he had asked about Margot. Her mother said she was fine. Neither had explored the matter further, and, after a few more minutes of small-talk, Fern returned to her laps. Before doing so, she had addressed him formally, 'See you around, Father'.

CHAPTER TWENTY-SIX

The Empty Chalice

That day in October began like any other for Father Philippe. After concelebrating Mass, he and Father Nolan met over breakfast to discuss the day's schedule. Father Nolan said he would make five hospital calls and four visits to parishioners ill at home. Father Philippe would handle the other visits, including allowing an hour at the hospital bedside of Perry Turner. He would also drive out to see Andy Cummings and be back in time for duty in the confession room.

Father Nolan tapped his list. 'Why don't you also drop in on Ma Schiff?'

'How is she?'

Father Nolan gave a little smile. 'You go see.'

Driving through the ghetto, Father Philippe saw there was a greater despair about the people than he remembered when he had last come here. Unemployment was higher, and so was resentment. He and Father Nolan between them must try and find more ways to help these underprivileged people.

He was all the more pleasantly surprised when he did not immediately recognize Ma Schiff's house. The mass of creeper had gone. In its place the woodwork was a gleaming white, the front door a dark green.

The change in Ma Schiff herself was even more striking. She must, he guessed, be at least sixty pounds lighter and looked twenty years younger. Even her goitre seemed to have shrunk. She greeted him warmly and ushered him inside, seating him in a new armchair.

Father Nolan, she said shyly, had arranged it all. Harry Clampit had sent his men over to repaint and Pete Power let her have the furnishings and carpets on extended credit.

She led him into her daughter's old bedroom. Before the window was an artist's easel and palette.

'I do landscapes,' Ma Schiff said.

There was a vital quality about the canvases leaning against the wall.

'This is wonderful, Mrs Schiff. Really wonderful.'

'I owe it to my girl. I really owe her that much, Father Philippe.'

He shook his head. 'You owe yourself.'

Ma Schiff was powerful evidence that Christian living is not a matter of human achievement, but fundamentally a question of divine grace. Without it nothing can be achieved.

Three hours later, two more house visits done, he was at the bedside of Perry Turner in the Chronical Dependency Unit. The youth's swollen eyes and nose were dripping, his face sallow and sweating.

'If you want to cry, that's okay. Tears are good for all of us,' Father Philippe said, picking up a box of tissues from the bedside locker.

The youth wiped his nose.

His room in the Unit was only a few doors from the one Father Philippe had himself occupied.

'Did my Dad send you?'

'No. Nobody sent me. I came because I want to try and help you.'

'My Dad doesn't understand.' Perry trembled uncontrollably, still in the early stages of withdrawal.

'He does, Perry. He really does. He just wants you to get better.'

Another spasm racked Perry's body.

'May I sit down?'

The boy nodded between his shivering. Father Philippe sat on the chair. 'Do you want to talk about it?'

'I want to die. I feel I want to die,' Perry moaned.

'You feel like that now. But tomorrow you'll feel a little stronger. And a little more the day after that. It'll get a little easier each day.'

Another spasm shook the boy's body. 'I'm scared, Father. I'm scared.'

Father Philippe sat on the edge of the bed. 'Would you like me to hold you?'

Perry nodded, tears streaming down his face. Father Philippe cradled him in his arms, letting Perry bury his head against his shirt.

'I can't take any more. I can't. It's killing me. I need a fix. Christ, I need a fix. It's killing me,' came the repeated moaning.

Father Philippe held Perry tight, feeling his trembling. 'Don't be afraid.'

'I want to die.'

Father Philippe kept his voice and tone certain. 'God wants you to live, Perry.'

For a while they remained locked in silent embrace. Gradually, Father Philippe felt Perry growing calmer.

'I want you to listen to me very carefully, Perry. Will you do that?'

After a lengthy pause came a muffled 'Yes.'

'There is no magic. No pill. Nothing. Only you can get through this. Cold turkey is hell. It's the pits. But it's better than dying. You must believe that. You have to. I'm going to close my eyes now and I want you to do the same. And then we're both going to pray. Will you do that with me?'

'Yes,' came the whisper.

'Let's say the Our Father together. It's the best prayer I know.'

They recited it slowly.

Father Philippe gently disengaged himself and looked at Perry. He took a clean tissue and wiped the youth's face.

'Now, I want to teach you something. A very wise man wrote these words. I want you to listen very carefully. I want you to not only hear what I'm going to say, but feel the words.'

Father Philippe began to recite the mantra he had been given by Dr Stanway.

An hour later, heading south to his next appointment, Father Philippe wondered whether Perry had the willpower to break the hold drugs had over him.

He left the parkway and joined the interstate. Dan had landed a job somewhere out here, tending the lawns at one of the office complexes carefully sculpted into the contours of the land. Dan had been a patient at the Unit the same time as he had. In their conversations, Dan had shown he knew how to kick the habit. If he was willing, Dan could act as Perry's mentor.

He'd call Dr Stanway and suggest it. It really could work, Father Philippe thought, as he turned on to the country road where Andy Cummings lived.

Andy was a widower who had taught carpentry at Holy Family, one of the diocesan schools. When he retired two years ago, he had opened a shop selling reconditioned farm furniture and had built up a good business.

Six months ago he'd gone into the General for tests. A malignant tumour was discovered in his abdomen. He had undergone surgery and follow-up chemotherapy and radiation treatment. All failed to control the cancer. Four weeks ago Andy had insisted on coming home to die. Every day either Father Nolan or Father Philippe came out to see him.

As usual, Andy was waiting on a rocker on the porch, his bald head seeming too large for his scrawny neck.

'How are you doing, Andy?'

'Fine, just fine, Father. The new shots help a lot.'

A nurse called every day to administer increased doses of pain killer.

'I ordered the book you wanted. The school's sending it over,' Father Philippe said, sitting on the chair opposite.

Andy had asked for a Holy Family yearbook to complete his set covering the twenty-five years he had taught there.

'Thanks, Father. 1970,' he gave a fragile cough. 'was the year public schools began to desegregate. I had a couple of my old students wounded when they joined a march on the governor's mansion. May 21st, it was.'

Father Philippe had noticed the closer a person was to death, the clearer their recall of the past.

'That was a bad time for us all, Andy.'

The old man nodded.

'Worse now. We didn't have a drug problem then. Now kids in sixth grade are hooked. Look at the Turner boy.'

They had spoken about the case. Andy had taught Perry the rudiments of carpentry.

'His Dad dropped by this morning. I guess Harry was trying to find out how the boy got started,' said Andy, staring out across the land to where a tractor left a wake of dust on the skyline.

Father Philippe described his visit to Perry.

'He's a good boy, Father.'

'I know.'

They both watched the tractor turn and begin ploughing another furrow.

'I told Harry I'd like to talk to his boy.'

'What would you say to Perry, Andy?' Father Philippe asked.

Andy gave another weak cough. 'What would I tell him? That he's got a whole life of living to do. That God didn't intend him to mess it up like this. And if he wants to talk about dying, I'll tell him what it's like to wait to die. I'll tell him it's not easy.'

'I know, Andy.'

The old man nodded. 'I was scared like a jack-rabbit until you and Father Nolan talked to me. But you're right. A man has to learn to die.'

Between them they had encouraged Andy to accept he must not blight his life with doubts as it drew to a close.

'Like I've said, Andy, for each of us the end is not dying. It's the beginning.'

The old man's voice was soft. 'Let me see the boy. I want him to win out, too.'

Father Philippe nodded. 'I'll drop by the hospital on the way back and fix it. In the meantime, I'd like to pray with you.'

For a while they remained with heads bowed and eyes closed.

Driving back into the city he thought Andy's courage was proof the gifts of the Spirit were only available to those certain in their faith. The apostle John had been right: Christ had overcome the world. So, in his own way, had Andy.

Turning on to State Way, he had no inkling that in the time it would take him to drive one and two-thirds of a mile along the highway to the shopping mall, his own life was once more about to change.

He parked his car outside the Home Bakery, realizing he was hungry.

As he walked towards the coffee shop, a voice rooted him to the spot.

''Lo, Phil.' Margot had come out of a boutique. She wore the green trouser suit she had bought on their last day in the Bahamas.

His initial response was a silent entreaty: *Jesus, don't desert me now. Jesus, not now.*

Margot was smiling at him. He stared at her expression of almost child-like delight. The look, he remembered, was part of her; she wore it the way other women wore make-up. He had forgotten how feminine, soft and desirable it could make her.

'How are you, Margot?'

'I'm fine. Mother said you were back. You look terrific.'

He managed to keep his voice calm. 'Thanks. So do you.'

She moved towards him, and he could smell the perfume on her body. She touched him on the arm, then quickly withdrew her hand.

He continued to be intensely aware of his every response, his mind racing.

Touching has always been important to me. I've always felt one of the great mistakes of the priesthood has been an unhealthy emphasis on the dangers of tactility. Christ was highly tactile. There is plenty of Gospel evidence to show he gave and received pleasure through touching.

'Phil, it's great to see you.'

'Same here.'

He wanted her to say more. He noticed her clasped hands gripping themselves a little harder. His own were behind his back, clenched. After they had made love, there would be silence between them, and the absence of words would contain its own special sort of contact. She had said that words, at such times, held no meaning for her, they were a barrier to her own deeply-felt emotions. Silence, she had added, was especially uplifting, a very special kind of intimacy.

She continued staring at him in silence.

She had, he thought, still the most beautiful eyes he had ever seen. He smiled at her.

I know I'm rushing for the ball. But I can't help it. I'm human. That's always been my trouble. I'm flesh and blood inside this priest's suit. To deny that would be to deny my own self-realization. Everyone wants to be loved. And loving is no longer being frightened, but understanding. O Lord, if I say I fear I am not worthy of your trust, it really means I am able to give or receive love. I still love her.

'Where are you going?' Her voice had a cadence he had always found exotic.

'To eat.'

Chastity is part of the virtue of temperance, the state which controls the pleasures of touch: eating, drinking and sexual satisfaction. But for a virtue to have any meaning, it must not be repressive. A virtue is meant to humanize living in Christ. Control over my passions is less possible when I'm condemned to pretend they don't exist. I don't think any virtue can work if it's repressive.

She smiled. 'Why don't you follow me and I'll cook you a steak?' Her eyes, framed by those incredibly long lashes, looked at him. 'Medium rare and a salad. With some wine. How does that sound?'

It was a statement rather than a question. He had forgotten until this moment that she had this knack of by-passing non-essentials.

Only pleasure based on evil intent is evil. I don't have a bad thought in my head. I'm human. It's the church that isn't. Instead of forcing me to suppress my feelings, it should help me Christianize my sexuality.

He touched her arm, saying to himself he was expressing a basic human need; that affectionate and tactile stimulation was essential for him to function as a healthy, emotionally integrated priest. It was more than merely physical. Through this one touch he wanted her to know he felt other and altogether more powerful emotions.

'Sounds terrific,' Father Philippe said.

As he drove down the highway, he went over all the things she could have said: Why had he not written from the halfway house, or called since he'd been back? He remembered it was not her style. She'd always said recriminations were negative.

It had been so long, ten months now, and yet here he was once more, driving to her apartment, thinking whoever said people can change had it all wrong. Margot hadn't altered. Her extraordinary ability to combine a vulnerable modesty with an open hunger, was still there.

He glanced in his driving mirror. The scared little-boy look had gone.

He knew he had never really stopped believing sexual fulfilment and chastity were incompatible, just as he also knew the church would continue to reject that reality. Margot had been right. *A priest was a man.* His sexuality was a gift from God, a sign of his love for him as a man, and as a priest. He was certain now there was not one kind of sexuality for celibates, another for everybody else. A priest is a man. He was his own person, driving behind the woman he had never stopped loving. That was his reality. That was *his* honesty.

Parking behind Margot's car, he knew he would no longer be ambivalent and hestiant, but eager and certain to show himself he could manage. And he was equally certain he would accept responsibility for his actions. That too, he saw, as a sign of his new-found self-realization. He had never felt more comfortable.

Watching Margot open the door of her apartment, he was full of love and grace. He reached forward and held Margot by the shoulders, turning her to face him.

'You're looking very, very beautiful – more beautiful than I've ever seen you,' he said.

She laughed.

He kicked the door behind them, his arms around her waist.

'Are you thinking what I'm thinking?' she whispered.

'You better believe it.'

She drew him to her, a sense of excitement more wonderful than he could remember experiencing, sweeping over him.

Margot led him into the bedroom. He stared at the kingsize bed.

'I didn't change a thing since you left. I guess I just knew you'd come back.' She kissed him lovingly on the mouth.

'I never went away. Not really.' He reached to undo the zipper on her suit. 'Show me. I want to see you.'

She stepped out of the suit. She was naked except for her panties.

He touched her gently as she undressed him, slowly, the way he had always liked, first removing his priest's collar, then unbuttoning his black clerical shirt, pressing her lips against his chest, keening softly with pleasure. She unbuckled his belt and his priest's trousers fell to the carpet. He stepped out of them, kicking off his shoes. She bent down and removed his socks, and finally, his shorts. He felt he was on fire as she guided him to the bed. He pressed his face against her neck, moaning under her touch.

'Wait. Don't be in such a hurry.'

'I've missed you, Margot. I've missed you so much.'

Her voice matched his whisper. 'I've missed you too. I want this to be beautiful. I want to make you happy again.' Her hands were everywhere, touching and exploring him.

He was kissing her eyes, her lips, her neck, her nipples, her stomach.

She softly commanded him to wait, laying him on his back, touching his lips with the tip of her tongue. He writhed and groaned. Suddenly she gasped, rolling on her back, ready for him.

An hour later, Father Philippe lay naked on the bed, listening to the sounds from the kitchen, talking to Harry Turner on Margot's bedside phone, explaining why he wanted Andy and Dan to see Perry.

He still felt he had a vocation, and was full of God's grace. Making love to Margot had been a beautiful experience that had not made him less of a priest. What had happened was striking proof he could not live a worthwhile life in Christ without taking into account his sexuality.

Margot was holding two goblets of chilled wine. She handed him one, listening as he told Harry why a dying old man and a reformed junkie might be able to help his son. Harry finally agreed.

He put down the phone and, after they finished the wine, they made love again.

Margot returned to the kitchen to cook their steaks. Lying on the bed, listening to her singing, he reminded himself that the underlying message of the Song of Songs was that physical love-making was the affirmation of a healthy relationship between two persons who genuinely love each other. He was determined his relationship with Margot would have a similar fidelity.

They ate in bed. He talked to Margot about his time in the Unit and at the halfway house. It felt natural and good to speak so freely. He told her he felt closer to her in mind as well as body than he had ever done before. Finally, he turned and looked at her seriously. 'It's going to be okay this time, Margot. It really is.'

Her hand moved possessively over his face. 'You better believe it. This time you better had.'

For thirty-two days, Father Philippe lived a dual life. The priestly side of him was more devoted than ever to his ministry. The man in him was never more evident than when he was with Margot.

He located Dan and brought him to see Perry. He sat at the bedside while Dan described what it was like to come up from addiction. He had driven over to Andy and brought him in to see the boy, and again listened while the teacher quietly explained why Perry must fight for his own survival.

Every day Father Philippe offered the sacrifice of the Mass, distributed Communion and delivered penances in the confession room. Once, he had administered extreme unction. Each night he luxuriated in the smell of Margot's body and the joys of her bed.

He resolved the paradox by telling himself there was nothing to resolve. There was no theological rule that any longer made sense to him about grace. The 'state of grace' the church spoke of was a poor substitute for the greater grace God offered. It was as simple as that.

He resumed jogging with Fern. She had looked at him appraisingly, but said nothing. The unspoken message was clear: he, and he alone, must walk his own tightrope.

He had slept deeply, not disturbed by the need to scratch or the return of his nightmare. He found this further reassuring proof God understood him. What had once seemed an impossibility – living without guilt because of his love for Margot – had become a joyous certainty. He could have a full loving relationship with her and, at the same time, live a full life in Christ. Man-made rules did not trouble him any more. God had made it clear there was space for both his ministry and Margot in his life. Loving her had released a vast and unsuspected dam of love within himself. He was so filled with love that it touched everything he saw and did. Discovering this, he had learned how much more he could still give to others.

One night, driving back from her apartment, he dropped by to see Perry. The boy was making slow but definite progress. He had been off drugs for six weeks and was no longer crying for a fix. Rung by rung, he was also climbing his own ladder to self-realization.

Together they said the mantra. Then Father Philippe told the boy the story of what Christ said to Nicodemus about hearing the wind, but not knowing from where it came, or where it was bound. He told Perry that God was like that. 'We just don't know on whom he will next bestow this light from heaven.'

At a little after 6.30 on his thirty-third morning, the telephone rang at his bedside in the rectory. He picked up the receiver. It was Margot.

'Can you come over? I need to talk to you.'

'Are you okay?'

'Come over. Please.'

She hung up before he could answer. He did not know why, but he felt suddenly apprehensive.

Forty minutes later, he faced her across the breakfast table. She told him her period was two weeks overdue.

He felt as though 'the kitchen door to the great world beyond had been wrenched open by a gust of icy wind, blowing into my mind the realization that my old guilt was back'.

From outside came the sound of morning traffic; people going to work, life going on. He asked her if she was absolutely certain she was pregnant.

Margot nodded.

For a moment he closed his eyes. As quickly as it had come, the chill wind had gone. The moment of guilt passed.

Her voice was so soft it was a mere thought. She asked him what they were going to do? He opened his eyes, a feeling of goodness coming over him. He walked to her chair. She pressed against him. He continued to cradle her head against his waist and endlessly smooth her hair, singing her favourite song: 'Love is Everywhere'.

She hugged him to her. When he had finished singing, he bent down and murmured: 'If ever two were one, then we are.'

They remained silent for a long moment.

When he began to speak, his voice was low and compelling. The most important thing was they loved each other. Everything else would stem from that. Loving each other must be their base line for all decision-making. But there was time to reflect on what was best for both of them. He had, he realized, placed the gentlest of emphasis on 'both'. He wanted her to understand this would not be her decision alone, but they would make it together. The first step, he concluded, would be to get a pregnancy test kit. He would go to the drugstore.

Margot looked up at him wonderingly. 'But, Phil. You're a priest. You just can't walk in and buy a test kit. The whole town will know.'

He smiled down at her. 'I'll disguise myself.'

She suddenly started to laugh.

He knew he had successfully negotiated a dangerous moment, showing her he was prepared to act decisively. For the moment, all she needed was reassurance; later, they could discuss the reality.

Driving back to the rectory, Father Philippe reviewed the options. He swiftly rejected an abortion. Both of them had always felt it was morally reprehensible. The baby could be adopted. But that, too, would be emotionally unsettling for them both. They would always know that, somewhere, their child was alive but abandoned to its own fate. And, for Margot, there would be the additional trauma of having to endure the pointing fingers in the community. She was not a teenager, but a mature woman close to thirty: the speculation of who the father was would be that much more intense. It was true that, with Fern's money, she could go away and wait out her confinement, but that would also be stressful. Margot would feel abandoned, having to move away to wait for a baby she would then have to give away. Besides, leaving the area would not end the gossip. People would guess, they almost always did. Yet, he could hardly admit fatherhoood and expect to remain in active ministry. While he still believed he was in God's grace, he was quite certain the church would show no mercy.

Arriving at the rectory, he considered another option. Margot could face the gossip, keep the child and raise it as a single parent. Its paternity would be their secret. He would see their child growing. He would continue to visit Margot and though, outwardly, he would seem no more than a caring priest, they would both know why he was there. Their child. He could be both a priest to his flock and a father to his child.

The more he thought about it, the more possible it seemed: he would give their child all the things he had himself been denied: parental love, security, understanding, support, encouragement. He was suddenly very excited. He still could have the best of both his worlds.

Buoyed by that possibility, Father Philippe started to disguise himself for the visit to the drugstore. He put on a sweat shirt and Levis and sandals. From a dresser drawer, he removed a box which contained greasepaint and cotton wool. A while ago an actor had given him the make-up kit as a memento of a backstage visit. Wadding cotton wool into balls, he inserted them inside his mouth, appreciably changing the shape of his face. He darkened his skin with the greasepaint. From a closet he took a battered fedora. The hat had belonged to his father; the only time he had worn it was at his funeral. He completed the transformation by putting on a pair of silver-tinted sun-glasses.

Driving across town, a new thought occurred to him. Margot could refuse to raise their child alone. What then? He drove for half an hour before he accepted if this was her reaction, he would marry her. But the thought drove all others from his mind except one. What about his ministry?

When he purchased the kit, the clerk's voice was low and conspiratorial. 'She'll need an early morning specimen. Then she must wait an hour. If the test is negative, the specimen will be cloudy. If it's positive, it will show clear. You remember to tell her. Fuzzy – and she's fine. Clear – and she starts knitting.'

Father Philippe repeated the instructions.

A little after 6.15 the following morning, Father Philippe's bedside telephone rang. Until the early hours, he had sat with Margot discussing their options. One minute she had wanted to have the baby adopted, the next to raise it herself. For a while she had spoken about moving to another part of the country and starting a new life. Then she had said she would remain and brave the gossip. Each time he thought she had come to a final decision, Margot reversed it. But not once had she even hinted they should marry. Neither had he raised the idea. Finally, he had said they could not really decide anything until she knew absolutely if she was pregnant.

Back in the apartment, he had fallen asleep, remembering he had told Perry that grace came in all sorts of mysterious and unpredictable guises.

For a moment longer he let the telephone ring, already seeing her face, their bed, where they had started a new life. He picked up the receiver. Margot said the result was positive.

From the apartment across the hall, he could hear the strong and unmistakable baritone of Father Nolan starting his day. Every morning when he arose, he sang the old evangelical hymn, 'Amazing Grace'.

> Amazing grace! How sweet the sound
> That saved a wretch like me!
> I once was lost, but now am found,
> was blind, but now I see.

Father Philippe felt a surge of confidence. 'Margot, listen. It's going to be okay. We'll work it out. Together.'

'Oh, Phil! I'm so glad.'

The voice from across the hall had grown louder.

> 'Twas grace that taught my heart to fear,
> And grace my fears relieved;
> How precious did that grace appear
> The hour I first believed!

Father Philippe spoke into the telephone. 'Margot. We're going to keep the baby. I want that.'

She started to weep.

'Margot. I want to sing to you.'

'What?'

His voice united with that of Father Nolan's.

> Through many dangers, toils and snares,
> I have already come;
> 'Tis grace hath brought me safe thus far,
> And grace will lead me home.

He asked her to join in the last verse. Together, over the telephone, they sang.

> And when we've been there ten thousand years,
> Bright, shining as the sun,
> We'll have no less days to sing God's praise
> Than when we first begun.

There was silence from across the hall and over the telephone. Then Father Philippe told Margot he loved her and would see her shortly.

Chalice case in one hand, Father Philippe knocked on the door of Father Nolan's apartment. From within came the slow, shuffling footsteps. The door slowly opened. Father Nolan stood there in his bathrobe and slippers. For a long moment, he stared at Father Philippe, his eyes going from the chalice case to his face and back again.

'I need to speak to you, Ray.'

Father Nolan opened the door wider, his eyes still firmly fixed on the chalice case, and led the way into his sparsely furnished living room. Father Philippe placed the case on a side table.

Father Nolan went to the kitchen and returned with a coffee pot and two cups. He busied himself pouring, saying nothing. He handed Father Philippe a cup. The only sound was the ticking of a wall clock.

'What's going on, Philippe?'

'I'm leaving.'

Father Nolan stared.

'I'm leaving to get married.' He explained why, and what had happened.

When he had finished, Father Nolan sat slumped in his chair, a finger moving back and forth over his lower lip.

'Have you thought this through? You're a fine priest. The church needs men like you to do God's work.'

'The church is run by men, Ray. A man in Rome decides what is fallible or infallible. I can't live my life any longer like that. I can't have other men split me down the middle about such an important matter as being a man. I can't go on living with myself, pretending.'

Father Nolan shifted in his chair. 'They'll never release you. There's hardly been a dispensation since this Pope came to office. You won't get one. As long as he's there, you'll still be a priest. Don't you see that?'

'Ray, listen to me. I know you mean well. You always have. And I'm grateful for that. I really am. But don't you understand? I want to live with my own passion for the first time, not the handed-down passions of the church. I can't go on living under the sort of regulations that are destructive to me as a man. Having to pretend my collar acts as a totem that keeps me from having normal healthy responses.'

Father Nolan looked away. 'But you made a vow.'

Father Philippe interrupted. 'Don't lay that one on me, Ray. When I took that vow, I didn't know what it really meant. You probably didn't. I doubt if a goddamn priest in the whole church knows. We get sucked along with the idea we are better than the angels. Then, one morning, we wake up and find we're human, with human responses. That we can actually love in a human way. Care in a human way. Feel in a human way. That we're not just hiding behind our collar.'

'Watch it, Philippe. Calm down.'

Father Philippe shook his head. 'Oh, sweet Jesus, Ray. I'm sorry. But don't you understand that what we are asked to do has nothing to do with God. It's all to do with men. God didn't say I could only be a good priest if I'm celibate. Men did. God didn't invent the blessed Mother. Men did. God didn't say we have to live outside our bodies to do his work. Men did. Don't you see, Ray? It is men who took away our passions. It is men who make us cheat on ourselves. It is men who created this whole myth of celibacy. Don't you see that?'

Father Nolan stared at him. Finally, he spoke. 'It's what makes our priesthood different from all the others. We are priests forever.'

For a moment Father Philippe stood still, then he walked over to his chalice case and handed it to Father Nolan.

'I don't need this anymore to be in God's grace.'

He turned and walked towards the door.

CHAPTER TWENTY-SEVEN

Certainties

After the taxi brought Clare home from the convent, her mother led her upstairs and opened the door to her old bedroom.

'I've put everything back as it was on the day you went in,' her mother said.

The books Clare had read as a teenager, her collection of records, the single bed with the crucifix above it, her wicker chair: the past all surged back as she remembered how she had left here, filled with a certainty she would never return. She smiled brightly at her mother and said how wonderful it was to see everything just as she remembered it. The other feeling was hers to share with no one – that she had failed to live up to God's expectations.

A few days later she went to her first party. Being asked to dance, having a man hold her close, one hand on her bottom, the other draped around her shoulder, his face buried in her neck, made her stiffen in panic. She abruptly pleaded a headache and went outside so no one would see her shaking. Her cousin, Barbara, found her and, being both quick and understanding, smiled sympathetically and said Clare needed a drink. Several whiskys later she allowed Barbara's husband, Sean, to dance with her. He grinned disarmingly and said some men could be very cloddish. She found herself smiling gratefully, and the fear of not knowing how to respond to that other man lifted.

A week after leaving, she telephoned the convent to enquire when she could start to teach. The Superior said it could be several weeks and she should use the time to readjust. Reverend Mother's voice had been barely audible, as if she was speaking from another world. 'I expect you're finding it very strange out there?'

Clare had said she was indeed finding it difficult. Before she hung up, the Superior sighed and said she hoped matters would improve.

The more well-meaning people were, the harder it was for Clare to shake off her feelings of guilt and doubts she had made the right decision. Rationally, she knew there were no grounds to feel like this. There had been no rush to judgement, she kept telling herself as she tried to integrate into the new life her family and their friends were planning for her.

There were the times she felt the pull of her old life most of all. The Rule, for all its strictness, had developed her sense of purpose, her prayer life, her ability to do without so many of the things people in the outside world found important. She didn't really mind what she ate or drank and wasn't anxious to buy some new item of clothing every week, or be invited out on dates. Instead, she still liked to spend a portion of her day alone and enjoyed going early to bed, awakening in the dark at the convent hour, waiting for her family to rise.

Those times her inner debate was most determined to shake her resolve. Had she, after all, done the right thing? In the first light of a new day the image of Reverend Mother dispensing her with immeasurable sadness from her sacred vows would often float into her consciousness.

In the weeks that followed – in between registering with a doctor, the tax office and placing herself on numerous bureaucratic lists – Clare faced other realities. Living a spiritual life in a world where all forms of religious values were under attack was the greatest of challenges. While her own home remained a bastion of faith, beyond it was a more profound upheaval than she had ever imagined.

Nearly all the women she knew, single or married, were practising some form of contraception. More Catholic girls than ever before, among them a high percentage of school girls, were going to England for abortions. Marriage itself was under attack. In the circle she was introduced to – middle- class, hard-working Dubliners – there were many unmarried couples living together; often one partner had deserted a husband or wife to set up home with someone else. Sex at every level was a casual matter.

Until now she had never had unrestricted access to television, radio or films; in the convent viewing was strictly controlled. But, at home, able to watch and listen when she liked; she was stunned at the promotion of sex: its crudeness, its explications, the frankness of its language. Everywhere she turned, the emphasis seemed to be on nakedness and sensual pleasures. The moral doctrine, which had sustained her for years, daily crumbled a little more before her eyes.

Years of chastity had instilled in her to always remember what the Rule said about the dangers of touching. Now she was casually kissed by her parents and sisters, and called 'darling' by one of her brother-in-laws. For so long she had been called 'sister', and that had never been a form of endearment. In her new world, everyone seemed to caress, hug, hold, cuddle, stroke, embrace and fondle. No one seemed able to survive without such stimulation. It was, she realized with a dawning sense of wonder, a natural way of showing love.

Initially she found it stifling to live in the confined space of her parent's home after the vastness of the Mother House. It needed a conscious effort to adjust to the sheer *closeness* of everybody, to realize a feeling of being crowded in was natural.

After a while she came to accept not having to wait until being spoken to, and that it was natural for people to cheerfully interrupt each other and talk whenever they felt like it. It had taken time to adapt to mealtimes being relaxed occasions with the television on and, more often than not, one of her sisters playing a tape of hard rock music in the kitchen. Clare had forgotten what a noisy place the world was.

Clare had been home for a month before the Deputy wrote with details of where she would teach. The school was an hour's journey away from home, the children no different to those she had taught before. At the end of her first term, she told her mother, 'You know, I can really hack this life.'

Seeing the surprised look on her mother's face, Clare smiled. 'One of the boys told me to *hack* it is *cool*. You know, cool as in *cool, man, cool*.'

She taught for six months before she moved out of her parent's house into her own apartment. She arranged a mortgage, opened a bank account and learned how to handle a weekly budget.

Most evenings, on the way back from school, she would drop in to see her father, confined to his day-bed downstairs. One evening, when she was there, his solicitor arrived and they spent an hour together alone. Afterwards her father breathed a small sigh and said how glad he was to have settled his will.

Through him, more than with any other member of the family, she continued to explore her spiritual needs. They amounted to this: truth, she told him was neither less true because it was old, or more true because it had been recently discovered. God for her was still now. Eternity his instant.

One evening he looked at her for a long moment and said that, while he so admired her values, she must stop this constant inner searching. She had done her share of that. God wanted her to do something else: relax. He motioned her to sit on the chair beside his bed.

Holding her hand the way he had when she was a child, he spoke gently. 'I can still sense the guilt in you that you've let your mother and myself down. You've no need to feel like that and the Order is getting what it wants. You spend almost three hours a day travelling to and from school. You work the sort of day most people would call exploitation. You've nothing to feel guilty about. God wanted you back in the world, Clare. He really did.'

She held him close, lying her face against his, feeling his hand softly stroking her hair.

A month after Clare moved into her apartment, Tom telephoned and asked if they could meet. After she overcame her surprise at his call, she hesitated. His part in her life had ended before it even had a chance to begin. The past, the might-have-been had gone up in flames when she burned his letter.

Tom had quietly pressed, and his tone, though still soft, held an assurance she had no need to worry. She had finally agreed.

Coming into the coffee shop, she recognized him at once. He embraced her quickly and, over tea, told her he was in a parish in the suburbs: a curate to an old priest; a petty tyrant whose meanness was only equalled by that of his housekeeper.

She had spent the afternoon laughing at his stories of life in the parochial house. Towards the end, Tom asked why she had left. She told him. He looked reflective. 'Chastity, maybe. But not obedience,' he finally said, saying no more.

After she insisted on settling the bill, he said he was free next weekend. Maybe they could go and see a film? She smiled – why not? What harm could there be?

So it began. Whenever Tom had a free weekend they met, going to a movie or a play, an art exhibition or a concert. Afterwards they would have supper together. Every weekend, Tom would drop by to see her father, spending an hour at his bedside.

Sometimes Tom brought troubling news to discuss. The number of vocations had now reached a record low, not only in the diocese but throughout the country. Clonliffe and Maynooth, the other great Irish seminary, were virtually deserted; convents often only had a handful of ageing nuns. Tom predicted that if present trends continued, Ireland, one of the great bastions of Catholicism, would be a vocational desert by the end of the century.

Her father had shaken his head and insisted that while there were priests like Tom, the church was still in safe hands.

Clare had known after their first meeting that she still loved Tom. Sometimes she had been tempted to tell him, but she knew instinctively that would be wrong. Other times she knew she would be able to live without him if their friendship ended. Only after a few months of being with him had she admitted to herself that to love a priest was like loving no other man.

She had been tempted to tell her father of her feelings for Tom. They had been speaking about how difficult it was to maintain a genuine friendship. Her father had gently held her face between his hands and whispered, his voice husky from his pain-killers, that like him she had very powerful emotions. Then, his words barely reaching her, he said that Tom was also filled with feelings. Her father had looked at her for a long moment, his gaze steady and searching.

'For a woman, a friendship with a priest is very special – and unusual, when the women is as young and pretty as she is.'

That was the moment she wanted to say what was in her heart. Instead, she told her father he need not worry because her faith would always guide her conscience.

Smiling, his voice rallying, he said he never, for a moment, meant to imply he thought otherwise.

Her father died while she was on the bus coming home from school. Her mother met her at the door and broke the news. Clare went to her father's bedside and knelt in prayer, half-listening to her mother explaining he had been wondering what little bit of news Tom would next bring when he had suddenly closed his eyes and was gone.

One of the first photographs she took with the new camera she bought from her wages was of her father's grave.

The following Saturday, she snapped Tom on the steps of the art museum. He had been reluctant to pose and, over dinner, she finally raised the question of their relationship, insisting he must never think she would expect more than he could give. He gave her a quick smile and changed the conversation.

In the weekends that followed, Tom increasingly spoke about his growing certainty he could face his own inner needs, that he positively enjoyed being able to turn away from the world from time to time, either through short periods of solitary prayer, or retreats. When she said, that while that was quite wonderful, she also wondered whether at times he felt lonely, Tom had shaken his head almost angrily and said he would never feel that.

In making her own adjustments, she had recognized a celibate tried to brush aside any negative feelings. It had taken her months to recognize that any form of healthy intimacy – her now easygoing relationships with her family and her fellow teachers – could also sometimes produce hostility. There were still times when she both loved and hated people simultaneously. There was nothing wrong in allowing those emotions to co-exist. It was a sign of maturity.

She wanted to say to Tom that, for any relationship to have more than a superficial meaning, there must always be present an element of risk. The more deeply felt the love given and received, the more important it was to understand the anger it could sometimes provoke. But Clare said none of these things.

She began to notice certain traits about Tom. When she held his arm, she could feel his body become rigid and see his eyes cloud over, almost as if he was hurting, as if her femininity was alien, as if it was wrong for her to want to be so close to him.

One time she tried to argue that tactility was healthy, and need not always be in a sexual context. She said it would equally demonstrate affection, caring support and selfless loving. Celibacy should not preclude touching. He had flushed and asked her, please, to take her arm away. From then on she stopped touching him, feeling a sense of defeat that she had been unable to make him see that touching was a positive sign of his sexuality.

After they had been seeing other for about nine months, Tom began to develop blinding headaches and crippling pains in his back. Then he started to break dates, phoning usually on a Friday evening when she was beginning to anticipate what they might do over the weekend, saying he felt too unwell, or that a sudden parish commitment had come up.

She noticed in particular then that he had a priest's way of talking, making *commitment* sound as if it was something very special, a pact he shared with God, something he had been asked to discharge on earth for him. Finally came that dreadful discovery that to save himself, Tom had lied to her. On that particular weekend he had not been ill as he said, but had gone away with another priest.

Two weeks later he drove her out into the countryside and said they could no longer go on meeting. Through the pounding in her head, she had thought afterwards: *Once a priest, always a priest.*

She never heard from Tom after that Saturday when her loneliness and aloneness became one. Much later, with a new archbishop in the diocese, she heard Tom had been given his own parish. She still loved him. She expected she would go on loving him for the rest of her days.

CHAPTER TWENTY-EIGHT

Decisions

Through his developing connections to the Vatican, Andrew had secured good seats for himself and Nancy, the petite, dark-haired girl at his side. They were close to the stage where Pope John Paul II would shortly address the vast gathering in St Peter's at his regular Wednesday audience.

Nancy was openly impressed with Andrew's influence. In his soutane and gleaming Roman collar he was a commanding figure, leading her confidently past the armed City of Rome policemen at the outer perimeter or St Peter's Gate. She was even more admiring of the smart salutes the papal Swiss Guards gave him at their checkpoint and the deferential bow from the Vatican court usher as he led them to their seats.

Nancy stared around, fascinated at the spectacle. There were already a dozen cardinals on the platform and perhaps another fifty church dignitaries; middle-aged men in red, purple, gold and greens: the colours of Roman clerical power.

Andrew knew why she wanted to come. To be so close to the very centre of the power of the church, the Pope, was to be in the presence of what Nancy saw as the inexplicable mystery of the church. In many ways Nancy saw Catholicism as a kind of magic, controlled by those who knew the right incantations. She would never understand, however much he explained, that the gifts of the Spirit were available to all those who accepted unconditionally. Yet, for all her education and position with a United Nations relief organization based in Rome, when it came to religion Nancy had very definite perceptions.

Yet, in her own special way, he freely conceded, she had enlivened his life. It would be hard for anyone, he knew, to recognize that this pretty girl, so demure in her modest long-sleeved dress, was the same one who sat opposite him in the ristorante where once Jane had said she was considering marrying Giles. On those occasions Nancy would wear a halter top and skirt, her eyes would be fixed on him continuously as she described her latest sexual escapade. Nowadays he would listen to her vivid descriptions with the same detachment he hoped, in years to come, he would display when hearing confessions.

He had convinced himself that listening to Nancy had enhanced his psychosexual development. Nancy was the woman friend he had always wanted, one who had helped him better understand all kinds of emotions while remaining true to his vow of celibacy.

He knew many of his fellow seminarians practised a conscious denial of their sexuality. They simply refused to concede they were angry because there was no optional celibacy. Instead, they pretended it did not matter, not realizing the damage that did to their personal growth. For his part, he had become a champion for optional celibacy. At every opportunity, he continued to raise it within the seminary and at the Greg. The more intense the opposition, the more relaxed and fulfilled he had felt. There was nothing better, he had told Nancy, to release tension than the swift and deadly cut and thrust of clerical debate.

There was a sudden distant cheer from the far side of the square. The roar grew. He helped Nancy to stand on her chair so that she had a better view. The *campagnola*, the white-painted pope-mobile, was slowly driving around the edge of the plaza, the Pope turning from side to side, waving and smiling.

The cheering reached a continuous roar as the *campagnola* stopped before the podium. Flanked by his aides, the Pope slowly climbed the steps to his massive throne. He turned to raise his hands. Silence instantly fell over the square.

Nancy whispered to Andrew, 'He doesn't need anything else with that power. It must be the biggest turn-on ever.'

Andrew grinned. 'That's why I'd like to be Pope.'

Then the voice of Pope John Paul II, amplified by scores of loudspeakers, boomed across the square.

'Our beloved predecessor, Pope Paul the Sixth, said that priestly celibacy has been guaranteed by the church for centuries as a brilliant jewel, and retains its value undiminished.'

It was Victoria's turn to cook breakfast. She fried the eggs over-easy, the way Jim liked them. She could hear him singing in the shower. Checking the coffee was percolating, she went to the bathroom, calling to him he had better hurry as she would have to leave in fifteen minutes.

Her first patient was Sister Ann whom she was hoping to finally convince that her lesbian feelings did not diminish her religious commitment and she must believe her deep spirituality still remained the core of her life.

Victoria went to the bedroom. Jim had made the double-bed. After he started to sleep over, she found he was very domesticated. He had finally accepted his ability to love, totally and without preconditions, as she loved him. The physical release they both enjoyed was only a very small part of their loving relationship. However, they both also agreed that, if penetration did occur, they would afterwards both feel unhappy. Instead, they continued to handle their sexual feelings in a way which left them both satisfied.

Because there was a self-imposed limitation on their sexual gratification, she was certain they had achieved a higher form of love than most married couples. By avoiding full physical intercourse – often with its attendant strains when one partner was more demanding than the other – their emotional attachment was deeper and less destructive, more free of tension and consequently more loving.

The fundamental dishonesty of the church, they both agreed, was that it had always known that psychosexuality was the very core of all human life. She was equally certain that, if she or Jim were not so well integrated and realized that celibacy was something they would never feel comfortable with, they would have given up vocations to which they were still deeply committed.

They both also agreed the church still took no real account of normal human responses. Consequently, people like them had been driven to hide perfectly healthy relationships because of a decision taken centuries earlier and which, from a modern psychological standpoint, was unsupportable. Yet, to dare to openly challenge that decision, to suggest that tens of thousands of nuns and priests were forced to live part of their lives in Christ as a subterfuge, to have their emotional growth arrested, and their emotions traumatized: that would only lead to swift and savage punishment.

The church, under its present pontiff, Victoria was certain, could do worse than ponder the early sayings of the fathers.

Judge not him who is guilty of fornication, if thou are chaste: or thou thyself wilt offend a similar law. For he who said thou shalt not fornicate said also 'though shalt not judge'.

She had already mailed a copy of the quotation to his Holiness, Pope John Paul II. She doubted if it ever reached him.

More certain is that sharing her life with Jim had made living her own life in Christ that much more meaningful. She was sure to be a good nun first required she be a fully aware and sexually integrated woman.

They would continue to live as they did until she returned to the Mother House. A week ago, Reverend Mother had telephoned to say that the Order wished her to return and counsel in the convent. No reason had been given – nor had Victoria expected one. Some things had not changed.

Father Philippe parked outside St Mark's on a Sunday morning. Some parishioners still greeted him as Father Philippe. Others chose to ignore him, a few were openly hostile. Some of the priests in the diocese were embarrassed when they met him, but Father Nolan had remained a steadfast friend.

He had come to the General to see Margot after Cap was born and, two years later, Daniel. He was one of the first guests invited to dinner when they bought a house with money Fern loaned them. Father Philippe was closer to his mother-in-law than he had ever been to his own mother.

Married life with Margot had, after an initial period of adjustment, run surprisingly smoothly. She was a loving, caring wife and mother, imbued with a fierce loyalty. She refused to take any interest in the church – feeling it alone was responsible for the years of trauma her husband had endured.

That was why Margot would not partake in Holy Communion. In the parked car provided by the company he now worked for as a sales executive, Father Philippe tried again to persuade his wife to accompany him.

'Just this once, Margot?'

She shook her head firmly. 'No, Phil. I don't need all that. I don't mind you taking Cap and Daniel. But it's not for me. Not while they've got men like the chancellor and this new man running the show.'

On the day the new bishop arrived in the diocese, a survey confirmed that the biggest single factor for priests and nuns within the United States deciding to leave religious life was still their unwillingness to accept the vow of celibacy. Almost half of those surveyed said they found the vow unrealistic and distasteful.

The great majority who abandoned their vocation had also turned their back on the church. Many sought other faiths and cults. Judaism was a popular choice. More thought-provoking had been the admission of many nuns and priests that they have turned to paganism, goddess worship, astrology and Oriental meditation. They had often redesigned church rituals to worship solstices, equinoxes and full moons.

The bishop had dismissed the survey as further evidence of a dangerous conspiracy by 'a handful of liberals' to destroy the church. There must be obedience, he had thundered in his first sermon.

The techniques for control remained as rigid as always, emanating from the flow of encyclicals, apostolic letters and commands from Rome. Absent from all the Vatican's outpourings was what Father Philippe saw as a total lack of understanding that the only way out of the most serious crisis the church had ever faced was to recognize that change was inevitable. Instead, there was only bleak condemnation and a narrowness often enforced with medieval harshness. Not a single priest in this diocese had received dispensation. Those, like Father Philippe, who had married outside the church, were regarded as having committed mortal sin, their unions unrecognized, their children branded as bastards.

Father Philippe tried one last time to persuade Margot to accompany him and their children to Mass.

Margot shook her head.

Finally accepting, he picked Daniel up with one arm and took Cap by the hand and walked towards St Mark's.

Margot called after him. 'You still walk like a priest.'

He smiled. He supposed he always would.

Driving away from a house call, listening to a mid-morning talk show, Father Breslin realized another year had slipped by. This pleasant day was the start of the forty-second year of his ministry. The anniversary fell at a time when, to him, the church seemed besieged by priests and nuns who wanted to turn it into a worldwide managerial system, a religious multinational with the Pope presiding over God Incorporated and his bishops acting as divisional heads with special responsibilities for finances, baptisms, bequests, betrothals and burials.

There were others who wanted the church to abolish the sins of masturbation, fetishism and transvestism, to allow women to be ordained; to turn dogmatic and moral theology and canon law itself inside out, making it no longer a matter of total obedience but a plaything for the revisionists. But the most vocal of all demands was for an alteration in the sacred vow of celibacy.

He crossed the road where, a few miles further along, Mary had died almost a year ago, killed instantly in a head-on collision with a truck. He had gone to the funeral, standing with the family mourners. Watching the coffin being lowered into the earth, he knew he would go on loving her.

On the car radio, a priest was insisting that the pontiff's latest pronouncement had brought the church ever closer to confrontation. The soft, persuasive voice claimed the church was moving into its twilight following the Pope's declaration he would never allow optional celibacy. The radio priest posed a question.

'If the golden law of sacred celibacy is to remain, what reasons are there to show it is holy and fitting?'

Father Breslin switched off the radio. The anarchy was spreading from within.

He had often thought how celibacy had been singled out to be isolated and scrutinized, more than any other sphere of religious human activity. It had somehow become the new challenge to a Pope who had shown that tough leadership need not be unimaginative and insensitive.

In a world ruled by leaders who promised anything in exchange for power, John Paul II had shown it was possible to govern without compromise, that to heed the clamour for change was to only increase the sense of insecurity, that to offer new hope was to remember old truths.

The Pope had shown the church was mercifully free of the domination of the measurable. He had shown he was prepared to fail gloriously instead of achieving victory at the expense of compromise. He was not a man like his predecessors, ready to appease the doubters or change his mind. Instead he had never forgotten his responsibility was steeped in tradition. He would continue to bear witness to a truth that for centuries had been strong enough to sustain itself, but now required every available defender.

Father Breslin had come to see how unimportant in the end was the issue of whether celibacy should be optional or scrapped. He felt immeasurable sadness for those nuns and priests who had left the church to either marry or live their lives with others, who had dreamed impossible dreams of changing the unchangeable. In the end they had only cheated themselves with their claims that unless they were allowed complete sexual freedom, they could not do God's work.

More clearly than ever, he saw that his priestly celibacy represented hope and a promise. It helped him to live by the unique experience of a deeply personal communion with God; living a celibate life was a passionate reminder that life was an unquestioning acceptance of failure and a commitment to redeem it. For a priest, living a full life in Christ was one based on the certain knowledge that the first and only intended goal of celibacy was to spiritually enhance those who have voluntarily accepted it.

Celibacy for Father Breslin, was neither desire or denial. It was acceptance.

CHAPTER TWENTY-NINE

Towards Tomorrow

On an October evening in 1996, Father Breslin stared in shock and disbelief, and then mounting anger, at the report on the television news. A man he personally believed had already done more lasting harm to the church than any other since that day Bishop Eamonn Casey had announced, in May 1992, to a stunned Irish nation that he had fathered a love-child, had now made an even more titillating confession.

Standing before a rented cottage in the Lake District, Scotland's newly resigned Bishop of Argyll and the Isles, Roderick Wright, admitted he and the woman standing beside him, his mistress, Kathleen MacPhee, had finally consummated their relationship. This revelation about their already headline-gathering lives, ensured the debate on celibacy would continue to be the plaything of the tabloid headline-writers.

The saga of Bishop Wright's affair with a mother of three, as well as having fathered a child by another woman, had surfaced on the day Father Breslin finally retired as parish priest. Due to poor health, he had been transferred to the less demanding duties of a curate in a parish overlooking the Irish Sea. The day he packed all his worldly possessions – mostly cardboard boxes of books and his precious audio cassette tapes – into a U-haul van, he had been a priest for forty-six years and thirty-four days. In all that time he had tried to see celibacy as a gift which many had once eagerly promised to receive, but increasingly more felt unable to keep.

By the time Father Breslin had settled into his modern bungalow home, the Wright affair had erupted into a sensation that had swept through the bronze doors of the Vatican's Apostolic Palace. That the Pope had swiftly accepted the Bishop's resignation had done nothing to quell the furore, much of it prurient.

For Father Breslin the issue was intensely more personal. First Casey and now Wright had delivered telling blows to his personal credo. For a mere priest to fail, and he had seen too many do so in his long ministry, was sad and tragic. But to see two princes of the church, men who had both once been tipped as candidates for perhaps even its highest office – was altogether another matter. How could those hundreds of priests the two bishops had been responsible for have expected leadership to live a 'full and proper life in celibacy, prayer and friendship, in which their sexuality had its proper place, when there had been no such leadership from Casey and Wright?' Father Breslin had asked himself.

Switching off the television, he went to his study and sat for a long time with his hands tightly clasped, the way he had taught himself to become calm. There were other reasons why the affair of Roderick Wright had upset him. Through his network of contacts within the Irish Hierarchy, he knew that further, equally embarrassing, revelations had surfaced.

Vocatio, an Italian organization that specialized in helping priests who had left the church specifically because of involvement with a woman, announced its latest survey placed the number of priests worldwide who had done so in the past twenty years was now well in excess of 120,000 – and growing daily. Add the number of priests who chose to remain in ministry, but maintained a secret relationship with a woman, and the figure exceeded 250,000. *Vocatio* further reported that '20 per cent of North American priests have a stable but secret relationship with a woman, while 50 per cent get involved in occasional sexual skirmishes'.

Worldwide, of the 404,000 priests in active ministry in October 1996, at least one-third had been, or were still engaged in, breaking their vow of compulsory celibacy, claimed *Vocatio*.

Unquestionably, potential recruits to Ireland's seminaries were being deterred by the rule. In late 1996, Father Breslin's old seminary, Clonliffe, had less than a dozen students and only eighteen young men had entered the training section of St Patrick's College, Maynooth, the lowest number for two centuries in that seminary's history.

Father Breslin also knew that many in the Irish laity believed enforced celibacy had also contributed to some of the appalling cases of paedophilia uncovered in the church in recent years. Just as Casey had paid off his mistress and son with funds he had secretly 'borrowed' from diocesan funds, it had emerged that other priests were giving payments to children they had abused.

Yet, the only Irish bishop to even propose there should be an open debate on celibacy, Brendan Comiskey, Bishop of Ferns, had been ordered to Rome and effectively silenced. In the midst of the burgeoning Wright affair, Ireland's twenty-four bishops were asked by *The Sunday Times* to take part in a confidential survey on their attitude to celibacy. Sixteen refused and the rest were said to be 'unavailable'. Bishop James McLoughlin, Casey's successor in Galway said, 'I consider that such types of survey achieve no good and only serve to trivialize important issues.'

It was that judgement which prompted Father Breslin, on that October evening, to once more reach for his trusty old cassette recorder and deal with the subject in his own way. Inserting a tape into the recorder, he cleared his throat and, in a voice still surprisingly strong considering how frail he had become, he began to speak.

Celibacy remains what it always was – an ideal and a challenge. At its best it can actualize our human potential, but this can only be achieved with God's grace. But it is the challenge part that interests me. To live in celibate love in today's world is not easy and even verges on the heroic.

He paused to consider the next point. Once the thought had become ordered in his mind, he delivered it with easy fluency.

Sexuality and spirituality are mutually compatible. Both flow from the very core of human life. For a priest and, I daresay, a nun, the goal must be to integrate both. It is not a matter of choosing to separate them but bonding them into one, in which the spiritual and the sexual, the holy and the sensual, are at one with each other. Living in the Spirit and in Christ does not mean an alienation of ourselves from our own physicality.

Once more he paused, wondering for a moment how much of this Casey and Wright, all those other priests who had cheated themselves, their vows and their church, had ever realized it was possible and necessary to speak of celibate sexuality.

The one thing I have learned is that a celibate is not asexual. But just as it can be said that sexuality is beautiful and Christian, so it must be added that sexuality is dangerous. It is understanding the balance between the two which allows a priest or nun to live a healthy life. At all times we must be realistic and positive. Sex is a danger. It can overtake the person. It will deaden us to living in the Spirit. And, above all, we must never delude ourselves that healthy integration of our sexuality is an excuse for sexual licence.

He replayed the tape to make sure this was what he really wanted to say. Satisfied, he continued to record.

The priesthood is in a mess because so many of us have forgotten about affective prayer. That requires a synthesis of our emotional and spiritual lives. Only through that can the ultimate goal of celibacy for a priest lead him to a fuller life in Christ. To achieve that, we must understand that the celibate life is based upon Jesus of Nazareth as fully man, as a man of faith, as God's man, as God's presence in all we do and think. Celibacy and sexuality both have the same goal, the fulness of life. It can never be a question of one or the other. Never celibacy or sexuality. It is an integration of both. My only wish is that for all of us who remain in the service of the church do so by remaining sexual celibates in the service of God.

Father Breslin switched off the recorder. He sat in his book-lined study, allowing the darkness to envelop him.

On an October afternoon in 1996, a month into the new term, there was a knock on Clare's classroom door. She frowned; she was going to a concert that evening with a male friend and wanted no delay in getting home. This was her fifth year in the apartment and, though she had never had a man stay over, she dated on a regular basis, enjoying a full and healthy relationship with a number of men. Her hair was styled, she wore make-up and varnish on her nails. Her skirt was tailored and her blouse made of silk. She had packed her tote bag, bought on a visit to Madrid, and was putting on her loden topcoat, purchased during a winter ski holiday in Austria, when the knocking came again.

The classroom door opened and Shelagh came in. The tall and graceful seventeen-year-old had been the winner of last term's scripture prize for her essay on St John being the apostle that Jesus had admired above all the others. It had been so well-argued that Clare had brought it to the Mother House on her next monthly visit. Sister Martha, who had become the Order's Superior four years ago, had read the essay, nodding appreciatively.

'Clare, you are doing wonders with these girls,' Sister Martha had said. 'I'd very much like to see this pupil and explore her views further.'

Clare had passed on the message to Shelagh shortly before the school had broken up for the long summer vacation. When class had reassembled in September, Shelagh had casually mentioned that she had seen Reverend Mother several times. In the new-term rush, Clare had shown no more than fleeting interest.

'Can you spare me a little time, Miss?' Shelagh asked.

'Well...'

'It won't take long, Miss.'

Clare smiled. 'Okay. What's this about?'

Shelagh closed the door and leaned against it. When she spoke, her voice was very certain. 'I want to be a nun. Reverend Mother said I should talk to you.' In the momentary stillness, Clare had a sudden vivid memory of that other time, and another classroom, when she had confided to Sister Imelda her own wish to enter religious life.

'Did Reverend Mother say why you should speak to me, Shelagh?' Clare asked carefully.

'Oh yes, Miss. She said you had been in the Order yourself.'

'She told you that?' Clare asked.

'Mind, she said, I wasn't to tell anybody. But that it was important that you should know that I knew.'

'I see.' Clare leaned against her desk, recovering. 'Very well. It's true. I was a member of the Community... but I left.'

'Why was that, Miss?'

'Because...' Suddenly and inexplicably a thought struck Clare. 'Come and sit down, Shelagh. We've a lot to talk about.'

'You sure you have the time, Miss?'

'Positive,' Clare said, putting all thoughts of the concert from her mind. She would become Shelagh's mentor, Shelagh her phoenix, kindling again those moments when she had first felt the pull of religious life irresistible.

That Shelagh wanted to follow in her footsteps was striking proof of God's continuing self-revelation. So much else had gone. But in a way it did not matter. Here, in this trusting teenager, was the exquisite promise of tomorrow. That Shelagh wanted to be part of the ultimate mystery meant there was hope for them both.

Clare began to explain why, indeed, Shelagh would make a fine nun.

In October 1996, Andrew, an ordained priest for the past eight years and now a curate in a West of England parish, had begun a new draft of a book that dealt with some of the questions, feelings and decisions that had arisen during and after his journey to ordination. Much of it was based on his diaries, which he still continued to write-up every night.

Once a month he visited Father Patrick, now in his eighty-second year and living in a home run by the church. Andrew's own parents had died during the past three years and Andrew had officiated at both their funerals. A year ago he had learned that Jane had divorced Giles. Jane had herself written to him at the seminary and the letter had been forwarded. He had been back to Rome twice in the time since he had been ordained. He had found his love affair with the city had cooled, not least because on his second visit, he was mugged while walking late one evening along a bank of the Tiber.

He doubted if his book would ever be published, though priest friends who had read the latest draft, and offered suggestions, felt it had particular importance in the chapter titled 'Loving and Releasing'.

The chapter began with the undeniable statement that 'men and women committed to religious celibacy fall in love. They have done so in the past, they do so today, and will do so in the future. It is the nature of all humanity. There is only one way to deal with such a situation. At the very first stirring, it must be resisted. Crushed and rejected and the cause of it removed. That is the only way.'

In a later passage, Andrew had argued that every day must be one 'of rededication to the celibate life for priests and nuns. To do so requires that his or her personal relationship to the Father, Son and Holy Spirit, is done through prayer. A committed celibate's experience of human love contains a remarkable potentiality for prayer. Celibacy has, and always will be, both a gift and a mystery. Through prayer life, love is refined so that it becomes compatible with celibate dedication.'

Andrew was positive he would be able to live his life by such standards until the very end of his priesthood.

October 1996 marked Victoria's second year as the Order's Deputy Superior. In accepting the post, she had made a number of conditions to which the Order had agreed. She would not live in the Mother House, but would join the other fifteen nuns in the first prayers of the day. She would leave after supper to return to her apartment a mile away.

Three days a week, she ran the out-patient's clinic for nuns and priests at a local hospital. She spent six weeks in every year away from the Mother House, visiting the Order's outposts in Europe and, most recently, a Community they had started in Argentina.

In 1993 she had ended her relationship with Jim by mutual consent. A year later Victoria had begun a new one with a priest she had met in Rome. Since then they had met two or three times a year, usually on holiday, sharing a bed, but not fully consummating the relationship.

In a recent comment she had put on paper, Victoria had rationalized her behaviour.

My private life as a celibate is as important to me as my public one. My public life is lived in a Community and through ministry, my private life in intimacy and solitude. All, I have discovered, are of equal importance if I am to continue to mature. Solitude makes me face my true self, to discover all the obscure forces within me. Solitude enables me to discover what conflicts there are in the depths of my heart and allows me the time to resolve them. It enables me to continue to have a healthy relationship. Sex for me is increasingly less important. There is something far more gratifying beyond that. In saying that, I am reminded of the lovers in the Song of Songs who, after every possible extravaganza of words, understand the inefficiency. At that moment, all I want to do is just to be – to be and do God's work.

Even in 1996, she accepted not everybody would accept her rationale or her way of living, that many, if they could, would ask of her one question: *Why do you remain in religious life?*

To that question, Victoria had one answer, 'Every day my life allows me new possibilities for prayer, loving and friendship.'

In October 1996, Father Philippe was in his tenth year of waiting to be formally dispensed from his vows. There was now a third member of his family, Mary Ellen, three years old, with his dark good looks and a smile that her father was convinced would turn heads in the next century. He doubted if, even by then, he would have received his dispensation from the Vatican. He had written a number of times requesting it. Each time there had been no response.

He thought only a miracle, 'akin to accepting the Virgin Birth in all its forms' would make the church understand the needs of committed men and women. He knew if there was optional celibacy he would resume his ministry at once.

In his last letter to the Vatican, he had written, 'My church continues to be a church of stultification, of blind dogmatism, of rigid cruelty, of self-righteousness, of inhibition, of fear, of morbid guilt, of hypocrisy, of ignorance, of superstition, of insensitivity and of self-destruction.' Once more, perhaps not surprisingly, there had been no response. But, to this day, he could still walk with confidence and certainty into his old church, despite knowing that, in the eyes of the Vatican, 'Margot is still no better than my concubine and our children illegitimate.'

He also continued to live his life in Christ fully as a man. That he would remain on Rome's books as a non-active priest almost certainly until he died, he had come to see as 'no more than an administrative fact. More important to me is that I know that God is a continuous part of my personal history. God made me who I am. I will remain what I firmly believe God wants me to be – a loving husband and caring father.'

It is hard to gainsay him when he says that the church is the ultimate loser in failing to allow him integrate his sexuality in the service of the kingdom of God.

How many more will have joined him by the time you have finished reading this book? How long can the Holy Roman Catholic and

Apostolic Church cling to a vow that has no realistic role to play in the truly Christian vision of the world today?

The reactions in October 1996 to the sad business of the Roderick Wright affair had many of the symptoms of an institution in deep crisis. There was an outpouring of self-examination that was characteristic at such times. The most interesting comment came from Cardinal Basil Hume, Primate of All-England and Wales who, in the heat of the matter, pointed out that 'celibacy is a matter of discipline not doctrine, of institutional, not divine law'. In other words it was a rule made by men and could be undone by them.

But his Eminence was not about to lead the charge to the Vatican to change matters. He was merely pointing out 'the reality'. Personally he would, he added, not wish to see a change in the rule of mandatory celibacy for a priest.

Pope John Paul II has remained committed to the status quo. In an address to the Congregation for the Doctrine of the Faith in November 1995, he condemned those theologians who had dared to criticize his view on the matter: 'It seems necessary to recover the authentic concept of authority in the church. Theology can never be reduced to the private reflections of a theologian or a group of theologians.'

The one certainty is that the further Rome is from its last jolting crisis over a supposed celibate breaking free from his sexual shackles, the closer it is to the next one. And ultimately, that cannot be good for not only the most important Christian church on earth, but for Christianity itself.

TRIAL
The Life and Inevitable Crucifixion of Jesus

Gordon Thomas

Soon to be a major feature film, this powerful book is a top-flight investigative journalist's detailed examination of the life and death of Jesus. Compellingly readable, it amounts to a modern dramatization of the known facts which leads to some startling conclusions and bears comparison with Frank Morison's classic *Who Moved the Stone?*

'Written with both enthusiasm and care... will appeal to anyone looking for the kind of freshness and vigour of detail that historical scholarship cannot supply. Readers will value it as enjoyable, even fascinating, education... One understands why the first Easter was not thought suitable for this style of treatment, but the message is shouted by the very eagerness with which the story is told up to this point: He lives!'

David L. Edwards, Church Times

ISBN 0 7459 3754 3

Also from Lion publishing

THE ORIGINAL JESUS
The Life and Vision of a Revolutionary

Tom Wright

Was Jesus of Nazareth a political upstart? Biblical historian and broadcaster Dr Tom Wright reveals new perspectives on the political and cultural context to Jesus' life and teachings. This book will intrigue anyone interested in the historical person of Jesus.

Nearly 2000 years after his execution, the enigmatic figure of Jesus Christ remains the subject of intense historical investigation. In this fascinating new book, Tom Wright draws on the latest scholarly findings to present startling new insights into the claims of this true revolutionary. He shows how understanding the environment in which the Gospels were written can shed fresh light on their message. Colour photographs throughout.

ISBN 0 7459 3707 1

Also from Lion publishing

BED OF NAILS

Peter Owen Jones

'*Bed of Nails*... could as well have been called *The Accidental Ordinand*. It is a Hornbyesque, postmodern religious confession, the tale of a typically modern man signing over his life to an untypically ancient institution... a tale of culture shock, as he travels, open-mouthed, from ad-land to church-land.'

   The Observer

Witty, passionate, iconoclastic, this sizzling diary does for the Church of England what Nick Hornby did for Arsenal.

'A warts and all account of what happens when you put an advertising director and proverbial bad boy into theological college... Frequently funny, sometimes spectacular to behold and often very moving.'

   Stephen Farish, Editor, PR Week

ISBN 0 7459 3627 X

All Lion paperbacks are available from
your local bookshop, or can be ordered
direct from Lion Publishing. For a free
catalogue, showing the complete list of
titles available, please contact:

Customer Services Department
Lion Publishing plc
Peter's Way
Sandy Lane West
Oxford OX4 5HG

Tel: (01865) 747550
Fax: (01865) 715152